The Economics of Consumption

THE ECONOMICS OF CONSUMPTION

Theory and Evidence

Tullio Jappelli

and

Luigi Pistaferri

OXFORD
UNIVERSITY PRESS

OXFORD
UNIVERSITY PRESS

Oxford University Press is a department of the University of Oxford. It furthers
the University's objective of excellence in research, scholarship, and education
by publishing worldwide. Oxford is a registered trade mark of Oxford University
Press in the UK and certain other countries.

Published in the United States of America by Oxford University Press
198 Madison Avenue, New York, NY 10016, United States of America.

Library of Congress Cataloging-in-Publication Data
Names: Jappelli, Tullio, author. | Pistaferri, Luigi, author.
Title: The Economics of Consumption: Theory and Evidence / Tullio Jappelli and
Luigi Pistaferri.
Description: New York, NY : Oxford University Press, [2017] |
Includes bibliographical references.
Identifiers: LCCN 2016042409| ISBN 9780199383146 (hardcover) |
ISBN 9780199383153 (pbk.) |ISBN 9780199383177 (updf) |
ISBN 9780199383184 (epub)
Subjects: LCSH: Consumption (Economics)
Classification: LCC HB801 .J36 2017 | DDC 339.4/7—dc23
LC record available at https://lccn.loc.gov/2016042409

9 8 7 6 5 4 3 2 1
Paperback printed by Webcom, Inc., Canada
Hardback printed by Bridgeport National Bindery, Inc., United States of America

To our parents: Ruggiero and Janna; Anna and Giuseppe

CONTENTS

PREFACE

Consumption decisions are crucial determinants of business cycles and growth. As a share of US gross domestic product (GDP), personal consumer expenditure has grown steadily since the early 1970s to reach, by 2008, 70 percent of GDP. Knowledge of how consumers respond to the economic environment and how they react to the risks that they encounter during the life cycle is therefore crucial for evaluating stabilization policies and the effectiveness of fiscal packages implemented in response to economic downturns or financial crises. Does the response depend on the nature and duration of income changes? Do anticipated income changes have a different impact on consumption than unanticipated shocks? And do transitory income shocks have a lower impact than permanent ones? Do all consumers respond in the same way, or does the response vary by the economic circumstances and consumers' characteristics? Do the rich increase consumption less than the poor when their income changes? In the past decades, economist have proposed many analytical perspectives, and studied these questions with a variety of data and approaches. This book attempts to assemble a vast research field in a coherent way, and in a way that is accessible to students and policy analysts. The 2015 Nobel Prize awarded to Angus Deaton, one of the most influential contributors to the field, is a good testament of the importance of the topics we attempt to survey in this book.

Economists have been interested in the effect of income changes on consumption at least since the Keynesian consumption function appeared in the literature. That function simply posits that consumption depends on current disposable income. This simple formulation neglects that past saving affects the current standard of living. The lack of dynamics of the Keynesian consumption function is relaxed in the approach based on intertemporal optimization, which is the subject of this book.

Our starting points are the Modigliani and Brumberg (1954) and Friedman (1957) celebrated life-cycle and permanent-income models. Both models posit that people use saving to smooth income fluctuations, and that consumption should respond little if at all to income changes that are predictable. In the life-cycle model, households save in anticipation of the income reduction that they will experience when they exit the labor market, or borrow when young in anticipation of increases in their future earnings induced by human capital investments. The permanent-income hypothesis emphasizes the role of short-run income fluctuations, focusing on income uncertainty as a determinant of saving. While the two models differ in some important aspects, they have many common themes. According to both models, consumption and saving decisions result from the maximization of a utility function subject to an intertemporal budget constraint. Both models identify a structural relationship between consumption and total (long-run) resources, not between consumption and current income as in the Keynesian tradition. The two models lead also to similar predictions about the short-run dynamics of saving, namely, that an unanticipated and transitory income shock is mainly absorbed by saving and very little by consumption.

Although the roots of the modern theory of consumption are in the 1950s, the 1970s represent a turning point for the study of intertemporal choice under uncertainty. In a key contribution, Hall (1978) proposed to estimate the first-order conditions of the consumer's intertemporal optimization problem. This approach has been applied in thousands of papers, using national accounts data or household surveys. In the 1980s and 1990s income risk and borrowing constraints have been fully integrated in the intertemporal model of consumption. Except for a few cases in which the optimization problem can be solved analytically, these studies rely on numerical simulation methods. From an empirical perspective, many authors have used microeconomic data on households, allowing for various sources of individual heterogeneity. The increasing availability of microeconomic data and the development of simulation methods have highlighted that the various types of risk and the characteristics of financial and insurance markets in which consumers operate deeply affect their intertemporal decisions. Aggregation of individual functions is also taken seriously in this literature, moving away from the paradigm of the representative agent, with profound implications for the evolution of aggregate consumption as well as for consumption inequality. At various points in time Deaton (1992), Browning and Lusardi (1996), Browning and Crossey (2001a), and Attanasio and Weber (2010) have reviewed these theoretical contributions and the empirical literature about intertemporal choice.

This book attempts to guide readers through the most important theoretical papers in the field, and to evaluate theoretical models using facts or available empirical estimates. It is divided into three parts.

CONTENT

The first seven chapters provide the basic ingredients of models with intertemporal choice, guiding the reader from a model without uncertainty to intertemporal models with income risk and borrowing constraints. The central part of the book (Chapters 8, 9, and 10) reviews recent empirical literature on the effect of income changes on consumption and on the relevance of precautionary saving. The last four chapters contain a selection of various extensions of the intertemporal model studied in the first part of the book.

In Chapter 1 we summarize the main implications of the life-cycle model and of the permanent-income hypothesis in the absence of uncertainty, a benchmark case that we will refer to often in subsequent chapters. Chapter 2 discusses the empirical implications of these models, particularly regarding the elasticity of intertemporal substitution, the relation between saving and the interest rate, and the age profile of consumption and wealth. The chapter introduces also stylized facts that emerge from a first glance at consumption data, pointing out the merits but also the drawbacks of the sources of information that researchers have available.

Chapter 3 presents a model with complete markets, a situation in which consumers can access a full set of insurance contracts and are protected against any possible risk. Although in this model consumers are exposed to risks, the complete-market assumption in fact neutralizes their effect on consumption. Indeed, many of the implications of this model are similar to the case without uncertainty considered in Chapter 1. The chapter also surveys some of the tests of the complete-market hypothesis, and the implication of the complete-market hypothesis for consumption inequality and for consumption mobility.

Chapter 4 removes the assumption of complete markets and studies the effect on consumption of income risk when consumers have a quadratic utility function. This assumption leads to the so-called certainty equivalence model: income shocks affect the dynamics and level of consumption, yet the assumption of quadratic utility implies that consumers do not react to risk. This model is also useful because it allows a closed-form solution for the level of consumption (a consumption function).

Chapter 5 examines how the consumer's problem changes in the presence of credit market frictions. The theory of intertemporal choice developed in previous chapters assumes that there are no imperfections in the credit market. This implies that consumers can borrow and save as much as needed (given only the intertemporal budget constraint). Credit market imperfections impose further constraints on the consumer, limiting the ability to transfer resources from the future to the present.

Chapter 6 removes the assumption of quadratic utility and examines situations in which consumers respond to income risk by increasing current saving to protect against future shocks to income. This motive for saving is called precautionary saving, and it provides an explanation for some of the empirical findings in the literature, such as the observation that people with more volatile incomes tend to save more than individuals with more stable income patterns.

While the previous two chapters analyze precautionary saving and liquidity constraints in isolation, Chapter 7 analyzes models that have combined them to provide a unified treatment of intertemporal decisions. In the buffer stock models of Deaton (1991) and Carroll (1997) liquidity constraints and precautionary saving interact, because consumers anticipate the risk of being denied credit in the future, and react by increasing current saving.

Chapters 8, 9, and 10 are three empirical chapters, surveying some of the papers that have tested the validity of intertemporal consumption models. In Chapter 8 the focus is on the implication of the model that consumption should not react to anticipated income changes. In Chapter 9 the focus is on the implication that unanticipated income changes should affect consumption, particularly if the shocks are permanent. Chapter 10 surveys empirical papers that have provided evidence for or against the precautionary motive. Each of these surveys of the empirical literature is selective, with no attempt to be exhaustive. The papers that we cite are not necessarily the most influential, but they are representative of a certain approach or methodology.

Chapter 11, on life uncertainty, is closely linked to Chapter 12, on bequests. Lifetime uncertainty heightens the incentive to accumulate resources to protect against longevity risk. In the absence of annuity markets, life uncertainty explains why consumers may choose to maintain a high level of wealth even in old age, and thus leave accidental (or unplanned) bequests. But a complete characterization of bequest motives must also comprise the possibility that altruistic consumers wish to transfer a portion of their wealth to their descendants in the form of gifts or voluntary bequests.

The final two chapters address topics that, alone, could be treated in monographs. Chapter 13 analyzes intertemporal choice when the utility function is not separable: in particular, we consider the case where utility depends on habits, durable goods, leisure, home production, and distinct consumption by household members. Chapter 14 presents various cases of non-standard preferences or behavior, such as mental accounting, time inconsistency, lack of financial sophistication, and social and collective preferences. These two chapters are designed not to provide a systematic treatment of the topics but, more modestly, to indicate interesting directions of recent research and avenues to modify or enrich the models presented in the book.

ORGANIZATION

The book avoids technical discussions about the econometrics of intertemporal choice and stochastic dynamic programming. Full analysis of these issues would require too much space and would ultimately distort our aim, which is to summarize the various theories of consumption and examine their empirical validity.

Each chapter starts with an overview highlighting important concepts developed in previous chapters and ends with a summary drawing its main message. When a result is highly technical we summarize it in a more qualitative way, omitting lengthy mathematical derivations and referring interested readers to the original sources. Where possible, the chapter begins with a presentation of the material, relying on a simple two-period model to describe the main insights of the theory and generalizing to many periods only later on.

On many issues we maintain a systematic link between the chapters. The Euler equation, which describes how consumption changes over time, allows estimation of the parameters of the utility function without making assumptions about the budget constraint or the sources of uncertainty. This equation is therefore a focal point of many chapters, and throughout the book we augment it to account for liquidity constraints, income risk, life uncertainty, labor supply, consumption habits, and so on. Where possible, we show how uncertainty and the structure of financial and insurance markets affect the level of consumption. This analysis is much more difficult than that of the dynamics of consumption, and only a few cases deliver closed-form solutions.

A second theme is the effect of anticipated and unanticipated income changes on consumption. While some models of intertemporal choice suggest that consumption growth should not be affected by anticipated changes in income, all consumption models suggest that consumption should react to unanticipated income shocks, particularly if they are long-lasting.

INTENDED READERSHIP

The book is designed for an advanced undergraduate course or a first-year Ph.D. course and requires only basic knowledge of mathematics and econometrics. It could be used as a reference in several courses, and in particular it is suited to:

- *An undergraduate course in macroeconomics.* Macroeconomists might want to use the initial chapters of the book, as part of a course that covers business cycle fluctuations.
- *A course in applied econometrics.* The central part of the book (Chapters 8, 9, and 10) guide students through the empirical literature, pointing to different datasets and empirical strategies.
- *Ph.D. courses.* The book could be used as an introduction to the literature for courses in macroeconomics, applied econometrics, and labor economics.

ACKNOWLEDGMENTS

Over the years, some chapters of the book have been used in the macro and labor classes that we have taught at Stanford University and at the University of Naples Federico II. Some of the chapters draw from an earlier book we wrote in Italian (Jappelli and Pistaferri, 2000a), and from a survey published in the *Annual Review of Economics* in 2010 on the consumption effect of income changes. Other material is based on our joint work, and we refer to it when appropriate. We wish to thank students who attended our courses and who provided a good many useful comments and criticisms, in particular Maria Carannante, Hannah Hironaka, Christian Julliard, Yichen Su, and Alessandra Voena. On the topics covered here, we have learned much over the years from a number of close friends and coauthors: Orazio Attanasio, Richard Blundell, Dimitris Christelis, Luigi Guiso, Narayana Kocherlakota, Hamish Low, Tom MaCurdy, Costas Meghir, Mario Padula, Marco Pagano, John Pencavel, Itay Saporta-Eksten, and Guglielmo Weber.

We also thank several anonymous referees for most useful feedback early on in the project, and Scott Parris for being so patient over the years. Finally, many of the papers we have worked on over time have been made possible by grants from a number of institutions: the National Science Foundation, the National Institutes of Health, the European Research Council Programme, the Stanford Institute for Economics and Policy Research, the 6th and 7th Framework Programmes of the European Union, and the Italian Ministry of University and Research. We gratefully acknowledge their continued support.

CHAPTER 1

Intertemporal Choice Under Certainty

This chapter introduces the basic intertemporal problem faced by a consumer who has to choose between consumption and saving when future incomes and interest rates are known with certainty. First we consider a model with only two periods and a fixed demographic structure; next we extend the analysis to a more realistic multi-period, finite-horizon model in which family composition changes over the life cycle; and finally we present the continuous-time version of the model and introduce the limiting case in which individuals have an infinite horizon. With appropriate assumptions about the individual income profile and productivity growth, we can derive the life-cycle model of Modigliani and Brumberg (1954) as a special case, and study how demographic variables and productivity growth affect national saving.

Essentially this chapter introduces basic aspects of the consumer choice problem that we will encounter in many subsequent chapters. For example, we discuss the relationship between the Euler equation and the consumption function, the effect on saving of changes in the interest rate, and the difference between the individual and the aggregate saving functions.

1.1. THE TWO-PERIOD MODEL

Suppose that a consumer has a planning horizon of only two periods, t and $t+1$. Before going into the details of the problem, it is important to distinguish between stocks and flows. In our case, there are two flows—income and consumption (y and c) in each period—and a single stock, assets (a). The stock of assets can be measured at the beginning or at the end of each period. Here our convention is that, unless otherwise noted, assets are measured at the beginning of the period. This is a discrete-time convention—the basic point is that assets measured at the beginning of a period coincide with the assets measured at the end of the previous period.

We assume that at the beginning of the period the consumer has some level of wealth a_t (initial condition). In each of the two periods, the individual earns some labor income, receives some interest income, consumes, and saves. The return on wealth is the interest rate (r), assumed constant and paid at the beginning of the period on the wealth transferred from the previous period. The consumer can borrow and lend at the same real interest rate (no credit market imperfections). Under this assumption, the interest rate thus coincides with the cost of debt if the wealth transferred from the first to the second period is negative. A further assumption we make is that the consumer has no bequest motive. Finally, we assume that labor income in the two periods (y_t, y_{t+1}) is exogenous and that there is no uncertainty about income or the interest rate.

The consumer's *dynamic* budget constraints determine the level of wealth at the beginning of each period:

$$a_{t+1} = (1+r)(a_t + y_t - c_t) \tag{1.1}$$

$$a_{t+2} = (1+r)(a_{t+1} + y_{t+1} - c_{t+1}). \tag{1.2}$$

The dynamic budget constraint is an accounting relationship: at the beginning of each period, wealth is equal to the wealth carried over from the previous period plus labor income and interest income accumulated during the period, minus consumption during the period.

Note that while the consumer is not alive in period $t+2$, equation (1.2) is needed to determine the level of wealth that remains after death (i.e., assets available at the beginning of period $t+2$ or end of period $t+1$). What is this level? Without further assumptions, the dynamic budget constraint does not rule out the possibility that consumers may borrow more than they will be able to repay over the course of their life. For the consumer problem to be well defined, we must specify a terminal condition. The requirement that the consumer cannot die in debt implies that $a_{t+2} \geq 0$; the assumption that the consumer does not want to leave bequests implies that $a_{t+2} \leq 0$. Combining the two inequalities, the terminal condition is:

$$a_{t+2} = 0. \tag{1.3}$$

Replacing this condition in equation (1.3) gives $a_{t+1} = c_{t+1} - y_{t+1}$, and substitution of this into equation (1.2) gives the consumers' *intertemporal* budget constraint:

$$c_t + \frac{c_{t+1}}{1+r} = a_t + y_t + \frac{y_{t+1}}{1+r} = a_t + h_t, \qquad (1.4)$$

where h_t represents the value of human capital, that is, the sum of current income and the discounted value of future earnings. The intertemporal budget constraint indicates that the present discounted value of future consumption is equal to the sum of initial wealth plus human capital.

We are now ready to study the consumer choice problem. The consumer chooses the optimal level of consumption by maximizing a utility function that takes as arguments the consumption of the two periods:

$$\max \ u(c_t, c_{t+1})$$

subject to the constraints:

$$c_t + \frac{c_{t+1}}{1+r} = a_t + h_t$$
$$a_t \text{ given}$$
$$c_t, c_{t+1} > 0.$$

From now on, we assume that the utility function is concave, that is, $\partial u(.)/\partial c_j > 0$, $\partial^2 u(.)/\partial c_j^2 < 0$, with $j = t, t+1$. In most of the book we leave the arguments of the maximization problem implicit, unless otherwise noted. The Lagrangean function of the problem is:

$$\max L = u(c_t, c_{t+1}) + \lambda \left[a_t + h_t - c_t - \frac{c_{t+1}}{1+r} \right]$$

with first-order conditions:

$$\partial u(.) / \partial c_t = \lambda \qquad (1.5)$$

$$\partial u(.) / \partial c_{t+1} = \frac{\lambda}{1+r}, \qquad (1.6)$$

which, combined, give:

$$\frac{\partial u(.) / \partial c_t}{\partial u(.) / \partial c_{t+1}} = (1+r).$$

The solution is represented graphically in Figure 1.1. If savings increase by one unit, the consumer obtains $(1+r)$ additional units of consumption in the next period. The term $(1+r)$ thus represents the price of consumption

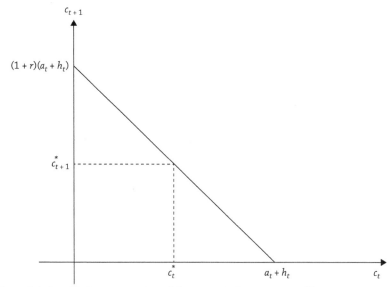

Figure 1.1: Graphical representation of the two-period consumer problem

in the first period, expressed in terms of units of consumption in the second period.

The solution is represented by two demand functions for optimal consumption (c_t^* and c_{t+1}^*) in the two periods:

$$c_t^* = f(r, a_t + h_t)$$
$$c_{t+1}^* = g(r, a_t + h_t).$$

We can now consider comparative statics exercises. Given our assumptions about the utility function, an increase in wealth ($a_t + h_t$) shifts the intertemporal budget constraint upward and to the right and increases both c_t^* and c_{t+1}^*.

The effect of the interest rate on the level of first-period consumption and saving is ambiguous in principle. A change in the interest rate has three effects on consumption: an income effect, a substitution effect, and a wealth effect. The total effect depends on whether the consumer is a net saver or a net borrower in the first period.

First, an increase in r reduces human capital, that is, the present discounted value of future earnings, and causes a fall in consumption in both periods. This is the *wealth effect*. Second, following the increase in r, the price of consumption in the first period increases and the individual will tend to reduce c_t^* in favor of c_{t+1}^*; this is the *substitution effect*. Finally, a rise in the interest rate increases income from assets (for net savers, i.e., those with $c_t^* < a_t + y_t$) or debt interest payments (for net borrowers, i.e., those with $c_t^* > a_t + y_t$) in the second period. In equilibrium both c_t^* and c_{t+1}^* increase or decrease depending on the asset position of the first period. This is the *income effect*. Hence, for a net saver the net effect of increasing the interest rate on first-period consumption is ambiguous, while for a net debtor it unambiguously decreases consumption.[1]

We now introduce the assumption that the utility function is additive and separable over time, so that the objective function can be rewritten as:

$$u\left(c_t, c_{t+1}\right) = u\left(c_t\right) + v\left(c_{t+1}\right) = u\left(c_t\right) + \frac{u(c_{t+1})}{1+\delta}, \tag{1.7}$$

where δ, the rate of time preference, can be interpreted as a measure of individuals' degree of impatience. The hypothesis of *intertemporal additivity* implies that the marginal utility of consumption today is independent of consumption in other periods—that is, that $u'(c_t)$ is independent of c_s, $\forall t \neq s$. As we shall see, this assumption greatly simplifies the analysis but fails when considering durable consumption (as the intensity of use of a given durable good affects the utility one can get from it in the future) or consumers' habits (as individuals assign particular value to being able to maintain their living standards unchanged). We discuss the issue of intertemporal non-separability in Chapter 13.

In the case of intertemporal additivity (1.7), the first-order conditions become:

$$u'(c_t) = \lambda \tag{1.8}$$

$$u'(c_{t+1}) = \lambda\left(\frac{1+\delta}{1+r}\right). \tag{1.9}$$

The Lagrange multiplier λ measures the marginal utility derived from increasing the consumer's resources by one unit, that is, the marginal utility of wealth $(a_t + h_t)$. If $r > \delta$ ($r < \delta$, respectively) the marginal utility of consumption falls (rises) from the first to the second period, so that second-period consumption is greater (or less) than first-period consumption. If instead $r = \delta$, the marginal utilities (and the levels of consumption themselves) are constant. Substituting (1.8) into (1.9) yields the Euler equation:

$$(1+\delta)\frac{u'(c_t)}{u'(c_{t+1})} = 1+r. \tag{1.10}$$

1. Empirical evidence on the sign of the relationship has also proved elusive. None of the studies that have tried to pin down this effect have found a convincing relationship between the two variables. The main empirical problem is the low variability of interest rates in microeconomic data. Chapter 2 shows that the same difficulty is encountered in estimating the effect on saving behavior of a tax incentive to save, which changes the after-tax return on assets. In principle, estimating the effect of the interest rate

In equilibrium, the ratio between the marginal utilities of consumption, discounted by the rate of time preference, is constant and equal to the price of first-period consumption. Alternatively, equation (1.10) indicates that the marginal rate of substitution between the levels of consumption in the two periods is equal to the marginal rate of transformation $(1+r)$.

Note the difference between the Euler equation and the consumption equation $c_t^* = f(r, a_t + h_t)$. The Euler equation describes how consumption varies over time; as we shall see, the only parameter that can be estimated from the Euler equation is the elasticity of intertemporal substituion. By contrast, the consumption function relates the level of consumption to the interest rate and lifetime resources. From this function, then, we can calculate the marginal propensity to consume out of wealth and the effect of a change in the interest rate on consumption.[2]

1.2. THE MULTI-PERIOD MODEL

It is easy to generalize the two-period model to the case of an individual who lives T periods, from 0 to $T-1$. In this case, the problem is to maximize the present discounted value of future utility,

$$\max \sum_{t=0}^{T-1} \frac{u(c_t)}{(1+\delta)^t},$$

subject to:

$$a_{t+1} = (1+r)(a_t + y_t - c_t) \quad \text{for } t = 0,1,...,T-1$$
$$a_0 \text{ given}$$
$$a_T = 0.$$

To derive the intertemporal budget constraint, we can divide the dynamic budget constraint $a_{t+1} = (1+r)(a_t + y_t - c_t)$ by $(1+r)^{t+1}$, and sum over the consumer horizon:

$$\sum_{t=0}^{T-1} \left(\frac{a_{t+1}}{(1+r)^{t+1}} - \frac{a_t}{(1+r)^t} \right) = \sum_{t=0}^{T-1} \left(\frac{y_t}{(1+r)^t} - \frac{c_t}{(1+r)^t} \right).$$

on consumption could be easier for samples of net debtors, where the effect is not theoretically ambiguous.

2. Here and in the rest of the book, we define the marginal propensity to consume with respect to variable x (income or wealth) as $\partial c / \partial x$.

Using the terminal condition $a_T = 0$, the intertemporal budget constraint is:

$$\sum_{t=0}^{T-1}\frac{c_t}{(1+r)^t} = a_0 + \sum_{t=0}^{T-1}\frac{y_t}{(1+r)^t} = a_0 + h_0. \qquad (1.11)$$

As usual, the intertemporal budget constraint tells us that the present discounted value of consumption is equal to the present discounted value of all the resources available to the individual, that is, initial wealth plus human capital.

The Lagrangean expression of the problem can be written as:

$$\max L = \sum_{t=0}^{T-1}\frac{u(c_t)}{(1+\delta)^t} + \lambda\left(a_0 + h_0 - \sum_{t=0}^{T-1}\frac{c_t}{(1+r)^t}\right).$$

In period t the first-order condition is:

$$u'(c_t) = \lambda\left(\frac{1+\delta}{1+r}\right)^t. \qquad (1.12)$$

Taking logarithms on both sides gives:

$$\ln u'(c_t) = \ln\lambda + t\ln\left(\frac{1+\delta}{1+r}\right). \qquad (1.13)$$

In the following period we have instead:

$$\ln u'(c_{t+1}) = \ln\lambda + (t+1)\ln\left(\frac{1+\delta}{1+r}\right). \qquad (1.14)$$

Subtracting equation (1.13) from equation (1.14) yields:

$$\Delta\ln u'(c_{t+1}) = \ln\left(\frac{1+\delta}{1+r}\right),$$

where Δ is the difference operator (such that $\Delta x_t = x_t - x_{t-1}$). Using a first-order Taylor expansion of $\ln u'(c_{t+1})$ around c_t, multiplying and dividing by c_t and using the approximation $\ln\left(\frac{1+\delta}{1+r}\right) \cong \delta - r$, we get:

$$c_t\frac{u''(c_t)}{u'(c_t)}\frac{c_{t+1}-c_t}{c_t} \cong \delta - r,$$

which can be solved for the growth rate of consumption,

$$\frac{c_{t+1}-c_t}{c_t} \cong -\frac{u'(c_t)}{c_t u''(c_t)}(r-\delta)= EIS(r-\delta),$$

where *EIS* denotes the elasticity of intertemporal substitution, a term that we will interpret below. The expression indicates that consumption increases over time when the interest rate (which measures the incentive to shift consumption forward in time) is higher than the rate of time preference (which measures instead the incentive to bring consumption to the present). In cases where the incentive to save is exactly balanced by the incentive to consume, the marginal utility of consumption is constant throughout the consumer's life (as in equation 1.10 with $r = \delta$), so consumption is constant.

Moreover, the greater the elasticity of intertemporal substitution, the greater the consumption growth. This elasticity measures how much the growth rate of consumption increases in response to an increase in the interest rate, namely:

$$\frac{d\left(\left(c_{t+1}-c_t\right)/c_t\right)}{dr} = -\frac{u'(c_t)}{c_t u''(c_t)} \geq 0.$$

Since this derivative measures the incentive to substitute consumption across time periods in response to a change in the interest rate, it is called the *elasticity of intertemporal substitution*.[3] Since in the Euler equation the marginal utility of consumption is kept constant, the foregoing derivative isolates the pure substitution effect of a change in the interest rate, keeping constant any change in the intertemporal budget constraint induced by a change in the interest rate (income and wealth effects).[4] The EIS is inversely related to the degree of concavity of the utility function (i.e., its second derivative). The greater the concavity, the less the willingness to substitute consumption across periods. Note that if the utility is of the form $u(c_t) = \frac{c_t^{1-\gamma}}{1-\gamma}$, EIS equals the constant γ^{-1}. This function is therefore called the isoelastic utility.

---

3. This concept is analogous to that of the elasticity of substitution between two goods (x, y) in response to a percentage change in their relative prices. The elasticity of substitution is defined as $d\ln(x/y)/d\ln(p_x/p_y)$. In our case, $d\ln(c_{t+1}/c_t) \cong (c_{t+1}-c_t)/c_t$ and the analogue of (p_x/p_y) in the intertemporal problem is $(1+r)$ (the relative price of consumption in period $t+1$ in terms of that of period t).
4. Elasticities that are derived when the marginal utility is kept constant (as in this case) are also known as Frisch elasticities, to distinguish them from Hicksian

1.3. THE LIFE-CYCLE MODEL

In this section, we derive the celebrated life-cycle model of Modigliani and Brumberg (1954) as a special case of the more general model discussed above. As before, we assume that individuals have a horizon of T periods, that their utility function is additive and separable over time, that they receive a certain income stream (y_t), and that there is no bequest motive for saving $(a_T = 0)$ (the possibility that individuals may derive utility from bequests is discussed in Section 1.5). For simplicity, we assume that both the rate of time preference δ and the interest rate r are zero $(r = \delta = 0)$. From (1.12), this implies that,

$$u'(c_t) = \lambda \quad \text{for every } t = 0,1,\dots,T-1$$

so that

$$u'(c_t) = u'(c_s) \quad \forall t,s.$$

It follows that $c_t = c$ for every t.[5] Substituting the first-order conditions into the intertemporal budget constraint (1.11) (with $r = 0$) yields the consumption function:

$$c = \frac{a_0 + \sum_{t=0}^{T-1} y_t}{T} = \frac{1}{T}(a_0 + h_0). \tag{1.15}$$

Equation (1.15) states that consumption is proportional to lifetime resources, the proportion depending on the planning horizon T.

To further specify the solution, suppose that the consumer's life is divided into two phases: work (from 0 to $N-1$), where labor income is constant and equal to y, and retirement, during which the consumer withdraws from the labor market and income is zero (from period N to $T-1$). The income profile is thus:

$$y_t = \begin{cases} y & \text{for } t \le N-1 \\ 0 & \text{for } t > N-1 \end{cases},$$

elasticities (in which utility is constant) and Marshallian uncompensated elasticities. This distinction will be useful when we analyze the case of non-separable preferences in Chapter 13.

5. Using the result from Section 1.2, we could have solved the problem by simply noting that consumption is constant when $r = \delta$, as in our case.

which immediately yields the consumption function derived by Modigliani and Brumberg:

$$c = \frac{N}{T}y + \frac{1}{T}a_0.$$

The marginal propensity to consume out of labor income is therefore equal to (N/T), the ratio of the length of working life to overall life, while the marginal propensity to consume out of wealth is much smaller $(1/T)$. Note that if we interpret T as the remaining life horizon in a cross section of consumers who differ by age, both propensities tend to increase with the age of the consumer; hence the life-cycle model implies that the propensity to consume is greater for the elderly than for the young. Note that this consumption function is quite different from the Keynesian function, $c_t = \alpha + \beta y_t$, in which consumption depends only on current income and the marginal propensity to consume cannot be microfounded, that is, derived as the outcome of an intertemporal choice problem.

Now that we have obtained an explicit solution for consumption, we can study the evolution of human capital, saving, and wealth over the life cycle. Assume for simplicity that initial wealth equals zero $(a_0 = 0)$. Recalling that wealth and human capital are measured at the beginning of the period, we know that in the initial period $(t = 0)$ human capital (h) is equal to the sum of current and future incomes (Ny). As time goes by, h declines, falling to zero in the year in which the individual retires (N):

$$h_t = \begin{cases} (N-t)y & \text{for } 0 \le t \le N \\ 0 & \text{for } t > N \end{cases}. \tag{1.16}$$

Using the consumption function $c = (N/T)y$, we can also characterize the profile of saving according to age. Saving $(s_t = y_t - c_t)$ is positive during the working phase and turns negative after the individual leaves the labor market:

$$s_t = \begin{cases} \left(1 - \dfrac{N}{T}\right)y & \text{for } t \le N-1 \\ -\dfrac{N}{T}y & \text{for } t > N-1 \end{cases}. \tag{1.17}$$

Finally, knowledge of the saving profile allows us to obtain the age profile of wealth, which is just the sum of the accumulated savings. Wealth grows from year to year at a constant rate (equal to the propensity to save) until retirement and then decreases at a rate equal to the propensity to consume:

$$a_t = \begin{cases} t\left(1 - \dfrac{N}{T}\right)y & \text{for } 0 \leq t \leq N \\[2ex] N\left(1 - \dfrac{N}{T}\right)y - (t - N)\dfrac{N}{T}y = N\left(1 - \dfrac{t}{T}\right)y & \text{for } t > N \end{cases} \qquad (1.18)$$

Accumulated wealth reaches a maximum $N\left(1 - \dfrac{N}{T}\right)y$ at the end of the working life, that is, at the beginning of period N. And the wealth accumulated during the working period is exactly equal to the resources used for consumption during the retirement period. Finally, one can verify that for $t = T$ wealth is zero, so the terminal condition is met. Comparing the path of wealth with that of human capital, one notices that total wealth, $a_t + h_t$, is greatest at the beginning of the individual's life and decreases each year at the rate (N/T), reaching zero after T years.

The age profiles of consumption, saving, and income are plotted in Figure 1.2 (see Modigliani 1986). The income profile is shown by the dashed line, the consumption profile by the solid line. Saving is positive during the working period and negative during retirement. Since the area of the rectangle of positive saving $N\left(1 - \dfrac{N}{T}\right)y$ is exactly equal to the area of the rectangle of negative saving $(T - N)\dfrac{N}{T}y$, aggregate life-cycle savings are exactly equal to zero.

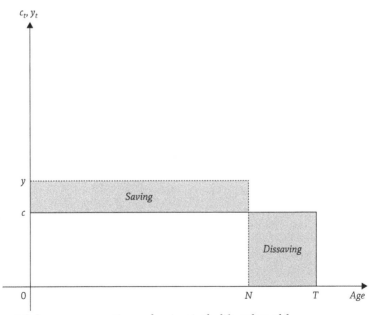

Figure 1.2: Income, consumption, and savings in the life-cycle model

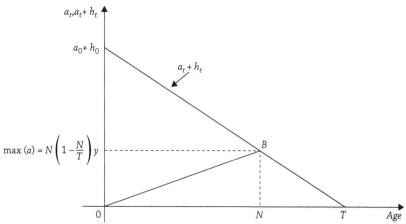

Figure 1.3: The age profile of wealth in the life-cycle model

In Figure 1.3 OBT represents the age profile of wealth during the life cycle, while the downward-sloping line indicates total wealth (including human capital, that is $a_t + h_t$). At any age, wealth a_t is positive, but the closer individuals are to retirement, the wealthier they are. The concave age profile of a_t is one of the life-cycle model's strongest empirical implications. In fact, many studies have tried to determine whether, holding lifetime resources (the term Ny) constant, individuals who are closer to retirement actually are richer than the young or the elderly, and whether wealth actually is reduced after retirement.

1.4. DEMOGRAPHIC VARIABLES

In the life-cycle model examined up to this point, each consumer acts in isolation and no attempt is made to distinguish between the individual and the family. But we know that reality is different: individuals live in households composed of several members, and the number of household members varies over time. The easiest way to account for the demographic structure of the consumer unit is to consider a utility function that depends on per capita consumption, not total household consumption. Alternatively, since the consumption of a child is not comparable to that of an adult, one can "deflate" household consumption by adult equivalence scales rather than the simple number of members (for instance, taking into account that adults consume more than children).

It should be noted that here and elsewhere in the book we follow the standard "unitary" approach, which assumes that a household acts as if it were a single decision maker, maximizing a well-behaved (single) utility function subject to a budget constraint. An alternative approach differs from this model in recognizing that the individual household members have their own, possibly divergent, rational preferences. The implications of these collective models for intertemporal models are discussed in Chapter 13.

Treating the household as a single entity and defining an appropriate equivalency scale, we consider the objective function of a family in which the utility function depends on per capita consumption adjusted to adult equivalence,

$$u\left(c_t, z_t\right) = u\left(\frac{c_t}{\alpha\left(z_t\right)}\right) = u\left(\bar{c}_t\right),$$

where z_t represents household size or information about household composition (such as number of adults and number of children), $\alpha(z_t)$ the equivalence scale described above, and $\bar{c}_t$ a measure of consumption per adult equivalent. The function z_t generally increases in the first part of the life cycle (when the household is formed and children are born) and declines later on (when children grow up and leave home). The utility function indicates that preferences are separable between but not within periods: the function depends on consumption, household size, and household composition.

Defining consumption per adult equivalent has two implications, one for the level of consumption and another for consumption growth. To see the implication for the level of consumption, assume that the interest rate is equal to the rate of intertemporal preference. In this case we know that the profile of individual consumption would be constant throughout the life cycle. But now the optimal choice for the family is to maintain constant consumption per adult equivalent $\bar{c}_t$, not the absolute level of consumption c_t. Since z_t is a concave function of age (and $\alpha(z_t)$ too is concave), the profile of the level of consumption c_t is also concave.

To see the implication for consumption growth, consider the case in which $r \neq \delta$. The interdependence between intertemporal consumption decisions and demographic variables also introduces a new incentive to replace current consumption with future consumption. To illustrate this effect, we assume that the evolution of z_t is perfectly anticipated and known from the first period and that the interest rate is constant. The problem is to maximize:

$$\max \sum_{t=0}^{T-1} \frac{u\left(c_t, z_t\right)}{\left(1+\delta\right)^t}$$
$$s.t. \quad a_{t+1} = \left(1+r\right)\left(a_t + y_t - c_t\right)$$
$$a_T = 0.$$

The first-order conditions are:

$$\frac{u'(c_t, z_t)}{u'(c_{t+1}, z_{t+1})} = \frac{1+r}{1+\delta}.$$

Let us assume that in each period the utility function is isoelastic with elasticity of intertemporal substitution equal to γ^{-1} and that the equivalence scale takes the simple form $\alpha(z_t) = \alpha z_t$. Hence $u(c_t, z_t) = \frac{1}{1-\gamma}\left(\frac{c_t}{\alpha z_t}\right)^{1-\gamma}$. The first-order condition of the problem can then be written as:

$$\left(\frac{c_{t+1}}{c_t}\right)^{-\gamma}\left(\frac{z_{t+1}}{z_t}\right)^{\gamma-1}\frac{1+r}{1+\delta} = 1.$$

Using the approximation that $\ln\left(\frac{1+r}{1+\delta}\right) \approx r - \delta$, we obtain an explicit solution for consumption growth:

$$\Delta \ln c_{t+1} = \gamma^{-1}(r - \delta) + \frac{\gamma-1}{\gamma}\Delta \ln z_{t+1}. \qquad (1.19)$$

According to equation (1.19), the rate of growth of consumption ($\Delta \ln c_{t+1}$) depends on the difference between the interest rate and the rate of time preference (as in equation 1.12), and the effect of the difference is stronger as the value of the elasticity of intertemporal substitution γ^{-1} increases. In this model, consumption can also grow if household size is expected to grow. If the elasticity of substitution is relatively low ($\gamma^{-1} < 1$), a positive change in the number of household members increases the growth rate of consumption and therefore encourages saving in the current period.

Considering household decisions instead of individual decisions opens up new scenarios for theory and applications. Besides the collective approach mentioned above, there is a large literature on the interdependence of family decisions on consumption and labor supply, observing that women's decision to work depends on husbands' income and/or the presence of children (see Chapter 13). Another active line of research studies the role of the family in sharing and insuring against risks. This function partly compensates for lack of formal insurance markets and is therefore widely cited by supporters of models with complete markets (see Chapter 3).

1.5. INTERTEMPORAL CHOICE IN CONTINUOUS TIME

In this section we complete the analysis of intertemporal choice without uncertainty, presenting a version of the model in continuous time that we are going to use later on (in particular, in Chapters 11 and 12). Although the insights do not differ from those under discrete time, the case of continuous time is useful to see how to derive the intertemporal budget constraint from the dynamic budget constraint and how to express the marginal propensity to consume out of lifetime resources. The model will also be used to derive an explicit solution for the level of consumption and to study the effect of a change in the interest rate on consumption when the utility function is isoelastic, a case that has received a good deal of attention in the empirical literature.

Consider a consumer who maximizes an additive and separable intertemporal utility function subject to a dynamic budget constraint. The consumer lives for T periods. The utility function is isoelastic with elasticity of intertemporal substitution equal to γ^{-1}. The consumer's objective function is:

$$\max \int_0^T \frac{c_t^{1-\gamma}}{1-\gamma} e^{-\delta t} dt$$

subject to the constraints:

$$\dot{a}_t = ra_t + y_t - c_t$$
$$a_0 \text{ given}$$
$$a_T \geq 0$$
$$c_t > 0,$$

where $\dot{x} = dx/dt$ denotes a time variation. The dynamic budget constraint in continuous time shows that at each moment in time the change in wealth is equal to the difference between income (from assets, ra_t, and labor, y_t) and consumption. Initial wealth is given, and last-period wealth has to be non-negative. The Hamiltonian function of the problem is:

$$H_t = \frac{c_t^{1-\gamma}}{1-\gamma} e^{-\delta t} + \mu_t \left[ra_t + y_t - c_t \right].$$

The necessary and sufficient conditions for a maximum are:[6]

$$e^{-\delta t} c_t^{-\gamma} = \mu_t \tag{1.20}$$

$$r = -\frac{\dot{\mu}_t}{\mu_t} \tag{1.21}$$

$$\mu_T a_T = 0.$$

6. Recall that the first-order conditions of the problem are $(dH_t / dc_t) = 0$ and $(dH_t/da_t) = -\dot{\mu}_t$. The condition $\mu_T a_T = 0$, instead, is the terminal condition, see Kamien and Schwartz (1981) for a formal proof.

Since from equation (1.20) we have $\mu_T = c_T^{-\gamma} e^{-\delta T} > 0$, and since $c_T > 0$, the terminal condition becomes $a_T = 0$, that is, the same condition that is imposed in the discrete time model. To obtain the growth rate of consumption, we take the logarithm on both sides of equation (1.20), then take the derivative with respect to time and use (1.21) to eliminate the terms in μ:

$$\frac{\dot{c}_t}{c_t} = \gamma^{-1}(r - \delta). \tag{1.22}$$

As in the discrete time model of Section 1.1, consumption grows over time if the interest rate exceeds the rate of time preference and declines in the opposite case. The effect is stronger as the elasticity of intertemporal substitution γ^{-1} rises. The solution of this differential equation is given by:

$$c_t = c_0 e^{\gamma^{-1}(r-\delta)t}, \tag{1.23}$$

where c_0 is the initial level of consumption.

We next integrate the dynamic budget constraint $\dot{a}_t = ra_t + y_t - c_t$ and use the terminal condition to obtain the intertemporal budget constraint. Multiplying the dynamic budget constraint by the integration factor e^{-rt} and integrating from 0 to T, we obtain:

$$\int_0^T e^{-rt}(\dot{a}_t - ra_t)\, dt = \int_0^T e^{-rt} y_t\, dt - \int_0^T e^{-rt} c_t\, dt.$$

Since the primitive of $e^{-rt}(\dot{a}_t - ra_t)$ is $a_t e^{-rt}$, the equation can be rewritten as:

$$a_t e^{-rt}\Big]_0^T = a_T e^{-rT} - a_0 = \int_0^T e^{-rt} y_t\, dt - \int_0^T e^{-rt} c_t\, dt = h_0 - \int_0^T e^{-rt} c_t\, dt,$$

where h_0 represents the value of human capital, that is, the present discounted value of future earnings. Finally, using the terminal condition, we obtain the intertemporal budget constraint:

$$\int_0^T e^{-rt} c_t\, dt = a_0 + h_0, \tag{1.24}$$

which states that the present discounted value of future consumption is equal to initial wealth plus human capital.[7] Substituting the consumption equation (1.23) into the intertemporal budget constraint (1.24), we get:

7. Note, however, that if the interest rate changes over time, the intertemporal budget constraint should be written as $\int_0^T c_t e^{-\int_0^t r_v dv}\, dt = a_0 + \int_0^T y_t e^{-\int_0^t r_v dv}\, dt$. For simplicity, we neglect this case here.

$$\int_0^T c_0 e^{\gamma^{-1}(r-\delta)t} e^{-rt}\, dt = a_0 + h_0.$$

Since $\int_0^T e^{-\alpha t}\, dt = -\dfrac{e^{-\alpha T}}{\alpha} + \dfrac{1}{\alpha} = \alpha^{-1}\left[1 - e^{-\alpha T}\right]$, assuming $\alpha = \left[r - \gamma^{-1}(r-\delta)\right] > 0$
(to ensure that consumption is positive), we obtain the consumption function:

$$c_0 = \frac{\left[r - \gamma^{-1}(r-\delta)\right]}{1 - e^{-\left[r-\gamma^{-1}(r-\delta)\right]T}}(a_0 + h_0) = \theta(a_0 + h_0). \tag{1.25}$$

The marginal propensity to consume out of total wealth, θ, depends on all the parameters of the model but not on the level of wealth.[8] This follows from the assumption that preferences are homothetic.[9]

Let us study the effect of the interest rate r, preferences (γ and δ), and planning horizon T on the propensity to consume. To evaluate the effect of T, assume for simplicity that $r = 0$ and the utility function is logarithmic, so $\gamma = 1$. In this case $\theta = \dfrac{\delta}{1 - e^{-\delta T}}$; hence the propensity decreases as remaining life T increases.[10] The elderly (individuals with low T) consume a larger share of their wealth than the young (individuals with high T). This prediction of the model was mentioned in Section 1.3.

To evaluate the effect of the other parameters, let us consider a case where the time horizon is infinite, $T \to \infty$, implying that the marginal propensity to consume is $\theta = r - \gamma^{-1}(r-\delta)$. In this case, note that the terminal condition $a_T = 0$ must be rewritten as $\lim\limits_{t\to\infty} a_t e^{-rt} = 0$. We can verify that the propensity to consume increases with the consumer's impatience, $\dfrac{\partial\theta}{\partial\delta} > 0$, and that the effect of the elasticity of intertemporal substitution depends on the sign of $(r-\delta)$. If $(r-\delta) > 0$, then $\dfrac{\partial\theta}{\partial\gamma^{-1}} < 0$, and vice versa. Moreover, if $\gamma^{-1} = 1$, then $\theta = \delta$, and the interest rate does not affect the propensity to consume, $\dfrac{\partial\theta}{\partial r} = 0$ (this is the case of logarithmic utility). If instead $\gamma^{-1} > 1$, the substitution effect dominates

---

8. From equation (1.25) we can obtain, as a special case, the life-cycle model studied in Section 1.3. If $y_t = y$ for $t = 0, \ldots, N$, $y_t = 0$ for $t > N$, then $h_0 = Ny$; furthermore, if $r = \delta$, the solution to the maximization problem is the same as in Section 1.3.

9. A function $f(.)$ is homogeneous of degree r if $f(kc_1, kc_2, \ldots, kc_T) = k^r f(c_1, c_2, \ldots, c_T)$ for $k > 0$. A homogeneous function has the property that the marginal rate of substitution between any two arguments (i.e., (f_{c_s}/f_{c_t}) for all $s \neq t$) does not vary in response to a proportionate change in consumption $c_1, c_2, \ldots, c_T$. The marginal rate of substitution depends on the *ratio* between consumptions of different periods but not on the *level* of consumption in any period. Functions that are monotonically increasing transformations of homogeneous functions (such as the utility functions that we use in this book) are called homothetic and have the same property. Indeed, if $u[f(c_1, c_2, \ldots, c_T)]$ is homothetic, then $(u_{c_s}/u_{c_t}) = (f_{c_s}/f_{c_t})$.

10. The assumption that $\alpha > 0$ ensures that $\delta > 0$ in the special case $\gamma = 1$.

the income effect and the derivative is negative. If $\gamma^{-1} < 1$, the income effect dominates and the derivative is positive. Finally, if $\gamma^{-1} = 0$, then $\theta = r$: there is no incentive to substitute future for present consumption and only the income effect is at work.

It should be noted that a higher r, besides influencing the marginal propensity to consume, also reduces the value of human capital (h_0) and, consequently, the level of consumption. This is what we called the "wealth effect" in Section 1.1. Thus for low values of the elasticity of intertemporal substitution, an increase in the interest rate is more likely to reduce consumption.

In future chapters we will focus on how the marginal propensity to consume is affected by relaxing several of our assumptions. Chapter 3 shows that the conclusions reached here basically apply even in the presence of uncertainty, provided that markets are complete. The results change considerably, however, in the presence of liquidity constraints (Chapter 5), income risk (Chapters 6 and 7), life uncertainty (Chapter 11), bequest motives (Chapter 12), and non-separable utility functions (Chapter 13). In all these cases closed-form solutions are commonly unavailable, so the analysis focuses primarily on the properties of the Euler equation.

1.6. INFINITE TIME HORIZON

The main difference between Modigliani and Brumberg's life-cycle model (1954) and Milton Friedman's permanent income hypothesis (1957) involves the planning horizon, which is finite in the former (hence the importance of saving for retirement) and infinite in the latter. A second difference, not considered here but fully developed in Chapter 4, is that Friedman's model explicitly considers the role of uncertain income fluctuations. Nevertheless, here we can obtain a first insight into that model by considering consumers with infinite horizons.

Obviously, no individual lives forever, but the assumption of an infinite horizon can be justified by positing that individuals belong to a dynasty linked by intergenerational transfers. To see this, suppose that individuals care not only about their own happiness but also about their descendants' happiness. The utility function of these so-called altruistic consumers can be written as:

$$U_b = v\left(c_b; U_{b+1}\right),$$

where c_b represents the sequence of consumption of cohort b over time (for example, from year zero to year T) and $U_{b+1} = v\left(c_{b+1}; U_{b+2}\right)$. The presence of descendants' utility in the individual's objective function makes the horizon effectively infinite. In a deterministic setting and with $v(.)$ being additive in its arguments, one can rewrite the objective function as:

$$U_b = \int_0^T u(c_t)e^{-\delta t}\,dt + \int_T^{2T} u(c_t)e^{-\delta t}\,dt + \ldots = \int_0^\infty u(c_t)e^{-\delta t}\,dt,$$

subject to the constraints:

$$a_0 = \int_0^\infty (y_t - c_t)e^{-rt}\,dt$$

$$\lim_{T\to\infty} a_T \geq 0.$$

With infinite horizon and the additional assumption that $r = \delta$, it is easy to show that the consumption function (1.25) can be rewritten as:

$$c_0 = r(a_0 + h_0) = y^p.$$

According to the model with an infinite horizon (or altruistic consumers), consumption is thus equal to permanent income y^p, which is defined as the annuity value of total wealth, that is, the fraction of wealth that can be spent indefinitely without depleting it. We shall encounter a similar expression for the consumption function in Chapter 4 in a model with discrete time and uncertain labor income.

1.7. AGGREGATE IMPLICATIONS OF THE LIFE-CYCLE MODEL

Our results to this point relate to the study of individual consumers in isolation. In many cases, however, study of national accounts variables is essential, as various economic policies (taxes, transfers, social security arrangements, etc.) affect all consumers simultaneously. Under what conditions can we apply these results to the behavior of the entire economy? In other words, under what conditions is aggregation valid?

The model with altruistic consumers or infinite horizon examined in Section 1.5 solves the problem of aggregation. As dynasties have an infinite horizon, they never age. If the economy is populated by identical dynasties, the behavior of one dynasty is equivalent to the behavior of all, and the national accounts data convey the same information as microeconomic data. In future chapters we shall see that aggregation also depends on the structure of individual preferences, uncertainty, and the possibility of insuring against individual risks.

In the life-cycle model, however, the aggregation process leads to quite different aggregate consumption, saving, and wealth functions. To see this, consider an economy with no growth in population or productivity $n = g = 0$, where n is the population growth rate and g the productivity growth rate). At each point in time, the economy is populated by $\int_{t-T}^{t} dk = T$ individuals, so there is one individual for each generation.[11] Making the same assumption about preferences and income profile as in Section 1.2, in the absence of growth one can interpret Figures 1.2 and 1.3 not as individual profiles but as aggregate income, consumption, and wealth in a given time period.

National consumption, income, saving, and wealth are the sum of the consumption, income, saving, and wealth of the individuals alive in period $t > T$:

$$X_t = \int_{t-T}^{t} x_k \, dk,$$

where k denotes the time of birth, $x = c, s, y, a$, and $X = C, S, Y, A$. We use lower-case letters to denote individual variables and upper-case letters for aggregate variables.[12]

With zero growth, the aggregate variables are constant over time. Using the consumption function, one can readily establish that $C = Y = Ny$. One can also verify from Figure 1.3 that aggregate wealth A is given by the area of the triangle with base T and height given by wealth of the consumer of age N who has just exited from the labor market, $N\left(1 - \dfrac{N}{T}\right)y$:

$$A = \frac{TN\left(1 - \dfrac{N}{T}\right)y}{2}.$$

It follows that the aggregate wealth-income ratio is constant over time and equal to:

$$\frac{A}{Y} = \frac{T - N}{2}.$$

In this simple model the length of retirement $(T - N)$ is the only parameter that determines the aggregate wealth-income ratio. It follows that a lowering

11. We assume that labor force entry and exit occur in continuous time, even if each individual makes choices in discrete time. For instance, the individual born in period τ plans consumption and saving in periods $\tau, \tau+1, \dots, T-\tau-1$.
12. The lower bound of the integral is the age of an individual born T periods ago (at time $t - T$). The upper bound is the age of an individual born today (at time t).

of the retirement age or a lengthening of life expectancy will increase the aggregate wealth-income ratio.

Using the individual saving function of Section 1.2, one can immediately show that in this stationary economy, national saving is zero:[13]

$$S_t = \int_{t-T}^{t} s_k\, dk = \int_{t-N}^{t} \left(1 - \frac{N}{T}\right) y\, dk - \int_{t-T}^{t-N} \frac{N}{T} y\, dk$$
$$= \left[N\left(1 - \frac{N}{T}\right) y - (T-N)\frac{N}{T} y\right] = 0. \tag{1.26}$$

The first integral is the saving of workers (born between $t-N$ and t), and the second integral is the dissaving of the retired (born between $t-T$ and $t-N$). In a stationary economy the saving of the young is therefore exactly offset by the dissaving of the old. The most important lesson of equation (1.26) is that, in contrast with the permanent income model of Section 1.5, microeconomic saving functions are very different from the individual functions.

Let us now consider growth of population and productivity. Modigliani and Brumberg assumed that the individual income profile is constant through life, and that productivity growth occurs between generations. Each generation is therefore larger and richer (in terms of lifetime income) than its predecessor,

$$L_k = L_0 e^{nk} \quad \text{and} \quad y_k = y_0 e^{gk},$$

where L_0 and y_0 denote the size of the initial generation and the income of its members, respectively. As in Deaton (1992), one can calculate national consumption by summing the consumption of all generations alive in the current period t (individuals whose age is between 0 and T):

$$C_t = \int_{t-T}^{t} \frac{N}{T} y_0 e^{gk} L_0 e^{nk}\, dk = \frac{N}{T} y_0 L_0 e^{(g+n)t} \left[\frac{1 - e^{-(g+n)T}}{g+n}\right].$$

National income is the sum of the incomes of the individuals who work in period t, that is, those whose age is between 0 and $(T-N)$:

$$Y_t = \int_{t-N}^{t} y_0 e^{gk} L_0 e^{nk}\, dk = y_0 L_0 e^{(g+n)t} \left[\frac{1 - e^{-(g+n)N}}{g+n}\right].$$

---

13. The results that aggregate wealth is constant and that aggregate saving is zero hold even if the interest rate does not equal the rate of time preference.

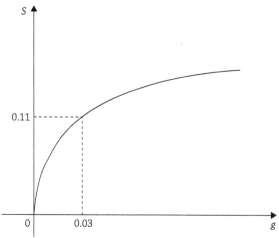

Figure 1.4: Aggregate saving and growth in the life-cycle model

Notice that national consumption and income grow at the common rate $(n+g)$, even if individual income and consumption are constant. Finally, the aggregate propensity to save is an increasing function of $(n+g)$:

$$\frac{S_t}{Y_t} = 1 - \frac{N}{T}\frac{1-e^{-(g+n)T}}{1-e^{-(g+n)N}}.$$

(1.27)

The reason the life-cycle model predicts a positive correlation between saving and growth is simple: an increase in either population or productivity growth implies that the saving of the young exceeds the dissaving of the old, so aggregate saving is positive.

Figure 1.4 plots the relationship between saving and growth implied in equation (1.27), assuming $T = 50$ and $N = 40$. In the postwar period the average economic growth rate of OECD countries has been approximately 3 percent. For this rate the model predicts a saving rate of 11 percent, not far from the actual historical average. And for growth values close to 3 percent, the derivative of equation (1.27) with respect to growth is approximately equal to 2: an increase of 1 percentage point in the growth rate is associated with a rise of 2 points in the propensity to save.

Empirically, many studies have discovered a strong correlation between the two variables; see, for instance, Loayza, Schmidt-Hebbel, and Servén (2000). Figure 1.5 documents the saving-growth correlation in a large sample (118 countries). The correlation is positive and significant, suggesting that a 1-percentage-point increase in the growth rate of per capita GDP is associated with a rise of about 2 points in the saving rate, in line with the life-cycle model predictions. However, one cannot simply ascribe the correlation to a genuine life-cycle effect (growth causing saving), rather than to other mechanisms.

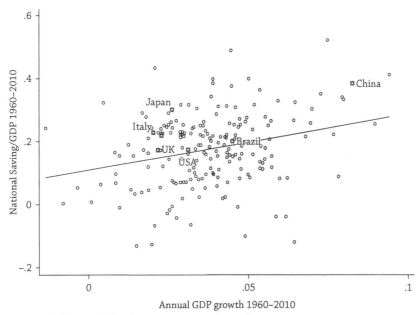

Figure 1.5: The correlation between saving and growth

Note: The figure plots the national saving rate against GDP growth in 1960–2010. Data are drawn from the World Bank Saving Database.

For instance, many growth models (including the Solow model and those with endogenous growth) predict that an increase in saving will be associated with higher subsequent growth, and therefore generate the same correlation through a completely different mechanism.

Furthermore, in more realistic versions of the life-cycle model the relation between saving and growth is not so clear-cut. In fact, productivity growth also occurs during the working life of an individual, and not just because income rises from one generation to the next, the case we examined here. When the age-income profile is upward-sloping, we must consider two possibilities. If young people can borrow against future earnings, an increase in the rate of productivity growth increases not only saving by the middle-aged but also borrowing by the young, making the overall effect on aggregate saving ambiguous. If instead young people are credit-constrained, an increase in productivity growth still raises aggregate saving. Like upward-sloping income profiles, bequest motives and concerns for future generations attenuate the link between growth and saving. As we shall see in later chapters, the possibility of insurance, different pension regimes, taxation, and other factors also affect the relationship.

This chapter has introduced the intertemporal problem faced by a consumer who has to choose between consumption and saving when future incomes and interest rates are known with certainty. We have derived the Euler equation and the consumption function in both discrete and continuous time. We have also shown the importance of aggregation, and why individual consumption and saving functions can differ from aggregate ones. In the next chapters we will extend the basic model to allow for uncertainty, credit market imperfections and other realistic features of preferences and of the economic environment.

CHAPTER 2

The Age Profile of Consumption and Wealth

The simple version of the life-cycle model studied in Chapter 1 yields a number of important empirical predictions about consumption and saving behavior. First, the growth rate of consumption depends on the difference between the expected real interest rate and the rate of time preference and varies with the elasticity of intertemporal substitution (EIS). Second, individuals seek to smooth the marginal utility of consumption over time. In the simplest case examined in Chapter 1, this means that they also try to smooth consumption. Third, young consumers should be accumulating resources for retirement, and hence have an adequate level of wealth at retirement. Finally, the elderly should be decumulating resources, ideally at a rate that implies zero remaining wealth at the date of decease.

To test these predictions, one can draw on a vast array of data on interest rates, consumption, income, and wealth. Some come from time series and national accounts, others from cross-sectional or longitudinal surveys of households. This chapter introduces stylized facts that emerge from a first examination of such data, pointing out the merits but also the drawbacks of the available sources.

2.1. CONSUMPTION GROWTH AND THE INTEREST RATE

The model discussed in Chapter 1 suggests that the key factor in consumption growth is the incentive to substitute consumption between different times. This incentive depends on the level of the interest rate and is measured by the elasticity of intertemporal substitution. This elasticity is also the key to understanding the role of monetary and fiscal policy in modern macroeconomic models. For example, if it is high, even a small reduction in the real interest rate (for example, one generated by a fall in government spending) induces a large increase in current consumption, resulting in output stabilization. For these reasons, precise estimates of this parameter are crucial for many policy applications.

In Section 1.2 we derived the Euler equation with an isoelastic utility function and constant real interest rate. This derivation can be generalized to the case of time-varying interest rate to obtain:

$$\frac{c_{t+1} - c_t}{c_t} = \gamma^{-1}\left(r_{t+1} - \delta\right).$$

The incentive to substitute future consumption for present consumption depends on the difference between the real interest rate and the rate of time preference. If $r = 0.03$, $\delta = 0.015$, and $EIS = 0.3$, the rate of consumption growth should be 0.45 percent per year. Even if we double the value of the elasticity of intertemporal substitution, the rate of growth of consumption is only 0.9 percent. This value is much lower than that found in United States national accounts data, as can be seen from Figure 2.1 (where the average consumption growth rate is 3.1 percent from 1970 to 2012). One can reduce the

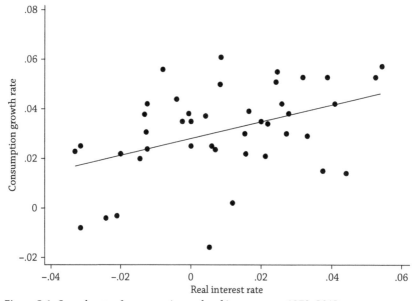

Figure 2.1: Growth rate of consumption and real interest rate, 1970–2012
Note: The real interest rate is measured as the difference between the return on three-month T-bills and the deflator of private consumption. Sources: NIPA and Global Financial Data (https://www.globalfinancialdata.com/index.html).

discrepancy between theory and the empirical data by assuming unrealistically low values for the discount rate. Alternatively, one can reconcile them by substantially increasing the elasticity of intertemporal substitution. But this conflicts with the microeconomic evidence (discussed below), which suggests that the elasticity of intertemporal substitution is less than 1. This inconsistency is known as the excess growth puzzle.

Estimating the EIS involves adding an error term to the Euler equation above, assuming that the rate of time preference δ does not vary over time so its effect on consumption growth is absorbed by a constant term, and then regressing the growth rate of consumption on the expected real interest rate:

$$\frac{c_{t+1} - c_t}{c_t} = k + \gamma^{-1} r_{t+1} + \varepsilon_{t+1}, \tag{2.1}$$

where k is a constant. Equation (2.1) is usually estimated by instrumental variables because, as will be shown in Chapter 4, the error term might be correlated with the interest rate in period $t+1$. This equation can be estimated either with aggregate data or with microeconomic data. One of the earliest and most complete studies based on aggregate data is Hall (1988), which uses various measures of the real interest rate and different sampling periods between 1924 and 1983 and concludes that when the endogeneity of the interest rate and other econometric problems are taken into account, the elasticity of intertemporal substitution is close to zero, at least in the United States.

More recent data on the relationship between consumption growth and the real interest rate are displayed in Figure 2.1. The figure, which refers to the period 1970–2012, shows that in the aggregate, consumption growth and real interest rates are positively correlated, although there are many years in which consumption growth was positive and the real interest rate negative (and vice versa). The ordinary least squares (OLS) estimate of the EIS in equation (2.1) is $\gamma^{-1} = 0.31$ and statistically significant; an instrumental variable regression using lags of consumption growth and the interest rate gives a similar result. This point estimate is in a range that many macroeconomists would consider plausible. In fact, with isoelastic utility, the EIS is the inverse of the coefficient of relative risk aversion. The implied risk aversion from Figure 2.1 is 3.2, which is well within the range that economists consider realistic.

In principle, equation (2.1) applies to an individual agent. Only under highly particular conditions (for instance, the existence of a representative agent) can time series data be used to estimate its parameters. Attanasio and Low (2004) make it clear that when such conditions do not obtain (see Chapter 3 for a discussion), the elasticity of intertemporal substitution can be estimated only with microeconomic data available for a long period. Attanasio and Weber (1995) use data from the Consumer Expenditure Survey for the

United States, getting estimates for the elasticity of intertemporal substitution that are in the 0.2–0.4 range, though rarely statistically significant. One limitation of their analysis is that all households are assumed to face the same interest rate. Zeldes (1989) uses variability in after-tax real interest rates induced by differences in marginal tax rates according to household income and obtains an estimate of the EIS of around 0.4, but with a large standard error. More recently, Gourinchas and Parker (2002) find higher values of the EIS, ranging between 0.7 and 2.0.

The range of estimates discussed here suggests that there is still considerable uncertainty surrounding the value of the EIS and that the Euler equation approach to pinning this parameter down has delivered only partial answers.

2.2. SAVING AND THE INTEREST RATE

We already know from Chapter 1 that the effect of an increase in the interest rate on saving depends on the relative importance of the income, wealth, and substitution effects. From an empirical point of view, the key parameter affecting the sign of the relationship between saving and the interest rate is the elasticity of intertemporal substitution. To see why, consider the two-period model of Section 1.1 with isoelastic utility. The saving function is simply:

$$s_t = y_t - c_t = y_t - \frac{h_t}{1 + (1+r)^{\gamma^{-1}-1}\beta^{\gamma^{-1}}},$$

where $h_t = y_t + y_{t+1}(1+r)^{-1}$ is human capital. Let $\theta = (1+r)^{\gamma^{-1}-1}\beta^{\gamma^{-1}}$. Hence the effect of the interest rate on saving is:

$$\frac{\partial s_t}{\partial r} = (\gamma^{-1}-1)\frac{\theta}{(1+\theta)^2}\frac{h_t}{(1+r)} - \frac{\partial h_t}{\partial r}\frac{1}{1+\theta}.$$

The first term on the right-hand side depends on the magnitude of the EIS. Since the second term is always positive (because $\partial h_t / \partial r < 0$ unambiguously), the overall effect is ambiguous. A positive relationship emerges only for relatively high values of the EIS (certainly values above 1). Since the EIS is believed to be relatively small (and unlikely to exceed 1), the strength and sign of the effect of interest rates on saving are empirical issues that theory does not help to resolve.

Estimating the Euler equation offers information on the value of the EIS, but by itself this provides only partial information about the overall effect of interest rates on saving. However, there is an ample literature designed to estimate the direct effect of asset returns on saving. A first approach specifies a reduced form for saving and estimates the interest rate elasticity controlling for other determinants of saving. Honohan (2000) reviews several studies based on aggregate data and concludes that "more studies have found a positive interest rate elasticity than a negative one, but the coefficients have generally been small and often insignificant" (83). Possible reasons this approach has been inconclusive are problems of aggregation (some investors might have positive elasticity of saving, others negative) and endogeneity of interest rates.

A second approach studies the portfolio and saving effect of specific tax reforms that change the after-tax return on certain assets, thus creating cross-sectional and time-series variation in the returns to individuals with different marginal tax rates. Many countries feature such tax incentives to save, particularly for retirement instruments. The specific tax provision and generosity of saving incentives vary considerably across countries, but the basic features are common. For instance, in the United States, households can contribute up to a specified ceiling to retirement saving accounts such as IRAs and 401(k)s, using pre-tax dollars, but withdrawals from the funds are taxed.

These plans have provided the grounds for empirical research that seeks to determine the extent to which contributions to tax-deferred saving accounts represent "new saving" rather than mere substitution between tax-favored assets and other types of assets. Our reading of this literature, as summarized by Poterba, Venti, and Wise (1996), Engen, Gale, and Scholz (1996), Besley and Meghir (1998), and Bernheim (2002), is that there is broad consensus that (at least in the United States) tax-deferred savings accounts have induced massive portfolio shifts toward tax-favored assets, but much less consensus that they have actually increased saving.[1] Chetty et al. (2014) use administrative data from Denmark, where measurement error is virtually absent. In one experiment, they study a reform that reduced substantially tax incentives for rich taxpayers to contribute to retirement accounts, and find that the reform had only a small impact on total saving. In a second experiment, they consider the importance of automatic contributions by looking at the behavior of people who switch from jobs with low contribution rates to jobs with high rates. They find that most individuals exhibit passive saving behavior, and they conclude that automatic enrollments that nudge individuals to save more may have larger impacts on national saving at a lower fiscal cost than saving incentives. This is one example in which economists advocate default solutions, an issue that we will address in Chapter 14. Analyses of tax reforms are quite useful to analyze the impact of specific events, but are not designed to recover the structural parameters of the model.

1. For Italy, Jappelli and Pistaferri (2003) find that savers' decisions to invest respond only modestly to variations in the return on saving policies induced by changes in tax deductibility of the premiums.

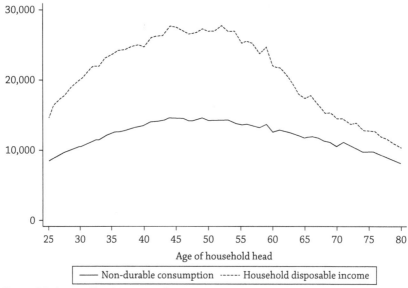

Figure 2.2: Age profile of income and consumption
Note: Data are drawn from the pooled 1980–2010 Interview Surveys of the Consumer Expenditure Survey (CEX).

2.3. THE AGE PROFILES OF INCOME, CONSUMPTION, AND WEALTH

According to the life-cycle hypothesis, consumers try to smooth a volatile income profile by choosing a constant profile of consumption over their life cycle. It follows that saving should be positive for individuals of working age and negative for the elderly, and that accumulated wealth should be a concave function of age and reach a peak around retirement age. These assumptions about consumer behavior can be verified only with the help of microeconomic data—for example, by constructing age profiles of income, consumption, and wealth.

How do applied economists go about constructing such age profiles? A simple approach is to compute the average consumption, income, and wealth of all consumers of a given age and plot the resulting profiles against age.

Figure 2.2 plots household disposable income and consumption against age. The data come from the pooled 1980–2010 Interview Surveys of the Consumer Expenditure Survey (CEX), the only US dataset with comprehensive information on household consumption. Disposable income is defined as the sum of labor income, capital income, and public and private transfers minus taxes. It represents the amount that families have to allot between consumption and saving in each period.[2]

2. Disposable income in the figure is the standard definition, excluding pension contributions of workers and including pension benefits for retired workers. We discuss the validity of this definition in Section 2.7.

The age profile of disposable income is increasing over the life cycle, peaking around age fifty. After sixty, many workers retire and disposable income declines significantly due to the loss of labor income. The consumption profile is more stable, with a first phase in which consumption is much lower than income and another in which households consume almost as much as their disposable income (during retirement). In the working stage of the life cycle the difference between income and consumption is used to increase real and financial wealth or pension entitlements (so-called pension wealth). Saving is positive even during retirement, although much less so than during the working period. Furthermore, both income and consumption profiles are concave, with consumption tracking income over much of the life cycle. However, our definition of consumption excludes all durable goods and the services associated with durables, so it underestimates true consumption and hence tends to overestimate saving quite substantially.

Figure 2.3 plots the cross-sectional profile of wealth, computed using data from the pooled Survey of Consumer Finances (SCF) for 1983–2007. The profile indicates that households accumulate wealth until retirement. Afterward wealth declines but does not fall to zero, which was predicted by the life-cycle model set out in Chapter 1. An important related issue is whether households accumulated enough wealth to finance their consumption during retirement.

There is clearly a discrepancy between the positive saving in old age implied by Figure 2.2 and the negative saving implied by Figure 2.3. This discrepancy may reflect several causes: the fact that changes in wealth do not always match the difference between income and consumption, cohort effects (which we

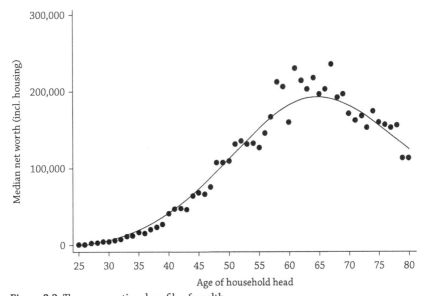

Figure 2.3: The cross-sectional profile of wealth
Note: Data are drawn from the pooled 1983–2007 Survey of Consumer Finances (SCF).

discuss in Sections 2.4–2.6), and the conventional definition of disposable income used in Figure 2.2 (which we discuss in Section 2.7).

2.4. ESTIMATING THE AGE PROFILE OF CONSUMPTION

A fundamental problem in interpreting the profiles of Figures 2.2 and 2.3 is the presence of cohort effects, that is, the fact that the people surveyed in a given cross section were born in different years and therefore may have different resources and preferences. This means one cannot interpret the consumption and wealth profiles as the life-cycle profile of an individual. For example, if we use data from a 2010 cross section, (future) average wealth at age sixty for those born in 1980 is not necessarily well approximated by average wealth of those who were born in 1950 and so are already sixty. In this section we discuss the problems that arise when one wants to account for such cohort effects in estimating the age profile of consumption. Similar methodological problems arise in estimating the age profile of wealth or income, so the discussion here is general.

The theory set out in Chapter 1 predicts that individual consumption and wealth should have distinctive age profiles. That is, consumption should be smoother than income and the wealth profile should be concave, reaching its maximum near retirement age. But in certain cases these age effects are hard (or impossible) to distinguish from effects due to the passage of time (year effects) or the presence at each point in time of different generations (cohort effects).

Why should there be cohort and year effects on top of age effects? Year effects arise because the business cycle may induce wealth destruction at an aggregate level, affecting all households equally. For example, the financial crisis of 2007–9 resulted in a massive decline in the prices of houses and stocks, which affected many individuals simultaneously. Cohort effects are due to shocks that affect some cohorts but not others. For example, the generation that came of age during the Great Depression (often called "Depression babies") may have developed a strong aversion to stockholding, and this may have affected their asset accumulation strategies later in life (Malmendier and Nagel, 2011). Or the postwar baby boom generation may have had fewer opportunities to accumulate assets due to increased competition in the market for education, the labor market, and so on, induced by their large numbers. But the most important reason wealth or consumption may differ across generations is productivity growth between generations, as analyzed in Section 1.7.

We indicate cohorts with the index b (year of birth), and consumption and wealth at age t of individuals born in year b as $c_{t,b}$ and $a_{t,b}$, respectively. In

Chapter 1 we show that, in general, consumption is an age-dependent function of lifetime resources (or human wealth) h_b (assuming no initial assets):

$$c_{t,b} = \theta(t)h_b. \tag{2.2}$$

In general, the propensity to consume out of lifetime resources, $\theta(t)$, depends not only on age t but also on the interest rate, the rate of time preference, and the elasticity of intertemporal substitution (which in this section we assume to be the same for all individuals). In more complex and realistic formulations of the life-cycle model, the propensity to consume depends on other factors as well, such as family composition and social security legislation.

The important point of equation (2.2) is that the propensity to consume, $\theta(t)$, depends on age but not on lifetime resources. Resources instead determine the level of consumption, regardless of age. These implications of the theory follow from the hypotheses of homothetic preferences and absence of uncertainty.

Estimation of equation (2.2) from a single cross section may confound the pure age effect $\theta(t)$ with the fact that productivity may be growing across cohorts (the h_b term).[3] To understand why, we consider a simple example.

In Figure 2.4 we plot the hypothetical age profile of consumption (the dashed lines) of individuals born in 1960, 1970, 1980, and 1990. Assume for simplicity that each individual enters the labor market at age twenty. In our example, the consumption of each individual is constant, as predicted by the life-cycle hypothesis, so the function $\theta(t)$ is independent of age, and hence $c_{t,b} = \theta h_b$. However, we assume that there is productivity growth across cohorts, which shifts the line of constant consumption depending on the individual's year of birth.

Now suppose that we survey consumers in 2010 and plot consumption data against age. We would find that consumption equals θh_{1990} for the twenty-year-olds (who are just entering the labor market), θh_{1980} for the thirty-year-olds (who entered the labor market in 2000), θh_{1970} for the forty-year-olds, and θh_{1960} for those who are fifty and entered the labor market in 1980. The resulting cross-sectional profile (the solid line in the graph) is downward-sloping and could be read as evidence that consumption declines over the life cycle (as in the $r < \delta$ case discussed in Chapter 1), whereas in fact consumption is constant; that is, the downward slope simply reflects the cohort effect (the growth in h_b that takes place across generations). The relationship between age and consumption that is estimated on the basis of cross-sectional data is thus utterly misleading.

3. In the simplified version of the model that we examine here, the cohorts differ only in productivity. In reality, however, their preferences, their mortality rates, and the institutions they face may also be different.

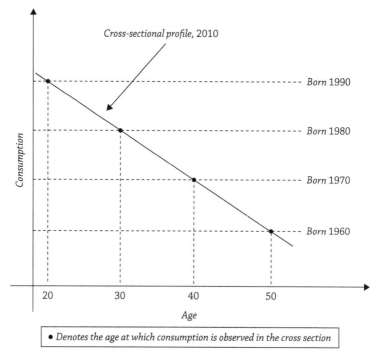

Figure 2.4: Age and cohort effects in consumption

To understand the issue econometrically, let us assume—consistent with Figure 2.4—that a cohort's resources grow at rate g, that is, $h_b = h_0 \exp(gb)$, where h_0 is the initial value of cohort resources, g is the growth rate of productivity, and there are no business cycle effects. Both the parameters h_0 and g are unknown and need to be estimated from the data. It is now useful to write equation (2.2) in logarithms:

$$\ln(c_{t,b}) = \ln\theta(t) + \ln(h_0) + gb. \tag{2.3}$$

Assume that $\theta(t) = \exp(\alpha t)$. This functional form accommodates the various cases studied in Chapter 1. In particular, the sign of α depends on the value of the interest rate relative to that of time preference. For example, if $r > \delta$, the consumption profile is always increasing and $\alpha > 0$. If $r < \delta$, $\alpha = 0$, and if $r < \delta$, the consumption profile is always decreasing and we should find $\alpha < 0$. We hence rewrite the consumption function (2.3) as:

$$\ln(c_{t,b}) = \ln(h_0) + \alpha t + gb. \tag{2.4}$$

Even if we observe the consumer's age t and year of birth b, we cannot separately identify the parameters α and g from the consumption equation using cross-sectional data. The reason is that t and b do not provide independent information about the individual: age is immediately given by year of birth and vice versa. From the econometric standpoint, it is therefore impossible to identify the age effect (the parameter attached to variable t) separately from the cohort effect (the parameter attached to variable b) because the survey year is obtained as $t + b$, that is, as the sum of age and year of birth. Hence, in our specific example, where for each individual $t + b = 2010$, one can rewrite equation (2.4) as:

$$\ln c_{t,b} = \ln h_0 + \alpha t + g(2010 - t)$$
$$= \underbrace{(\ln h_0 + 2010g)}_{\text{constant}} + \underbrace{(\alpha - g)}_{\text{coeff. on age}} t.$$

A regression of consumption on age would identify the difference between the age and the cohort effect, not the two separately.

The literature has proposed several ways to attack this identification problem. One simple strategy relies on outside information. King and Dicks-Mireaux (1982) propose an ingenious method to account for cohort effects when only cross-sectional data are available. They use out-of-sample information to obtain a proxy for the term h_b in equation (2.2). The method was originally proposed for estimating the profile of wealth but is also valid for consumption. King and Dicks-Mireaux measure the resources of each cohort by using information on productivity growth from national accounts and then pass on the relationship between wealth and lifetime resources as a function of age and other demographic variables. The major limitation of this method is that cohort effects are assumed and not estimated from the data, which precludes the possibility that cohorts may differ not only in productivity but also in preferences. Furthermore, the reliability of the implied age effect is conditional on the validity of the out-of-sample assumption.

Alternative solutions consist in increasing the dimensions of the data, that is, moving from single cross sections to repeated cross sections or panels. In both cases, additional survey years make possible independent variation between b and t; that is, one observes individuals of the same age at different times. In panel data they are the same individuals, whereas in repeated cross sections they belong to a representative sample of the same cohort. In principle, the best choice is panel data, because they follow the same individuals over time (i.e., we could observe all the points in the dashed lines of Figure 2.4).[4] However, the choice is not obvious in this context, because panel data suffer from attrition and the data may become increasingly unrepresentative as time goes by. The advantage of repeated cross sections is that, unlike panel

---

4. A panel is called *continuous* if the households surveyed are always the same (as in the Panel Study of Income Dynamics in the United States and the British Household Survey) and *rotating* if households are interviewed for a number of periods and then

data, they are available in many countries, and generally with large samples. Repeated cross-sectional surveys include the Family Expenditure Survey in the United Kingdom and the Current Population Survey in the United States. Deaton (1985) develops the econometrics of such data, providing the conditions under which repeated cross section data can be used to track cohorts over time and estimate panel data relationships.

The identification of age and cohort effects from panel or repeated cross section data depends crucially on the hypothesis that there are no business cycle effects. Including the latter breaks the identification argument once more. From an econometric viewpoint, consider an extension of the econometric model (2.4) that adds time effects:

$$\ln\left(c_{t,b}\right) = \ln h_0 + \alpha t + g b + d_m \delta, \tag{2.5}$$

where d_m is a matrix of dummy variables that capture time or business cycle effects related to the survey year $m = t + b$. These effects may arise from extending the model of Chapter 1 to allow for uncertainty. To see the identification problem most clearly, assume that the time effects consist of a simple time trend: $d_m = m$. Equation (2.5) can be rewritten as:

$$
\begin{aligned}
\ln\left(c_{t,b}\right) &= \ln h_0 + \alpha t + g b + m \delta \\
&= \ln h_0 + \alpha t + g b + (t + b)\delta \\
&= \underbrace{\ln h_0}_{\text{constant}} + \underbrace{(\alpha + \delta)t}_{\text{coeff. on age}} + \underbrace{(g + \delta)}_{\text{coeff. on cohort}} b,
\end{aligned}
\tag{2.6}
$$

showing that the age and cohort effects are contaminated by the presence of year effects.

In estimating equation (2.6), a better approach is to use a flexible specification for age and cohort effects. In Figure 2.5, we report the results from a regression of log consumption against a full set of age dummies. The dashed line represents the fitted profile obtained omitting cohort effects, the solid line the fitted profile obtained controlling for a full set of year-of-birth dummies. The age profile is normalized to be zero at age 25. Assuming that time effects are absent, the difference between the two can be interpreted as the bias arising from cohort effects. It is apparent that in CEX data the bias affects

replaced with others in order to maintain a representative sample (as in the US Consumer Expenditure Survey); it is *balanced* if all the households it comprises are interviewed for the same number of periods. Recently, some *cohort* panel surveys have been conducted, interviewing not only the household of origin but also those formed from it (as children create their own families, say).

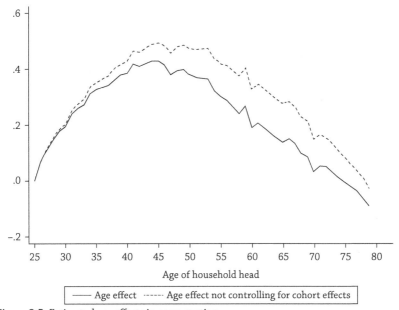

Figure 2.5: Estimated age effects in consumption

Note: The dashed line represents the fitted consumption profile obtained omitting cohort effects, the solid line the fitted profile obtained controlling for a full set of year-of-birth dummies. Data are drawn from the pooled 1980–2010 Interview Surveys of the Consumer Expenditure Survey (CEX).

mostly older generations, so the cross-sectional age profile is more hump-shaped than the cohort-adjusted profile.

One point worth stressing is that there is no solution to the multi-collinearity involving age (t), year of birth (b), and year of the survey (m). Age, cohort, and time effects can be identified only by imposing non-testable identifying assumptions.

Deaton and Paxson (1997) proposed to circumvent the problem by assuming that the year effects add up to zero and are orthogonal to a time trend (m), hence $\sum_m d_m = 0$ and $\sum_m m d_m = 0$. This is equivalent to assuming that any trend in the data reflects a combination of age effects and cohort effects and thus can be predicted from the first year in which the individual makes consumption plans. The assumption is therefore that d_m captures only the effect of additive macroeconomic shocks or the presence of non-systematic measurement error.[5]

5. The method is restrictive for another reason as well. In the presence of uncertainty, the effect of macroeconomic shocks on consumption and wealth depends on age (for example, a young consumer responds differently to an unexpected change in income than an individual close to retirement). These interaction effects are absent in the Deaton-Paxson assumption.

2.5. DEMOGRAPHIC VARIABLES AND EQUIVALENCE SCALES

Another problem in interpreting the profiles of Figures 2.2 and 2.3 is that household structure varies over the life cycle. In the baseline life-cycle model described in Chapter 1 we assumed that each consumer acts in isolation, not distinguishing between individual and family. In Section 1.4 we took into account the fact that household structure changes over time and that consumption patterns may reflect changes in the size and composition of the household. This led us to reformulate the consumer problem in terms of per capita consumption rather than total household consumption.

To show the importance of changes in household structure, Figure 2.6 plots family size against the age of the household head. The profile is hump-shaped, with marriage taking place early in the life cycle, followed by the arrival of children, a peak around age forty-five, and a decline thereafter as children leave home.

Empirical researchers typically use the age of the head of the household as a proxy for the "age" of the household and consider a utility function that depends on per capita household consumption. However, there are drawbacks to this proxy, as the definition of "household head" is somewhat arbitrary and may depend on survey conventions, and the head's identity can change

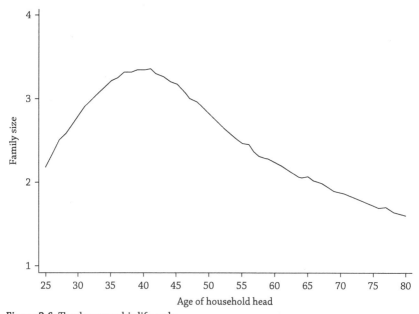

Figure 2.6: The demographic life cycle
Note: Data are drawn from the pooled 1980–2010 Interview Surveys of the Consumer Expenditure Survey (CEX).

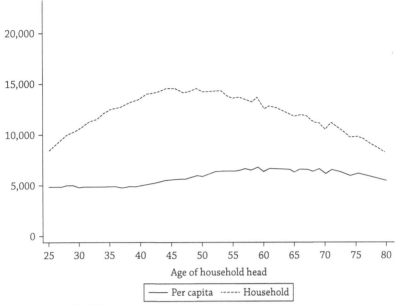

Figure 2.7: Non-durable consumption
Note: Data are drawn from the pooled 1980–2010 Interview Surveys of the Consumer Expenditure Survey (CEX).

owing to, say, divorce or death. Applied researchers have not yet satisfactorily accounted for these problems.[6]

One way of taking demographic effects into account is to discard total household consumption in favor of per capita consumption. This is done in Figure 2.7, which shows that the per capita consumption profile is much flatter than the total consumption profile. However, this procedure also poses complex problems, because it assumes that the consumption of a child is comparable to that of an adult. A more appropriate approach is to use equivalence scales, that is, assign different weights to different household members. Such weights typically depend on age and family size. For example, the Organisation for Economic Co-operation and Development (OECD) scale assigns a weight of 1 to the first adult in the household, 0.7 to any other adult, and 0.5 to any child. Equivalence scales can thus convert units of household consumption into adult-equivalent units. They also play an important role in public policy. For example, welfare payments (food stamps, Temporary Assistance to Needy Families, etc.) vary with household size and composition.[7]

6. Deaton and Paxson (2000) took a significant step in this direction by ingeniously allocating household consumption to the consumption of individual members and applying the life-cycle model to individuals, not to households. There is no simple way to implement their approach because of economies of scale, public goods, and family transfers.

7. For a comprehensive overview of equivalence scales, see Deaton (1997, ch. 4).

2.6. THE AGE PROFILE OF WEALTH

The life-cycle model with finite horizon suggests that wealth increases until retirement and then falls:

$$a_{t,b} = \lambda(t)h_b, \qquad (2.7)$$

where $\lambda(t)$ is a concave function of t independent of h_b. The wealth equation (2.7) generalizes the life-cycle model studied in Chapter 1. In particular, equation (1.18) shows that wealth increases linearly until retirement age, $a_{t,b} = \frac{t}{N}\left(1 - \frac{N}{T}\right)h_b$, for $t = 0,\ldots,N-1$, and then becomes $a_{t,b} = \left(1 - \frac{t}{T}\right)h_b$ for $t = N,\ldots,T$. Versions of the model where $r \neq \delta$ change the shape of the function $\lambda(t)$ but not the fact that it is concave and independent of h_b.

Do assets actually follow a concave profile over the life cycle of an individual? And do they fall after retirement? These fundamental predictions of the model are apparently simple to test, but in practice they have proved to be very difficult to answer convincingly. The reason is that again, as in the case of consumption, the estimation of the wealth profile is contaminated by time and cohort effects.

One of the earliest efforts to study the life-cycle pattern of wealth accumulation was made by Diamond and Hausman (1984). Using panel data from the US National Longitudinal Survey of Mature Men, they found that the wealth of the elderly declined at a rate of around 5 percent per year. Estimates from Hurd (1989) from the Retirement History Survey indicate decumulation rates ranging from 1.5 to 3 percent a year (and more for couples without children). The results obtained by King and Dicks-Mireaux (1982) with Canadian data indicate wealth reductions by the elderly ranging between 2 and 8 percent a year, depending on the specification used.

Rather than wealth data, many studies use data on saving to test the hypothesis that individuals run down assets after retirement. In principle, the change in assets should equal saving, so the type of data used should be immaterial. In practice, however, saving is measured as disposable income minus consumption, and wealth as the sum of real and financial assets. In survey data, there is no guarantee that the two measures deliver the same results, especially because wealth is heavily affected by capital gains and losses, which are not usually recorded in measures of disposable income. Furthermore, the resulting definitions of saving might be affected by various measures of income and consumption, including the treatment of durable goods, and the misreporting of income and some spending categories.

Recent evidence comparing asset decumulation as gauged by the two measures (change in wealth and the difference between income and consumption) comes from Hurd and Rohwedder (2010), based on the Health and Retirement Study. Using wealth changes, they find that decumulation by singles is faster than by couples. Using the difference between income and consumption, they find lower dissaving rates for singles and no decumulation at all by couples.

In recent decades two large international projects have investigated the issue of whether wealth diminishes (or saving is negative) after retirement. The NBER project in the early 1990s (Poterba, 1994) focused on the G7 economies. It concluded that there is no evidence of wealth decumulation in old age and, further, that it is difficult to explain the cross-country differences in household saving rates. Almost twenty years later, another project addressed similar issues, relying on repeated cross-sectional data. This work confirmed many of the earlier findings: there is little wealth decumulation after retirement, and discretionary saving—carefully distinguished from mandatory saving in pension funds and social security contributions—is positive even in old age (Borsch-Supan, 2003).

The first column of Table 2.1 reports some of the findings of the more recent project. In virtually all the nations covered, saving is positive well beyond retirement. In the United States, Italy, the Netherlands, and Japan, saving declines with age but, except for Japan, is still positive at old ages, and in some countries (France, Germany) saving actually increases with age. In a number of countries the pattern contrasts with the evidence on saving as measured by the first difference of wealth. For instance, discretionary wealth appears to decline in the Netherlands, Italy, and the United States. This divergence of changes in wealth from saving confirms the significant discrepancies between the wealth and saving measures.

The table also provides information on the composition of wealth around retirement. Everywhere, annuitized wealth (in the form of pension funds or social security assets) is quite substantial. For instance, social security wealth is about twice as great as discretionary wealth in Japan and in Italy and about 50 percent greater in the United Kingdom, Germany, and the Netherlands; in the United States, annuitized wealth accounts for about 40 percent of total wealth at retirement.

The counterpart of this is that the income of the elderly consists mainly of annuities (see in particular the careful evidence on the source of retirement income in the US, Dutch, and British studies). Thus, given the high contribution rates to pension funds and social security, the difference between earned income and disposable income is very large in all countries (positive during the working span and negative during retirement). And a proper account of saving would show that the elderly do decumulate assets, in that their consumption is financed in large part by annuities. To take just one example, in the Netherlands median wealth at retirement is only €35,000. This tiny stock of wealth is slowly depleted during retirement but not drained down to zero, perhaps to guard against health and longevity risks or for bequest motives.

Table 2.1. FINDINGS OF THE INTERNATIONAL SAVING PROJECT (VALUES IN EUROS)

Country	Discretionary saving during retirement	Evidence on decumulation of discretionary wealth	Real plus financial wealth around retirement	Pension wealth around retirement	Social security wealth around retirement
France	Increasing with age (between 3,000 and 4,000)	No evidence of decumulation (age profile is flat after age 70)	200,000	NA	NA
Germany	Mean saving is about 3,500, median is 1,000, and both are rather flat after age 65	No evidence of decumulation (age profile is flat after age 60)	150,000	NA but modest; pension funds finance only 6% of retirement income	225,000
Italy	Declining from about 2,000 but still positive in old age	Evidence of wealth decumulation (Modigliani and Jappelli, 2006)	90,000	NA but modest given limited role of pension funds	180,000 (including the severance pay fund)
Japan	Negative saving rates after age 60 or 70, depending on definitions	NA	128,000	NA	215,000 to 320,000, depending on assumptions about the internal rate of return
Netherlands	Low and declining, but still positive in old age	Evidence of wealth decumulation	Average wealth at age 60–64 is 83,000, median is 35,000	NA but very important (90% of the workers are covered)	Between 100,000 and 177,000, depending on household composition
United Kingdom	Median saving after age 65 is about 1,000	NA	NA	NA but very important (87% of workers are covered)	109,200 (about as important as private wealth)
United States	Median saving declines with age but remains positive	Financial wealth declines with age	According to Gokhale, Kotlikoff, and Sabelhaus (1996), for males in the 60–69 age group 41% of total wealth is annuitized; for females in the same age group 46% of total wealth is annuitized		

Note: Except where indicated, the data are taken from the papers in Borsch-Supan 2003.

But the bulk of retirement consumption is financed by the buildup of private pension funds covering 90 percent of workers and a generous pension system.

2.7. THE MEASUREMENT OF SAVINGS AND WEALTH

Section 2.5 makes it clear that a large part of wealth is in the form of pension entitlements and that a large part of saving is through mandated pension systems. Discretionary saving accordingly represents only part of the resources accumulated for later consumption.

For this reason, disposable income as conventionally defined (plotted in Figure 2.2) may not be an appropriate variable for checking the validity of the life-cycle model. In fact, the conventional definition treats pension fund and social security contributions as taxes and pension benefits as transfers. But since contributions entitle workers to a retirement pension, they should be regarded as a (mandatory) component of life-cycle saving and hence added back to income. On the other hand, income from pension funds and social security benefits accruing to the retired represent not income produced but rather a depletion of the pension wealth accumulated previously. The greater the amount of mandatory saving, the greater the difference between earned income and disposable income.

Jappelli and Modigliani (2006) argue that where mandatory contributions to pension funds and social security are sizable (as in all the countries shown in Table 2.1), the age profile of saving as conventionally measured cannot be taken as evidence either for or against the life-cycle model. To illustrate this point and the relationship between discretionary and mandatory saving (or between discretionary wealth and pension wealth), it is useful to start from the individual dynamic budget constraint, assuming for simplicity that the real interest rate is zero (dropping the time subscripts):

$$\Delta x = \Delta a + \Delta p = w - c,$$

where x is total wealth, w earnings, and c consumption. Total wealth is the sum of discretionary wealth a and pension wealth p. However, the two forms differ in that a is bequeathable while p is annuitized and disappears when the individual dies. The right-hand-side variables indicate that total saving (or change in total wealth) is the difference between earnings and consumption.

Earned income (w) includes mandatory contributions to pension funds and social security contributions (τ) and excludes pension benefits (b). From the standpoint of the life-cycle model, this is the relevant income measure. The conventional measure of disposable income is instead $y = w - \tau + b$. Given the two definitions of income, one can compute two measures of saving, discretionary and mandatory:

$$s_d = \Delta a = w - \tau + b - c$$

$$s_m = \Delta p = \tau - b.$$

The former is the conventional measure of saving; the latter is the difference between mandated pension contributions and benefits. Finally, total saving is the sum of discretionary and mandatory saving $s_T = \Delta x = s_d + s_m$.

To understand the importance of the different definitions, consider the case of a worker with a constant age-earnings profile of $15,000 (before contributions) who starts working at age twenty, retires at age sixty, and receives a pension until age seventy-five. The worker contributes a constant fraction of earnings (25 percent) to a pension fund (or to social security) and receives a constant benefit of 66 percent of pre-tax, pre-retirement income, so the present value of benefits equals the present value of contributions (the pension is actuarially fair). Suppose also that desired consumption is flat (at $10,900) and that the interest rate and the growth rate of earnings are both equal to zero.

Retirement income includes only pension benefits. So while earned income is $15,000 until retirement and zero afterward, disposable income is $11,250 before retirement and $10,000 afterward. Given the large contributions and corresponding benefits, discretionary saving represents a tiny share of income ($350 before retirement and –$900 afterward). Mandatory saving before retirement accounts for $3,750, while mandatory dissaving during retirement amounts to the pension received, –$10,000. Even though life-cycle savings are $4,100 before retirement and –$10,900 after, in this example the large swings in this variable are practically eliminated if one goes instead by the conventional definitions of disposable income and saving. If the contribution rate is raised to 27.3 percent, discretionary saving would actually be zero through life. But it would be a mistake to conclude that the flat saving profile contrasts with the predictions of the life-cycle model: in fact, the consumer adheres exactly to that model.

In more general settings, mandatory saving affects the path of discretionary saving, although the impact might not be one for one, as in the foregoing example. However, allowing for different returns on discretionary and pension wealth, individual income growth, imbalances in the social security system, and life uncertainty does not change the qualitative conclusion: namely, that where pension wealth is a substantial component of total wealth, the path of discretionary saving is a very poor indicator of retirement saving.

Several lessons can be drawn from the current state of the literature on estimating consumption, wealth, and saving profiles. First, applied economists need to go beyond the use of repeated cross-section data to control properly for individual heterogeneity. Second, to estimate the relation between discretionary and mandatory wealth, one needs information on pension wealth, which depends heavily on labor market histories. Third, pension wealth is affected by the family's labor supply (for instance, one vs. two income earners), the age gap between spouses, their expected retirement ages, their employment status, and so on. For these reasons, only panel data with information on individual retirement transitions and work histories can measure the substitution between mandatory and discretionary saving. The need for panel data is particularly important in a period like the present, when the distribution of retirement ages and pension benefits is being altered.

A final point is that the annuitization of future medical expenses is not usually included in any measure of saving or wealth of the sort discussed in this chapter. Like pension contributions, public health taxes such as those dedicated to universal health care in many European countries or Medicare in the United States pose important definitional and economic issues. Like pension contributions, payments to the health care fund are also a form of mandatory saving and, as in any pay-as-you-go system, they transfer resources from the young to the old. It is hard to impute these transfers to households (or individuals), because contributions are often paid out of the general income tax and benefits are provided in kind. Still, this is an exercise that is worth attempting, because differences in health care arrangements may help to explain different patterns of consumption, saving, and wealth according to households, time periods, and countries.

CHAPTER 3
Complete Markets

The assumption that consumers face no uncertainty greatly simplifies analysis, but it is unrealistic. Individuals may lose their job without notice, or the firm they work for may suddenly go out of business. Stock markets may boom or bust unpredictably. Unanticipated social security reforms may affect the age of retirement or the size of the pension people are entitled to when they retire. To account for these vagaries of life, the modern theory of intertemporal consumption choice makes explicit assumptions about the nature of the uncertainty that consumers face (in regard to income, asset returns, duration of life, and so forth). When considering economic models under uncertainty, however, one must first determine whether there are markets in which individuals can insure against the risks they face.

An extreme hypothesis considered by economists is that markets are complete. Under complete markets, *all* idiosyncratic risks to individuals can be insured. This is possible only if there is a complete set of contingent consumption claims that are traded at time zero behind the veil of ignorance (i.e., before uncertainty is revealed).[1] What does this mean exactly?

Suppose that the economy has only two consumers (Irving and Joe), two states (good and bad), and a single consumption good. Assume for simplicity that the earnings of the two consumers are perfectly negatively correlated. When consumer i's state is good, he earns $y + 1,000$ (and j earns $y - 1,000$). When consumer i's state is bad, consumer i earns (and $y + 1,000 j$ earns $y + 1,000$).[2] Both Irving and Joe expect to earn y on average, but they face

---

1. Under some technical conditions, it can be shown that the same allocations can be achieved through a sequential market equilibrium using only a full set of one-period-ahead securities (so-called Arrow-Debreu securities) that pay off only if a given event occurs (see Section 3.1).

2. To help intuition, you can think of Irving and Joe as two farmers planting a homogeneous crop (e.g., wheat) on two sides of a hill. Their earnings are given by the value

considerable uncertainty (the standard deviation of their earnings is $1,000).[3] If the two consumers know the characteristics of the economy (i.e., the nature of the shock to the other consumer), they will have a strong incentive to share their income risk through a complete set of contingent consumption claims. A contingent consumption contract could be designed as follows: if Joe turns out to be in the good state, he transfers $1,000 worth of consumption to Irving. If it is Joe who is in the bad state, he receives a $1,000 consumption transfer from Irving. At time 0 the contracts are signed, and at time 1 (when the state is revealed) the contracts are simply executed, and no more trades occur. Irving and Joe still earn (and consume) y on average but face no uncertainty at all (they consume y no matter what). The ex ante contract they sign is Pareto efficient, as it can be easily verified. If consumers are risk-averse (a property common to all the utility functions we shall consider), they would choose exactly this solution. The example can be extended to the case of many consumers, many states, many periods, and many commodities without altering the basic insights.

While the theory of complete markets is elegant and useful, it flies in the face of reality. Obviously, we do not have all the markets that the theory requires for full consumption insurance. As many authors have noted, however, such insurance can be achieved in many ways, embracing formal markets (insurance contracts), informal channels (e.g., implicit or explicit agreements between private parties), and even public intervention (income redistribution programs).

The assumption of complete markets has two consequences for the analysis of intertemporal choice. First, it neutralizes the effect of uncertainty on the distribution of individual consumption over time. Individuals behave *as if* there were no uncertainty. Optimal allocations will resemble those obtained in the case of certainty examined in Chapter 1. Second, it makes individual behavior coincide with aggregate behavior, so we can study either one indifferently. In this chapter we discuss the validity of these two corollaries of the theory.

In later chapters we will analyze the effect of incomplete credit and insurance markets on intertemporal choices. The comparison will be particularly interesting in cases where individuals have a precautionary motive for saving or when they cannot smooth consumption by borrowing from financial intermediaries. Here, instead, we analyze a model similar to the one discussed in Chapter 2, but under the assumption of complete markets and uncertainty

---

of the wheat they harvest. Wheat also represents the only good they consume (in the form of bread, say). What is uncertain is the effect of moles on yield. Randomly, moles choose one side of the hill to eat the wheat (which reduces the yield, $y-1,000$) and one side of the hill for their droppings (which increases the yield through manuring, $y+1,000$).

3. We assume that each event has a 0.5 probability of occurring.

about future income. Below we illustrate some extensions of the model, such as in the presence of heterogeneous individual preferences, and some empirical tests of the complete-market hypothesis. We conclude with a discussion of why the assumption fails.

3.1. A MODEL WITH TWO STATES AND TWO PERIODS

In this section we analyze the decisions of a consumer who decides how to allocate resources between different states of the world and periods of time. Unlike the example used in the introduction, in which consumers trade contingent consumption claims, here we develop a case in which they trade securities. We assume that there are only two periods and two states of the world. The generalization to many periods and many states will be considered in Section 3.2.

In the first period there is no uncertainty and the consumer receives income (or an endowment) equal to y_t; in the second period there are two possible states of the world, g and b (good and bad), with associated incomes $y_{t+1,g}$ and $y_{t+1,b}$. The two states have respective probabilities of:

$$\Pr\left(y_{t+1} = y_{t+1,g}\right) = \pi$$
$$\Pr\left(y_{t+1} = y_{t+1,b}\right) = (1 - \pi).$$

Assuming that markets are complete is equivalent to positing a number of contingent markets exactly equal to the number of contingent goods (in addition, of course, to spot markets). In our example, accordingly, we assume three markets: one spot market for present consumption and two contingent markets for future consumption in the two states of the world. Denote the competitive prices in the spot market and futures markets in the two different states of the world g and b by p_t, q_g, and q_b, respectively. For simplicity, assume that $r = \delta = 0$. We normalize $p_t = 1$, that is, we assume that present consumption is the numeraire and therefore interpret the prices q_j $(j = g,b)$ in relative terms. In practice, q_j is the price of a security that pays off 1 unit of consumption only if state j occurs. That is, the payoff of this security is $x_j = 1\{j \text{ occurs}\}$. Denote with s_j the net purchase of these securities. If $s_j < 0$, consumers sell securities rather than buy (short sales). Note finally that we could allow for a risk-free bond (as in Chapter 1), but in this context it would be redundant, because a risk-free bond that pays off 1 unit of consumption in each state can be replicated by purchasing contingent bonds $s_g = 1$ and $s_b = 1$.

The consumer's problem is to maximize expected utility:

$$u\left(c_t, c_{t+1,g}, c_{t+1,b}\right) = u\left(c_t\right) + \pi u\left(c_{t+1,g}\right) + (1 - \pi)u\left(c_{t+1,b}\right) = u\left(c_t\right) + E_t u\left(c_{t+1}\right), \quad (3.1)$$

where E_t is the expectation conditional on the information available in period t. Equation (3.1) assumes that utility is separable over time and between states of the world. The hypothesis of double additivity between periods and states is reasonable and greatly simplifies the analysis. However, it is important to bear in mind that it implies that the marginal utility of consumption at time t and state j is not affected by consumption in a different period or state. There are cases in which separability over time is hard to defend (as in the case of consumption habits, durables consumption, etc.) and cases in which it is the separability across states of nature that may be violated (as when enjoyment of consumption differs between states of good and poor health). We defer discussion of non-separability to Chapter 13.

The budget constraints faced by the consumer are:

$$c_t = y_t - q_g s_g - q_b s_b$$
$$c_{t+1,g} = y_{t+1,g} + s_g \quad \text{with prob. } \pi$$
$$c_{t+1,b} = y_{t+1,b} + s_b \quad \text{with prob. } (1-\pi),$$

which give the intertemporal budget constraint:

$$c_t + q_g c_{t+1,g} + q_b c_{t+1,b} = y_t + q_g y_{t+1,g} + q_b y_{t+1,b}.$$

Replacing the two period constraints in the objective function gives:

$$\max u\left(c_t, c_{t+1,g}, c_{t+1,b}\right) = u\left(y_t - q_g s_g - q_b s_b\right) + \pi u\left(y_{t+1,g} + s_g\right) + (1-\pi)u\left(y_{t+1,b} + s_b\right).$$

The first-order conditions with respect to s_g and s_b are:

$$-q_g u'\left(c_t\right) + \pi u'\left(c_{t+1,g}\right) = 0$$
$$-q_b u'\left(c_t\right) + (1-\pi)u'\left(c_{t+1,b}\right) = 0,$$

which imply the state-specific Euler equation:

$$u'\left(c_t\right) = \frac{\pi}{q_g} u'\left(c_{t+1,g}\right) = \frac{(1-\pi)}{q_b} u'\left(c_{t+1,b}\right).$$

To specify the solution, we assume that the pricing of security j is actuarially fair. This is equivalent to assuming that the price equals the probability of event j occurring, for example, $q_g = \pi$ and $q_b = (1-\pi)$.[4] Under this

4. Actuarial fairness implies that an insurance company issuing securities s_g and s_b purchased by consumers in period t at prices q_g and q_b and paying off in period $t+1$

restriction, the optimal allocation of resources between periods and between states satisfies:

$$u'(c_t) = u'(c_{t+1,g}) = u'(c_{t+1,b}).$$

It is easy to verify that the optimal consumption plan satisfies the condition:

$$c_t^* = c_{t+1,g}^* = c_{t+1,b}^*, \qquad (3.2)$$

that is, full consumption insurance. By substituting this condition into the intertemporal budget constraint with $q_g = \pi$ and $q_b = (1-\pi)$, we get:

$$c_t^* = c_{t+1,g}^* = c_{t+1,b}^* = \frac{1}{2}(y_t + E_t y_{t+1}).$$

Consider the example of the introduction, where $y_t = y$, $y_{t+1,b} = y - 1{,}000$, $y_{t+1,b} = y - 1{,}000$, and $\pi = 0.5$. What the consumer does in this case is purchase 1,000 units of s_b and sell 1,000 units of s_g. If the good state occurs, the consumer pays a return $s_g = 1{,}000$ to whoever bought the securities. If the bad state occurs, the consumer receives a return, $s_b = 1{,}000$ from the securities purchased in the first period. The optimal consumption plan thus distributes the expected value of total income uniformly over time *and* across states of nature, exactly the same solution found in Chapter 1 in the case of certainty: individuals consume exactly the same amount in the good and bad states of the world. In subsequent chapters we will clarify that in the absence of contingent markets it is always possible to shift resources between the two periods but not between the two states of the world: in order to smooth consumption, individuals will have to rely solely on their savings, not on insurance markets. In other words, consumption will be equalized in expectation,

$$c_t^* = E_t c_{t+1}^* = \pi c_{t+1,g}^* + (\pi + 1) c_{t+1,b}^*, \qquad (3.3)$$

but not state by state. In this case (i.e., in the absence of contingent insurance contracts) the consumer would transfer the same amount of assets to the second period, regardless of the state of the world. This is clearly inefficient, because in the good state of the world there would be far too much consumption relative to the bad state. A final consideration relates to the variability of

depending on the state that occurs makes zero profits. In other words, the insurance company solves the following profit maximization problem with respect to s_g and s_b:

$$\max q_g s_g + q_b s_b - \pi s_g - (1-\pi)s_b.$$

future consumption. With complete markets, the variance of future consumption is zero, as is clear from equation (3.2). If markets were incomplete and saving in the first period were still zero, then the variance of future consumption would coincide with that of future income and could therefore be very high.

3.2. THE MULTI-PERIOD MODEL

We can now generalize the foregoing example to the case in which there are S states of the world, the horizon is infinite, and the economy is populated by N consumers. The ith consumer maximizes:

$$\max \sum_{s=1}^{S} \sum_{t=0}^{\infty} (1+\delta)^{-t} \pi_{s,t} u(c_{i,s,t}),$$

where $\pi_{s,t}$ is the probability of state s occurring in period t (we assume this is the same for all individuals), δ is the rate of time preference, and $u(c)$ is concave. Note that for every t, $\sum_{s=1}^{S} \pi_{s,t} = 1$ must hold.

For simplicity, we assume that all consumption choices are delegated to a central planner, who has the task of implementing the optimal allocation of resources for the N consumers in the economy. It can be shown that this result is identical to that of a decentralized market economy where decisions are taken individually (the case examined in Section 3.1 with only two periods and two states of the world). The planner's objective function is:

$$\max \sum_{i=1}^{N} \lambda_i \sum_{s=1}^{S} \sum_{t=0}^{\infty} (1+\delta)^{-t} \pi_{s,t} u(c_{s,t}), \tag{3.4}$$

where λ_i is the weight the planner attaches to the utility of the ith individual. For now, we assume that the sum of the weights is equal to 1, that is, that the planner maximizes a weighted average of the objective functions of the N consumers. The economic significance of the weights will be clarified below. The planner maximizes the objective function (3.4) subject to the resource constraint that the sum of individual consumptions (aggregate consumption) is equal to the sum of individual incomes (aggregate income) in each period and in each state of the world:

$$\sum_{i=1}^{N} c_{i,s,t} = \sum_{i=1}^{N} y_{i,s,t} \quad \text{for all } s,t. \tag{3.5}$$

The Lagrangean function of the problem is therefore:

$$L = \sum_{i=1}^{N} \lambda_i \sum_{s=1}^{S} \sum_{t=0}^{\infty} (1+\delta)^{-t} \pi_{s,t} u(c_{i,s,t}) + \sum_{s=1}^{S} \sum_{t=0}^{\infty} \mu_{s,t} \left(\sum_{i=1}^{N} y_{i,s,t} - \sum_{i=1}^{N} c_{i,s,t} \right),$$

where $\mu_{s,t}$ is the Lagrange multiplier of the resources of the economy in state s and period t. The first-order condition of the problem in the generic period t is then:

$$\lambda_i (1+\delta)^{-t} \pi_t u'(c_{i,t}) = \mu_t,$$ (3.6)

where we have dropped the subscript s, since in each period only one state of the world occurs. Dividing equation (3.6) for any two consumers (i and j), we obtain:

$$\frac{u'(c_{i,t})}{u'(c_{j,t})} = \frac{\lambda_j}{\lambda_i}$$ (3.7)

for $i \neq j$ and for every t. Although the levels of consumption may be (and usually are) different, the ratio of marginal utility between any two consumers is constant over time.[5]

To better understand the implications of the model, consider a case where the utility function is isoelastic, namely, $u(c) = \dfrac{c^{1-\gamma}}{1-\gamma}$. Taking logarithms of both sides of equation (3.6) gives an expression for the logarithm of consumption:

$$\ln c_{i,t} = \frac{1}{\gamma} \ln \lambda_i + \frac{1}{\gamma} [\ln \pi_t - \ln \mu_t - t \ln(1+\delta)].$$ (3.8)

Lagging the expression by one period,

$$\ln c_{i,t-1} = \frac{1}{\gamma} \ln \lambda_i + \frac{1}{\gamma} [\ln \pi_{t-1} - \ln \mu_{t-1} - (t-1)\ln(1+\delta)],$$ (3.9)

and subtracting equation (3.9) from equation (3.8) gives the growth rate of individual consumption:

$$\ln c_{i,t} - \ln c_{i,t-1} = \frac{1}{\gamma} [\Delta \ln \pi_t - \Delta \ln \mu_t - \ln(1+\delta)] = g_t,$$ (3.10)

where Δ represents a first difference (that is, $\Delta x_{t+1} = x_{t+1} - x_t$). The growth rate of individual consumption depends solely on aggregate components, common to all individuals, not on individual resources. Since everyone's consumption grows at the same rate, those who have higher consumption than average will

5. If the utility function is isoelastic or exponential, the ratio of consumption levels of any two individuals is constant over time. If instead the utility function is quadratic, this is no longer true.

continue to have it in any subsequent period.[6] Note that although individual consumption is not constant but varies over time in response to aggregate fluctuations, as the planner diversifies all individual risks, consumption grows at the same rate for everyone.[7]

Equation (3.10) clarifies that the complete-market assumption entirely neutralizes individual uncertainty: individual (idiosyncratic) income shocks do not affect changes in consumption over time. The main empirical prediction of the model with complete markets is that the growth rate of individual consumption depends solely on aggregate variables and not on individual characteristics (e.g., family income). To check the validity of the hypothesis, one can regress the growth rate of individual consumption on variables that measure shocks to household resources (for example, the rate of income growth or periods of unemployment). Under the null hypothesis of complete markets, these variables should have a coefficient equal to zero. We discuss later how applied economists have used variants of this idea to test the full risk-sharing hypothesis.

Some authors have noted that differences in individual preferences may induce false rejection of full insurance. To see why this is so, we generalize the isoelastic utility function to include a set of demographic variables z: $u(c,z) = \dfrac{c^{1-\gamma} - 1}{1 - \gamma} e^{-\theta z}$. The variables z affect the marginal utility of consumption. For example, z may include household composition (as in Section 1.4), in which case the marginal utility of the same level of consumption increases with household size. In this case, equation (3.8) is rewritten as:

$$\ln c_{i,t} = \frac{1}{\gamma} \ln \lambda_i + \frac{1}{\gamma}\left[\ln \pi_t - \ln \mu_t - t\ln(1+\delta)\right] - \frac{\theta}{\gamma} z_{it}$$

and equation (3.10) becomes:

$$\ln c_{i,t} - \ln c_{i,t-1} = \frac{1}{\gamma}\left[\Delta\ln \pi_t - \Delta\ln \mu_t - \ln(1+\delta)\right] - \frac{\theta}{\gamma}\Delta z_{it}. \qquad (3.11)$$

6. With complete markets the differences in the distribution of the level of consumption are implicitly determined by the initial endowment of skills. More-skilled workers will have higher-than-average income and consumption, and thus their utility is weighted (with weight λ) more by the planner. This can be seen from equation (3.7): if consumer i is weighted more than consumer j, then $\dfrac{u'(c_{i,t})}{u'(c_{j,t})} < 1$ and hence $c_{i,t} > c_{j,t}$ due to concavity of the utility function.

7. If the utility function is exponential, the conclusion is similar: changes in individual consumption depend only on an aggregate component. But if the utility function is quadratic, then changes in consumption are also affected by past levels of consumption.

With this utility function, the growth rate of individual consumption depends not only on aggregate components but also on the growth rate of the individual demographic variables z_{it} that shift individual preferences. With complete markets, individual risk can still be insured with contingent contracts. If z_{it} is the number of household members, for example, larger families may enter into contracts with smaller ones. However, it is not clear that these implementation strategies are realistic.

3.3. TESTS OF COMPLETE MARKETS

Most of the studies that have sought to verify the validity of the model with complete markets are based on regressions of the type:

$$\Delta \ln c_{it} = \beta \Delta \ln c_t + \delta \Delta \ln y_{it} + u_{it}, \tag{3.12}$$

where c_{it} indicates individual consumption, c_t aggregate consumption, and y_{it} a variable that measures the shocks to individual or family income (or in some cases family income as such). In the simplest version of the test, the error term u_{it} can be interpreted as reflecting measurement error in consumption. The null hypothesis of complete markets requires $\beta = 1$ and $\delta = 0$. The latter restriction follows from the fact that with complete markets idiosyncratic changes in income should not affect consumption, the former from the fact that consumption grows at the same rate for all households. To see this more clearly, let us go back to equation (3.6), now assuming that the utility function is isoelastic and there are no preference shifts ($\theta = 0$ in equation (3.11)),

$$\lambda_i \left(1+\delta\right)^{-t} \pi_t c_{i,t}^{-\gamma} = \mu_t,$$

and rewrite it as the product of an individual component and an aggregate component:

$$c_{i,t} = \kappa_i m_t, \tag{3.13}$$

where $\kappa_i = \lambda_i^{1/\gamma}$ and $m_t = \left[\dfrac{\pi_t}{\mu_t (1+\delta)^t} \right]^{1/\gamma}$. Aggregate consumption is given by $\sum_{i=1}^{N} c_{i,t} = \kappa m_t$, namely:

$$c_{i,t} = \frac{\kappa_i}{\kappa} \sum_{i=1}^{N} c_{i,t} = \rho_i \sum_{i=1}^{N} c_{i,t}. \tag{3.14}$$

Table 3.1. A TEST OF COMPLETE MARKETS FOR THAILAND, THE UNITED STATES, AND ITALY

	Thailand	United States		Italy
Growth rate of aggregate consumption	0.74	1.06	—	1.32
	(9.25)	(13.25)		(3.30)
Growth rate of household income	0.34	0.04	0.16	0.53
	(2.00)	(4.00)	(9.88)	(5.30)

Note: The regression for Thailand is reported in Townsend (1989, table 2, 93). The regressions for the United States are reported in Mace (1991, table 3, 947), and Schulhofer-Wohl (2011, table 2, 946). The regression for Italy is estimated with data from the Survey of Household Income and Wealth (SHIW) for the years 1987–1991. The *t*-statistics are reported in parentheses.

Taking logs on both sides and then taking first differences, this implies that individual consumption should move in lockstep with aggregate consumption (or $\beta = 1$ in equation (3.12)).

Table 3.1 shows the results of this regression for three countries: Thailand, the United States, and Italy. In each regression, variable y_{it} represents the disposable income of the family. The coefficient of the growth rate of aggregate consumption is not far from 1, particularly in the United States, but the coefficient of the growth rate of income is positive and statistically different from zero in all three countries. The rejection of the complete-market hypothesis is extremely clear for Thailand and Italy, while for the United States the income coefficient is statistically significant but smaller in absolute value in both studies reported.[8]

The hypothesis that $\delta = 0$ in equation (3.12) is valid only under a number of specific assumptions. First we need to assume that there are no correlated measurement errors between consumption and income. Second, income must be cross-sectionally orthogonal to unobserved preference shifts or heterogeneous discount rates (see equation (3.11)). If leisure is endogenous and preferences are non-separable, changes in income may be induced by changes in leisure and the test will correctly reject the null. In other words, changes in income may appear significant simply because they serve as proxies for the omitted growth in the leisure variable.

Another reason for the rejection of the complete-market hypothesis test is preference heterogeneity. Suppose that people differ in risk aversion: the risk-loving will be more willing to tolerate fluctuations in consumption than

---

8. Mace (1991) shows that the complete-market hypothesis is not rejected when preferences are posited to reflect constant absolute risk aversion (CARA), so the levels rather than the growth rates of consumption and income are used. These results have been criticized by Nelson (1994), who shows that they are sensitive to sample selection and the way consumption data are constructed.

the risk-averse. Hence the regression one should run is not equation (3.12) but rather:

$$\Delta \ln c_{it} = \beta_i \Delta \ln c_t + \delta \Delta \ln y_{it} + u_{it}, \qquad (3.15)$$

where β_i reflects the heterogeneity in risk aversion. Schulhofer-Wohl (2011) notes that under preference heterogeneity, the regression that is typically run in the literature can be rewritten as:

$$\Delta \ln c_{it} = \beta \Delta \ln c_t + \delta \Delta \ln y_{it} + \left[u_{it} + (\beta_i - \beta) \Delta \ln c_t \right],$$

where the term in square brackets is the new error term. The point is that $\Delta \ln y_{it}$ is correlated with the omitted variable $(\beta_i - \beta)\Delta \ln c_t$ if more risk-loving households have income that responds more to aggregate shocks, meaning that the test will signal failure of the complete-market hypothesis even when risk-sharing arrangements are in place. A final explanation for the failure of the hypothesis is that income measurement error biases the test in favor of the null. This may explain the evidence in support of complete markets in developed countries, where measurement issues may be more important.

To overcome some of these problems, Cochrane (1991) seeks to identify exogenous shocks to individual labor income, that is, changes that are outside the agent's control (such as days of illness and involuntary job loss). Cochrane uses the Panel Study of Income Dynamics (PSID), regressing the growth rate of food consumption (the only type of consumption the study specifies) on a number of variables assumed to serve as proxies for exogenous shocks to individual income. The results of some of these regressions are reported in Table 3.2. In most cases the complete-market hypothesis is rejected. For

Table 3.2. THE EFFECT OF INDIVIDUAL RISK ON CONSUMPTION GROWTH

	Households that did not experience changes in size	Households that experienced changes in size
Sick days	−0.05	−0.06
	(−2.36)	(−3.74)
Layoff	−24.03	−26.74
	(−4.95)	(−7.81)
Strike days	−0.21	−0.05
	(−1.24)	(−0.37)
Income growth	0.05	0.10
	(2.43)	(7.09)

Source: Cochrane (1991, table 2, 970–71). The *t*-statistics are reported in parentheses. The estimates come from separate regressions.

example, being laid off reduces the growth rate of consumption by 24 percent on average, while the effect of income growth is of comparable magnitude, as in Table 3.1. In principle, these variables might still be correlated with individual preferences, that is, the random term u in equation (3.12), so the results may not necessarily conflict with the model. For example, one could argue that those who are ill or lose their job become depressed, lose appetite, and therefore voluntarily reduce their food consumption. However, the evidence on whether a dramatic event such as job loss leads to higher or lower consumption is mixed at best.

Regressions similar to Cochrane's are considered by Dynarski and Gruber (1997). The most interesting aspect of this paper is its focus on the different channels that may allow individuals to insure income risks. Using data drawn from the Consumer Expenditure Survey and the PSID, they conclude that the income of the spouse provides little insurance with respect to changes in the income of the breadwinner, while the contribution of public transfers (food stamps, unemployment benefits, etc.) does have a substantial effect. Even the tax system provides implicit insurance by virtue of the redistributive role of progressivity. Dynarski and Gruber found that 35 percent of any change in income is buffered by changes in the marginal tax on labor income. Since only 50 percent of change in income is actually insured, they conclude that households must provide for the remaining 50 percent through their own resources (i.e., by accumulating or decumulating wealth in response to individual risks, contrary to the complete-market hypothesis). Saving is therefore an alternative to risk sharing.

As noted above, one reason for the rejection of the null hypothesis is that households have heterogeneous preferences. Mazzocco and Saini (2012) show that if households have different degrees of risk aversion, the standard tests will reject the complete-market model even when households do share risk efficiently. In particular, in equation (3.12) individual consumption growth will not track aggregate consumption growth perfectly but will respond to idiosyncratic income shocks. Empirically, the expenditure functions (household consumption as a function of pooled resources) of any two households should cross if they differ in degree of risk aversion and share risk efficiently. The intuition is that when times are bad the less risk-averse consumers "insure" the more risk-averse by allowing them to take more of the pooled resources, whereas in good times the opposite occurs.[9] Mazzocco and Saini propose two ingenious non-parametric tests for preference heterogeneity and, using Indian data, conclude that the null hypothesis of identical risk preferences is strongly rejected. They then test efficiency with and without the assumption of preference homogeneity. With it, confirming previous results, they reject

9. These agreements are reminiscent of the "implicit contracts" mechanisms linking a risk-averse worker with a (less) risk-averse firm (Azariadis, 1975).

efficient risk sharing at the village and caste levels; without it, they still reject efficiency at the village level but cannot reject it at the caste level. Their study accordingly suggests that the relevant risk-sharing unit in rural India is caste and not village.

3.4. IMPLICATIONS FOR CONSUMPTION INEQUALITY AND MOBILITY

Equation (3.10) can also be used to derive some distributional implications of the complete-market hypothesis. First, since individual consumption growth depends only on aggregate variables, consumption inequality (as measured, for instance, by the cross-sectional variance of individual consumption) should be constant over the life cycle of a given cohort of individuals. This idea, originally proposed by Deaton and Paxson (1994), has been generalized by Blundell and Preston (1998) and Attanasio and Jappelli (2001). Deaton and Paxson, based on cohort data for the United States, the United Kingdom, and Thailand, strongly reject the null hypothesis. In fact, in all countries the consumption inequality of a given cohort is not constant but fans out as people age.

The second distributional implication of the complete-market hypothesis is that we should observe no consumption mobility. We saw that under this hypothesis changes in individual consumption depend only on aggregate fluctuations common to all individuals. The distribution of consumption at a given point in time is therefore a sufficient statistic for consumption in all subsequent periods. The model with complete markets suggests that the distribution of consumption is stable in time. If in period t households are ranked according to their level of consumption, in period $t + 1$ (and in all subsequent periods) the ranking should remain unchanged: the consumption of each family can grow or shrink as a result of changes in the aggregate resources of the economy, but the increase or reduction is the same for all families. One way to verify the validity of the model with complete markets is to construct a transition matrix for the distribution of consumption in two periods of time and calculate an index of consumption mobility. The advantage of this approach, developed by Jappelli and Pistaferri (2006), is that one could find no changes in consumption inequality even if there were considerable mobility from one year to the next (think of poor and rich simply switching places). Thus simple cross-sectional measures (such as the variance of consumption) may not capture all deviations from full insurance, whereas the transition matrix does. The disadvantage of the approach is that it requires proper panel data on consumption, which are generally hard to come by.

Table 3.3, drawn from Jappelli and Pistaferri (2006), shows that there is quite a lot of consumption mobility in Italy (one of the few countries for which panel data on consumption are available for a non-negligible number of years).

Table 3.3. THE TRANSITION MATRIX OF CONSUMPTION

1993 consumption quartile	1995 consumption quartile			
	1st	2nd	3rd	4th
1st	0.67	0.25	0.07	0.01
2nd	0.24	0.43	0.27	0.07
3rd	0.07	0.27	0.43	0.23
4th	0.02	0.05	0.23	0.69

Note: Data are drawn from the Italian Survey of Household Income and Wealth (SHIW). Source: Jappelli and Pistaferri (2006).

Only 67 percent of households in the first consumption quartile are in the same quartile two years later. About 30 percent of households in the top or bottom quartile are in a different quartile only two years later, and about half of those in the middle two quartiles have moved to a different quartile two years later. A mobility index (such as the Shorrocks index, which is based on the trace of the transition matrix) formally rejects the null hypothesis of no consumption mobility.[10] While measurement error might explain part of the mobility observed, the authors show that in order for the data to be consistent with the complete-market model the measurement error must be implausibly high.

3.5. THE AGGREGATION PROBLEM

One of the most difficult problems in macroeconomics is determining the conditions under which it is possible to apply microeconomic models conceived and developed to characterize the behavior of individual decision-making units (consumers or firms, say) to explain aggregate variables such as total consumption or wealth. Empirically, aggregate data are useful because they provide a long-term perspective on the macroeconomy and because they are more readily available than microeconomic data and less subject to measurement error, attrition problems, and so on. Furthermore, dynamic stochastic general

10. To summarize the amount of mobility in a distribution, one can compute several indices. Denote by M a stochastic transition matrix, and by q the number of quantiles of the distribution (in Table 3.3, quartiles). The Shorrocks index of mobility is defined as $S(M) = \frac{q - trace(M)}{q}$. In Table 3.3 the index can be interpreted as the proportion of households moving across the consumption distribution between t and $t+1$. Since $0 \leq trace(M) \leq q$, the index satisfies the condition $0 \leq S(M) \leq 1$. The lower bound of the index corresponds to zero mobility; in this case $trace(M) = q$ and $S(M) = 0$. The upper bound is total mobility, that is, a case in which all households move to a different quantile in period $t+1$, so that $trace(M) = 0$ and $S(M) = 1$.

equilibrium macroeconomic models are usually based on the representative-agent assumption and calibrated to match aggregate phenomena.

In Chapter 1 we saw that in the life-cycle model the aggregate consumption function does not mirror the individual function. In a number of cases, however, aggregate variables are informative about the underlying individual behavior. For example, it can be shown that this occurs if the planning horizon is infinite and there is no uncertainty. Provided that there are no differences in individual preferences, individual behavior and aggregate behavior coincide even in the presence of uncertainty, as we show in this section, as long as markets are complete. A further important case (which we examine in later chapters) is that of a quadratic utility function, regardless of market completeness.

To see the implications of the complete-market model for the aggregate economy, suppose we append an error term to equation (3.10) to capture measurement error:

$$\ln c_{i,t} - \ln c_{i,t-1} = g_t + \varepsilon_{i,t}. \tag{3.16}$$

If one had individual data, the objective would be to estimate the parameters g_t, the common growth rate experienced in each period by individuals who share risks perfectly. This could be achieved by pooling data for all individuals and times and running a regression of individual growth rates of consumption on a dummy for each period. But suppose that individual data are not available. Equation (3.14) gives us a relationship linking individual consumption to aggregate consumption,

$$c_{i,t} = \frac{\kappa_i}{\kappa} \sum_{i=1}^{N} c_{i,t} = \rho_i \sum_{i=1}^{N} c_{i,t}, \tag{3.17}$$

where $\sum_{i=1}^{N} c_{i,t}$ is aggregate consumption at time t. Individual consumption is a share of aggregate consumption ρ_i that is constant over time. It follows that studying the evolution of consumption in the aggregate is fully equivalent to studying the evolution of consumption of individuals. In fact, taking logs of both sides of equation (3.17) and first differencing to eliminate the individual effect yields:

$$\ln c_{i,t} - \ln c_{i,t-1} = \ln \left(\sum_{j=1}^{N} c_{j,t} \right) - \ln \left(\sum_{j=1}^{N} c_{j,t-1} \right).$$

This implies that one can replace individual consumption data with aggregate consumption data in equation (3.16) to estimate the parameters g_t. Aggregation works perfectly because the growth rate of each individual's consumption is equal to that of aggregate consumption. It is straightforward to calculate this growth rate with national accounts data and track individual behavior even if microeconomic data are not available. In our example, we could use aggregate growth of consumption in period t as an estimate of g_t.

In circumstances where the complete-market hypothesis does not hold, however, the level (or the logarithm) of consumption cannot be decomposed into individual and aggregate components, as in equation (3.14). With incomplete markets, the growth of individual consumption differs from that of national consumption. And in practice the logarithm of aggregate consumption is easily calculated from the national accounts, but not from the average of the logarithms of individual consumption.

To understand the effect of this non-linearity in the aggregation process when markets are incomplete, suppose we want to compute the growth rate of aggregate consumption from the microeconomic data, and that individual consumption evolves according to the Euler equation as:

$$\ln c_{it} - \ln c_{it-1} = g_{it} + \varepsilon_{it} \quad \text{for } i = 1,...,N.$$

In later chapters we develop various models in which, as in this case, the growth rate of consumption is different for each individual. Summing across individuals on both sides of the Euler equation yields:

$$\sum_{i=1}^{N} \ln c_{it} - \sum_{i=1}^{N} \ln c_{it-1} = \sum_{i=1}^{N} g_{it} + \sum_{i=1}^{N} \varepsilon_{it}. \tag{3.18}$$

National accounts data, however, only give us the sum of consumption of N individuals—the terms $\sum_{i=1}^{N} c_{it}$ and $\sum_{i=1}^{N} c_{it-1}$—and not the sum of the logarithm of consumption of the N individuals, as in equation (3.18). Since,

$$\sum_{i=1}^{N} \ln c_{it} - \sum_{i=1}^{N} \ln c_{it-1} \neq \ln \sum_{i=1}^{N} c_{it} - \ln \sum_{i=1}^{N} c_{it-1}, \tag{3.19}$$

the estimates of the Euler equation based on consumption from national accounts are incorrect. As Attanasio and Weber (1993) point out, while we can calculate the logarithm of aggregate consumption (the right-hand side of equation (3.19)) from national accounts, the theory suggests that we should calculate the sum of the logarithms of individual consumption (the left-hand side of equation (3.19)).

To see the relation between the logarithm of the average and the average of logarithms, consider the following second-order Taylor approximation:

$$\ln c \approx \ln E(c) + [c - E(c)]\frac{1}{E(c)} - \frac{1}{2}[c - E(c)]^2 \frac{1}{E(c)^2}.$$

Hence,

$$\ln E(c) \approx E(\ln c) + \frac{1}{2} CV(c)^2.$$

The difference between the logarithm of the average and the average of logarithms is known as the *Theil index of inequality*, which in this approximation is half the squared coefficient of variation. In general, the index depends also on the distribution of resources in the economy and varies with the business cycle. These observations, together with the discussion in Section 1.7, reinforce the need to use microeconomic rather than aggregate data to analyze consumption behavior.

3.6. WHY DON'T WE OBSERVE COMPLETE MARKETS?

Given the overwhelming empirical evidence against complete markets, in the chapters that follow we work on the assumption that markets are incomplete. In particular, in most cases we assume that consumers only have access to a simple form of self-insurance, namely, borrowing and saving through a risk-free bond. It is interesting, however, to understand what it is that impedes complete markets—in other words, to understand what induces violation of the first-best Pareto-optimal solution described in Sections 3.1 and 3.2.

A first issue is that certain risks, by their very nature, cannot be diversified. Aggregate risks, insofar as they affect all pool members equally, are fundamentally uninsurable. A second issue is the distinction between risk and uncertainty, drawn by Knight (1921). An event can be defined as "risky" when we can assign a probability to its occurrence, "uncertain" when we cannot. Risky events may be insurable, while uncertain events may not be, since it is harder to "price" them. But more important, there may be different types of friction preventing the realization of a complete-market equilibrium: informational asymmetries or problems in enforcing risk-sharing agreements.

First let us consider problems involving private information. The model with complete markets posits that all individual shocks are publicly observable, so anyone suffering a negative shock to income is compensated with a positive transfer (and conversely for a positive shock). But if shocks are not observable, then every individual has the incentive to claim having been hit by a negative shock: Irving and Joe, in the example given in the introduction, would both have an incentive to report a negative earnings shock of $1,000 and claim a transfer from the other party (and a judge called to establish the truth would be unable to determine who is entitled to receive the transfer contracted).[11]

11. More generally, market failure can be explained by moral hazard or adverse selection. Consider the hypothetical case of a private market in unemployment insurance.

A second problem is that in many cases contingent contracts are hard to enforce; that is, there is a problem of limited commitment. In the same example, Irving may have no incentive to repay Joe when he gets a positive $1,000 shock to his own income. More generally, in the case of limited commitment full risk sharing may fail for four reasons: (a) high persistence of income shocks, (b) low time preference, (c) near-zero variance of income shock, and (d) low risk aversion (Alvarez and Jermann, 2000). These conditions are quite intuitive. For example, individuals with very persistent incomes are poor risk-sharing partners. Those with persistently low income give back to the pool very rarely, while those with persistently high incomes have greater incentives to walk away from the pool. Similarly, the incentive for risk sharing diminishes when risks are rarer or when aversion to these risks declines.

Some works have tested the importance of private information and limited commitment to understanding deviations from the full-risk-sharing model. The research strategy is to test the complete-market model under circumstances in which private information or limited commitment problems are unlikely to be important. For example, Hayashi, Altonji, and Kotlikoff (1996) have proposed a distinction between risk-sharing within and outside the family. In their terminology, "family" is understood to mean an *extended* family, that is, several households linked by blood or co-residence (for example, parents and children, each with their own households). They assume a set of contingent contracts that can be made and adhered to only by individuals who belong to the same family of origin. The reason is that many of the problems that prevent formal insurance markets from operating (such as information asymmetries or limited commitment) are absent or easier to circumvent within the family. Other authors also believe that the possibility of risk diversification as such constitutes a significant incentive for marriage and household (Becker, 1981). For example, if both spouses work, the variability of household income decreases, reducing precautionary saving (see Chapter 6). However, Hayashi, Altonji, and Kotlikoff (1996) reject the hypothesis of insurance both between and within families.

If employees knew their income would be fully replaced in the event of unemployment, they might simply try to be fired (i.e., put out little effort on the job), and the insurance company might have no way of observing their actions (moral hazard). Alternatively, the demand for unemployment insurance might come primarily from individuals with high unobserved ex ante unemployment risk (adverse selection). In either case, the private market collapses. Government unemployment insurance may resolve the problem of adverse selection by making contributions to the unemployment insurance fund mandatory, but it still cannot eliminate moral hazard. Note that in the case of unemployment insurance and other social insurance programs such as disability benefits, another source of moral hazard is the lack of incentives to exit the program; for instance, jobless workers receiving benefits may turn down job offers, or individuals on disability insurance may remain in the program even when their health status improves.

Attanasio and Davis (1996) follow a similar strategy. As noted above, one possible reason the test for complete markets fails is that private information prevents a complete-market equilibrium from arising. To test this idea formally, they consider publicly observable shifts in the wage structure. During the 1980s and 1990s there was a large increase in wage inequality, driven primarily by an increase in the return to observable and unobservable skills. These wage changes are presumably exogenous with respect to idiosyncratic shocks to taste; moreover, because they are large and publicly observable (newspapers ran numerous articles on the phenomenon), a test that uses such changes as a proxy for income shocks on the right-hand side of equation (3.15) can hardly be said to suffer from private information problems. Attanasio and Davis use data on cohorts (defined on the basis of year of birth and level of education) and find a "spectacular failure" of the complete-market hypothesis: in contrast to the model, which predicts no correlation, cohort-level consumption growth is strongly correlated with cohort-level wage growth.

While the assumption of complete markets seldom passes empirical tests, many economists believe that the self-insurance model, which we introduce in Chapter 4 (and which most of the literature relies on to explain intertemporal consumption behavior), may in some circumstances be equally extreme. Moreover, while the tests of the complete-market hypothesis discussed so far reject the null, they do not specify any clear alternative: is it self-insurance, where no other insurance besides saving and borrowing is available, or something in between self-insurance and full insurance?

While it is true that private information or limited commitment may prevent full risk sharing and that in reality consumers cannot sign contracts against all contingencies, they often do have access to some types of insurance beyond self-insurance, such as formal insurance markets covering specific risks (car accidents or natural disasters, for instance), as well as other formal or informal mechanisms. For example, in many cases the government rescues consumers through a system of transfers (such as unemployment benefits, a form of partial insurance against the risk of being laid off). Other public transfers partially insure against sickness or disability risks. In other cases, informal contingent contracts may provide protection against risks. Examples include implicit contracts between workers and employers and the safety net that parents often provide for their children.

This chapter has taken the complete-market model as a benchmark, but the empirical evidence that we have surveyed shows that a variety of testing strategies and data sets thoroughly reject it. The failure of this hypothesis calls for studying models in which consumption allocations are affected by uncertainty. It further implies that the representative agent framework is inappropriate for studying intertemporal consumption decisions.

CHAPTER 4

The Certainty Equivalence Model

In Chapter 3 we relaxed the assumption that consumers know their future labor incomes with certainty. However, we also showed that the assumption of complete markets entirely neutralizes individual uncertainty. Now we examine the effects of uncertainty on intertemporal consumer choices when markets are incomplete.

The literature has paid considerable attention to the model known as "certainty equivalence," which is obtained when the marginal utility of consumption is linear. This approach allows a closed-form solution for consumption even with uncertainty, but the model also has a number of unrealistic features, notably the postulates that consumers do not respond to increases in risk and that preferences are characterized by increasing risk aversion and the existence of a "bliss point" in consumption.

In Section 4.1 we derive the Euler equation for consumption under uncertainty. We then study optimal consumption decisions with linear marginal utility and discuss the model's implications for saving and for consumption inequality.

4.1. INTERTEMPORAL CHOICE UNDER UNCERTAINTY

In this section we study the problem of a consumer who must maximize expected utility over the rest of his or her life cycle (assumed to end with certainty at T).[1] Labor income and the interest rate (which for simplicity we

---

1. Note that, unlike Chapter 1, which for simplicity of notation assumed consumers die at the end of period $T-1$, this discussion assumes that they start their consumption planning in a generic period t and live until the end of period T.

assume paid on a single asset) are uncertain. To simplify notation, we drop the individual subscript. The objective function is to maximize expected utility:

$$\max E_t \sum_{\tau=0}^{T-t} (1+\delta)^{-\tau} u(c_{t+\tau}),$$ (4.1)

subject to the dynamic budget constraint:

$$
\begin{aligned}
a_{t+\tau+1} &= (1+r_{t+\tau+1})(a_{t+\tau} + y_{t+\tau} - c_{t+\tau}) \quad \text{for } \tau = 0,1,...,T, \\
a_t \ & \text{given} \\
a_{T+1} &\geq 0
\end{aligned}
$$ (4.2)

and where E_t denotes the expectation conditional on the information available in period t. Note that, ex post, the intertemporal budget constraint is satisfied exactly, but at the beginning of each period one can formulate only expectations about the variables comprised by the budget constraint (for instance, the exact value of $a_{t+\tau+1}$ is uncertain if $r_{t+\tau+1}$ is a random variable). This differs from the formulations examined in Chapters 1 and 3.

Researchers typically assume that the terminal condition on wealth in period $T+1$ is satisfied with equality $(a_{T+1} = 0)$. The idea is that in a model with no bequest motive, dying with a positive amount of wealth does not provide any utility gain; in fact, any residual wealth at the end of the last period of life could instead have been used to increase consumption, producing a net increase in utility. Hence there is no incentive to "leave money on the table".[2]

The problem can be solved by dynamic programming (Stokey and Lucas, 1989), which requires defining the value function of the problem, namely:

$$V_t(a_t) = \max E_t \sum_{\tau=0}^{T-t} (1+\delta)^{-\tau} u(c_{t+\tau}),$$ (4.3)

subject to equation (4.2).

The left-hand side of equation (4.3) represents the maximum expected utility (discounted at time t) that the consumer obtains from the optimal sequence of consumption associated with an initial endowment of wealth equal to a_t (the state variable). Hence if $c*$ denotes the optimal solutions to the problem, we have $V_t(a_t) = E_t \sum_{\tau=0}^{T-t} (1+\delta)^{-\tau} u(c_{t+\tau}^*)$. By defining the value function, the multi-period problem becomes a recursive sequence of two-period problems that can be represented by the Bellman equation,

---

2. As we shall see, this reasoning does not necessarily apply to quadratic utility, which is characterized by a bliss point in consumption.

$$V_t(a_t) = \max_{c_t, a_{t+1}} u(c_t) + (1+\delta)^{-1} E_t \left[V_{t+1}(a_{t+1}) \right]$$

$$= \max_{c_t} u(c_t) + (1+\delta)^{-1} E_t \left\{ V_{t+1} \left[(1+r_{t+1})(a_t + y_t - c_t) \right] \right\}, \quad (4.4)$$

substituting the dynamic budget constraint into the second expression and using the fact that $E_t E_{t+1} x = E_t x$ by the law of iterated expectations.

How can a multi-period problem be reduced to a sequence of two-period problems? Equation (4.4) shows that, given the information available in period t, the consumer formulates expectations on future income and interest rates and chooses consumption as if these expectations are to be realized. In other words, c_t is a *sufficient statistic* for the optimal consumption plan for the remaining periods. In period $t + 1$, once the realizations of income and interest rate are observed, the consumer updates the expectations that determine the consumption choice in that period. The solution method continues in the same way until period T.

Differentiating (4.4) with respect to the control variable c_t, we obtain the first-order condition for a maximum:

$$u'(c_t) - (1+\delta)^{-1} E_t \left[(1+r_{t+1}) V'_{t+1}(a_{t+1}) \right] = 0. \quad (4.5)$$

The term $V'_{t+1}(a_{t+1})$ is not observable. Suppose that the optimal solution to problem (4.5) is $c_t^*(a_t)$. Then, by definition of value function (or of indirect utility), we have:

$$V_t(a_t) = u\left[c_t^*(a_t) \right] + (1+\delta)^{-1} E_t \left\{ V_{t+1} \left[(1+r_{t+1})(a_t + y_t - c_t^*(a_t)) \right] \right\}. (4.6)$$

Differentiating equation (4.6) with respect to the state variable a_t and using (4.5) and the envelope theorem, we obtain:

$$V'_t(a_t) = (1+\delta)^{-1} E_t \left[(1+r_{t+1}) V'_{t+1}(a_{t+1}) \right]. \quad (4.7)$$

Substituting (4.7) into (4.5), we obtain:

$$V'_t(a_t) = u'(c_t),$$

that is, the marginal utility of wealth coincides with that of consumption, a condition known as the *envelope condition*. Moving forward one period, we get:

$$V'_{t+1}(a_{t+1}) = u'(c_{t+1}).$$

Substituting this expression into (4.5), we finally get the Euler equation:

$$u'(c_t) = (1+\delta)^{-1} E_t \left[(1+r_{t+1}) u'(c_{t+1}) \right]. \qquad (4.8)$$

This equation gives the conditions under which a given consumption plan is intertemporally optimal. In equilibrium, an infinitesimal reallocation of consumption between two successive periods cannot result in a gain in utility. In other words, in equilibrium the reduction in utility due to the decrease in consumption in period t by one unit is balanced by a corresponding increase in discounted expected utility obtained by postponing consumption to period $t+1$.

The Euler equation (4.8), together with the dynamic budget constraint, provides important information about an individual's life-cycle consumption profile. If the interest rate is constant and equal to the rate of time preference (i.e., $r_t = r = \delta$ for every t), (4.8) becomes:

$$E_t u'(c_{t+1}) = u'(c_t). \qquad (4.9)$$

According to (4.9), marginal utility follows a martingale stochastic process:[3] the expected value of the marginal utility of consumption in period $t+1$ is equal to the marginal utility in period t. This property of the solution was first noted by Hall (1978). While the best predictor of marginal utility is thus the marginal utility of the previous period, ex post marginal utility changes only if the expectations deviate from realizations.

In the absence of specific assumptions about the utility function, equation (4.9) is a stochastic difference equation that is not easy to solve and provides no information concerning the level of consumption. To solve this equation, in Section 4.2 we formulate specific hypotheses concerning the functional form of utility and the labor income process.

4.2. THE EULER EQUATION WITH QUADRATIC UTILITY

The certainty equivalence model depends on strong assumptions about individual preferences and the functioning of capital markets. To our earlier assumptions, namely, that the utility function is additive and separable (between periods and between states of the world) and that the consumer maximizes expected utility[4] and can lend and borrow at the same interest rate (i.e., that there are no imperfections in the credit market), we now add the

3. A stochastic process given by $E_t x_{t+1} = x_t$ is called a random walk if the variance of the innovation $(x_{t+1} - E_t x_{t+1})$ is constant over time. In the more general case of heteroscedasticity, the stochastic process is called a *martingale* (Hamilton, 1994).
4. This assumption implies additivity for the utility function both across periods of time and across states of the world.

assumption that the instantaneous utility function is quadratic. The results under these assumptions are similar (albeit not identical) to those obtained previously in the absence of uncertainty, justifying the term "certainty equivalence model".

For simplicity, we assume that the rate of return on savings is constant, and we rewrite equation (4.8) as:

$$\frac{1+\delta}{1+r}u'(c_t) = E_t u'(c_{t+1}). \tag{4.10}$$

If instantaneous utility is quadratic, $u(c_t) = ac_t - \frac{b}{2}c_t^2$ (with $a,b > 0$), then marginal utility is equal to $u'(c_t) = a - bc_t$. Such a utility function has very convenient analytical properties, but also some unrealistic features. One is that consumption has a "bliss point" (utility reaches a maximum at a value of consumption $c_t = a/b$). This implies that in the last period of life consumers may want to "leave money on the table" (in the form of involuntary bequests) if income realization exceeds the bliss point of consumption. Another drawback is that when the utility function is quadratic, risk aversion is increasing in consumption; in other words, richer consumers are more risk-averse than poorer ones. Finally, as we shall see in detail, with quadratic utility a mean-preserving spread in expected income does not affect consumption or saving choices; that is, individuals do not save for precautionary motives.

The main advantage of quadratic preferences is that given the linearity of the expectation operator $E(.)$, the expected value of the marginal utility of consumption equals that of expected consumption, that is, $E[u'(c)] = u'.[E(c)]$. Since marginal utility is a linear function of consumption, we can invert it. The first-order condition becomes:

$$E_t c_{t+1} = \frac{a}{b}\frac{r-\delta}{1+r} + \frac{1+\delta}{1+r}c_t, \tag{4.11}$$

that is, consumption follows a first-order autoregressive process with drift. Defining an innovation (or forecast error) in consumption as the difference between realized and expected consumption ($\varepsilon_{t+1} \equiv c_{t+1} - E_t c_{t+1}$, with $E_t(\varepsilon_{t+1}) = 0$ by definition), we can rewrite equation (4.11) as:

$$c_{t+1} = \frac{a}{b}\frac{r-\delta}{1+r} + \frac{1+\delta}{1+r}c_t + \varepsilon_{t+1}. \tag{4.12}$$

If the interest rate coincides with the rate of time preference, equation (4.12) becomes simply:

$$c_{t+1} = c_t + \varepsilon_{t+1}. \tag{4.13}$$

This is a first important result of the certainty equivalence model: consumption itself, and not just marginal utility (as in the general case), follows a martingale stochastic process (typically, the variance of innovation does not have to be constant). Ex ante, the best predictor of consumption is previous-period consumption. Ex post, consumption varies only because of forecast errors.

To find an explicit solution for the level of consumption, we must consider the intertemporal budget constraint. As income (hence future consumption) is a random variable, we must consider the expected value of the intertemporal budget constraint:

$$\sum_{\tau=0}^{T-t} \frac{E_t\left(c_{t+\tau}\right)}{(1+r)^{\tau}} = a_t + \sum_{\tau=0}^{T-t} \frac{E_t\left(y_{t+\tau}\right)}{(1+r)^{\tau}}. \tag{4.14}$$

We know from the first-order condition (4.13) that $E_t c_{t+\tau} = c_t$ for all τ. Substituting this condition into the intertemporal budget constraint, we get:

$$c_t \sum_{\tau=0}^{T-t} (1+r)^{-\tau} = a_t + \sum_{\tau=0}^{T-t} \frac{E_t\left(y_{t+\tau}\right)}{(1+r)^{\tau}}. \tag{4.15}$$

Using the properties of geometric series, one can show that $\sum_{\tau=0}^{T-t}(1+r)^{-\tau} = \varphi_t \frac{1+r}{r}$, with $\varphi_t = \left[1 - \frac{1}{(1+r)^{T-t+1}}\right]$. Using this result, (4.15) becomes:

$$c_t = \frac{r}{1+r} \varphi_t^{-1} \left[a_t + \sum_{\tau=0}^{T-t} \frac{E_t\left(y_{t+\tau}\right)}{(1+r)^{\tau}}\right]. \tag{4.16}$$

If the time horizon is infinite, the above expression simplifies even further.[5] Since $\varphi_t \to 1$ when $T \to \infty$, we have:

$$c_t = \frac{r}{1+r}\left[a_t + \sum_{\tau=0}^{\infty} \frac{E_t(y_{t+\tau})}{(1+r)^{\tau}}\right] = \frac{r}{1+r}\left(a_t + E_t h_t\right) \equiv E_t y_t^P, \tag{4.17}$$

where $E_t h_t$ is the expected value of human capital and y_t^P is permanent income. Equation (4.17) is the fundamental equation of the certainty equivalence model, and we will refer to it quite often further on.

---

5. The terminal condition of the maximization problem in this case is $\lim_{t \to \infty} a_t (1+r)^{-t} = 0$.

The consumption function (4.17) that comes out of the certainty equivalence model has several interesting properties. First, the distribution of resources over time does not affect consumption choices. Second, consumption is a linear function of the expected value of lifetime resources, since the term in square brackets in (4.17) indicates total wealth (the sum of the consumer's human capital and financial wealth).[6] Other moments of the distribution of future income (e.g., the variance of future resources) do not affect current consumption; the consumer behaves as if the future resources were known with certainty.[7]

The marginal propensity to consume out of total wealth is given by the term $r/(1+r)$, which is known as the *annuity value* of wealth. When r is small, as it often is in reality, this term is very close to zero. Equation (4.17) indicates that individuals consume only the flow of resources that leaves their level of wealth (their "endowment") unchanged.[8] This flow is the product of wealth and the annuity factor, which is exactly the definition of permanent income. Consumption is equal to the expected value of permanent income, as shown by the last term of (4.17), a result already obtained in Section 1.6 in the case of certainty. For this reason, the certainty equivalence model, in the case of an infinite horizon, is also called the *permanent-income hypothesis*.

If the planning horizon is finite (see equation (4.16)), the marginal propensity to consume out of total wealth increases with age, because older people have fewer periods than young people over which to spread changes in lifetime wealth. In the last period, the marginal propensity to consume is equal to 1.[9] In Section 4.3 we examine some specific examples of the income process.

To solve for the level of consumption, one can use specific assumptions about the income process and solve equation (4.17). For instance, suppose

6. Why do we divide by $(1+r)$? By assumption the interest is received in the subsequent period, so in order to calculate h_t and a_t in period t, we have to discount in period $t+1$ by the interest rate, which in our case is constant.

7. Consider two consumers, one whose future income is 101 with probability 0.5 and 99 with probability 0.5, and another whose future income can be 0 or 200 with equal probability. The two processes have the same mean, but for the second consumer the variability of future income is clearly greater. According to the certainty equivalence model, however, consumption choices are identical.

8. This is equivalent to investing every dollar owned in financial markets and consuming only the return on the investment, r. The return needs to be discounted by one period because the interest is earned at the beginning of the next period. Hence, a one-dollar change in lifetime wealth produces a change in consumption of $r/(1+r)$ dollars.

9. Note that the marginal propensity to consume when the planning horizon is finite is greater than when it is infinite. Indeed, in the case of a finite horizon, the consumer will have to spend by period T not only the flow of interest but also the accumulated wealth.

that income is an independently and identically distributed process, $y_t \sim$ i.i.d. (μ, σ^2). Then lifetime income is:

$$E_t h_t = y_t + \frac{\mu}{r} \qquad (4.18)$$

and the level of consumption can be conveniently expressed simply as a function of the sum of current income and wealth (that is, "cash on hand"):

$$c_t = f(a_t + y_t) = \frac{\mu}{1+r} + \frac{r}{1+r}(a_t + y_t). \qquad (4.19)$$

With different income processes, one can still express consumption as a function of current income and assets, but not necessarily of their sum. We apply this characterization of the consumption function in Chapters 5–7, where we analyze models that go beyond certainty equivalence (that is, models with liquidity constraints or precautionary saving).

4.3. THE CONSUMPTION FUNCTION AND INCOME INNOVATIONS

We will now use the fundamental equation of the certainty equivalence model (equation (4.17)) to further clarify the properties of the solution. Substituting the dynamic budget constraint into equation (4.17) gives:

$$c_t = r\left(a_{t-1} + y_{t-1} - c_{t-1}\right) + \frac{r}{1+r}\sum_{\tau=0}^{\infty}(1+r)^{-\tau}E_t y_{t+\tau}. \qquad (4.20)$$

Lagging the consumption function by one period and multiplying by $(1+r)$, we get:

$$(1+r)c_{t-1} = ra_{t-1} + r\sum_{\tau=0}^{\infty}(1+r)^{-\tau}E_{t-1}y_{t-1+\tau}.$$

Finally, subtracting (4.19) from (4.20) yields an expression for the change in consumption:

$$c_t - c_{t-1} = \varepsilon_t = \Delta c_t = \frac{r}{1+r}\sum_{\tau=0}^{\infty}(1+r)^{-\tau}\left(E_t y_{t+\tau} - E_{t-1} y_{t+\tau}\right). \qquad (4.21)$$

Equation (4.21) gives a structural interpretation for the error term in the Euler equation. Changes in consumption occur only because of changes in expectations about future income; if expectations do not change, neither does consumption. New information available in period t, instead, induces consumers to revise their income expectations and adjust their consumption plans. Equation (4.21) thus indicates that the change in consumption is equal to the annuity value of the change in total wealth (i.e., the discounted value of the difference between the new and the old income profiles). In sum, c_t is constant only when expectations are realized and differs from c_{t-1} only when there are unexpected changes in income. This differential response of consumption to anticipated and unanticipated changes in income is the basis of the modern tests of the permanent-income hypothesis.

4.4. INCOME SHOCKS AND THE MARGINAL PROPENSITY TO CONSUME

Equation (4.21) shows that changes in consumption depend on innovations or shocks to the income process. To see how the income-generating process affects the relationship between consumption and innovations to income, in this section we consider a number of specific income processes. We start with the case in which the planning horizon is infinite and income follows an ARMA(1,1) process—a popular characterization when using macroeconomic time series data:

$$y_t = \rho y_{t-1} + v_t + \kappa v_{t-1}$$

(with ρ possibly equal to 1). Equation (4.21) rewrites as:

$$\Delta c_t = \frac{r}{1+r} \frac{1+r+\kappa}{1+r-\rho} v_t. \qquad (4.22)$$

In equation (4.22) consumption changes depend on the degree of persistence of the income process. The more persistent the process, the more volatile consumption is from one year to the next. To simplify the discussion, consider the case of AR(1) ($\kappa = 0$) and ask how the AR coefficient (ρ) affects the sensitivity of consumption with respect to income shocks. If $\rho = 0$ (the income process is not serially correlated), the marginal propensity to consume with respect to income shocks is $r/(1+r)$. This is because when $\rho = 0$ all variations in income are transitory and individuals consume only the annuity value of the income revision. Hence in this case consumption is much less volatile than income. If instead $\rho = 1$ (income follows a martingale process), all changes in income are permanent, and the marginal propensity to consume with respect to income shocks is equal to 1.

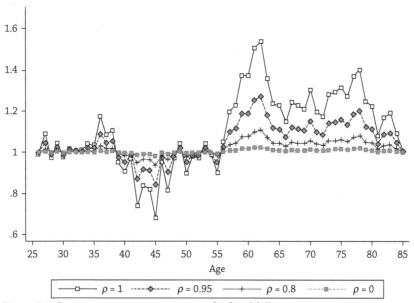

Figure 4.1: Consumption response to income shocks of differing persistence

Note: The figure plots consumption against time for income processes with different degrees of persistence ($\rho = 1.0, 0.95, 0.8$, or 0 and $\kappa = 0.2$ throughout) starting from a normalized initial consumption value of 1, assuming $v = 0.1$ and $r = 0.05$.

Figure 4.1 plots consumption against time for income processes with different degrees of persistence ($\rho = 1.0, 0.95, 0.8$, or 0 and $\kappa = 0.2$ throughout) starting from a normalized initial consumption value of 1, assuming $\sigma_v = 0.1$, and $r = 0.05$. Note that we are using, as an illustration, a single realization of the income process. The figure shows that consumption is much more variable when the process that generates income is more persistent. Quite clearly, the volatility of consumption depends heavily on the size of the autoregressive coefficient, because shocks tend to have a more lasting impact on consumption.[10]

If the horizon were finite, we would have a generalized expression:

$$\Delta c_t = \left(\frac{r}{1+r}\right)\left[1 - \frac{1}{(1+r)^{T-t+1}}\right]^{-1}\left\{1 + \frac{\rho + \kappa}{1+r-\rho}\left[1 - \left(\frac{\rho}{1+r}\right)^{T-t}\right]\right\}v_t \quad (4.23)$$

$$= \theta(r, \rho, \kappa, T-t)v_t.$$

10. This observation is at the heart of the critique set forth by Lucas (1976), namely, that the relationship between consumption and income (or even the relationship between consumption and the interest rate) depends on a parameter that can potentially be affected by policy interventions (in our case, the degree of income persistence, for example because collective bargaining agreements can induce changes in the nature of persistence of income to reflect tax reforms or inflation).

Table 4.1. THE MARGINAL PROPENSITY TO CON-
SUME (MPC) WITH RESPECT TO INCOME SHOCKS

ρ	κ	$T{-}t$	λ
1	−0.2	40	0.81
1	0	10	1.00
0.99	−0.2	40	0.71
0.95	−0.2	40	0.46
0.8	−0.2	40	0.19
0.95	−0.2	30	0.50
0.95	−0.2	20	0.56
0.95	−0.2	10	0.66
0.95	−0.1	40	0.51
0.95	−0.01	40	0.56
1	0	∞	1.00
0	0	∞	0.05

Note: The table shows the value of the marginal propensity to con-
sume (λ) for various combinations of ρ, κ, and $T{-}t$ (setting $r = 0.05$).

Table 4.1 above shows the value of the marginal propensity to consume,
λ, for various combinations of ρ, κ, and $T{-}t$ (setting $r = 0.05$). A number
of implications emerge. If the income shock represents an innovation to a
random walk process ($\rho = 1$, $\kappa = 0$), then consumption responds to it one-
to-one regardless of the horizon (compare the second and penultimate row
of Table 4.1). The response could be attenuated only if shocks were to end
at some point of the life cycle, for instance if the only source of income
uncertainty was earnings, and shocks (permanent or transitory) ended at
retirement. This may not be plausible, though, in that fluctuations in asset
values, intergenerational transfers to children or other relatives, medical
expenditures, and so on all combine to create some income risk even after
retirement.

A decrease in the persistence of the shock lowers the value of λ. When
$\rho = 0.8$ (and $\kappa = -0.2$), for example, the value of λ is a modest 0.19. A
decrease in the persistence of the MA component works in the same direction, but the magnitude of the response is greatly attenuated. Finally, a useful
limiting case is when the income process is i.i.d. (corresponding to $\rho = \kappa = 0$)
and the horizon is infinite: now the marginal propensity to consume is equal
to the annuity value $r / (1+r)$, which is approximately 5 percent.

The limitation of the ARMA characterization of the income process is that it restricts shocks to be of only one kind. But ever since Friedman (1957), economists have recognized that some income shocks are transitory (mean-reverting), while others are persistent (non-mean-reverting), with an effect that is cumulative over time. Examples of transitory shocks are fluctuations in overtime work, bonuses, lottery prizes, and bequests. Permanent innovations are generally associated with job mobility, job loss, promotions, and severe health shocks.

In keeping with these ideas, a very popular characterization among applied economists assumes that income is the sum of a random walk and a transitory i.i.d. component:

$$y_t = p_t + u_t$$
$$p_t = p_{t-1} + \zeta_t.$$

The appeal of this characterization is that it is closely related to Friedman's Permanent Income Hypothesis (PIH).[11] In this case, the equivalent of (4.23) is:

$$\Delta c_t = \lambda_t u_t + \zeta_t,$$

where $\lambda_t = \left(\dfrac{r}{1+r}\right)\left[1 - \dfrac{1}{(1+r)^{T-t+1}}\right]^{-1}$. This shows that consumption responds one-to-one to permanent shocks, but its response to a transitory shock depends on the time horizon. In particular, one can show that the response is small for young consumers (those with a long horizon) and increases with age.

Figure 4.2 plots the marginal propensity to consume out of a transitory shock for a consumer who lives to age seventy-five. Clearly, it is only in the last decade or so of life that there is a substantial response of consumption to a transitory shock. The graph also plots, for comparison, the response given an infinite horizon. An interesting implication is that a transitory unanticipated stabilization policy is likely to have a substantial effect only on older consumers (unless liquidity constraints are important, which may well be the case for younger consumers).

The importance of the stochastic nature of the income process also can be elucidated by considering another significant theoretical point. In the data, consumption is less variable than income (see, for example, Figure 2.2). Is this fact always consistent with the permanent-income hypothesis? It turns out that there are some income processes that imply the opposite of what we observe in the data. These are non-stationary income processes. Let us consider

---

11. See Friedman (1957). Meghir (2004) provides an analysis of how the PIH has influenced the modern theory of consumption.

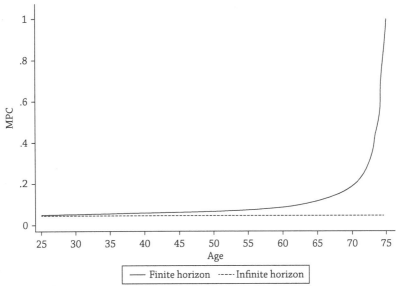

Figure 4.2: The response of consumption to a transitory income shock
Note: The figure plots the marginal propensity to consume (MPC) out of a transitory shock for a consumer who lives to age 75 and for an infinite-lived consumer.

a case studied by Campbell and Deaton (1989) where income follows an AR(2) process:

$$y_t = \mu + (1+\rho)y_{t-1} - \rho y_{t-2} + \varepsilon_t.$$

If $\rho > 0$ (a case that Campbell and Deaton consider possible based on the stochastic process for aggregate labor income in the United States), we can substitute the AR(2) process into (4.21) to obtain:

$$\Delta c_t = \frac{1+r}{1+r-\rho}\varepsilon_t.$$

If we now compute the ratio between the variances of the innovations in consumption and in income, we obtain:

$$\frac{\text{var}(\Delta c_t)}{\text{var}(\Delta y_t)} = \left(\frac{1+r}{1+r-\rho}\right)^2 > 1.$$

In this case, then, the model predicts that the variability of consumption will be *greater* than that of income, an implication that clashes with the empirical evidence, creating what Campbell and Deaton term the *excess smoothness puzzle*.

4.5. SAVING FOR A RAINY DAY

The certainty equivalence model makes it possible to derive a closed-form solution also for the level of savings (Campbell, 1987). Suppose that the planning horizon is infinite and define saving as:

$$s_t = \frac{r}{1+r}a_t + y_t - c_t. \qquad (4.24)$$

Disposable income is the sum of the first two terms on the right-hand side of (4.24). Saving is then the difference between consumption and disposable income.[12] From (4.24), consumption is thus:

$$c_t = \frac{ra_t}{1+r} + y_t - s_t. \qquad (4.25)$$

Equating the two definitions of consumption given by (4.17) and (4.25) (and hence maintaining the assumption that $r = \delta$), we obtain:

$$\frac{ra_t}{1+r} + \frac{r}{1+r}\sum_{\tau=0}^{\infty}(1+r)^{-\tau}E_t y_{t+\tau} = \frac{ra_t}{1+r} + y_t - s_t.$$

Isolate y_t from the sum of the left-hand side to get:

$$-s_t = -y_t + \frac{r}{1+r}\sum_{\tau=1}^{\infty}(1+r)^{-\tau}E_t y_{t+\tau} + \frac{r}{1+r}y_t = -\frac{1}{1+r}y_t + \frac{r}{1+r}\sum_{\tau=1}^{\infty}(1+r)^{-\tau}E_t y_{t+\tau}.$$

Again isolating the term $E_t y_{t+1}$ from the summation and simplifying, we get:

$$-s_t = -\frac{1}{1+r}y_t + \frac{r}{1+r}\frac{E_t y_{t+1}}{1+r} + \frac{r}{1+r}\sum_{\tau=2}^{\infty}(1+r)^{-\tau}E_t y_{t+\tau}$$

$$= -\frac{1}{1+r}y_t + \frac{E_t y_{t+1}}{1+r} - \frac{E_t y_{t+1}}{(1+r)^2} + \frac{r}{1+r}\sum_{\tau=2}^{\infty}(1+r)^{-\tau}E_t y_{t+\tau}$$

$$= \frac{E_t \Delta y_{t+1}}{(1+r)} - \frac{E_t y_{t+1}}{(1+r)^2} + \frac{r}{1+r}\sum_{\tau=2}^{\infty}(1+r)^{-\tau}E_t y_{t+\tau}.$$

12. The return on capital is $ra_t/(1+r)$ and not ra_t. As is explained in Chapter 1, this depends on the assumption that interest on capital is received at the beginning of the subsequent period and must be discounted accordingly.

Repeating for $E_t y_{t+2}$ we have:

$$-s_t = \frac{E_t \Delta y_{t+1}}{(1+r)} + \frac{E_t \Delta y_{t+2}}{(1+r)^2} - \frac{E_t y_{t+2}}{(1+r)^3} + \frac{r}{1+r} \sum_{\tau=3}^{\infty} (1+r)^{-\tau} E_t y_{t+\tau}.$$

Recursive substitutions yield the saving function:

$$s_t = -\sum_{\tau=1}^{\infty} (1+r)^{-\tau} E_t \Delta y_{t+\tau}. \tag{4.26}$$

Equation (4.26) indicates that saving is equal to the present discounted sum of expected *declines* in income. If a consumer expects income to rise, the optimal course is to finance current consumption by borrowing or running down assets in anticipation of higher future incomes $(s_t < 0)$. If instead income is expected to decline (for example, if the probability of unemployment increases or if taxes are expected to go up), saving is positive, as consumption is reduced and resources are accumulated to cope with the expected income decline $(s_t > 0)$.[13] This equation is therefore also referred to as *saving for a rainy day*. In fact, Campbell's original paper uses the expression "rainy day" to describe the saving effect of an expected change in income, not the response to an increase in income risk (which is absent, by definition, in the certainty equivalence model).

4.6. CONSUMPTION INEQUALITY

Deaton and Paxson (1994) examine the implications of the certainty equivalence model for the dynamics of inequality in consumption. The model posits that consumption follows a martingale process. This is a prediction that holds for any agent in the economy, so we can write it as:

$$c_{it} = c_{it-1} + \varepsilon_{it}, \tag{4.27}$$

where the index i denotes a generic individual $(i = 1,2,...,n)$. Suppose further that we distinguish between B cohorts $(b = 1,...,B)$, and denote with n_b the number of individuals in cohort b.

Taking the variance of both sides of equation (4.27) yields:

$$\text{var}_{i \in b}(c_{it}) = \text{var}_{i \in b}(c_{it-1}) + \sigma_{bt}^2, \tag{4.28}$$

13. If c_t and y_t have unit root, then saving is stationary.

where $\text{var}_{i\in b}\left(c_{i,t}\right)=\sum_{i\in b}\dfrac{\left(c_{it}-c_{bt}\right)^2}{n_b}$, $c_{bt}=\sum_{i\in b}\dfrac{c_{it}}{n_b}$, $\sigma_{bt}^2=\text{var}_{i\in b}\left(\varepsilon_{it}\right)$. We have assumed that $\text{cov}_{i\in b}(c_{it-1},\varepsilon_{it})=0$ for all t. Deaton and Paxson show that this holds if aggregate consumption is part of the information set of each individual. Notice that this assumption is unrelated to the orthogonality restriction $E_{t-1}(\varepsilon_{it})=0$. The covariance $\text{cov}_{i\in b}(c_{it-1},\varepsilon_{it})=0$ is taken over a cross section of individuals, while the restriction $E_{t-1}(\varepsilon_{it})=0$ applies to each individual over a time series. For simplicity of notation, from now on we omit the cohort subscripts.

Since the variance is a measure of inequality, and since $\sigma_{bt}^2\geq 0$, equation (4.28) suggests that the inequality of consumption in a group of individuals born in the same year increases over time, so the distribution spreads out as the cohort ages. This result derives from the fact that consumption innovations—that is, the term ε_{it} in (4.27)—are cumulative over time owing to the martingale pattern of the consumption process.

It is also possible to obtain a structural relationship between the cross-sectional variance of consumption and that of income. If the planning horizon is finite and income is the only source of uncertainty up to a retirement age N, the equivalent of equation (4.21) relates the change in consumption to the present discounted value of income innovations:

$$\Delta c_{it}=\left[1-\dfrac{1}{(1+r)^{T-t+1}}\right]^{-1}\dfrac{r}{1+r}\sum_{\tau=0}^{N-\tau}(1+r)^{-\tau}\left(E_t-E_{t-1}\right)y_{it+\tau}=\lambda_t\eta_{it}.$$

The term λ_t is a discount factor that takes account of the fact that the horizon is finite, and η_{it} is the income innovation term. Rewriting the equation in terms of past income innovations $c_{it}=c_{i0}+\sum_{\tau=0}^{t}\lambda_\tau\eta_{i\tau}$ and taking the variance on both sides, as before, we obtain:

$$\text{var}\left(c_{it}\right)=\text{var}\left(c_{i0}\right)+\sum_{\tau=0}^{t}\lambda_\tau^2\sigma_{\eta_\tau}^2.$$

For any given initial distribution of resources $\text{var}(c_{i0})$, the increase in the dispersion of consumption is related directly to the variance of income shocks. When the planning horizon is finite, the cross-sectional variance of consumption increases monotonically with age until retirement, at which point it ceases to rise because income is no longer subject to shocks.[14]

14. In the complete market model all shocks are insurable, and hence the variance of consumption is constant throughout life—a strong empirical prediction.

Computing consumption inequality for the United States, the United Kingdom, and Taiwan, Deaton and Paxson find that the evidence is broadly consistent with the permanent income model: the cohort variance of consumption does fan out as people age, and the spreading slows down considerably after retirement.

Battistin, Blundell, and Lewbel (2009) go one step further and consider the implications of the model for the distributions of income and consumption as such, not just their variances. Using cohort data, they observe that empirically the shape of the income distribution is approximately log-normal, while that of consumption is log-normal. They explain the difference between the two distributions by noting that in the permanent income model, consumption depends on accumulated permanent income shocks, so Gibrat's law—that if a variable is equal to the accumulation of a series of proportional shocks, it follows a log-normal distribution—applies. However, income is also affected by transitory shocks, which are rarely log-normally distributed, reflecting the skewedness of events such as wealth transfers, overtime work, and temporary layoffs, and therefore the mixture distribution of income deviates more strongly than consumption from log-normality.

To sum up, in the model studied in this chapter there is income uncertainty, but people do not change their consumption decisions when uncertainty changes. The model is analytically convenient, it helps to gain intuition into the forces that affect consumption decisions, and it delivers a closed-form solution for consumption and consumption inequality. However, in this model changes in income risk have no effect on saving, and credit markets are assumed to be perfect. To study how consumption responds to risk or credit market imperfections, we need to modify consumers' preferences or introduce borrowing constraints. This leads naturally to Chapters 5, 6, and 7, in which the model is extended to allow for liquidity constraints and precautionary behavior.

CHAPTER 5
Liquidity Constraints

The theory of intertemporal choice that we have developed so far assumes that there are no imperfections in the credit market. The ability to borrow and save as much as needed—imposing only the intertemporal budget constraint—allows the transfer of resources over time and thus maintenance of a stable consumption profile through the life cycle. Now we will study how the consumer's problem changes in the presence of credit market frictions. As we shall see, the latter may explain why consumption growth is sensitive to expected changes in income (excess sensitivity of consumption) and why it is greater than predicted by the certainty equivalence model (excess growth of consumption).

Before discussing a model with *liquidity constraints*, we need to clarify the concept of imperfect credit markets. We consider constraints on the amount a consumer can borrow. We ignore cases in which the borrowing rate is higher than the rate of return on consumers' assets. And we focus on borrowing to finance consumption of non-durables, not expenditure on consumer durables or house purchase.

A consumer is subject to a liquidity constraint if he or she cannot borrow as desired, given the terms of the loan contract (interest rate, loan maturity, installments, etc.) and the time profile of expected income. The constraint can be written as a requirement that assets cannot fall below a fixed level b:

$$a_t \geq -b.$$

If $b = 0$, the constraint is equivalent to imposing the condition that wealth must be non-negative, preventing the consumer from borrowing. If $b > 0$, the consumer can borrow (and wealth can be negative), but only up to a certain limit. For instance, the consumer may have a current account overdraft facility.

We have not posited that the constraint must be imposed in every period t or that b is constant. In fact, a consumer can perfectly well be subject to a constraint in some stages of the life cycle (early in one's working life, say, or during a spell of unemployment) and not others. Furthermore, the constraint may depend on consumer characteristics (income, employment status, etc.), on whether the loan serves to purchase durable goods (which can be used as collateral), and on supply factors, such as efficiency and competition in the financial industry.

To analyze the effect of liquidity constraints on intertemporal consumption decisions, we start with a simple two-period model positing no uncertainty (Section 5.1) and study the effect of expected income changes in Sections 5.2–5.4. In Section 5.5 we derive the Euler equation with liquidity constraints in a multi-period setting.

5.1. A TWO-PERIOD MODEL

Suppose that initial wealth is zero $(a_t = 0)$ and that the rate of time preference and the interest rate are both zero as well, $r = \delta = 0$. The objective function of the consumer in the case of certainty is:

$$\max u(c_t) + u(c_{t+1}),$$

subject to the dynamic budget constraint $a_{t+1} = y_t - c_t$. Given the terminal condition $a_{t+2} = 0$, it follows immediately that the intertemporal budget constraint is $c_t + c_{t+1} = y_t + y_{t+1}$.

When there are no liquidity constraints, the solution is a constant level of consumption, namely:

$$c_t^* = c_{t+1}^* = \frac{y_t + y_{t+1}}{2}. \tag{5.1}$$

We take this as the benchmark solution. Now suppose we impose the liquidity constraint $a_{t+1} \geq 0$: this implies that in the first period the consumer can save but not borrow. Since $a_{t+1} = y_t - c_t$, the constraint is equivalent to imposing $c_t \leq y_t$. The problem can be solved by writing the Lagrangean function:

$$L = u(c_t) + u(c_{t+1}) + \lambda(y_t + y_{t+1} - c_t - c_{t+1}) + \psi(y_t - c_t),$$

where ψ, the Kuhn-Tucker multiplier associated with the liquidity constraint, can be interpreted as the shadow price of debt, that is, the increase in utility that follows from relaxing the borrowing constraint. The first-order conditions are:

$$u'(c_t) - \lambda - \psi = 0$$
$$u'(c_{t+1}) - \lambda = 0 \qquad (5.2)$$
$$\psi(y_t - c_t) = 0 \quad \text{if } \psi \geq 0.$$

Combining the first two conditions, we obtain:

$$u'(c_{t+1}) = u'(c_t) - \psi. \qquad (5.3)$$

Since $\psi \geq 0$, liquidity constraints reduce the marginal utility of consumption over time (that is, consumption increases over time). In other words, given the assumptions on the utility function, $u''(c_t) > 0$ and $u''(c_t) \leq 0$, the rate of growth in consumption is higher with credit rationing than with perfect credit markets (where, given the assumption $r = \delta$, consumption growth is zero):[1] the consumer would like to borrow but cannot and is accordingly forced to consume less in the first period and more in the second than if there were a perfect credit market.

The solution is simple. If $\psi = 0$, then the liquidity constraint is not binding, the Euler equation is identical to that obtained in Chapter 1, and consumption is equal in the two periods, as in equation (5.1). If instead $\psi > 0$, the solution is simply $c_t = y_t$ and $c_{t+1} = y_{t+1}$. Since the consumer lives for only two periods, exactly the resources available are consumed in each period.

But what determines the value of ψ? That is, when will $\psi = 0$ or $\psi > 0$? Since the constraint is imposed on wealth at the beginning of the second period, $\psi < 0$ (the constraint is binding) only if $a^*_{t+1} < 0$, where a^*_{t+1} is planned wealth in the absence of liquidity constraints. Since $a^*_{t+1} = y_t - c^*_t$, then the constraint binds ($\psi > 0$) only if income is expected to be higher in the second period, $y_t < y_{t+1}$. For it is precisely when future income exceeds current income that consumers want to borrow.

Analytically, the optimal solutions for consumption in the two-period model with liquidity constraints are:

$$c_t = \min\left\{ y_t ; c^*_t \right\}$$
$$c_{t+1} = \max\left\{ y_{t+1} ; c^*_{t+1} \right\}.$$

Figure 5.1 illustrates the effect of the liquidity constraint: if it is not binding, the budget set (all the possible combinations of consumption allowed by

1. A simple first-order approximation of equation (5.3) gives $\dfrac{c_{t+1} - c_t}{c_t} \cong \dfrac{\psi}{u'(c_t)} \; EIS \geq 0$.

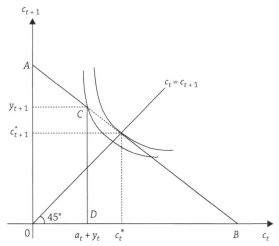

Figure 5.1: The effect of liquidity constraints in the two-period model

the intertemporal budget constraint) is given by the area below segment *AB*. Adding the liquidity constraint, the set shrinks to the area *ACD0*.[2] If planned consumption c_t^* (the amount that would be chosen in the absence of liquidity constraints) exceeds current income y_t, the consumer is constricted to a corner solution that corresponds to $c_t = y_t$ *(and $\psi > 0$)*. If instead $c_t^* \leq y_t$, the liquidity constraint $a_{t+1} \geq 0$ has no effect because the consumer would choose not to borrow *even* in the absence of credit constraints (and hence $\psi = 0$).

To summarize, in a model with two periods and no uncertainty, the consequences of liquidity constraints are clear. The optimal solution of the constrained maximization problem may be a *corner solution* (in mathematical terms, the tangency between the indifference curve and the budget line is at a corner, point C in Figure 5.1). Liquidity constraints bear only on the consumption of those who wish to borrow $(y_t < y_{t+1})$, while net savers $(y_t \geq y_{t+1})$ are not affected. Since earnings increase with age, the constraint is more likely to affect the behavior of the young.

5.2. THE SENSITIVITY OF CONSUMPTION TO EXPECTED INCOME CHANGES

In a model without liquidity constraints, the distribution of resources over the consumer's lifetime does not matter. For example, someone who expects to

---

2. The budget set when the consumer is subject to a liquidity constraint is given by the intersection of the two subsets $c_{t+1} = y_t + y_{t+1} - c_t$ (the intertemporal budget constraint) and $c_t \leq y_t$ (the liquidity constraint).

Table 5.1 THE EFFECT OF EXPECTED INCOME CHANGES

	Perfect credit markets		Liquidity constraints	
	Baseline	Promotion	Baseline	Promotion
y_t	1	1	1	1
y_{t+1}	3	4	3	4
c_t	2	2.5	1	1
c_{t+1}	2	2.5	3	4
Borrowing in period t	1	1.5	0	0
$\dfrac{E_t(c_{t+1}-c_t)}{E_t(y_{t+1}-y_t)}$	-.-	0	-.-	1
MPC period t	-.-	0.5	-.-	0
MPC period $t+1$		0.5		1

receive a promotion in the future will increase current consumption immediately by borrowing. In the model with liquidity constraints, however, the timing of the income change matters, in that the consumer can increase consumption only when the promotion actually occurs.

To show how the timing of income affects that of consumption, consider again the two-period model with $r = \delta = 0$. In the absence of liquidity constraints, the optimal solution is to keep consumption constant and equal to average income in the two periods. To illustrate with a simple numerical example, in Table 5.1 we assume $y_t = 1$ and $y_{t+1} = 3$. If capital markets are perfect, the consumer borrows an amount equal to 1 in the first period so that consumption equals 2 in both periods.

Suppose now that in period t the consumer learns of a forthcoming promotion in period $t+1$, so expected income increases from 3 to 4. Given the income innovation, consumption rises to 2.5 in both periods. At the optimum, the change from first- to second-period consumption is equal to 0 against an expected income change of 3 units. Since the consumer smooths expected income fluctuations, the sensitivity of consumption to expected income changes is nil, $\dfrac{E_t(c_{t+1}-c_t)}{E_t(y_{t+1}-y_t)} = 0.$[3] Also note that after the news of the promotion is received, first-period consumption increases by 0.5 unit compared with a change in expected income of 1 unit (from 3 to 4). It follows that

3. We use the ratio of expected consumption changes to expected income changes even though there is no uncertainty in the model. In fact, in our setting second-period income is known, so expected and realized income changes are always equal. In later chapters we link this discussion with the empirical literature distinguishing the consumption effects of expected and unexpected income changes.

the marginal propensity to consume with respect to the income innovation is 0.5 in both periods. In general, with $r = \delta = 0$ and a T-period model, the marginal propensity to consume is much lower, $1/T$, and in a model with infinite horizon it is zero.[4]

When the consumer cannot borrow in the first period, the constraint $a_{t+1} \geq 0$ holds with equality. Both before and after getting news of the promotion, the consumer is forced to consume exactly the income earned in each period. The change in consumption now depends on expected changes in income, $\dfrac{E_t(c_{t+1} - c_t)}{E_t(y_{t+1} - y_t)} = 1$, contrary to what is predicted by the model without constraints. Also note that the marginal propensity to consume with respect to the income news is 0 in the first period and 1 in the second. In other words, consumption responds too little in the first period and too much in the second.

With perfect credit markets, the ability to shift resources freely over time breaks the link between the timing of income and consumption. It is not surprising that when there is less capacity to borrow, the distribution of resources affects both the level and the slope of the consumption curve.

Liquidity constraints contradict some other predictions of the theory as well, such as the hypothesis that the marginal propensity to consume out of permanent changes in income is greater than out of transitory changes. To see why, let us use the same numerical baseline example as in Table 5.1, comparing a temporary increase in income (only in the first period, i.e., $y_t = 1.5$ and $y_{t+1} = 3$) with a permanent change (increases in both periods, i.e., $y_t = 1.5$ and $y_{t+1} = 3.5$). It is easy to verify that in the absence of constraints consumption is constant and equal in each period to average income, 2.25 (when the change is transitory) and 2.5 (when it is permanent). The marginal propensities to consume in the first period are then 0.5 (or $[2.25-2]/[1.5-1]$) and 1 (or $[2.5-2]/[1.5-1]$) for transitory and permanent changes, respectively. The reason is that a transitory change in income is evenly distributed over the entire life cycle and leads to a smaller increase in consumption than in income, while a permanent change is entirely consumed, because the income gain recurs in all future periods.

Consider now imposing the constraint $a_{t+1} \geq 0$. Regardless of income changes (transitory or permanent as they may be), the marginal propensity to consume is 1: in order to achieve the optimal solution, any change in income is entirely consumed (unless it is so great that consumers want to save rather than borrow, a situation discussed in Section 5.4).

---

4. If $r \neq 0$, the marginal propensity to consume in the infinite-horizon model is equal to the perpetual annuity factor $r/(1+r)$.

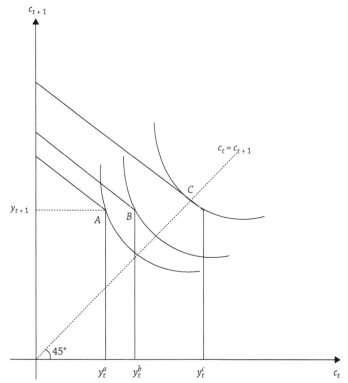

Figure 5.2: The effect of an increase in first-period income with liquidity constraints

5.3. THE TIMING OF INCOME AND CONSUMPTION

What is the effect of liquidity constraints when the timing of income changes? Figure 5.2 shows how consumption responds to a change in first-period income, given second-period income. The 45-degree line is the locus of all solutions in which consumption is constant over time $(c_t = c_{t+1})$. Initially the distribution of resources is $\{y_t^a, y_{t+1}\}$. As in Section 5.2, with $r = \delta = 0$, the optimal solution in the absence of constraints is therefore $c_t^* = c_{t+1}^* = (y_t^a + y_{t+1})/2$. If a liquidity constraint is imposed, it will be binding, and consumers will choose $c_t = y_t^a$ and $c_{t+1} = y_{t+1}$ (the corner solution corresponding to point A in Figure 5.2).

Suppose now that first-period income increases from y_t^a to y_t^b, so the constraint is relaxed. Since lifetime income increases, the optimal consumption plan is revised upward. But despite rising income, the liquidity constraint is still binding and the solution is still a corner (point B in Figure 5.2). It is important to note that the marginal propensity to consume is 1, whereas in the model without liquidity constraints it would be 0.5, because the increase in income is equally divided between the two periods.

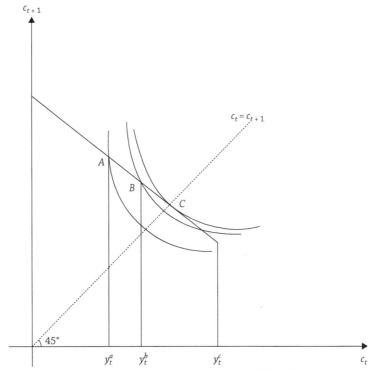

Figure 5.3: The effect of a change in the timing of income with liquidity constraints

With liquidity constraints, the consumer attempts to close the gap between desired and actual consumption. To reduce this intertemporal distortion, income changes are entirely consumed, that is, the marginal propensity to consume equals 1.

To overcome the distortions induced by liquidity constraints, income has to increase substantially. For example, if income rises to y_t^c, the increase is so large that the constraint no longer binds. In this situation, the consumer decides to save in the first period $\left(\text{so } a_{t+1} > 0\right)$ and the marginal propensity to consume is less than 1.[5]

Similar conclusions are reached in Figure 5.3, where we change the *timing* of income, keeping lifetime resources constant. That is, an increase in first-period income is offset by an equivalent reduction in second-period income, as with a temporary tax rebate followed by an equal tax hike in the following period. As before, small changes in current income (that is, variations that cannot close the gap between actual and desired consumption) offset by equal and opposite

5. Where might the changes in income in the first period come from? In a model with endogenous labor supply, one way to ease liquidity constraints is to work more in the current period.

changes to future income do not bring the consumer to the first-best solution (they are still at the corner, as when they move from point A to point B in Figure 5.3). Hence the marginal propensity to consume is still 1. However, larger redistributions in favor of current income (for example, from y_t^b to y_t^c) overcome the liquidity constraint and allow the consumer to attain the unconstrained optimum. This is another example in which an increase in current income translates one-to-one into an increase in consumption.

5.4. THE NATURAL BORROWING CONSTRAINT

If income is uncertain and the Inada condition holds (so that consumers' utility approaches minus infinity as consumption approaches zero), the intertemporal budget constraint implies what is known as the "natural borrowing constraint," which holds even in the absence of formal credit rationing.

In keeping with the two-period model, we assume that income can take a minimum value, y_{min}, with positive probability in both periods. Initial wealth is a_t. The dynamic budget constraint (when $r = \delta = 0$) is:

$$a_{t+1} = a_t + y_t - c_t.$$

Since the resources that remain in the second period are spent completely (no bequest motive), it follows that $c_{t+1} = a_{t+1} + y_{t+1}$. Note that a_{t+1} is known before the consumer learns the realization of income in the second period. Moreover, its value must be such that $c_{t+1} \geq 0$ even if y_{min} occurs. Therefore, to prevent the possibility of zero consumption, consumers would never borrow an amount greater than y_{min} in the first period, which leads to the constraint:

$$a_{t+1} \geq -y_{min}.$$

Substituting this inequality into the dynamic budget constraint, we obtain a constraint on consumption in period t:

$$c_t \leq a_t + y_t + y_{min}.$$

In the multi-period case, the constraint generalizes to take into account the sequence of minimum incomes that will be realized in the future:

$$c_t \leq a_t + y_t + \sum_{s=t+1}^{T} y_{s,min}.$$

Note that if $y_{min} = 0$, that is, if income can drop to zero, the natural borrowing constraint implies that consumers will never borrow. As we will see in Chapter 7, this assumption is applied by Carroll (1997) to develop his version of the buffer stock model.

5.5. THE EULER EQUATION WITH LIQUIDITY CONSTRAINTS

To extend the analysis of liquidity constraints in a multi-period setting, we now study the case in which the consumer lives until period T and there is uncertainty about future labor income. In keeping with the notation of Chapter 4, we assume that consumers solve:

$$\max E_t \sum_{\tau=0}^{T-t} (1+\delta)^{-\tau} u(c_{t+\tau}),$$

subject to the constraints:

$$a_{t+\tau+1} = (1+r)(a_{t+\tau} + y_{t+\tau} - c_{t+\tau})$$
$$a_t \text{ given}$$
$$a_{t+\tau+1} \geq 0 \quad \text{for every } \tau = 0, 1, ..., T-t.$$

The constraint $a_{t+\tau+1} \geq 0$ requires that wealth can never be negative at any point in the life cycle. We can rewrite the problem by defining the value function as:

$$V_t(a_t) = \max_{c_t, a_{t+1}} u(c_t) + (1+\delta)^{-1} E_t V_{t+1}(a_{t+1}) + \psi_t a_{t+1},$$

subject to the budget constraint $a_{t+1} = (1+r)(a_t + y_t - c_t)$, and where ψ_t is the Kuhn-Tucker multiplier associated with the period t borrowing constraint. The first-order condition is therefore:

$$u'(c_t) - (1+\delta)^{-1}(1+r)E_t V'_{t+1}(a_t) - \psi_t(1+r) = 0.$$

As in Chapter 4, we denote the optimal (and unique) solution to the problem by $c_t(a_t)$. Hence, by the definition of the value function, it must be that:

$$V_t(a_t) = u[c_t(a_t)] + (1+\delta)^{-1} E_t V_{t+1}\{(1+r)[a_t + y_t - c_t(a_t)]\}$$
$$+ \psi_t\{(1+r)[a_t + y_t - c_t(a_t)]\}.$$

Differentiating both sides with respect to the state variable a_t, we get:

$$V_t'(a_t) = u'(c_t)c_t'(a_t) + \frac{1+r}{1+\delta}\left[1 - c_t'(a_t)\right]E_t V_{t+1}'(a_{t+1}) + \psi_t(1+r)\left[1 - c_t'(a_t)\right];$$

rearranging terms, we get:

$$V_t'(a_t) = c_t'(a_t)\left[u'(c_t) - \frac{1+r}{1+\delta}E_t V_{t+1}'(a_{t+1}) - \psi_t(1+r)\right]$$
$$+ \frac{1+r}{1+\delta}E_t V_{t+1}'(a_{t+1}) + \psi_t(1+r).$$

The first-order condition implies that the expression in square brackets is equal to 0, so,

$$V_t'(a_t) = u'(c_t).$$

Since this envelope condition applies in each period,[6] then lagging by one period and considering again the first-order condition, we get the Euler equation modified to take account of the liquidity constraint:

$$u'(c_t) = \frac{1+r}{1+\delta}E_t u'(c_{t+1}) + \psi_t(1+r) \geq \frac{1+r}{1+\delta}E_t u'(c_{t+1}). \qquad (5.4)$$

This relationship applies with equality only if the liquidity constraint does not bind.

An analytical solution with liquidity constraints can be derived assuming that utility is quadratic (and $r = \delta$ for simplicity). Then,

$$(a - bc_t) = E_t(a - bc_{t+1}) + \psi_t(1+r).$$

Rearranging terms, we obtain an expression for the change in consumption:

$$\Delta c_{t+1} = \psi_t b^{-1}(1+r) + \varepsilon_{t+1}.$$

If the constraint does not bind in period t ($\psi_t = 0$), the Euler equation reduces to the martingale equation (4.13). When the liquidity constraint does not bind ($\psi_t > 0$), consumption is no longer a martingale, that is, a statistical

---

6. The envelope condition is the same even when the liquidity constraint is binding. This is because liquidity constraints create only intertemporal distortions, not intratemporal ones. This feature of the problem has been used in empirical analysis by Meghir and Weber (1996).

process whose innovations are unpredictable on the basis of current information, or $E_t \Delta c_{t+1} = 0$. On the contrary, when the constraint binds, expected consumption changes are not equal to zero because the consumer is aware that the constraint will change the slope of the consumption path, or $E_t \Delta c_{t+1} > 0$. Furthermore, expected consumption will be correlated with all the variables that are related to the presence of liquidity constraints, such as expected income changes and the level of current resources.

Empirically, detecting liquidity constraints from the Euler equation is difficult in the extreme, because the constraint is not always operative and may bind only occasionally during the life of the consumer.

The model with liquidity constraints presented in this chapter offers two general results. First, the timing of income affects the timing of consumption. Second, if the borrowing constraint is binding, consumers must defer consumption, meaning that consumption grows more over time than it would with perfect credit markets. There is another important reason why consumers may want to postpone consumption, which is the desire to protect against income risk. This leads us, in the next chapter, to a discussion of the precautionary saving model.

CHAPTER 6
The Precautionary Saving Model

The certainty equivalence model is analytically tractable and yields many insights into the problem of intertemporal choice under uncertainty. For example, it delivers a closed-form solution for the consumption function. But it excludes saving driven by income uncertainty, the so-called precautionary motive. In the certainty equivalence model of Chapter 4, individuals save only if they expect their income to decline in the future, but they are indifferent to risk (whether income is more or less uncertain).[1]

As we shall see, the theory of precautionary saving, besides adding realism, provides an intuitive explanation for some of the empirical findings in the literature, such as the observation that people whose income is more volatile tend to save more. Moreover, it can also explain the excess sensitivity of consumption to expected income changes mentioned in Chapter 5. Indeed, a model with precautionary saving produces a good many predictions similar to those of the model with liquidity constraints. In this chapter we maintain the assumption of perfect credit markets. In Chapter 7 we combine the two models.

6.1. INCOMPLETE MARKETS AND PRECAUTIONARY SAVING

We know from Chapter 3 that with complete markets, individuals are wholly insured against income shocks. When markets are incomplete,

---

1. The certainty equivalence model with $r \neq \delta$ suggests that there are only two motives for saving: an intertemporal motive (related to the difference between the interest rate and the discount rate) and a life-cycle motive (due to expected declines in income, such as that associated with retirement).

however, consumers cannot fully diversify shocks and must count on self-insurance (i.e., saving). We need to distinguish between two cases, that in which the marginal utility of consumption is linear (the case of certainty equivalence, studied in Chapter 4) and that in which it is convex (precautionary saving, studied in this chapter).[2] To appreciate the differences, we focus initially on a two-period model where second-period income is uncertain. Specifically, we assume that income in period $t+1$ takes only two possible values, $y_{t+1,g}$ (the good state) and $y_{t+1,b}$ (the bad), with probability π and $(1-\pi)$, respectively. We also assume that $y_t = E_t(y_{t+1})$, so under certainty equivalence consumers have no incentive to "save for a rainy day".[3]

The consumer solves the problem:

$$\max u(c_t) + E_t u(c_{t+1}), \tag{6.1}$$

subject to the budget constraints:[4]

$$c_t + s_t = y_t$$
$$c_{t+1} = \begin{cases} s_t + y_{t+1,g} & \text{with prob. } \pi \\ s_t + y_{t+1,b} & \text{with prob. } (1-\pi) \end{cases}$$

The first-order condition is:

$$u'(c_t) = E_t u'(c_{t+1}),$$

that is,

$$u'(y_t - s_t) = E_t u'(y_{t+1} + s_t).$$

2. The importance of the shape of the utility function for optimal consumption decisions is clarified in the appendix to this chapter, which defines key concepts such as risk aversion and prudence for different utility functions.

3. In this chapter we assume that individuals make decisions with clear estimates of the probabilities of the possible specific outcomes. Here the terms "risk" and "uncertainty" are interchangeable. But in many situations, people don't know the probability structure of the possible events. Many economists refer to the situation posited here as risk, the other as uncertainty or ambiguity. In recent years various studies have laid a theoretical basis for ambiguity aversion and characterized the preferences that distinguish ambiguity aversion from risk aversion (Klibanoff, Marinacci, and Mukerji, 2005). Under these preferences it is possible to generate "precautionary saving" in response to an increase in ambiguity.

4. Saving s_t represents a storage of value, such as tangible or financial assets. However, given that markets are incomplete, it allows the consumer to transfer purchasing power only between periods, not between different states of nature.

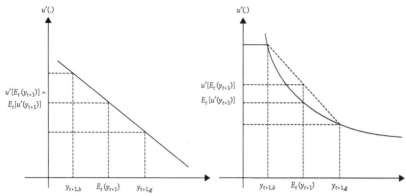

Figure 6.1: Linear and convex marginal utility of consumption

Since we assume that $y_t = E_t(y_{t+1})$, the equation can be rewritten as:

$$u'\left[E_t\left(y_{t+1}\right) - s_t\right] = E_t u'\left(y_{t+1} + s_t\right). \tag{6.2}$$

In the certainty equivalence model, marginal utility is linear. In fact, with quadratic utility, $u(c) = ac - (1/2)bc^2$ and the first-order condition (6.2) can be rewritten as:

$$a - b\left[E_t\left(y_{t+1}\right) - s_t\right] = E_t\left[a - b\left(y_{t+1} + s_t\right)\right].$$

The equality obtained in this case between the expected value of marginal utility and the marginal utility of the expected value is illustrated in the left-hand panel of Figure 6.1, where we set $\pi = 0.5$. Given the linearity of the expected value operator, we can write:

$$a - bE_t y_{t+1} + bs_t = a - bE_t y_{t+1} - bs_t,$$

which leads to the optimal solutions:

$$s_t^* = 0$$

$$c_t^* = E_t c_{t+1}^*.$$

Although consumers are risk-averse (the second derivative of the quadratic utility function is negative, i.e., $u'' < 0$), they do not react to risk. What matters is only expected income: the consumer does not save in the first period even if income in the second period in the bad state is very low, even nil.

What happens if the marginal utility function is not linear in consumption? In the right panel of Figure 6.1 we assume that it is convex. By Jensen's inequality, $u'E_t(y_t + 1) < E_t u'(y + 1)$, that is, the marginal utility of the expectation is lower than the expected value of marginal utility. To satisfy the first-order condition (6.2), consumers must reduce consumption in the first period and increase it in the second, so as to reduce the expected marginal utility of consumption in the second period and increase it in the first. The convexity of $u'(.)$ requires that $u'''(.) > 0$, because the second derivative of marginal utility is the third derivative of the utility function. From this it follows that the individual chooses positive saving only if the third derivative of the utility function is positive. In fact, to satisfy equation (6.2) with $u'''(.) > 0$ requires $s_t^* > 0$.

In sum, if marginal utility is linear, $u'''(.) = 0$ and there is no precautionary saving, but if it is convex, $u'''(.) > 0$ and there is an incentive to respond to risk. How can we measure the strength of this precautionary motive? Kimball (1990) proposed a criterion known as *absolute prudence*. While the Arrow and Pratt measure of absolute risk aversion, $A(c) = -\dfrac{u''(c)}{u'(c)}$, is the ratio between the second and first derivatives of the utility function, absolute prudence is the ratio between its third and second derivatives, $P(c) = -\dfrac{u'''(c)}{u''(c)}$. Absolute prudence is equal to zero for the quadratic utility function and positive when marginal utility is convex, that is, when the third derivative is positive. In analogy with the concept of relative risk aversion, $a(c) = cA(c)$, Kimball also defines the concept of *relative prudence*, $p(c) = cP(c)$. In the appendix to this chapter we report the coefficients of risk aversion and prudence (absolute and relative) for the utility functions most frequently used in the literature (quadratic, exponential, isoelastic).

6.2. A NUMERICAL EXAMPLE

In Table 6.1 we consider a simple numerical example that illustrates the main differences in terms of saving behavior in three relevant cases: complete markets, certainty equivalence, and precautionary saving.

Suppose that first-period income $y_t = 8$ and that the distribution of second-period income is given by:

$$y_{t+1} = \begin{cases} y_{t+1,g} = 10 & \text{with prob. } 0.6 \\ y_{t+1,b} = 5 & \text{with prob. } 0.4 \end{cases}. \qquad (6.3)$$

It follows that $y_t = E_t y_{t+1} = 8$. In the case of complete markets, as we know from Chapter 3, the optimal solution for consumption across states and over time is:

$$c_t^* = c_{t+1,g}^* = c_{t+1,b}^* = 8.$$

In the second period, consumption is completely stabilized by contingent contracts signed in the first period. The contracts stipulate that the consumer receives 3 in the bad state and pays 2 in the good state. This also implies that there is no need to save, hence optimal saving is zero.

To illustrate the effect of uncertainty on saving, we now relax the complete-market assumption and consider two hypotheses on consumer preferences. The first is that utility is quadratic (and therefore marginal utility is linear), as in the certainty equivalence model of Chapter 4. The second is that utility is logarithmic (so marginal utility is convex, giving rise to precautionary saving).

If utility is quadratic, marginal utility is $u'(c) = a - bc$, and therefore,

$$s_t^* = 0$$

$$c_t^* = E_t c_{t+1}^* = 8.$$

Compared to complete markets, under certainty equivalence consumption is smoothed only ex ante. Consumption in the second period will in fact be equal to $c_{t+1} = 10$ with probability 0.6 and $c_{t+1} = 5$ with probability 0.4. While in the case of certainty or complete markets the expected variance of consumption growth (reported in the last column of Table 6.1) is zero, now it is 0.09.[5]

Suppose finally that the utility function is logarithmic, with marginal utility given by $u'(c) = \dfrac{1}{c}$. Since $u'''(.) > 0$, the individual is prudent, as defined by Kimball, and relative prudence is $p(c) = (2)$. The first-order condition for an optimum is:

$$u'(y_t - s_t) = E_t u'(y_{t+1} + s_t),$$

or, given the assumptions on income distribution in (6.3),

$$\frac{1}{8 - s_t} = \frac{0.6}{10 + s_t} + \frac{0.4}{5 + s_t}.$$

One can easily verify that if $s_t = 0$, the first-order condition is violated. In fact,

$$u'(E_t y_{t+1}) = 0.125 < E_t u'(y_{t+1}) = 0.14,$$

as a consequence of Jensen's inequality. To satisfy the condition, we need to increase the marginal utility of consumption in the first period and

5. Note that $\operatorname{var}_t\left(\dfrac{c_{t+1} - c_t}{c_t}\right) = E_t\left(\dfrac{c_{t+1} - c_t}{c_t}\right)^2 - \left[E_t\left(\dfrac{c_{t+1} - c_t}{c_t}\right)\right]^2.$

Table 6.1. THE EFFECT OF INCOME UNCERTAINTY
ON CONSUMPTION AND SAVING

	c_t	s_t	$c_{t+1,g}$	$c_{t+1,b}$	$E_t\left(\dfrac{c_{t+1}-c_t}{c_t}\right)$	$\mathrm{var}_t\left(\dfrac{c_{t+1}-c_t}{c_t}\right)$
$y_t=8$						
$y_{t+1}=\begin{cases}y_{t+1,g}=10 & \text{with prob. 0.6}\\ y_{t+1,b}=5 & \text{with prob. 0.4}\end{cases}$						
Complete markets	8.0	0.0	8.0	8.0	0.00	0.00
Certainty equivalence	8.0	0.0	10.0	5.0	0.00	0.09
Precautionary saving	7.6	0.4	10.4	5.4	0.11	0.10
$y_t=8$						
$y_{t+1}=\begin{cases}y_{t+1,g}=12 & \text{with prob. 0.6}\\ y_{t+1,b}=2 & \text{with prob. 0.4}\end{cases}$						
Complete markets	8.0	0.0	8.0	8.0	0.00	0.00
Certainty equivalence	8.0	0.0	12.0	2.0	0.00	0.37
Precautionary saving	6.4	1.6	13.6	3.6	0.50	0.58

Note: In the table we assume that under certainty equivalence utility is quadratic and under precautionary saving it is logarithmic.

reduce the expectation of the second period so as to close the gap between $u'(E_t y_{t+1})$ and $E_t u'(y_{t+1})$. This is done by reducing first-period consumption to 7.6 and increasing saving to $s_t^* = 0.4$.

Compared to the case with complete markets, there is now an excess of resources in the good state of the world. Because consumers cannot change the amount of saving between two states of the world to protect against low income (5 in this example), they are forced to save even when they would not need to, that is, in the case of a good state of the world (here, 10). Complete markets allow people to transfer savings between states of nature. We are therefore faced with two different forms of consumption smoothing: precautionary saving equalizes consumption between periods, while complete markets enable smoothing *also* between states of nature. The first three rows of Table 6.1 summarize the results of the example in the three scenarios: complete markets, certainty equivalence, and precautionary saving.

Given the timing of the expected values of income and the assumption that $r = \delta$, in our example saving is due solely to the precautionary motive. In more realistic cases (e.g., if expected income is lower than current income or if the interest rate is higher than the rate of time preference) the precautionary motive explains only part of total saving.

In the lower half of Table 6.1 we consider another example, namely, a mean-preserving spread in income, in which expected income does not change (still 8, as above) but future income is now more uncertain and given by:

$$
y_{t+1} = \begin{cases} y_{t+1,g} = 12 & \text{with prob. } 0.6 \\ y_{t+1,b} = 2 & \text{with prob. } 0.4 \end{cases}. \tag{6.4}
$$

With complete markets the allocation of consumption is identical to the previous case. This is achieved by new contingent contracts such that the consumer receives 6 in the bad state and pays 4 in the good state. In the certainty equivalence model, there is no incentive to change the distribution of consumption (expected consumption growth is still 0), but the expected variability of consumption increases. Finally, if the individual is prudent, consumption in the first period decreases to 6.4 and saving grows to 1.6.

Let us now focus on the case of precautionary saving, comparing the expected value and expected variance of consumption growth before and after the increase in income risk. The last two columns of Table 6.1 show that the expected variance rises from 0.10 to 0.58. The increase in the variability of income is also reflected in the expected growth rate of consumption, which goes up from 0.11 to 0.50. It would be a mistake, however, to conclude that there is a causal relationship between the consumption growth rate and the expected variance. True, the growth rate of consumption increases with the variance of its expected growth rate, but in reality this is an equilibrium relationship. In other words, the variance of the expected growth rate of consumption is an endogenous variable, as it depends on consumption in the first period (which is chosen by the consumer). As we shall see, it is precisely the endogeneity of the variance that poses serious econometric and conceptual difficulties in estimating the Euler equations on the hypothesis of precautionary saving.

6.3. THE EULER EQUATION WITH PRECAUTIONARY SAVING

In this section we derive an explicit solution for consumption growth in two ways: (a) considering a second-order approximation to the optimal consumption rule with constant interest rates and (b) making distributional assumptions about the joint behavior of consumption growth and interest rates.

Start with the usual Euler equation and assume that the interest rate is non-stochastic:

$$
u'(c_t) = \frac{1+r}{1+\delta} E_t u'(c_{t+1}). \tag{6.5}
$$

Blanchard and Mankiw (1988) approximate (6.5) with a second-order Taylor series expansion of $u'(c_{t+1})$ around c_t:

$$u'(c_t) \cong \frac{1+r}{1+\delta} E_t \left[u'(c_t) + u''(c_t)(c_{t+1} - c_t) + \frac{1}{2} u'''(c_t)(c_{t+1} - c_t)^2 \right]. \quad (6.6)$$

Dividing equation (6.6) by c_t^2, we get:

$$\frac{u'(c_t)}{c_t^2} + \frac{u''(c_t)}{c_t} E_t \left(\frac{c_{t+1} - c_t}{c_t} \right) + \frac{1}{2} u'''(c_t) E_t \left(\frac{c_{t+1} - c_t}{c_t} \right)^2 \cong \left(\frac{1+\delta}{1+r} \right) \frac{u'(c_t)}{c_t^2}.$$

Solving for the expected growth rate of consumption, we finally get:

$$E_t \left(\frac{c_{t+1} - c_t}{c_t} \right) \cong EIS \left(\frac{r - \delta}{1+r} \right) + \frac{1}{2} p(c) E_t \left(\frac{c_{t+1} - c_t}{c_t} \right)^2, \quad (6.7)$$

where $p(c) \equiv -\dfrac{u'''(c_t) c_t}{u''(c_t)}$ is Kimball's coefficient of relative prudence and $EIS \equiv -\dfrac{u'(c_t)}{u''(c_t) c_t} = a(c)^{-1}$ is the elasticity of intertemporal substitution. Note that EIS is also equal to the inverse of the coefficient of relative risk aversion. Finally, $E_t \left(\dfrac{c_{t+1} - c_t}{c_t} \right)^2$ is a measure of the expected variability of consumption (the second uncentered moment).

Equation (6.7) shows that the variability of future consumption reduces current consumption: uncertainty makes the profile of consumption steeper. Furthermore, the sensitivity of consumption growth to uncertainty depends on the coefficient of relative prudence.[6]

A second way to obtain an analytical solution for consumption growth in the precautionary saving model, developed by Hansen and Singleton (1983), is to make a specific assumption about the joint probability distribution of future consumption growth and interest rates. The solution so obtained is exact, not an approximation.

Suppose that the utility function is isoelastic. The objective of the consumer is:

$$\max E_t \sum_{\tau=0}^{T-t} (1+\delta)^{-\tau} \frac{c_{t+\tau}^{1-\gamma} - 1}{1-\gamma},$$

---

6. If utility is quadratic, $u'''(.) = 0$, and then $p(c) = 0$. As in the certainty equivalence model, expected consumption growth depends only on the elasticity of intertemporal substitution, the interest rate, and the rate of time preference. Also, if $r = \delta$, we obtain equation (4.13) in Chapter 4.

subject to the dynamic budget constraint:

$$a_{t+\tau+1} = (1 + r_{t+\tau+1})(a_{t+\tau} + y_{t+\tau} - c_{t+\tau}),$$

and the terminal condition $a_{T+1} = 0$. The Euler equation in this case is:

$$E_t\left[\left(\frac{c_{t+1}}{c_t}\right)^{-\gamma}\frac{1+r_{t+1}}{1+\delta}\right] = 1. \qquad (6.8)$$

Now assume that the joint conditional distribution of consumption growth and interest rates is normal,[7]

$$\begin{bmatrix} \Delta \ln c_{t+1} \\ \ln(1+r_{t+1}) \end{bmatrix} \Big| I_t \sim N\left[\begin{pmatrix} \mu_c \\ \mu_r \end{pmatrix};\begin{pmatrix} \sigma_c^2 & \sigma_{cr} \\ \sigma_{cr} & \sigma_r^2 \end{pmatrix}\right],$$

where the first and second moments of the joint distribution are conditional on the information available in period t (e.g., $\mu_c = E_t \Delta \ln c_{t+1}$). Recalling that $e^{\ln x} = x$, we can now write (6.8) as:

$$E_t \exp\left[-\gamma\Delta \ln c_{t+1} + \ln(1+r_{t+1}) - \ln(1+\delta)\right] = 1.$$

Note that (using properties of the log-normal distribution) we can rewrite this equation as:[8]

$$\exp\left[-\gamma\mu_c + \mu_r + \frac{1}{2}\gamma^2\sigma_c^2 + \frac{1}{2}\sigma_r^2 - \gamma\sigma_{cr} - \ln(1+\delta)\right] = 1.$$

Taking logarithms yields:

$$-\gamma\mu_c + \mu_r + \frac{1}{2}\gamma^2\sigma_c^2 + \frac{1}{2}\sigma_r^2 - \gamma\sigma_{cr} - \ln(1+\delta) = 0.$$

Rearranging and using the approximation $\ln(1+x) \cong x$, we finally obtain:

$$E_t\Delta \ln c_{t+1} = \gamma^{-1}(E_t r_{t+1} - \delta) + \frac{\gamma}{2}\text{var}_t(\Delta \ln c_{t+1} - \gamma^{-1}r_{t+1}),$$

7. Note that $\ln(1+r_{t+1}) \cong r_{t+1}$.

8. Using the fact that if $X\sim N(\mu,\sigma^2)$, then $E(e^x) = \exp\left(\mu + \frac{1}{2}\sigma^2\right)$; similarly, if $\ln X\sim N(\mu,\sigma^2)$, then $E(X) = \mu + \frac{1}{2}\sigma^2$.

which is an explicit solution for expected consumption growth in the presence of precautionary saving. Since $\Delta \ln c_{t+1} \equiv E_t \Delta \ln c_{t+1} + \varepsilon_{t+1}$, we have:

$$\Delta \ln c_{t+1} = \gamma^{-1}\left(E_t r_{t+1} - \delta\right) + \frac{\gamma}{2} \text{var}_t\left(\Delta \ln c_{t+1} - \gamma^{-1} r_{t+1}\right) + \varepsilon_{t+1}. \qquad (6.9)$$

The first term on the right-hand side of (6.9) represents the effect of the expected interest rate on the growth rate of consumption. The greater the elasticity of intertemporal substitution (γ^{-1}), the greater this effect. The second term, absent in the certainty equivalence model, is always positive and is proportional to the coefficient of relative prudence (which in the case of the isoelastic utility function is $1 + \gamma$). Equation (6.9) indicates that in equilibrium an increase in uncertainty (i.e., the conditional variability of the consumption growth rate) is associated with higher consumption growth: the individual will consume less in period t and more in period $t+1$ and thus increase current saving.

In the case of isoelastic utility, both the terms on the right-hand side of (6.9) depend on γ. Hence a single parameter determines the elasticity of intertemporal substitution, the degree of risk aversion, and prudence.

The term that measures the importance of the precautionary motive, $\text{var}_t(\Delta \ln c_{t+1} - \gamma^{-1} r_{t+1})$, depends on the conditional variance of consumption growth, the variance of the interest rate, and the covariance between two. In the model we present in Section 6.4, the variance of consumption growth depends only on the variance of income, in that we assume that the interest rate is constant and that income is the only source of uncertainty. In more general models, however, the conditional variance may also reflect uncertainty about other random variables, such as demographics, medical expenses, and other unforeseen events.

6.4. AN EXPLICIT SOLUTION FOR PRECAUTIONARY SAVING

Under specific assumptions about the utility function and the stochastic income process, one can derive an explicit solution not only for the growth rate of consumption but also for the levels of consumption, saving, and wealth. The model developed by Caballero (1991) is particularly interesting, because it shows that the precautionary motive might explain not only why people save but in principle also a sizable fraction of aggregate wealth.

For simplicity, assume that the rate of time preference (δ) and the interest rate (r) are both zero. The utility function is exponential (see the appendix to this chapter). The objective of the consumer is:

$$\max E_1 \sum_{t=1}^{T} -\frac{e^{-\alpha c_t}}{\alpha},$$

subject to the constraints:

$$a_t = a_{t-1} + y_t - c_t$$
$$a_T = 0,$$

where we follow Caballero's convention in measuring wealth at the end of the period and not (as elsewhere in this book) at the beginning.[9] The consumer receives an uncertain income in each period, and there is no retirement, a condition that makes it clear that the sole motive for saving is precautionary. We assume that income follows a random walk, a special case of that considered in Chapter 4,

$$y_t = y_{t-1} + \zeta_t,$$

where the innovation of the income process, ζ_t, is normally distributed with mean zero and constant variance σ^2. Under these assumptions (in particular, no retirement and $r = \delta$, saving would be zero in the absence of uncertainty, and consumption would exactly track income (because any variation in income would be permanent).

In the specific case of the exponential utility function, the first-order condition for a maximum is:

$$e^{-\alpha c_t} = E_t e^{-\alpha c_{t+1}}. \tag{6.10}$$

Caballero shows that the solution to the problem is the following consumption rule:

$$c_{t+1} = c_t + \frac{\alpha \sigma^2}{2} + \zeta_{t+1}. \tag{6.11}$$

If $\sigma^2 = 0$ (i.e., if there is no uncertainty), equation (6.11) shows that expected consumption is constant over time, as in the certainty equivalence model. But if $\sigma^2 > 0$, expected consumption grows over time. The term $\dfrac{\alpha \sigma^2}{2}$ represents the so-called *risk premium*, which is what the consumer is willing to pay to avoid income risk.[10] Equation (6.11) can be rewritten as:

$$E_t \left(\frac{c_{t+1} - c_t}{c_t} \right) = \frac{1}{2} \alpha c_t \left(\frac{\sigma}{c_t} \right)^2,$$

9. For this reason, we also assume that the consumer lives from period 1 to period T rather than from 0 to $T-1$.

10. In general, the risk premium η satisfies the equation $uE(c-\eta) = Eu(c)$, where $E(c-\eta)$ is called the certainty equivalent of c and η is the price that the consumer is willing to pay to avoid the risk of the random variable c.

that is, expected consumption growth is equal to the product of the coefficient of relative prudence ($p(c) = \alpha c$) and the variance of income normalized by current income.[11]

We can now derive the consumption function using equation (6.11). The ex ante intertemporal budget constraint as of period t is:

$$\sum_{\tau=0}^{T-t} E_t c_{t+\tau} = a_{t-1} + \sum_{\tau=0}^{T-t} E_t y_{t+\tau},\tag{6.12}$$

given the random walk assumption, $E_t y_{t+\tau} = y_t$. Defining $\chi \equiv \dfrac{\alpha \sigma^2}{2}$, one can rewrite the expected value of (6.11) as:

$$E_t c_{t+\tau} = c_t + \tau \chi.$$

The difference between this model and the certainty equivalence model is immediately apparent: even if $r = \delta = 0$ (i.e., in the total absence of an incentive to substitute consumption intertemporally), consumption is no longer constant but grows at rate χ. Substituting the expressions for $E_t c_{t+\tau}$ and $E_t y_{t+\tau}$ into (6.12) yields the consumption function in period t:[12]

$$c_t = \frac{a_{t-1}}{T-t+1} + y_t - \frac{(T-t)}{2}\chi.\tag{6.13}$$

The first two terms on the right-hand side of this equation represent the level of consumption that would be achieved with certainty and a finite horizon.[13] The last term is negative and captures the precautionary motive for saving. Its contribution is even more evident when we consider the saving function directly.

Using the *dynamic* budget constraint, $a_t = a_{t-1} + s_t$, and by repeated substitution of equation (6.13), one obtains a useful expression for saving,

$$s_t = y_t - c_t = \left(\frac{T-t}{2}\right)\chi - \left(\frac{t-1}{2}\right)\chi,\tag{6.14}$$

11. Since $(\sigma/c_t)^2 \cong (\sigma/y_t)^2$ the variance of income is approximately equal to the variance of consumption.

12. It is useful to remember that $\sum_{k=0}^{N} k = \dfrac{N(N+1)}{2}$.

13. Note, in the consumption equation (6.13), one of the problems arising from the assumption of exponential utility. For young consumers (high $T-t$) facing a high level of uncertainty (high σ^2), in this equation there is a remote possibility that consumption could be negative.

which also allows us to rewrite the consumption function (6.13) as:

$$c_t = y_t - \left(\frac{T-2t+1}{2}\right)\chi. \tag{6.15}$$

Equation (6.14) shows the remarkable result that even if income and consumption are random variables, saving is a deterministic function of age. However, the variance of income plays an essential role in determining the shape of the saving profile.

The two terms of opposite sign appearing in (6.14) represent, respectively, the effect of uncertainty (which stimulates saving) and the effect of the planning horizon (which stimulates consumption). Until period $(T+1)/2$, the effect of uncertainty dominates and hence $s_t > 0$. After $(T+1)/2$, the effect of the planning horizon dominates, and the consumer draws down the wealth accumulated previously, hence $s_t < 0$. As the individual continues to receive income from work, there is no saving due to the prospect of leaving the labor market by retirement. However, income risk leads to a saving pattern resembling that of the life-cycle model: the young save and the elderly run down their savings.

Caballero also shows that individual wealth is hump-shaped and evolves according to:

$$a_t = \sum_{j=1}^{t} s_j = \sum_{j=1}^{t}\left(\frac{T-2j+1}{2}\right)\chi = \frac{t(T-t)}{2}\chi.$$

In the absence of uncertainty (i.e., when $\sigma^2 = 0$, so $\chi = 0$), $a_t = 0$ for all t. When $\sigma^2 > 0$, the profile of wealth is a concave function of age, just as in the life-cycle model, but because the individual never retires, the explanation for the hump shape is completely different. Young workers accumulate until midlife (period $T/2$) because risk dominates the horizon effect, and older workers decumulate until wealth is exhausted at $a_T = 0$, for the converse reason.

Adding up the wealth of all consumers in the economy gives an aggregate measure of wealth, as in Section 1.7. Assume that each individual lives for T periods and that the size of each cohort is constant and equal to $1/T$.[14] Since in each period t there are T cohorts alive, and recalling that $\chi = \dfrac{\alpha\sigma^2}{2}$, we have:[15]

$$A_t = \int_0^T \frac{1}{T} a_k \, dk = \int_0^T \frac{1}{T} k(T-k)\frac{\chi}{2} \, dk = \frac{\alpha\sigma^2 T}{24}.$$

14. Population is constant and normalized to 1.

15. It is useful to remember that $\sum_{k=1}^{N} k^2 = \dfrac{N(N+1)(2N+1)}{6}$.

The equation indicates that aggregate wealth, A_t, is constant over time and proportional to income risk. As in the life-cycle model, net aggregate saving, $S_t = A_t - A_{t-1}$, is zero if there is no population or productivity growth. Furthermore, the ratio between aggregate wealth and aggregate consumption is proportional to the product of the coefficient of prudence and the variance of national income:

$$\frac{A_t}{C_t} = \frac{\alpha\sigma^2 T^2}{24 C_t}\frac{C_t}{C_t} = \alpha C_t \frac{T^2}{24}\left(\frac{\sigma}{C_t}\right)^2. \tag{6.16}$$

Caballero considers some numerical examples showing how much of aggregate wealth can be explained by the precautionary motive. If $T = 50$, the coefficient of relative prudence (αC_t) is equal to 3, and $(\sigma / C_t) \cong (\sigma / Y_t) = 0.05$, then the ratio $(A / C) = 0.78$; if $(\sigma / Y_t) = 0.10$, $(A / C) = 3.12$. Since in the main industrialized countries aggregate wealth is generally between four and six times aggregate consumption, Caballero concludes that with realistic parameter values the model potentially explains a large share of national wealth.

The model's crucial assumption is that income shocks are permanent. If income was an AR(1) process without a unit root, or if part of the shocks had only transitory impact, the innovation in the income process would be less persistent, which would greatly reduce uncertainty and hence the share of aggregate wealth explained by the precautionary motive. For example, if $(\sigma / C_t) = 0.02$, the (A / C) share in equation (6.16) would be only 0.13. Furthermore, the assumption of exponential utility is convenient for obtaining an analytical solution but implausible, as it entails increasing risk aversion.

6.5. THE MARGINAL PROPENSITY TO CONSUME WITH PRECAUTIONARY SAVING

One of the main questions addressed in the literature is how consumption responds to income shocks. The advantage of the certainty equivalence model studied in Chapter 4 is that it yields very sharp predictions on the consumption impact of various types of income shock. For example, it entails the strong prediction that permanent shocks are entirely consumed (i.e., the marginal propensity to consume equals 1), while transitory shocks have limited or no impact. However, quadratic preferences also have drawbacks, implying as they do both increasing risk aversion and lack of a precautionary motive for saving. The Caballero model with exponential utility delivers a closed-form solution with precautionary saving, but as observed at the end of Section 6.4, it too has significant shortcomings.

In this section we discuss attempts to model precautionary saving, positing more realistic utility functions and a more realistic income process that allows for both permanent and transitory shocks. As we saw in the sections above, the problem with more realistic preferences (isoelastic, say) is that they cannot produce closed-form solutions for consumption. That is, there is no analytical expression for the consumption function, so it is not easy to derive the propensity to consume in response to income shocks. The problem of estimating this response cannot be handled by the Euler equation, which in fact says nothing about the sources of uncertainty (including, crucially, the stochastic structure of the income process). Furthermore, in the Euler framework the only parameters that can be estimated are the elasticity of intertemporal substitution and the rate of time preference.[16] For policy purposes, often the point is not the parameters per se but how consumers respond to interventions that change income permanently or temporarily. As we shall see in this section, this response is a function of structural parameters, the consumer's horizon and resources, and the market environment.

Recent research has sought to characterize the marginal propensity to consume, either by estimation or by numerical simulations. The estimation approach relies on the first-order condition for consumption and the dynamic budget constraint to approximate the dynamics of consumption. Blundell and Preston (1998) and Blundell, Pistaferri, and Preston (2008) use this approximation to derive a relation between the expectation error of the Euler equation and income shocks. Numerical simulations rely on specific assumptions about preferences and the income process to generate their results. Let us discuss the two approaches in turn.

Blundell, Pistaferri, and Preston (2008) consider the consumption problem faced by an individual with isoelastic preferences, whose objective is:

$$\max E_t \sum_{\tau=0}^{T-t} (1+\delta)^{-\tau} \frac{c_{t+\tau}^{1-\gamma}-1}{1-\gamma}.$$

The first-order condition of the problem is:

$$u'(c_t) = \frac{1+r}{1+\delta} E_t u'(c_{t+1}).$$

This Euler equation can be approximated as follows:

$$\Delta \ln c_t \cong f_t + \varepsilon_t, \tag{6.17}$$

16. And even this modest objective has proved difficult to attain, owing to limited cross-sectional variability in interest rates and short panels. See Attanasio and Low (2004).

where ε_t is a consumption innovation with $E_{t-1}\varepsilon_t = 0$, and f_t captures any slope in the consumption path due to interest rates, impatience, and the variance of consumption growth (similar to the first two terms on the right-hand side of equation (6.9)). Note that the approximation of the Euler equation also generates an approximation error, which we omit here to keep the model simple.

Equation (6.17) is still not very useful from an empirical or policy standpoint. While f_t could be captured by observable variables such as age, demographics, and interest rates, equation (6.17) also contains an innovation term (ε_t) about which we know very little. To make the equation empirically operational, Blundell, Pistaferri, and Preston adopt a further assumption, namely, that log income is the sum of a permanent component and a transitory component:

$$\log y_t = p_t + u_t$$
$$p_t = p_{t-1} + \zeta_t. \tag{6.18}$$

Using this assumption and a log-linear approximation of the dynamic budget constraint, they show that equation (6.17) can be rewritten as:

$$\Delta \log c_t \cong f_t + \eta_t \left(\lambda_t u_t + \zeta_t \right), \tag{6.19}$$

where λ_t is an annuitization factor and $\eta_t = \dfrac{\displaystyle\sum_{\tau=0}^{T-t} \dfrac{E_t y_{t+\tau}}{(1+r)^\tau}}{\displaystyle\sum_{\tau=0}^{T-t} \dfrac{E_t y_{t+\tau}}{(1+r)^\tau} + a_t}$ is the ratio of

human wealth (the present discounted value of future earnings) to total wealth (human plus financial wealth). During working life, the term η_t declines for two reasons: (a) financial wealth rises due to precautionary saving and retirement saving and (b) human wealth declines because remaining work life shortens as the consumer ages.

Note that here the model is expressed in logs, so what is estimated in the model is an elasticity, $\partial \ln c / \partial \ln y = (\partial c / \partial y)(y / c)$, with respect to the different components of the income process (transitory and permanent). Since (y / c) is on average not far from 1, here and in the rest of the book we refer loosely to the response of consumption to income (in levels and logs) as the *marginal propensity to consume*. This is roughly correct if the aim is to evaluate the response at the sample mean, but inaccurate in general because the (y / c) ratio varies substantially across individuals.

Equation (6.19) provides a straightforward interpretation of the impact of income shocks on consumption growth. For people far from the end of the life cycle (the young), financial wealth is small relative to human wealth, hence $\eta_t \simeq 1$. Permanent shocks accordingly translate almost completely into consumption changes, whereas transitory shocks have a negligible impact. This result is qualitatively similar to the prediction derived from the certainty equivalence model. However, in this model people have a precautionary motive for saving and η_t is close to, but strictly less than, 1. Most important, η_t is not constant over time. For consumers closer to retirement, financial wealth is large relative to human wealth, which is to say that η_t is appreciably smaller than 1; hence the response of consumption to permanent shocks diminishes as people age, owing to the precautionary accumulation of wealth.

In equation (6.19) the effect of an income shock on consumption depends not only on its persistence (whether it is permanent or transitory) and the length of the planning horizon but also on the preference parameters. More prudent individuals respond less sharply to income shocks because they can use accumulated wealth to smooth the impact. Equation (6.19) also guides the empirical estimation of the marginal propensity to consume (see Chapters 9 and 10).

A second approach to characterizing the marginal propensity to consume was developed by Kaplan and Violante (2010). Their study investigates this issue by simulating a life-cycle model in which consumers have isoelastic preferences, face income risk during their working life, and retire at age sixty-five. After retirement they receive a pension according to the rules of the US social security system and have a given probability of dying in each period (drawn from life tables). The income process, given by equation (6.18), is the same as in Blundell, Pistaferri, and Preston (2008).

Figure 6.2 plots the simulated marginal propensity to consume, given transitory and permanent income shocks, against age. A number of interesting findings emerge. First, the propensity with respect to transitory shocks is fairly low throughout the life cycle. Along the lines of Figure 4.2 in Chapter 4, it increases with age as the planning horizon shortens. In these simulations the marginal propensity to consume, averaged over the life cycle, is 0.06 (not too far from the assumed real interest rate of 0.03). Second, however, the consumption response with respect to permanent shocks varies a great deal. The response of the young is close to 1, but the marginal propensity to consume of people close to retirement is as low as 0.2 (the average is 0.77).[17] There are two reasons for this heterogeneous response. First, people accumulate financial wealth over the life cycle, implying that the term η_t in equation (6.19) declines with age (for a given amount of human wealth). Second, the impact of a permanent income shock on human wealth is much reduced for people close to retirement, owing to a horizon effect, which is a further reason for a decline of η_t.

17. Carroll (2009) simulates a buffer stock model (discussed in Chapter 7) assuming that consumers face both transitory and permanent income shocks, and shows that the marginal propensity to consume in respect of permanent shocks is between 0.75 and 0.92 for a wide range of plausible parameter values.

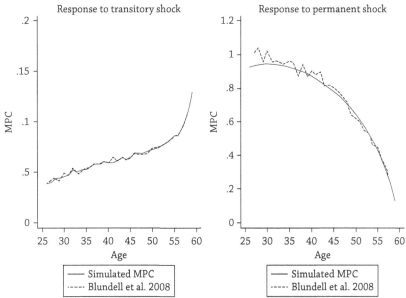

Figure 6.2: The marginal propensity to consume in the precautionary saving model
Note: The figure is constructed using simulated data from Kaplan and Violante (2010).

As we shall see in Chapter 9, Blundell, Pistaferri, and Preston (2008) find empirical estimates of the marginal propensity to consume with respect to income shocks that are not too far from these theoretical benchmarks.

It should be noted that in order to use these estimates of the marginal propensity to consume to simulate the impact of a policy change, one must assume that preferences and the income generating process are not affected by the policy change. That is, the estimates described in this section are not immune to Lucas's critique.

Here and in Chapter 5 we have studied liquidity constraints and precautionary saving in isolation. For quite different reasons, both these factors increase the expected rate of growth in consumption and lead to similar predictions regarding the sensitivity of consumption growth to expected income growth. In Chapter 7 we will see how they interact in buffer stock models, which include both liquidity constraints and precautionary saving.

APPENDIX

Risk aversion and prudence

A *risk-averse* individual is someone who, when asked to choose between two lotteries, chooses the one that awards a sum *x* with certainty, rather than one that awards the same sum x on average, but has a random component that can make the payoff greater or smaller. We define *risk-loving* as someone who prefers the uncertain lottery and *risk-neutral* as someone who is indifferent between the two.

Analytically, let $E(.)$ be the mathematical expectation operator, c random consumption, and $u(.)$ its associated utility function. Suppose that there are only two states of nature, in which consumption can equal c_1 or c_2 with probabilities π and $(1-\pi)$, respectively. We define the utility of average consumption and expected utility as:

$$u\left[E(c)\right] = u\left[\pi c_1 + (1-\pi)c_2\right]$$
$$E\left[u(c)\right] = \pi u(c_1) + (1-\pi)u(c_2).$$

We say that people are risk-averse if $u\left[E(c)\right] > E\left[u(c)\right]$, that is, if they prefer to receive $E(c)$ with certainty instead of the realization of the lottery. We define them as risk-loving if $u\left[E(c)\right] < E\left[u(c)\right]$, and risk-neutral if $u[E(c)] = E[u(c)]$.

By the definition of concavity, $u\left[E(c)\right] > E\left[u(c)\right]$. It follows that a risk-averse (risk-loving) consumer has a concave (convex) utility function. Figure 6.3 illustrates the three concepts graphically.

Since the individual is risk-averse if $u''(.) < 0$, the simplest measure of risk aversion is the degree of concavity of the utility function. The Arrow-Pratt measure of risk aversion is the ratio between the second and first derivatives of the function:

$$A(c) = -\frac{u''(c)}{u'(c)}.$$

This ratio is a local measure of risk aversion, because it varies depending on the point at which the derivative is computed (that is, it may depend on the level of consumption). A second measure of risk aversion is the degree of relative risk aversion:

$$a(c) = -c\frac{u''(c)}{u'(c)}.$$

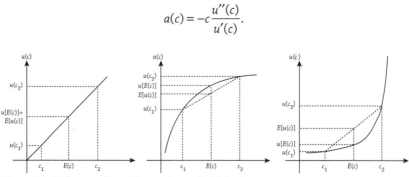

Figure 6.3: Risk neutrality, risk aversion, and risk loving

As consumption increases, absolute risk aversion may remain constant, increase, or decrease. This distinction is important, because only utility functions with decreasing or constant risk aversion give rise to precautionary saving. In fact, the derivative of absolute risk aversion with respect to consumption is:

$$\frac{dA(c)}{dc} = \frac{-u'''(c)u'(c) + [u''(c)]^2}{[u'(c)]^2}.$$

Since $u'(c) > 0$ and $u''(c) < 0$, a necessary (but not sufficient) condition for decreasing risk aversion is $u'''(c) > 0$, meaning that the marginal utility is convex. Decreasing absolute risk aversion is a plausible feature of preferences. Indeed, if risk aversion is decreasing, consumers tend to accept higher risk as consumption increases.

Along the lines of measures of absolute and relative risk aversion, Kimball (1990) has proposed to use the degree of convexity of marginal utility to measure the intensity of the precautionary motive for saving. The two measures, known respectively as the coefficient of absolute prudence and that of relative prudence, are:

$$P(c) = -\frac{u'''(c)}{u''(c)} \quad \text{and} \quad p(c) = -c\frac{u'''(c)}{u''(c)}.$$

Table 6.2 reports the four measures of attitude toward risk for the three utility functions used in most of the chapters of this book.

Quadratic utility: $u(c) = ac - \frac{b}{2}c^2$, defined in the interval $0 < c < \frac{a}{b}$. The first, second, and third derivatives with respect to c are $u'(c) = a - bc$, $u''(c) = -b$,

Table 6.2. RISK AVERSION AND PRUDENCE

Utility function	Absolute risk aversion $-\frac{u''(c)}{u'(c)}$	Relative risk aversion $-\frac{u''(c)}{u'(c)}c$	Absolute prudence $-\frac{u'''(c)}{u''(c)}$	Relative prudence $-\frac{u'''(c)}{u''(c)}c$
Quadratic: $u(c) = ac - \frac{b}{2}c^2$	$\frac{b}{a-bc}$	$\frac{b}{a-bc}c$	0	0
Exponential: $u(c) = -\frac{e^{-\alpha c}}{\alpha}$	α	αc	α	αc
Isoelastic: $u(c) = \frac{c^{1-\gamma}-1}{1-\gamma}$	$\frac{\gamma}{c}$	γ	$\frac{1+\gamma}{c}$	$1+\gamma$

and $u'''(c)=0$. Note that if the utility function is quadratic, risk aversion is increasing. The fact that risk aversion increases with consumption is viewed as an implausible feature of preferences and is one of the chief perceived weaknesses of the certainty equivalence model.

Exponential utility: $u(c)=-\dfrac{e^{-\alpha c}}{\alpha}$, where $\alpha>0$. The first, second, and third derivatives are, respectively, $u'(c)=e^{-\alpha c}$, $u''(c)=-\alpha e^{-\alpha c}$, and $u'''(c)=\alpha^2 e^{-\alpha c}$.

Note that if the utility function is exponential (as in Caballero, 1991), absolute risk aversion and prudence are constant (equal to α), while relative risk aversion is $a(c)=\alpha c$ and is therefore increasing. This property too is unrealistic, because it implies that the consumer is willing to take fewer risks as consumption increases. Furthermore, with exponential utility, it is possible to obtain an optimal solution with negative consumption.

Isoelastic utility: $u(c)=\dfrac{c^{1-\gamma}-1}{1-\gamma}$ with $\gamma>0$. The first, second, and third derivatives are, respectively, $u'(c)=c^{-\gamma}$, $u''(c)=-\gamma c^{-\gamma-1}$, and $u'''(c)=\gamma(\gamma+1)c^{-\gamma-2}$. The degree of absolute risk aversion is decreasing, while relative risk aversion and relative prudence are constant. The logarithmic utility function is a special case of isoelastic utility $\left(\lim\limits_{\gamma\to 1}\dfrac{c^{1-\gamma}-1}{1-\gamma}=\ln c\right)$.

CHAPTER 7

The Buffer Stock Model

Chapters 5 and 6 analyze precautionary saving and liquidity constraints in isolation. Now we will study models that combine these two factors to provide a unified, more realistic treatment of intertemporal decisions. We start off with a simple three-period model to illustrate how the expectation of future borrowing constraints can induce precautionary saving even in scenarios in which marginal utility is linear.

A more general model that allows liquidity constraints and precautionary saving to interact fully is the buffer stock model, of which there are two versions. One, developed by Deaton (1991), emphasizes the possibility that a prudent and impatient consumer may face credit constraints. The other, by Carroll (1997), features the same type of consumer but allows for the possibility of income falling to zero and so generating a natural borrowing constraint.

7.1. EXPECTED LIQUIDITY CONSTRAINTS

In Chapter 6 we have shown that with perfect credit markets precautionary saving arises only if the utility function exhibits prudence (i.e., the marginal utility function is convex). In this section we discuss a case in which credit market imperfections challenge this view, demonstrating that if the consumer faces liquidity constraints, precautionary saving may occur even with quadratic preferences. The basic intuition is provided by the simple three-period model proposed by Besley (1995).

Consider an individual whose utility function is quadratic (so that $u'''(.) = 0$ and the coefficient of prudence is equal to zero) and assume for simplicity $r = \delta = 0$. The only source of uncertainty is income, y, which is identically and independently distributed with mean μ and variance σ^2 over the support $[y_{min}, y_{max}]$. The consumer's objective is to maximize:

$$\max u(c_t) + E_t u(c_{t+1}) + E_t u(c_{t+2}),$$

subject to the dynamic budget constraints:

$$c_t + s_t = y_t$$
$$c_{t+1} + s_{t+1} = s_t + y_{t+1}$$
$$c_{t+2} = s_{t+1} + y_{t+2}$$

and to a liquidity constraint imposed on saving in period $t+1$:[1]

$$s_{t+1} \geq 0.$$

The constraint on saving prevents wealth from being negative in the second period. Substituting the constraints into the objective function, the consumer's problem can be rewritten as:

$$\max_{s_t, s_{t+1}} u(y_t - s_t) + E_t u(y_{t+1} - s_{t+1} + s_t) + E_t u(y_{t+2} + s_{t+1}) + \lambda E_t s_{t+1},$$

where $u(c_t) = ac_t - \dfrac{b}{2}c_t^2$. It can be solved by first finding the solution for the last period and then working backward to solve for the previous periods. The choice in the third period is simple, in that consumption exactly equals resources, that is, the accumulated savings from the previous period plus the income of the current period. In the second period the problem is:

$$\max_{s_{t+1}} u(y_{t+1} - s_{t+1} + s_t) + E_{t+1} u(y_{t+2} + s_{t+1}) + \lambda s_{t+1},$$

with first-order condition:

$$-u'(y_{t+1} - s_{t+1} + s_t) + E_{t+1} u'(y_{t+2} + s_{t+1}) \geq 0.$$

This condition applies with equality only if the constraint does not bind, that is, $\lambda = 0$. Using the assumptions on the utility function and the stochastic process of income, one obtains:

1. In this example we define the dynamic budget constraints in terms of the flow of saving rather than in terms of the stock of wealth. The two concepts are related through the identity: $s_t = a_{t+1} - a_t$.

$$-2s_{t+1} + (y_{t+1} + s_t) - \mu \geq 0.$$

This condition, together with the constraint $s_{t+1} \geq 0$, implies:

$$0 \leq s_{t+1} \leq \frac{1}{2}\left[(y_{t+1} - \mu) + s_t\right],$$

which yields the optimal solution for saving in the second period:

$$s_{t+1}^* = \begin{cases} \frac{1}{2}\left[(y_{t+1} - \mu) + s_t\right] & \text{if } y_{t+1} \geq \mu - s_t \\ 0 & \text{otherwise} \end{cases} \qquad (7.1)$$

Saving in period $t+1$ is positive only if the realization of income in the period (y_{t+1}) is sufficiently high. Equation (7.1) indicates that saving depends only on average income and not on its variance. In other words, in period $t+1$ there is no precautionary saving motive, just as in the certainty equivalence model.

The solid line in Figure 7.1 is the saving function with liquidity constraints, that is, the relation between saving and income in period $t+1$. For values of income greater than $\mu - s_t$, saving is proportional to income. For lower values, the liquidity constraint imposes zero saving. Because of the liquidity constraint, saving is a convex function of income. The dashed line in Figure 7.1 shows instead the amount of saving that the consumer would have chosen in

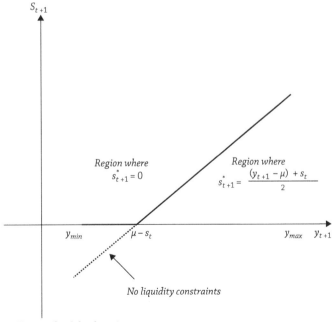

Figure 7.1: The graph of the function s_{t+1}

the absence of the liquidity constraints for low realizations of income. Unlike the model with liquidity constraints, the saving function is always linear, whatever the realization of income.

Figure 7.1 is the mirror image of a concave piece-wise linear consumption function. Consumption equals income up to $y_t = \mu - s_t$ (equivalently, consumption equals current resources, or cash on hand, $y_{t+1} + s_t$). Above this critical value, consumption is still a linear function of income, but the slope is lower; in other words, the consumption function is concave, a concept that recurs frequently in this chapter.

Using the optimal solution for s_{t+1} given by (7.1), we can now solve the problem for the first period:

$$\max_{s_t} u\left(y_t - s_t\right) + E_t u\left(y_{t+1} - s^*_{t+1} + s_t\right) + E_t u\left(y_{t+2} + s^*_{t+1}\right).$$

The first-order condition is:

$$-u'\left(y_t - s_t\right) + E_t u'\left(y_{t+1} - s^*_{t+1} + s_t\right) = 0.$$

Since $u(c_t) = ac_t - \dfrac{b}{2}c_t^2$, this condition can be rewritten as:

$$-2s_t + \left(y_t - \mu\right) + E_t\left(s^*_{t+1}\right) = 0. \tag{7.2}$$

Calculating the expected value of equation (7.1) gives:

$$E_t\left(s^*_{t+1}\right) = \int_{\mu - s_t}^{y_{max}} \frac{1}{2}\left[\left(y_{t+1} - \mu\right) + s_t\right] f(y_{t+1})\, dy_{t+1}.$$

This term depends not only on average income but also on higher moments of the income distribution. For example, if y_{t+1} is uniformly distributed over the interval $[y_{min}, y_{max}]$, and $y_t = \mu$, then substituting $E_t(s^*_{t+1})$ into equation (7.2) gives optimal saving in the first period,

$$s^*_t = \Phi\left(y_{max} - y_{min}\right),$$

with $\Phi = \dfrac{7}{2} \pm 2\sqrt{3} > 0$. Holding the mean constant, an increase in income risk (i.e., an increase in the difference $y_{max} - y_{min}$) increases current saving.[2] Since we

---

2. The result depends on the specific shape of the income distribution. The case of uniform distribution is the simplest one that generates a closed-form solution.

know from Figure 7.1 that s_{t+1}^* is a convex function of y_{t+1}, and since s_t^* is a linear function of s_{t+1}^*, then s_t^* is also a convex function of y_{t+1} in the interval $[y_{min}, y_{max}]$.

The result of the foregoing is that a mean-preserving spread in the income distribution increases saving even if utility is quadratic. The consumer anticipates the possibility of a liquidity constraint in the subsequent period and reacts by increasing current saving. If there were no liquidity constraint, the saving function would be linear (the dashed line in the figure), and there would be no incentive for precautionary saving, as in the certainty equivalence model.

7.2. PRECAUTIONARY SAVING WITH LIQUIDITY CONSTRAINTS

In this section we explore the case of imperfect credit markets and prudent consumers, first studied by Deaton (1991). As we shall see, although this model is based on different assumptions, it delivers implications similar to those of Carroll's buffer stock model.

Deaton considers the Euler equation that results when consumers' wealth is constrained not to be negative (equation (5.4) in Chapter 5), namely,

$$u'(c_t) \geq \frac{(1+r)}{(1+\delta)} E_t u'(c_{t+1}), \tag{7.3}$$

which holds with equality only if the liquidity constraint does not bind. But when the constraint is binding, current consumption is equal to current resources and, if the constraint is of the form $a_{t+1} \geq 0$, then $c_t = a_t + y_t$. We will then have $u'(c_t) = u'(a_t + y_t)$, and therefore (7.3) can be rewritten as:

$$u'(c_t) = \max\left\{u'(a_t + y_t); \frac{(1+r)}{(1+\delta)} E_t u'(c_{t+1})\right\}. \tag{7.4}$$

To understand equation (7.4), consider Figure 7.2. The liquidity constraint does not bind if optimal consumption in the absence of constraint is given by $c_t^* \leq a_t + y_t$. This level of consumption satisfies the Euler equation (7.4) with equality and corresponds to point A in the top panel of Figure 7.2. If preferences are such that optimal consumption exceeds current resources (i.e., the unconstrained consumer would choose point C), the liquidity constraint binds and the consumer chooses a corner solution (point B) and entirely consumes current resources.

The bottom panel of Figure 7.2 shows that a liquidity-constrained consumer cannot reduce the marginal utility of consumption to below $u'(a_t + y_t)$. Thus, attainable marginal utility is a vertical line at point $a_t + y_t$. The graph

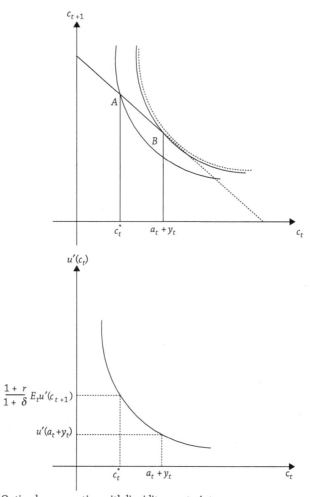

Figure 7.2: Optimal consumption with liquidity constraints

shows that for the unconstrained consumer, the marginal utility of current consumption equals $\dfrac{(1+r)}{(1+\delta)}E_t u'(c_{t+1})$.

With isoelastic preferences, there is no closed-form solution for consumption and one must solve numerically on the basis of specific assumptions about preferences, the income process, and the nature of the borrowing constraint. We provide a brief summary of the numerical simulation approach in the appendix to this chapter.

Deaton considers impatient consumers, those who have a strong incentive to consume earlier rather than later (i.e., he imposes $\delta > r$), which may require borrowing early in the life cycle—something that is precluded by the formal

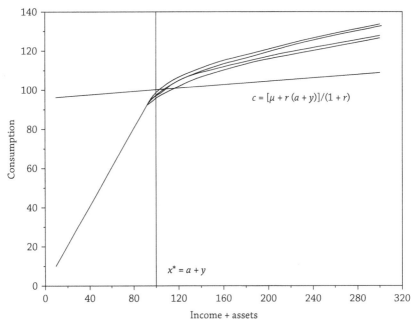

Figure 7.3: The consumption function in Deaton's model
Note: The figure is reproduced from Deaton (1992) with permission.

borrowing constraint. Deaton shows that consumption can be expressed as a function of current resources, or cash on hand:

$$c_t = f_t(a_t + y_t).$$

We have encountered this expression in Chapter 4 in connection with the certainty equivalence model. While in that case the consumption function has a closed-form expression, here there are no analytical solutions. However, the functional expression holds even with liquidity constraints. In fact, if the constraint binds, consumption equals current resources (i.e., there is a corner solution similar to point B in Figure 7.2).

As is observed in the appendix to this chapter, one can find the optimal policy function $f_t(a_t + y_t)$ by numerical simulations, making assumptions about preferences, the stochastic income process, and the parameter values. With Deaton's assumptions, one obtains the consumption function shown in Figure 7.3.[3] The line labeled $c = [\mu + r(a+y)]/(1+r)$ is the consumption

---

3. Deaton assumes that the utility function is isoelastic, the coefficient of risk aversion is 2, the interest rate is 5 percent, the rate of time preference is 10 percent, and income is independently and identically normally distributed with mean 100 and standard deviation of 10.

function that would obtain under certainty equivalence (equation (4.19) in Chapter 4). For low levels of cash on hand, consumption equals cash on hand, $a_t + y_t$, hence the consumption function is a 45-degree line. Above some critical level of cash on hand (x^*, a value that depends on the parameter assumptions), consumers have an incentive to accumulate some resources for the future, that is, to use wealth as a buffer (hence the term *buffer stock model*) against adverse fluctuations in income and the risk of future liquidity constraints. The concavity of the consumption function depends on the fact that above x^* the fraction of cash on hand that is not consumed increases with cash on hand—that is, people save a rising proportion of their resources.

Note that Deaton assumes that the consumer receives income in each period. Therefore, the accumulation of wealth does not follow, as in the life-cycle model, from the desire to maintain a constant level of consumption in anticipation of income declines (upon retirement, say). The main insight here is that even if consumers cannot borrow, they still seek to smooth consumption. They cannot draw on external sources (debt), but they do use their own savings (the wealth accumulated up to the current period). The model generates a precautionary saving motive that is reinforced by the possibility that a liquidity constraint may bind in the future.

Note that Figure 7.3 is not a graph of consumption against time but a relationship between consumption and cash on hand based on the function $f_t(a_t + y_t)$. Deaton shows that this function has two characteristics. First, consumption varies much less than income; second, due to liquidity constraints, changes in consumption are asymmetric, in that the probability of a decline is greater than that of an increase.

Deaton's simulations also show that wealth seldom falls to zero, and thus that the consumer is exactly at a corner solution only occasionally. This point is important, because it suggests that in most periods (if not always) the Euler equation (7.3) may be satisfied with equality even for consumers who are *always* subject to liquidity constraint (i.e., can never borrow) but who circumvent it by using wealth as a buffer. The model thus indicates that estimating the Euler equation is unlikely to produce evidence of binding liquidity constraints.[4]

7.3. THE BUFFER STOCK MODEL

Like Deaton (1991), Carroll (1997) assumes that the utility function is isoelastic and that consumers are impatient ($\delta > r$). However, rather than

---

4. Aiyagari (1994) considers the importance of precautionary saving and liquidity constraints in a general equilibrium framework to quantify their impact on the aggregate saving rate and inequality in wealth.

impose a borrowing limit, he assumes that income can be zero with some positive probability. As we know from the discussion of the natural borrowing constraint in Chapter 5, the possibility of zero income implies that consumers will never want to borrow, so the optimal solution will resemble that of a model with explicit liquidity constraints. The consumer's problem is:

$$\max E_t \sum_{\tau=0}^{T-\tau} (1+\delta)^{-\tau} \frac{c_{t+\tau}^{1-\gamma}-1}{1-\gamma},$$

subject to:

$$a_{t+1} = (1+r)(a_t + y_t - c_t)$$

$$\ln y_t = p_t + u_t$$

$$p_t = g + p_{t-1} + \zeta_t,$$

where the log of income is the sum of a permanent random walk component p_t and a transitory component u_t. Moreover, in each period there is a small probability that $y_t = 0$.

In this model consumers have a unique and stable ratio between cash on hand (wealth plus income) and the permanent component of income, which Carroll terms the target wealth-to-permanent-income ratio. Carroll also shows that a necessary condition for buffer stock behavior is $\gamma^{-1}(r-\delta) < g$, that is, the rate of growth of consumption in the case of certainty, $\gamma^{-1}(r-\delta)$, is lower than that of income g. To see the significance of this condition, suppose there is no uncertainty and initial assets are zero. Since consumption grows less than income, and since the present discounted value of consumption must eventually equal the present discounted value of income, it must be that the optimal *level* of consumption today is higher than the *level* of income today, that is, consumers want to borrow (note that if $g = 0$, the condition is simply $\delta > r$).[5]

In the buffer stock model, consumers balance the desire to spend induced by impatience against the incentive for precautionary saving to guard against the possibility of low income realizations (to prevent the marginal utility of consumption from becoming infinitely negative). The incentive to save therefore depends on the strength of the precautionary motive.

One important implication of the model is that buffer stock savers have a target for the ratio of their wealth to permanent income "such that if actual

---

5. Carroll (1997) shows that the sufficient condition for buffer stock saving also depends on the variance of the permanent income shock.

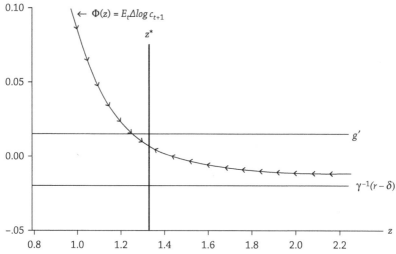

Figure 7.4: The target wealth-income ratio in the buffer stock model
Note: The figure is reproduced from Carroll (1997) with permission.

wealth is below the target, the precautionary saving motive will dominate impatience, and the consumer will save, while if actual wealth is above the target, impatience will dominate prudence, and the consumer will dissave" (Carroll, 1997, 2). In Figure 7.4, this ratio is denoted by $z_t = \dfrac{a_t + y_t}{P_t} = \dfrac{x_t}{P_t}$, where $P = \exp(p)$. If cash on hand $z_t > z^*$, impatience outweighs prudence, the consumer reduces wealth relative to permanent income, and consumption growth in the figure is negative (the arrows point upward). If instead $z_t < z^*$, the precautionary saving motive outweighs impatience and wealth increases relative to permanent income (the arrows point downward). It can also be shown that if $z_t = z^*$, the expected growth rate of consumption is approximately equal to the growth rate of income.[6]

It is also easy to see that if the growth rate of income increases, the wealth target is lowered (the intersection with the curve of expected consumption shifts to the left). If the rate of time preferences increases (or if the interest rate falls), the curve will also shift down, and so will target wealth.

The buffer stock model does not produce an analytic solution for consumption and wealth. Carroll's simulations of the age-wealth profile indicate that in the buffer stock model there is relatively little wealth accumulation by the young (see Figure 7.5). They will never borrow, instead holding consumption within current income so that consumption will track income over

---

6. Jappelli, Padula, and Pistaferri (2008) use self-reported data on target wealth. They test and reject the implication of the model that when wealth is below target, people save to get back on target (and vice versa).

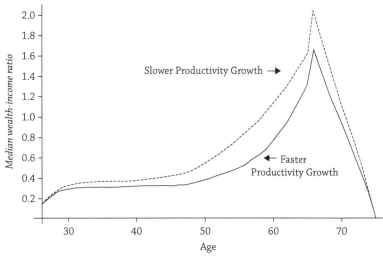

Figure 7.5: The age profile of the wealth-income ratio in the buffer stock model
Note: The figure is reproduced from Carroll (1997) with permission.

most of their working life. In the literature, this is often referred to as "high-frequency" income smoothing, as opposed to the "low-frequency" or "life-cycle frequency" smoothing that was postulated by Modigliani and Brumberg.

In Chapter 10 we shall see that in life-cycle models simulated with realistic preferences and income process, the wealth-income ratio increases over the course of working life, and target wealth is reached around retirement, implying that the consumption and income profiles are completely detached throughout life. The age profile of the wealth-income ratio during working life therefore provides a useful avenue for distinguishing different classes of models of intertemporal choice.

7.4. THE CONCAVITY OF THE CONSUMPTION FUNCTION

To sum up the topics discussed so far in the book, it is useful to review how liquidity constraints and precautionary saving affect the shape of the consumption function, that is, the relation of consumption to resources, by comparison with the case of certainty equivalence.

We know already that the certainty equivalence model delivers a linear relation between consumption and cash-on-hand. For instance, we know from Chapter 4 that if income follows a simple (albeit unrealistic) i.i.d. process, consumption is proportional to cash on hand, as in equation (4.19), which we repeat here:

$$c_t = \frac{\mu}{1+r} + \frac{r}{1+r}\left(a_t + y_t\right).$$

In this simple case the propensity to consume out of cash on hand equals the "wealth effect", that is, the propensity to consume out of total resources. For values of the interest rate between 0.02 and 0.05, the equation indicates that the marginal propensity to consume is quite low, between 0.0196 and 0.0476.

However, the relation between consumption and cash on hand also depends on individual preferences as well as the income process. To take another example, if income is a random walk, the permanent-income hypothesis yields a linear relation between consumption and the components of cash on hand:

$$c_t = \frac{r}{1+r}a_t + \frac{r}{1+r}\left(y_t + \frac{E_t y_{t+1}}{1+r} + ...\right)$$

$$= \frac{r}{1+r}a_t + y_t,$$

since for random walks $E_t y_{t+\tau} = y_t$ for all τ. In this example the marginal propensity to consume is much higher (actually, it is equal to 1) for a change in income than for a change in wealth.[7] Note, however, that the relation between consumption and each of the components of cash on hand remains linear given the assumption of quadratic utility.

In the model set out in Chapter 6 with constant absolute risk aversion and a random walk income process, we found again that consumption is a linear relation function of income, equation (6.15):

$$c_t = y_t - \left(\frac{T-2t+1}{2}\right)\chi.$$

In this equation there is no role for assets, because we assume that the interest rate is zero, so the marginal propensity to consume is again 1.

A linear consumption function, however, is the exception rather than the rule, and in more general models the marginal propensity to consume depends on the income process, individual preferences, and any liquidity constraints. For example, in Section 7.2 we observed that the consumption function in period t is concave in income because the consumer reacts to the possibility of a future liquidity constraint by increasing current saving. Carroll and Kimball (1996) show that adding income uncertainty to the standard optimization problem with preferences characterized by prudence induces a concave

---

7. An alternative way to analyze wealth effects is to assume that the returns to assets are stochastic and study how shocks to the rate of return affect consumption. See Contreras and Nichols (2010), which finds that the marginal propensity to consume out of wealth increases with the persistence of shocks to the interest rate.

consumption function in which the marginal propensity to consume out of cash on hand declines with wealth.[8]

The intuitive way to explain the concavity of the consumption function is that consumers with less wealth have less ability to shield their consumption against income shocks. So as their wealth declines, their fear of low income realizations intensifies, making their precautionary saving motive stronger and stronger. It is the increasing desire to reduce spending as wealth falls that compresses consumption by ever larger amounts (in absolute terms) as wealth diminishes.

In Chapters 5–7 we have enriched the certainty equivalence models to allow for liquidity constraints and precautionary saving. These more sophisticated models retain some of the implications of certainty equivalence—for instance, that consumption responds more strongly to permanent income shocks than to transitory ones—and also yield new ones, such as that liquidity-constrained consumers react excessively to anticipated income changes and that income risk affects consumption and the accumulation of wealth (saving). In Chapters 8–10 we present a selective review of the empirical evidence for the various models of intertemporal consumption behavior we have discussed so far.

APPENDIX

Solving consumption stochastic dynamic programming problems

As noted in Section 7.4, in all the models considered so far consumption can be written as a function of cash on hand:

$$c_t = f_t\left(a_t + y_t\right)$$

where the subscript t indicates that the relationship between consumption and cash on hand can vary with age (for instance, equation (4.16) in Chapter 4). In some cases the relationship is linear and available in closed form (as under certainty or certainty equivalence, or in models with exponential utility and random walk income). In other cases we know that consumption is a concave function of cash on hand, but there is no closed-form analytical solution. For this reason, researchers use numerical solutions.

---

8. Notable cases in which the consumption function is linear are: (a) where the utility function is isoelastic and there is interest rate risk but no labor income risk, and (b) where the utility function is CARA with labor income risk but no interest rate risk (the case we analyze in Section 7.4).

To see how this is done, start from the Euler equation with $r = \delta$ for simplicity:

$$u'\left[f_t(x_t)\right] = E_t u'\left\{f_{t+1}\left[(1+r)(x_t - f_t(x_t)) + y_{t+1}\right]\right\} \qquad (7.5)$$

where $x_t = a_t + y_t$ denotes cash on hand.

The only uncertain variable at time t is income in period $t+1$, which we assume to be distributed over the support $[0, +\infty]$ with density function $h(y_{t+1})$. For example, suppose that $y_t \sim$ i.i.d.(μ, σ^2) for all t. Equation (7.5) can then be rewritten as:

$$u'\left[f_t(x_t)\right] = \int_0^\infty u'\left\{f_{t+1}\left[(1+r)(x_t - f_t(x_t)) + y_{t+1}\right]\right\}h(y_{t+1})dy_{t+1}. \qquad (7.6)$$

We want to find the parameters of the consumption policy function, that is, the relationship between consumption and cash on hand in each period of life. If the horizon is finite, this problem can be solved by backward induction. The consumption policy function in the last period, T, can be found easily, as consumers exhaust all the resources that are available at the beginning of the period:

$$c_T = f_T(x_T) = x_T.$$

This function can now be substituted into (7.6) to find the policy function in period $T-1$:

$$u'\left[f_{T-1}(x_{T-1})\right] = \int_0^\infty u'\left\{(1+r)\left[x_{T-1} - f_{T-1}(x_{T-1})\right] + y_T\right\}h(y_T)dy_T. \qquad (7.7)$$

To give an intuitive example of how one can go about finding the policy function, suppose that $u(.)$ is isoelastic and that income can take only two values, good and bad, with associated probabilities π and $(1-\pi)$, so that (7.7) becomes:

$$\left[f_{T-1}(x_{T-1})\right]^{-\gamma} = \pi\left\{(1+r)\left[x_{T-1} - f_{T-1}(x_{T-1})\right] + y_{g,T}\right\}^{-\gamma}$$
$$+ (1-\pi)\left\{(1+r)\left[x_{T-1} - f_{T-1}(x_{T-1})\right] + y_{b,T}\right\}^{-\gamma}.$$

To find the policy function $f_{T-1}(x_{T-1})$, set values for γ and r and the distribution of income (i.e., π, $y_{g,T}, y_{b,T}$), choose a grid of possible values of cash on hand x_{T-1}, and find the parameters of the function $f_{T-1}(x_{T-1})$ that satisfy (7.7) with equality. Since numerically the grid is specified over a finite number of points, $f_{T-1}(x_{T-1})$ is typically found by interpolation between the values of the various points. Given the optimal policy function $f_{T-1}(x_{T-1})$, substitution of the latter into the Euler equation for the previous period gives the optimal policy function in period $T-2$, $f_{T-2}(x_{T-2})$. This algorithm continues up to the initial period t.

Once the policy functions for all the periods have been found, you can simulate life-cycle consumption paths by assuming an initial value for cash on hand and drawing income shocks from the assumed distribution. Since a_t is given, a random draw from the distribution of income provides y_t, and therefore x_t, and hence optimal consumption for that period through the policy function $f_t(x_t)$. The intertemporal budget constraint then determines wealth in the *next* period, a_{t+1}. A new random draw from the income distribution gives y_{t+1}, and therefore x_{t+1}. The optimal policy function $f_{t+1}(x_{t+1})$ gives c_{t+1}, and so forth.[9] This procedure is repeated until the last period, T. One advantage of these simulation techniques is that you can run policy experiments; for example, you can study how consumption responds to changes in the value of parameters (the interest rate, the distribution of random variables, taxes affecting the mean value of income, etc.).

The procedure described above "picks" values for the parameters γ, π, y_g, and y_b (assuming $y_{g,t} = y_g$ and $y_{b,t} = y_b$ for all t). Often, though, the purpose is precisely to obtain estimates of these parameters. In these cases, simulation methods can be used. The method of simulated moments (MSM) and indirect inference (II) are two examples of estimation by simulation.[10]

The idea behind these two estimation methods is as follows. Suppose the vector of unknown parameters of interest is $\lambda = (\gamma, \pi, y_g, y_b)$. Pick an initial guess for this vector, say λ_0. Given this and the policy functions, one can generate some simulated moments, such as the mean and the variance of consumption at different points of the life cycle (reflecting the age profile of consumption and consumption inequality over the life cycle, respectively). These moments are typically chosen to reflect important features of the behavior under study and to depend on the parameters of interest λ (which is an identification condition). Call these moments $m^s(\lambda_0)$. To avoid the influence of special draws, repeat the simulations S times and average these moments across simulations to obtain $\bar{m}(\theta_0) = S^{-1} \sum_{s=1}^{S} m^s(\theta_0)$. The same moments can, of course, also be computed in the actual data, which we denote as m_{data}.

If the guess on the parameters is "right," the difference between $\bar{m}(\theta_0)$ and m_{data} reflects only sampling error (i.e., the difference should be close to zero). If the difference is large, however, one can make another guess λ_1, compute

9. To prevent the solution from being influenced by extreme values, this procedure is usually repeated a number of times.
10. In some cases, only a subset of parameters is estimated, while others are taken from other studies or calibrated.

$\bar{m}(\theta_1)$ in a similar way, compare it with m_{data}, and so forth. In practice, a formal distance minimization algorithm is used,

$$\hat{\theta} = \arg\min_{\theta} \left[\bar{m}(\theta) - m_{data} \right]' \Omega \left[\bar{m}(\theta) - m_{data} \right],$$

where Ω is an appropriate weighting matrix. We refer readers to McFadden (1989) and Gourieroux, Monfort, and Renault (1993) for more technical econometric details on the method of simulated moments, Carroll (2012) for a set of technical notes and programs, and Gourinchas and Parker (2002) and Attanasio and Weber (1995) for early applications with consumption data.

CHAPTER 8

The Response of Consumption
to Anticipated Changes in Income

H ow does household consumption respond to changes in economic resources? Does the response depend on the nature and duration of the changes? Do anticipated changes in income have a different impact than unexpected shocks? And do transitory shocks have less impact than permanent ones? We have discussed the theoretical relationship between income changes and consumption. In this chapter and in Chapter 9 we examine the implications of models studied earlier in the light of the data, reviewing some of the empirical approaches researchers have taken to estimate the response of consumption to income changes. The emphasis is on method, the discussion focusing on the most important approaches and empirical results. To put matters in perspective, Figure 8.1 diagrams the main links between income changes and consumption, underscoring the questions that will be examined in these two chapters. The main distinction is between anticipated and unanticipated changes.

The intertemporal models studied in Chapter 3 (complete markets), Chapter 4 (certainty equivalence), and Chapter 6 (precautionary saving) postulate that people use savings in order to smooth income fluctuations, and that unless there are liquidity constraints (as in Chapters 5 and 7), consumption responds little if at all to changes in income that were expected. When this major theoretical prediction is violated, researchers conclude that consumption is excessively sensitive to anticipated income changes. This is indeed a clear implication of the theory, but designing a clean test of it encounters two types of problem, one empirical and one theoretical. Empirically, it is very hard to identify situations in which income changes in a predictable way. But even if the empirical difficulties can be surmounted, there are many plausible

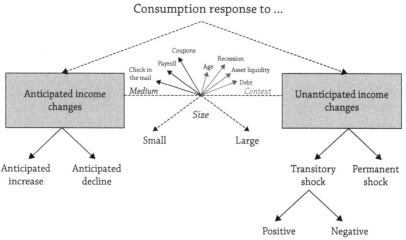

Figure 8.1: A diagram of the response of consumption to income changes

explanations for the rejection of the implications of the theoretical models, including liquidity constraints, non-separability between consumption and leisure, home production, the persistence of habits, aggregation bias, and the durability of goods.

More recently, the literature has sought to gain insight by distinguishing whether consumers expect income to decline or to increase. While credit constraints may be responsible for a correlation of consumption with expected income increases, they cannot explain why consumption reacts to expected income declines, as with retirement. A further distinction that has proven to be useful is between large and small anticipated changes, as consumers might be expected to react to the former and ignore the latter.

The branch on the right-hand side of Figure 8.1 focuses instead on the impact of unanticipated income shocks. Here the main distinction is between transitory shocks, which in theory should have only a modest impact on consumption, and permanent shocks, which should lead to major revisions. As with anticipated changes, the literature has sought to pin down the empirical estimates identifying positive and negative shocks. Since econometricians can study how consumption responds to income changes, the interest is in estimating the marginal propensity to consume as well as in testing the main tenets of the theory. Finally, Figure 8.1 indicates that context too may be relevant to the consumption impact of income shocks: small shocks might go unnoticed, while large ones could be more salient and have a stronger impact; consumption might respond differently in recessions and expansions; it might be age-dependent; the form in which income is received might also be relevant (for instance, via a reduction in the payroll tax or a check in the mail). Therefore, there is no single precise definition of what applied economists mean when they talk generally about the marginal propensity to consume.

The previous chapters have made it clear that consumption should react to unexpected income shocks, to an extent that depends on the characteristics and persistence of the shocks and on the degree of completeness of credit and insurance markets. Furthermore, models with perfect credit markets and quadratic utility imply that consumption should not vary with income changes that have been anticipated, but in models with liquidity constraints and precautionary saving, consumption may respond to such changes.

As an organizing framework, we can summarize our diagram by means of the following expression for the change in consumption:

$$\Delta c_{it} = z'_{it}\lambda + \alpha E_{t-1}\Delta y_{it} + \sum_{k=1}^{K} \phi_k \pi_{it}^k + \xi_{it}, \qquad (8.1)$$

where the z_{it} variables capture the effect of preference shifts (due perhaps to age or family size) on consumption, $E_{t-1}\Delta y_{it}$ denotes the expected value of income changes, and π^k are income shocks of different persistence; ϕ_k denotes the marginal propensity to consume out of shock π^k, and ξ_{it} is an approximation error (which may also include measurement error in consumption).

Depending on the purpose of the analysis, equation (8.1) can be used in two ways. In this chapter we test the hypothesis that an expected rise in income does not affect the growth of consumption (the so-called orthogonality test, or $\alpha = 0$), distinguishing between positive and negative expected income changes but making no specific assumption about the income process (i.e., treating $\sum_{k=1}^{K} \phi_k \pi_{it}^k + \xi_{it}$ as a composite error term). In Chapter 9, instead, we focus on estimating the marginal propensity to consume with respect to income shocks, that is, the parameters ϕ_k.

8.1. THE EXCESS SENSITIVITY TEST

According to the certainty equivalence model, consumption should follow a martingale stochastic process, making it impossible to predict changes in consumption between period t and period $t+1$ based on the information available in period t. The earlier literature used aggregate data to test this implication.[1]

The hypothesis that consumption follows a martingale was tested in a seminal contribution by Robert Hall (1978). Hall's test is also known as the *orthogonality condition test*. It was originally applied to aggregate data, and hence we

---

1. While in general one cannot use aggregate data to test the implications of microeconomic models, in the certainty equivalence case, under appropriate circumstances, this is possible.

drop the individual subscript i for simplicity. To understand the logic of the test, suppose that consumption follows a martingale,

$$\Delta c_{t+1} = \varepsilon_{t+1}, \tag{8.2}$$

with $E\left(\varepsilon_{t+1}|I_t\right) = E(\Delta c_{t+1}|I_t) = 0$. Under the null hypothesis that consumption is a martingale, this equation provides an orthogonality condition.

Let us consider a set of variables that belong to the consumer's information set, $x_t \in I_t$. Under the null hypothesis, the condition $E\left(\varepsilon_{t+1}|x_t\right) = E(\Delta c_{t+1}|x_t) = 0$ holds. It follows that no variable known in period t should be correlated with the change in consumption between t and $t+1$. In other words, in a regression of Δc_{t+1} on x_t, the coefficient of x_t should not be statistically different from zero.

Using US national accounts data, Hall did not reject the orthogonality condition for lagged income but did reject it for the stock price index. The orthogonality test was generalized by Marjorie Flavin (1981), using specific assumptions about the income process. She rejected the null hypothesis, finding that consumption responds to lagged income changes, which certainly belong to the consumer's information set.

A different approach to orthogonality testing regresses the growth rate of consumption (or the change in consumption), Δc_t, on the expected growth rate of income (or the expected change in income), $E_{t-1}\Delta y_t$. This is known as the *excess sensitivity test*, and it consists of testing the null hypothesis that $\alpha = 0$ in equation (8.1). Since expected income is not typically observable, one can use instrumental variables estimation, where lagged values of income (for example, y_{t-1} or Δy_{t-1}) act as instruments for changes in current income Δy_t (see the appendix to this chapter for details). That is, $E_{t-1}\Delta y_t$ is obtained as the projection of Δy_t onto these lagged values.

Campbell and Mankiw (1989) propose a test that is similar to those of Hall and Flavin, but they interpret the coefficient of expected income changes as the share of aggregate income received by households who simply set consumption equal to income in each period (dubbed "rule-of-thumb" behavior in the literature). Suppose that there are two groups of consumers. One group consumes all their income $\left(c_{1,t} = y_{1,t}\right)$, the second chooses consumption as in the certainty equivalence model. Thus, according to (8.2), $\Delta c_{2,t} = \varepsilon_{2,t}$ for each individual in this group. Denote by μ the share of aggregate income received by the first group of consumers (i.e., $y_{1,t} = \mu y_t$). Adding the two consumption functions, since $c_t = c_{1,t} + c_{2,t}$, we get:

$$\Delta c_t = \mu \Delta y_t + (1-\mu)\varepsilon_t. \tag{8.3}$$

Since Δy_t contains both anticipated and unanticipated components, Campbell and Mankiw estimate equation (8.3) by instrumental variables, using lagged values of income (dated $t-1$ and earlier) as instruments. Based on national accounts data for the United States, they find $\mu = 0.4$. Their interpretation is that 40 percent of aggregate income goes to individuals who follow the simple rule of thumb of consuming all their income. Campbell and Mankiw explain that rule-of-thumb behavior may stem from two distinct causes: some consumers may be myopic or passive, while others may be subject to liquidity constraints.

Jappelli and Pagano (1989), using OECD data, find large international differences in the degree to which consumption responds to expected changes in income. They find high values of μ in Italy, Spain, and Greece, intermediate values in Japan and England, and the lowest values in Sweden and the United States. The countries' μ rank is inversely correlated with their rank in the ratio of household debt to consumption. The study concludes that liquidity constraints are a possible explanation for the sensitivity of consumption.

Campbell and Mankiw's approach has several limitations. First, their test is subject to an identification problem if their instruments have little power (which may occur if, for example, income is a random walk). Second, it is only under particular assumptions (such as those of the certainty equivalence model) that one can use aggregate data to estimate relationships that describe microeconomic consumer behavior.[2] Finally, the reading of μ as reflecting liquidity constraints may be misleading, because while these constraints do prevent people from borrowing, they do not keep them from saving. In Campbell and Mankiw's model, however, such asymmetry is not mentioned.

An alternative way to test the orthogonality condition is to examine the implication of the certainty equivalence model that saving is equal to expected reductions in income (Campbell's "saving for a rainy day" hypothesis, outlined in Chapter 4). Since on this hypothesis people save because they expect their labor income to decline, saving should be at least as good a predictor of declines in labor income as any other forecast that can be constructed from publicly available information. Campbell designs a vector autoregressive model in which the two dependent variables are changes in income and saving and then tests whether past saving is a cause (in the Granger sense) of changes in income. Using aggregate data for the United States, he concludes that there is only weak evidence for excess sensitivity of consumption to income (which he interprets as insufficient variability of saving rather than as a correlation between changes in consumption and lagged changes in income). In particular, he finds that saving helps to forecast declines in labor income, but not as much as predicted by the strict version of the permanent-income hypothesis.[3]

2. This is also a problem for the tests proposed by Hall and Flavin.
3. The test proposed by Campbell has been conducted also on panel data by Alessie and Lusardi (1997). They use Dutch panel data and find that saving has very limited forecasting power.

8.2. IMPLEMENTING AND INTERPRETING THE EXCESS SENSITIVITY TEST

The empirical testing and interpretation of the restriction $\alpha = 0$ in equation (8.1) faces several difficulties. The test of excess sensitivity suffers from both econometric and theoretical problems. Econometrically, there can be difficulties when the data are generated by the permanent-income model but the econometric specification or the type of data used create spurious evidence of excess sensitivity. Theoretically, problems arise when the data used are generated by a different model. We examine these two cases in turn.

Early attempts to test for excess sensitivity relied on aggregate data, which could generate a spurious correlation between aggregate consumption growth and aggregate income growth even when there is no such correlation at the individual level. For instance, in the life-cycle model of Chapter 1 individual consumption is constant, regardless of individual income. But if income grows across generations, then national consumption will be perfectly correlated with national income.

The problems in interpreting excess sensitivity tests with microeconomic data are no less daunting, however. First of all, finding viable instruments for income growth that are truly exogenous and yet have good predictive power is difficult in the extreme, so that empirical economists have generally elected to use out-of-sample information about consumers' expectations of income changes, rather than pure statistical procedures. The instruments chosen for income growth might be poor because the econometrician has less information than the individual, who may be better informed about impending promotion or job loss. Hence, it may be more fruitful to identify episodes of evident, large, expected changes in income that are observable to both the individual and the econometrician. We discuss this approach in Sections 8.6 and 8.7.

Finally, a third econometric problem is that excess sensitivity may also arise spuriously from the misspecification of the stochastic structure of the forecasting errors (see the appendix in this chapter). Under the permanent income hypothesis with rational expectations, the conditional expectation of the forecast errors must be zero, that is, $E_{t-1}(\xi_{it}) = 0$ in equation (8.1). The empirical analogue of this expectation is an average taken over long periods of time, not across a large number of households. In fact, as Chamberlain (1984) points out, there is no guarantee that the cross-sectional average of forecast errors will converge to zero as the cross section gets larger. For instance, if the error is the sum of an aggregate and an idiosyncratic shock, then in a short panel the orthogonality condition fails even if the permanent income model is true: aggregate shocks induce a cross-sectional correlation between expected consumption growth and predicted income growth. The problem is sometimes dealt with by including time dummies in the Euler equation. But these do not solve the problem either, because aggregate shocks might be unevenly distributed across the population.

On the theoretical side, several different models create a correlation between consumption and income growth. Some extend the framework of the permanent income hypothesis to include, for example, precautionary saving or non-separabilities; others, however, are based on radically different assumptions, such as deviations from dynamic consistency.

A first important case is that of binding liquidity constraints. As noted in Chapter 5, in models with liquidity constraints the timing of the income is relevant: consumers who expect their income to grow and cannot borrow are not able to expand consumption in anticipation of the income increase, but only when additional income actually comes. The empirical implications of this model for excess sensitivity are discussed in the next section.

Excess sensitivity also arises in models with precautionary saving. As we know from Chapter 6, in this model the Euler equation also includes the conditional variance of consumption growth. If one omits this variable from equation (8.1), the excess sensitivity coefficient may be significant simply because $E_{t-1} \Delta y_{it}$ may be correlated with the omitted conditional variance term.

Excess sensitivity may result from failure to control properly for non-separable preferences with respect to leisure, an issue first raised by Heckman (1974). If leisure is an argument of the utility function, and if consumption and leisure are non-separable, today's consumption decisions will be affected by predictable changes in households' labor supply.[4] This implies that consumption growth is positively correlated with predictable growth in working hours. Since predicted growth in hours will almost surely correlate with predicted income growth, failure to control for labor supply indicators may lead to spurious evidence of excess sensitivity (that is, it could bias the estimated α coefficient upward), as Attanasio and Weber (1995) show with panel data drawn from the Consumer Expenditure Survey (CEX).

Other models depart more drastically from the framework we have studied so far. For example, Mazzocco (2007) relaxes the unitary models (in which the household is treated as a single entity) and assumes that decisions are made separately by each household member. He shows that in such a framework the Euler equation holds only for singles but not for couples, and confirms this on the basis of CEX data. In a different departure from the traditional model, Laibson (1997) shows that excess sensitivity can arise in equilibrium for consumers with hyperbolic preferences, a model covered in Chapter 14.

---

4. A similar dependence may arise from neglecting home production. As is shown by Baxter and Jermann (1999), excess sensitivity may arise because in the data expected income growth is correlated with home production over the business cycle.

8.3. TESTS FOR LIQUIDITY CONSTRAINTS

We have seen, then, that finding evidence for excess sensitivity does not help to discriminate between alternative consumption models. The test described in this section, devised by Zeldes (1989), links the excess sensitivity test to credit market imperfections using direct information on household wealth. In particular, the test compares the consumption behavior of two groups, those who are potentially subject to liquidity constraints and those who are not (low-wealth and high-wealth households, respectively).

To understand Zeldes's test, let us consider the Euler equation for consumption under the hypotheses that the utility function is isoelastic, the growth rate of consumption is normally distributed, and the consumer faces a borrowing constraint:

$$E_t \Delta \ln c_{t+1} = \gamma^{-1}(r - \delta) + \frac{\gamma}{2} \text{var}_t (\Delta \ln c_{t+1}) + \gamma^{-1} \ln(1 + \psi_t'). \qquad (8.4)$$

Zeldes draws his data from the Panel Study of Income Dynamics (PSID). He assumes that the variance term is constant and that a consumer is not subject to liquidity constraints ($\psi_t' = 0$) if financial assets (af) exceed two months' income ($af / y > 0.17$). *If instead financial assets are below this threshold, the term ψ_t' might be greater than zero. The econometric problem is that for these individuals the term $\gamma^{-1} \ln(1 + \psi_t')$ is an omitted variable that is correlated with household resources. According to this criterion, 38 percent of the PSID sample is classified as high-wealth and 62 percent as low-wealth.*

Zeldes then proposes two tests for the existence of liquidity constraints. The first relies on the thesis that the Euler equation should hold for the high-wealth group but not necessarily for the group potentially subject to liquidity constraints. To make the test operative, he adds lagged income to a standard Euler equation. Under the null hypothesis of no liquidity constraint, the income coefficient should not be statistically different from zero in either group. Under the alternative hypothesis that liquidity constraints do affect consumption, the income coefficient should be zero only in the high-wealth group, because the income of the low-wealth sample may be negatively correlated with the error term, which includes $\gamma^{-1} \ln(1 + \psi_t')$.[5] Zeldes finds that in the high-wealth group the coefficient of lagged income is not statistically different from zero, but in the low-wealth group it is negative and statistically significant.

One of the limitations of Zeldes's test is that wealth is only an imperfect indicator of liquidity constraints, which could reduce the precision

---

5. Income is negatively correlated with ψ_t because a positive income change relaxes the liquidity constraint.

of the estimates. Using direct information from the Survey of Consumer Finances (SCF) on consumers who were turned down for credit or discouraged from borrowing, Jappelli (1990) points out that any sample split based on wealth is likely to be contaminated by misclassification. In particular, the low-wealth sample will include a good many households who have access to credit and have chosen to have low wealth, and are therefore not liquidity-constrained. An additional source of sample split misclassification is measurement error.

Jappelli, Pischke, and Souleles (1998) extend the test using two indicators of access to credit as measures of liquidity constraints: (a) turned down for credit or discouraged from borrowing, and (b) lack of access to a credit line or a credit card. According to these indicators, the fraction of credit-constrained households ranges from 14 to 24 percent. Combining data from the SCF and the PSID, they find that in the unconstrained group the income coefficient is close to zero, while in the constrained group it is negative and statistically different from zero.

The test just described shows that income affects the consumption growth of credit-constrained consumers. However, the sensitivity of consumption among these consumers is not very high and is sometimes imprecisely estimated. As Deaton (1992) observes, it is not easy to find evidence for liquidity constraints using tests based on the Euler equation. Consumers anticipate future liquidity constraints by saving more, so the equation is not violated. Occasionally the constraint binds and the equation fails. Most of the time the test does not find any violation of the Euler equation not because credit markets are perfect but because consumers allow for the probability of future constraints.

To understand Zeldes's second test for liquidity constraints, assume that the sample split correctly identifies constrained and unconstrained consumers. Since $\psi'_t = 0$ for the unconstrained group, it follows that the term $\gamma^{-1} \ln(1 + \psi'_t)$ in equation (8.4) can be interpreted as the excess growth in consumption explained by liquidity constraints. The test first estimates the Euler equation for the unconstrained group and then uses the estimated coefficients to predict consumption growth for the constrained group. The difference between actual and predicted consumption growth is an estimate of $\gamma^{-1} \ln(1 + \psi'_t)$. Its sample average should be positive and statistically different from zero in the presence of binding liquidity constraints. Zeldes finds that the average consumption growth difference is positive, as predicted by the model with liquidity constraints, but statistically insignificant.

Misclassification of the sample split rule is not the only problem with Zeldes's test. Carroll (1997) notices that equation (8.4) also includes the conditional variance of consumption growth from the Euler equation. Omitting this variable might produce a spurious correlation between consumption growth and income that is stronger for low-wealth households. In fact, in models with precautionary saving wealthy households have greater capacity to buffer income fluctuations by drawing down assets, so a finding of excess sensitivity among poor households (as in Zeldes) is consistent with precautionary saving models. Table 8.1 summarizes the empirical strategies and main findings of some studies that have tested for excess sensitivity of consumption to anticipated income changes.

Table 8.1. SUMMARY OF LITERATURE FINDINGS ON EXCESS SENSITIVITY

Authors	Data	Empirical strategy	Main findings
Hall (1978)	1948–77 U.S. time series	Used quadratic preferences	Coefficient on lagged income growth statistically insignificant, but orthogonality restriction rejected for stock market prices.
Flavin (1981)	1949–79 U.S. time series	Specified an income process and estimated jointly the consumption and income equations	Evidence of excess sensitivity.
Altonji and Siow (1987)	1968–81 PSID	Used various measures of income determinants to account for measurement errors in income	Coefficient on lagged income growth statistically insignificant.
Zeldes (1989)	1968–82 PSID	Relied on an asset-based sample separation rule to investigate the impact of credit constraints on consumption	Excess sensitivity was associated with credit constraint due to violation of the Euler equation for the observations for which a constraint is likely to be binding and not for the others.
Attanasio and Weber (1995)	1980–90 CEX	Used labor supply variables as determinants of the marginal utility of consumption to account for non-separable preferences	Failure to control for labor supply indicators may have led to spurious evidence of excess sensitivity.
Shea (1995)	1981–87 PSID	Exploited union contracts (public information) to construct a household-specific measure of expected wage growth	Predictable wage movements were significantly correlated with consumption. Consumption responded more strongly to predictable income declines than to predictable income increases (inconsistent with liquidity constraints and myopia).

Table 8.1. CONTINUED

Authors	Data	Empirical strategy	Main findings
Garcia, Lusardi, and Ng (1997)	1980–87 CEX and PSID	Predicted the probability of being liquidity-constrained using a switching regression framework	Liquidity-constrained consumers were excessively sensitive to past information (but unconstrained consumers also exhibited behavior inconsistent with the theory).
Jappelli, Pischke, and Souleles (1998)	1983 SCF and 1971–87 PSID	Estimated probabilities of being constrained using Survey of Consumer Finances data and Euler equation for food consumption in the PSID	No evidence for much excess sensitivity associated with the possibility of constraints. The pattern of the conditional distribution of consumption in the constrained and unconstrained regimes was consistent with the hypothesis that liquidity constraints affect food consumption allocations.
Parker (1999)	1980–93 CEX	Used security payroll cap as an anticipated income increase (in the middle of the year) and decrease (in January)	$1.00 anticipated rise in income increased non-durable consumption by about .20 (unlikely to be due to liquidity constraints, because the sample included only high-income taxpayers).
Jappelli and Pistaferri (2000b)	1989–93 Italy Survey of Household Income and Wealth (SHIW)	Used subjective quantitative income expectations as an instrument for income growth	No evidence for excess sensitivity to either income increases or declines.

8.4. DIRECT EVIDENCE FROM CREDIT MARKETS

So far we have focused on borrowing to finance the purchase of non-durables. Given the mixed evidence for liquidity constraints in tests based on the Euler equation, an alternative avenue is to examine how credit market imperfections affect purchases of consumer durables and housing. The main difference between borrowing to finance non-durable goods and borrowing for durables or house purchase is that in the latter case the goods can serve as collateral.

Despite the secured nature of the debt, however, households typically do face some borrowing constraints in the mortgage market. For example,

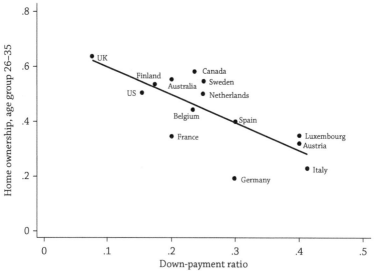

Figure 8.2: Proportion of home ownership among young households
Note: The figure is reproduced with permission from Chiuri and Jappelli (2003).

when a family decides to buy a house and seeks a mortgage, the bank typically finances only a fraction of the cost $(1-\alpha)$, not the entire amount. The rest, α, has to be paid by the buyer, who therefore faces a down-payment constraint. Similar considerations often apply to the purchase of consumer durables.

In the absence of imperfections in the credit market, the fraction α should be close to zero. In deciding whether or not to own their own homes, families should compare the cost of renting and the cost of owning (which includes mortgage payments, property taxes, depreciation, etc.). In equilibrium these costs should be equal. If there is a down-payment constraint, the family must have enough assets to cover it, that is, $a_t \geq \alpha H_t$, where a_t is accumulated wealth and H_t the price of the house. Since it takes time to accumulate the assets for the down-payment, the first effect of this constraint is to raise the age of first home-ownership.[6]

Figure 8.2 graphs the effect of mortgage finance availability on home ownership rates in those twenty-six to thirty-five years old in OECD countries. An increase in the down payment from 20 percent (as in Australia or France) to 40 percent (as in Italy) is associated with a reduction in the owner occupancy

6. A second effect of credit rationing in the mortgage market is an aggregate one. The constraint changes the optimal path of consumption and alters the distribution of savings by age: young families are forced to save more than they would in the absence of a constraint. In a growing economy, aggregate saving is greater than in the absence of constraints. The effect of the down-payment constraint on aggregate saving and wealth was studied by Jappelli and Pagano (1994), who found that in countries where banks demand relatively low down payments saving rates too are low.

rate of 20.2 percentage points in that age group. Of course, some individuals receive help from parents and friends in the form of loans, inheritance, or gifts and so at least partly overcome credit market imperfections. We return to this issue in Chapter 12.

Gerardi, Rosen, and Willen (2010) propose to test the relevance of mortgage market imperfections by measuring the extent to which households with higher expected future income purchase larger houses. Their thesis is that the higher a household's expected future income is, the higher its desired consumption will be. When credit markets work well, desired consumption equals actual consumption and current spending on housing is a good forecast of future expected income. Because credit market imperfections drive a wedge between actual and desired consumption, the extent to which spending on house purchase predicts future income can serve as a gauge of mortgage market imperfections. Using micro data for the United States, Gerardi, Rosen, and Willen find that since the early 1980s mortgage markets have become less imperfect and that securitization in the secondary mortgage market has played an important role.

Further evidence on the role of credit constraints in consumers' choices comes from a number of recent contributions. Gross and Souleles (2002) use proprietary credit card data to analyze how consumption responds to changes in credit supply. They estimate the marginal propensities to consume out of liquidity (measured by increases in credit card limits) and interest-rate elasticities. The permanent-income hypothesis says that consumers who are not credit-constrained should not increase credit card use when the ceiling is raised. Instead the authors find that increases in the maximum generate a significant rise in debt, particularly for people near the limit.

In a similar vein, Adams, Einav, and Levin (2009) use data from a large auto sales company in the subprime market and find that short-term liquidity is an important determinant of consumer behavior. In particular, demand for auto loans increases during tax rebate season, and purchases are highly sensitive to down-payment requirements. Attanasio, Goldberg, and Kyriazidou (2008) use data from the Consumer Expenditure Survey on auto loan contracts to estimate the elasticity of the demand for loans with respect to the interest rate, and find a very low elasticity (except for high-income households), which is consistent with the presence of binding credit constraints.

Finally, Aaronson, Agarwal, and French (2012) find that when the minimum wage is raised, minimum-wage households' spending on autos and debt increases. Much of this debt is in auto loans. These facts stand in sharp contrast to certainty equivalence models but are consistent with models in which households can borrow against durable goods. Intuitively, if the down-payment rate on autos is 20 percent, each additional dollar of income can purchase five dollars' worth of new car.

8.5. ASYMMETRIC RESPONSE TO INCOME INCREASES AND DECLINES

One reason pure statistical procedures to measure excess sensitivity provide a very weak test of the theory is that the instruments used to predict income growth (lagged income growth and the like) may not be powerful enough. Applied researchers have accordingly sought to identify specific episodes in which predicted income changes are observable by the consumer as well as the econometrician. Such episodes can also be classified into expected increases and decreases.

Why is the distinction between positive and negative income change important? We know from Chapter 6 that liquidity constraints should have asymmetric effects on consumption: they should affect consumers who want to borrow (for instance, those who expect positive income growth) but not those who want to save (such as those who expect their income to decline). Hence, in a regression of consumption growth on expected positive and negative income change, the coefficient of the former should be positive and statistically significant, while that of the latter should not be statistically different from zero if consumers cannot borrow against future income.

Shea (1995) was the first to focus on the asymmetric effects of liquidity constraints. Unlike the Zeldes test, Shea's procedure does not split the sample into two groups. In general, it is hard to gauge expected changes in income (whether positive or negative), because people form expectations on the basis of variables that surveys are unlikely to capture (such as news of promotions, the decision to change jobs, or the risk of job loss). To overcome this problem, Shea combines data from the PSID with information about negotiated wage increases from collective bargaining agreements. Using information on industry, occupation, and state of residence, and so imputing an expected wage to about 650 workers who can be matched to a collective bargaining agreement, he finds that the coefficient of expected positive wage growth is statistically insignificant, while that of expected wage declines is positive and statistically different from zero. This result clashes not only with the hypothesis of perfect credit markets but also with that of liquidity constraints (which predict the opposite pattern).[7]

Instead of external information on wage growth, Jappelli and Pistaferri (2000b) use subjective quantitative income expectations for a sample of Italian households and find no evidence of excess sensitivity with respect to either income increases or declines. Other studies examine episodes of expected income increases and expected income declines separately; these are discussed in Sections 8.6 and 8.7.

---

7. Shea argues that his result is consistent with *loss aversion,* that is, consumers consider even a small reduction in consumption as a great psychological loss. In the model with loss aversion, utility is concave down to a certain threshold of consumption and turns convex when consumption falls below the threshold.

8.6. EPISODES OF ANTICIPATED INCOME INCREASES

Table 8.2 summarizes the empirical strategies for addressing the consumption effect of anticipated income increases. The first to identify a specific episode of expected income increase to form a test of the permanent income hypothesis

Table 8.2. SUMMARY OF LITERATURE FINDINGS:
ANTICIPATED INCOME INCREASES

Authors	Data used	Empirical strategy	Main findings
Wilcox (1989)	1965–85 US macro series and Social Security Bulletin	Used pre-announced social security benefits increases as a measure of predicted income increase	Consumption increased not when the income increase was announced but when it actually took effect.
Shapiro and Slemrod (1995)	Telephone survey in 1992	Exploited 10-month reduction in income tax as a case of predictable transitory income increase	40% of interviewees planned to spend the extra take-home pay.
Souleles (1999)	1980–91 CEX	Exploited the anticipated income increase induced by tax refunds	10% of the refunds was spent on non-durables and 65% on total consumption; i.e., most went for durable-goods purchases.
Browning and Collado (2001)	1985–95 ECPF panel (Spanish households)	Used institutionalized June and December extra wage payments to full-time workers as a case of anticipated income increase	No evidence of excess sensitivity, suggesting bounded rationality as a reason earlier researchers found large response of consumption to predicted income changes.
Souleles (2002)	1982–83 CEX	Exploited the anticipated income increase induced by pre-announced tax cuts of the Reagan administration	Significant evidence of excess sensitivity in the response of consumption to the tax cuts.
Hsieh (2003)	1980–2001 CEX	Used both annual payments from the Alaska Permanent Fund and tax rebates as cases of predictable income increase	Evidence of excess sensitivity with respect to tax refunds but not with respect to payments from the Alaska Permanent Fund (can be explained using the magnitude argument).
Shapiro and Slemrod (2003)	Three surveys in 2001–2	Used 2001 tax rebates as a case of predictable income increase	22% of interviewees planned to spend the tax rebate. Little evidence of myopia or liquidity constraints.

(continued)

Table 8.2. CONTINUED

Authors	Data used	Empirical strategy	Main findings
Johnson, Parker, and Souleles (2006)	2001 CEX (included questions about rebates)	Used the exact timing of tax rebates to identify the causal effect	Average household spent 20–40% of the rebate on non-durable goods during the three-month period in which the rebate was received. Expenditure responses were largest for low-liquid-wealth and low-income households (consistent with liquidity constraints).
Agarwal, Liu, and Souleles (2007)	Proprietary panel from a large financial institution that issues credit cards nationally	Used exact timing of tax rebates to identify the causal effect of the rebate	Consumers initially saved part of the rebate, but soon afterward their spending increased, counter to the implications of the permanent-income model.
Stephens (2008)	1984–2000 CEX	Used predictable increases in discretionary income following the final payment of a vehicle loan	A 10% increase in discretionary income led to a 2–3% increase in non-durable consumption. Additional analysis suggested that these findings might be explained by the presence of borrowing constraints.
Shapiro and Slemrod (2009)	A survey in 2008	Used tax rebates as a case of predictable income increase	20% of survey respondents said that the 2008 tax rebates would lead them mostly to increase spending.

was Wilcox (1989), who examined the response of aggregate consumption to pre-announced increases in social security benefits. He found that consumption grows not when the increase is announced but when it takes effect. In particular, he estimated that a 10 percent rise in social security benefits induces a 1 percent increase in retail sales in the same month and a 3 percent increase in durable goods purchases. The limitation of this particular test is that it is difficult to analyze major changes in tax policy using aggregate data on the components of retail sales.

In a series of papers Shapiro and Slemrod (1995, 2003, 2009) use instant-survey data to measure individual responses to actual or hypothetical tax policies. For example, their 1995 paper examined the effectiveness of President George H. W. Bush's temporary reduction in income tax withholding in 1992.[8] One month after the change, they asked about 500 taxpayers

8. The change was transitory, as it would be offset by smaller tax refunds in 1993.

(a) whether they had realized that income tax withholding had decreased and (b) what they were planning to do with the extra money in their paycheck, that is, mostly save it or mostly spend it. Shapiro and Slemrod found that 40 percent of the people interviewed planned to spend the extra take-home pay, suggesting that even a temporary tax change could be moderately effective in increasing household spending. Their analysis of the 2001 income tax rebate gave a lower estimate of the marginal propensity to consume (only 22 percent of the households interviewed planned to spend it) and little evidence of myopia or liquidity constraints, and their study of the 2008 tax stimulus reached similar conclusions. Some problems with these studies—which are common to all research based on subjective responses or expectations—are that respondents have little incentive to answer correctly, may not understand the questions, and may in practice behave differently from their survey responses.

Other studies have used actual consumption data to study temporary tax changes that increase disposable income. Parker (1999) considers the effect on consumption of the anticipated income increase induced by reaching the cap on income subject to social security tax ($106,800 in 2009) at some point during the calendar year.[9] Souleles (1999) studies the anticipated income increase from tax refunds, and also (Souleles, 2002) analyzes how consumption responded to the widely pre-announced tax cuts of the Reagan administration. All of these studies use data from the CEX, all find evidence of excess sensitivity, and most do not attribute the failure of the theory to liquidity constraints.

In Parker's study, an anticipated $1.00 rise in income increases non-durable consumption by about $0.20. This result is unlikely to be due to liquidity constraints, because the sample includes only high-income taxpayers. Souleles (1999) finds that 10 percent of federal tax refunds is spent on non-durables, but that the response of total consumption is much stronger, or 65 percent of the refund, suggesting that most of it goes for durable goods. Since it is high-wealth individuals who use the tax refund mainly to purchase durables, he concludes that borrowing constraints explain only part of the result.[10] Souleles (2002) also points out that liquidity constraints are unlikely to explain his excess sensitivity finding.

Further insight from tax refunds is offered by Johnson, Parker, and Souleles (2006), who study the large income tax rebates under the Economic Growth

9. He also exploits the expected decline in income that high-income taxpayers face in January of each year when the social security tax kicks back in.
10. Hsieh (2003) studies two episodes affecting the same households: tax refunds (as in Souleles, 1999) and payments from the Alaska Permanent Fund, which go only to Alaska residents. He finds excess sensitivity with respect to tax refunds but not with respect to fund payments.

and Tax Relief Reconciliation Act of 2001. The program sent tax rebates, typically between $300 and $600, to about two-thirds of all U.S. households. According to the permanent-income hypothesis, a single rebate should have little effect on spending. Further, in the absence of liquidity constraints, spending should increase as soon as consumers begin to expect some tax cut, not just when they actually receive the check. Johnson, Parker, and Souleles's analysis exploits an unusual feature of the rebate program. Because it was administratively difficult to print and mail the checks all at once, they were mailed out over a ten-week period between late July and the end of September. Most important, the particular week in which a check was mailed depended on the second-to-last digit of the taxpayer's Social Security number, which is effectively random (the timing of receipt of the tax rebate was observed in their CEX data thanks to the addition of a special survey module). This randomization allowed the authors to identify the causal effect of the rebate by comparing the households that received the rebate earlier with those that received it later. The average household spent 20–40 percent of its 2001 tax rebate on non-durable goods during the three-month period in which the rebate was received. And the expenditure responses were largest for households with relatively low liquid wealth and low income, which is consistent with liquidity constraints.

In a related paper, Agarwal, Liu, and Souleles (2007) used a panel dataset of credit card accounts to analyze how consumers responded to the tax rebate analyzed by Johnson, Parker, and Souleles (2006). They estimated the month-by-month response to the rebate of credit card payments, spending, and debt, exploiting the randomized timing of disbursement to identify the causal effects. They found that, on average, consumers initially saved part of the rebate by increasing their credit card payments and thereby paying down debt and increasing liquidity. But soon afterward spending increased, counter to the implications of the permanent income model.

A paper that stands in contrast to these is Browning and Collado (2001), who used Spanish micro data to examine the consumer response to the payment of institutionalized extra wage payments to full-time workers in June and December. They detected no evidence of excess sensitivity, and argued that the reason earlier researchers had found a substantial response of consumption to predicted income changes was bounded rationality: consumers tend to smooth consumption and validate the theory when expected income changes are large, but less so when the changes are small and the cost of adjusting consumption is not trivial.[11] Suppose, for example, that

11. This argument from magnitude could also explain the puzzling findings of Hsieh (2003). Tax refunds are typically smaller than payments from the Alaska Permanent Fund (although the actual amount of the latter is somewhat more uncertain).

consumers who want to adjust their consumption upward in response to an expected income increase face the cost of negotiating a loan with a bank. It is likely that the utility loss from not adjusting fully to the new equilibrium is relatively small when the expected increase is small, so that if the transaction cost of negotiating a loan is high enough, no adjustment at all should take place.[12]

This "magnitude hypothesis" has been tested formally by Scholnick (2010), using a large dataset from a Canadian bank that includes information on both credit card spending and mortgage payments. Like Stephens (2008), Scholnick argues that the final mortgage payment represents an expected shock to *disposable* income. His test of the magnitude hypothesis seeks to determine whether the response of consumption to expected income increases depends on the relative size of the mortgage payments.

Overall, the main limitation of the approach discussed in this section is that it offers little guidance on how consumers would react to different shocks and environments. However, it does suggest ways of judging why consumption theories fail. For instance, some of the studies examined found that low-wealth consumers react more to predictable income changes than high-wealth consumers do. This points to the existence of liquidity constraints.

8.7. ANTICIPATED INCOME DECLINES AND THE RETIREMENT CONSUMPTION PUZZLE

The chief advantage of analyses that consider the effect of anticipated income *declines* on consumption is that in this case excess sensitivity cannot be attributed to liquidity constraints, because models with credit constraints predict that consumers will not borrow (but rather save) when they expect their income to decrease. While borrowing can and does have limits, saving does not.

The most important case of predictable income decline is retirement. A powerful test of whether consumption is insensitive to predictable changes in income is thus to compare consumption before and after retirement. The first paper to examine this issue is Banks, Blundell, and Tanner (1998), who used repeated cross-sectional data drawn from the UK Family Expenditure Survey (FES) and found a notable drop in consumption after retirement. Bernheim, Skinner, and Weinberg (2001) repeated the test for the United States using the PSID and also found evidence of a substantial consumption

---

12. Another factor that is potentially relevant but neglected in the literature is the time that elapses between the announcement and the actual income change. The shorter the interval, the smaller the utility loss from inaction.

decline. Furthermore, they sorted households into quartiles according to wealth and income-replacement rate. They found sharper decreases in consumption among households with less wealth and lower replacement rates. For example, consumption drops by 24 percent for the bottom income-replacement quartile, 15 percent for the second quartile, and 9 percent for the third and fourth. The main limitation is that the PSID has detailed information on only one type of consumption, namely, food.[13]

How do we explain the finding that consumption diminishes after retirement? One possibility, of course, is that the life-cycle theory is not valid and that consumers are myopic or lack self-control. That is, they fail to anticipate that retirement will mean a steep drop in income, and when they do realize it, they are forced to adjust their consumption downward. However, there are also explanations that do not imply a rejection of the theory. A good part of the fall in consumption at retirement may be due to a reduction in work-related expenses (such as transportation, meals, etc.), rather than a decline in all consumption categories. Another possibility is that retirement may not be perfectly expected after all, so consumption may legitimately fall because retirement comes as a shock. Haider and Stephens (2007) emphasize that for most workers the timing of retirement is uncertain, and that it is sometimes forced on people by events such as prolonged unemployment or disability.

A further explanation for a decline in consumption at retirement is home production, which is stressed by Hurd and Rohwedder (2006) and Aguiar and Hurst (2007). The idea is that consumption (in particular food consumption) is just an input to a home production function, the other factors in which are leisure time, shopping, and housework. Retirement sharply increases the amount of time available for shopping and housework, so individuals may choose to substitute, say, home-grown for store-bought tomatoes. Similarly, they may spend more time looking for cheaper items, or cooking a meal at home instead of eating at restaurants. Indeed, Aguiar and Hurst (2005) use the Continuing Survey of Food Intake of Individuals (CSFII), which has data on food expenditure as well as calorie intake, and the National Human Activity Pattern Survey (NHAPS) to show that while food expenditure does decline at retirement, food intake does not, consistent with the home production story. In a follow-up paper, Aguiar and Hurst (2006) use individual scanner data on grocery expenses from the ACNielsen Homescan Survey to show that the elderly shop more frequently and buy cheaper goods (or manage to

13. Studies based on more comprehensive consumption measures find little or no consumption decline in the United States. Hurd and Rohwedder (2006), using a special module in the Health and Retirement Survey (HRS), find that for the average household there is no decrease at all. However, their sample is rather small. Attanasio, Meghir, and Aguila (2008), using panel data from the CEX, find that food consumption declines by 6 percent, but detect no decline in non-food consumption. These papers also provide a detailed survey of the relevant literature.

find the same goods at a lower price) than younger individuals who have less leisure time.

Retirement is not the only situation in which households expect future resources to decline. Souleles (2000) studies the consumption effect of expected disposable income declines related to college tuition. Using CEX data, Souleles tests whether non-educational consumption decreases in proportion to households' college expenditures. He finds that, in keeping with the life-cycle hypothesis, households do a relatively good job of smoothing their consumption over the college years, despite the large expenses.

Retirement and college tuition expense are cases in which income declines in a predictable way, so the excess sensitivity test is free of complications due to liquidity constraints.

All in all, the evidence surveyed in this section and summarized in Table 8.3 favors the thesis of consumption smoothing and the basic tenets of the permanent income hypothesis. In Chapter 9 we shall see whether this conclusion still holds when we confront the model with the hypothesis that unexpected income changes should affect consumption, and

Table 8.3. SUMMARY OF LITERATURE FINDINGS: ANTICIPATED INCOME DECLINES

Authors	Data	Empirical strategy	Main findings
Gruber (1997)	1968–87 PSID	Used unemployment as cases of unanticipated and anticipated income shocks	For anticipated layoffs unemployment insurance (UI) did not have a smoothing effect. For unanticipated layoffs UI had a large smoothing effect. A 10% rise in the replacement rate reduced the fall in consumption upon job loss by about 3%.
Banks, Blundell, and Tanner (1998)	1968–92 FES	Controlled for demographics in preferences and non-separabilities with respect to labor supply	A life-cycle model could not fully explain the fall in consumption at retirement even when controlling for labor-market participation.
Souleles (2000)	1980–93 CEX	Used college tuition as a case of anticipated income decrease	Households were smoothing their consumption over the college years, despite large expenses, consistent with the life-cycle hypothesis.

(continued)

Table 8.3. CONTINUED

Authors	Data	Empirical strategy	Main findings
Bernheim, Skinner, and Weinberg (2001)	1978–90 PSID and CEX	Investigated testable implications of explanations for the variation in retirement savings for wealth and for consumption levels and growth	Evidence was found of a substantial consumption drop at retirement (24% for the first income quartile, 15% for the second quartile, and 9% for the third and fourth quartiles). The data are consistent with "rule of thumb," "mental accounting," or hyperbolic discounting theories rather than with life-cycle models.
Aguiar and Hurst (2005)	1989, 1994 Continuing Survey of Food Intake of Individuals (CSFII) and 1992–94 National Human Activity Pattern Survey (NHAPS)	Differentiating consumption and consumption expenditures using calorie intake and time use surveys	While food expenditure declined at retirement, food intake did not decline (consistent with home production theory).
Hurd and Rohwedder (2006)	HRS and Consumption and Activities Mail Survey (CAMS)	Used data on expected fall and realized fall in spending with retirement	Prior to retirement, workers anticipated on average a decline of 13.3% in spending; after retirement, they recollected a decline of 12.9%, suggesting no income surprise.
Aguiar and Hurst (2007)	1993–95 Denver ACNielsen Homescan Panel and 2003 American Time-Use Survey (ATUS)	Used price data and detailed data on time spent in home production to investigate the home production function	The elderly shop more frequently and buy cheaper goods (or manage to find the same goods at a lower price) than younger individuals who have less leisure.
Haider and Stephens (2007)	1969–77 Retirement History Survey (RHS) and 1992–2000 Health and Retirement Study (HRS)	Used workers' subjective beliefs about their retirement dates as an instrument for retirement	Estimates of consumption decrease were about a third less than when relying on the instrumental variables strategy used in prior studies.
Aguila, Attanasio, and Meghir (2008)	1980–2000 CEX	Linear difference-in-difference	Food consumption declined by 6%; no decline in non-food consumption.

that the response should depend on the persistence and magnitude of the shocks.

APPENDIX

Econometric problems in estimating the Euler equation

Given the strong assumptions that are needed to obtain consistent estimates of the parameters of the Euler equation using aggregate data, most empirical analyses are based on household panel data. Estimation with micro data is not problem-free, however. In this appendix, we examine two econometric problems that may affect the interpretation of excess sensitivity tests, measurement error and short panel data, and discuss strategies to address them.

MEASUREMENT ERROR

Suppose we want to test the sensitivity of consumption to expected income changes using panel data, that is, to determine whether the parameter β is statistically different from zero in the following regression:

$$\Delta c_{it} = \alpha + \beta E_{it-1}\left(\Delta y_{it}\right) + e_{it}. \tag{8.5}$$

As discussed in section 7.1, the permanent income hypothesis (PIH) predicts that $\beta = 0$. Since we can always decompose a stochastic variable into the sum of its expected value and its innovation, that is, $\Delta y_{it} = E_{it-1}\left(\Delta y_{it}\right) + v_{it}$, we can rewrite equation (8.5) as:

$$\Delta c_{it} = \alpha + \beta \Delta y_{it} + \varepsilon_{it}, \tag{8.6}$$

where $\varepsilon_{it} = e_{it} - \beta v_{it}$. Since Δy_{it} is correlated with the forecast error ε_{it} (unless the PIH is literally true, or $\beta = 0$), equation (8.6) needs to be estimated using an instrumental variables procedure. As is well known, an instrument is valid if it is correlated with the endogenous variable and not with the error term. In empirical studies, the endogenous variable Δy_{it} is often instrumented with lagged variables such as Δy_{it-1}. By the definition of rational expectations, both variables are uncorrelated with the error term (since $E_{t-1}\left(v_{it}\right) = 0$); moreover, unless income is a random walk process, they are both correlated with the endogenous variable.

Now suppose that income is measured with an error, that is, $y_{it}^* = y_{it} + u_{it}$, where y_{it} is true income, y_{it}^* observed income, and u_{it} a measurement error. In this case, instruments lagged by one period are no longer valid. Indeed, the Euler equation rewritten in terms of observable variables is:

$$\Delta c_{it} = \alpha + \beta \Delta y_{it}^* + \left(\varepsilon_{it} - \beta \Delta u_{it} \right). \tag{8.7}$$

The instrumental variable Δy_{it-1}^* is correlated with the error term in the Euler equation (8.7). If we ignore this problem, we get the familiar attenuation effect induced by measurement error and could end up confirming the null hypothesis $\beta = 0$ even when it is false. Hence, we may find no excess sensitivity even when in fact the PIH is false.

SHORT PANELS

Estimation of Euler equation parameters may be inconsistent when the time dimension of the panel is short (Chamberlain 1984). To understand the problem, let us consider the orthogonality condition discussed in Section 7.2: $E_{it-1}(\varepsilon_{it}) = 0$, where ε_{it} is the forecast error of the growth rate of consumption. A researcher would test the orthogonality condition by writing the regression:

$$\Delta c_{it} = \beta X_{it-1} + \varepsilon_{it}, \tag{8.8}$$

where X_{it-1} is a variable known to the consumer (for example, income) and the orthogonality condition predicts $\beta = 0$.

However, it is important to understand the conditions under which the estimator for β is consistent. Since the theory applies to any individual, in principle it could be tested using data on a single individual at a time. Since forecast errors should not exhibit systematic trends, if the PIH is correct they should average out to zero over a long enough horizon. Following this logic, the empirical equivalent of $E_{it-1}(\varepsilon_{it})$ is an individual average taken over T periods, with $T \rightarrow \infty$ to ensure the consistency of the estimator of β. However, panel data typically have a short horizon, so researchers assume that consistency is achieved with $N \rightarrow \infty$, that is, assuming that forecast errors average out to zero in the cross section.

This assumption may not hold in the case of an aggregate shock that causes all individuals to make forecast errors in the same direction. Now the cross-sectional average of the forecast error is not zero but instead is equal to the aggregate shock and invalidates the test of the orthogonality condition, creating spurious evidence of excess sensitivity.

To see this, consider the ordinary least squares (OLS) estimator of β in the regression (8.8) above:

$$\hat{\beta} = \frac{\sum_{i=1}^{N} X_{it-1} \Delta c_{it}}{\sum_{i=1}^{N} X_{it-1}^2}.$$

Suppose that the forecast error is $\varepsilon_{it} = \lambda_t + v_{it}$, where λ_t is an aggregate shock and v_{it} an idiosyncratic shock such that:

$$\plim_{N \to \infty} \frac{\sum_{i=1}^{N} v_{it}}{N} = 0$$

$$\plim_{N \to \infty} \frac{\sum_{i=1}^{N} v_{it} X_{it-1}}{N} = 0.$$

The probability limit of the OLS estimator is:

$$\plim_{N \to \infty} \hat{\beta} = \frac{\plim_{N \to \infty} N^{-1} \sum_{i=1}^{N} X_{it-1} \Delta c_{it}}{\plim_{N \to \infty} N^{-1} \sum_{i=1}^{N} X_{it-1}^2} = \beta + \frac{\plim_{N \to \infty} N^{-1} \sum_{i=1}^{N} X_{it-1} \varepsilon_{it}}{\plim_{N \to \infty} N^{-1} \sum_{i=1}^{N} X_{it-1}^2} = \beta + \lambda_t \frac{\mu}{\sigma},$$

with $\mu = \plim_{N \to \infty} N^{-1} \sum_{i=1}^{N} X_{it-1}$ and $\sigma = \plim_{N \to \infty} N^{-1} \sum_{i=1}^{N} X_{it-1}^2$. If one neglects the stochastic structure of the forecast error, the estimator of β is inconsistent. In particular, we may conclude erroneously that there is evidence of excess sensitivity of consumption even if the true $\beta = 0$. Also note that in this example it is impossible to determine the sign of the bias in the OLS estimator.

One way to overcome this problem is to add year dummies to the Euler equation, attempting to obtain a direct estimate of λ_t. It can be shown that adding time dummies is equivalent to a within-group regression, in which one regresses $\left(\Delta c_{it} - N^{-1} \sum_{i=1}^{N} \Delta c_{it} \right)$ against $\left(X_{it-1} - N^{-1} \sum_{i=1}^{N} X_{it-1} \right)$.

The drawback to this simple solution is that it may still fail to deliver consistent estimates of β if the aggregate shock is unevenly distributed across consumers, so time dummies do not completely absorb its impact.[14]

---

14. Altug and Miller (1990) note that the estimator that adds time dummies is consistent when markets are complete. In fact, if markets are complete, idiosyncratic shocks are insurable and adding time dummies eliminates the problem. Of course, how plausible the hypothesis of complete markets is remains an open question.

An alternative solution to the short panel problem is *synthetic panels* (Deaton, 1985). While panel data are rare and often of relatively short duration, many countries conduct large cross-sectional surveys that are repeated over many years. Prominent examples are the Family Expenditure Survey in the United Kingdom and the Current Population Survey in the United States. Synthetic panels can be constructed by aggregating data for individuals who are born in the same year, on the assumption that the behavior of a group of individuals can be studied via a representative agent of the group. The use of synthetic data attenuates both the problems discussed here. First, averaging over many individuals reduces measurement error. Second, synthetic panels often have a much longer time dimension than genuine panels. For instance, the Consumer Expenditure Survey in the United States has only a short panel dimension (at most four quarters), while a synthetic panel constructed in the Consumer Expenditure Survey can cover as much as 120 quarters (as of 2010). Synthetic panels have problems of their own, however. For example, estimating Euler equations with such data requires strong assumptions about the individual information set, such as that each consumer knows the level and dynamics of cohort resources.

CHAPTER 9

The Response of Consumption to Unanticipated Changes in Income

In this chapter we examine tests of the hypothesis that consumption will respond to unanticipated income changes and that the response will depend on the persistence of the shock and on the degree of imperfection in the credit and insurance markets. Recall our organizing framework from Chapter 8, adapted to the case of isoelastic preferences (hence consumption and income changes are replaced by growth rates):

$$\Delta \ln c_{it} = z'_{it} \lambda + \alpha E_{t-1} \Delta \ln y_{it} + \sum_{k=1}^{K} \phi_k \pi^k_{it} + \xi_{it}, \tag{9.1}$$

where as before the π^k represent different types of shock to log income. A special case that we focus on in this chapter is characterized by the income process:

$$\ln y_{it} = p_{it} + u_{it} + v_{it}$$

$$p_{it} = p_{it-1} + \zeta_{it} = p_{i0} + \sum_{j=1}^{t} \zeta_{ij},$$

where $\pi^1_{it} = \zeta_{it}$, $\pi^2_{it} = u_{it}$, and $\pi^3_{it} = v_{it}$ represent a permanent income shock, a transitory shock, and a measurement error, respectively, and p_{i0} is the initial draw of the permanent component.

This chapter discusses the estimation of the marginal propensity to consume with respect to these shocks, that is, the parameters ϕ_k. These parameters not only reflect the impact of income shocks on consumption but also may be informative about the structure of credit and insurance markets. For example, in the case of complete markets $\phi_k = 0$ for all k, because all shocks are insured. As has been observed in previous chapters, the permanent-income model suggests that consumption responds strongly to permanent income shocks, while transitory shocks have negligible effects. In models with partial insurance—provided by governments, firms, family networks, or other channels—consumers are able to insure against shocks more fully than in models with just self-insurance (so that ϕ_k assumes intermediate values between the complete-market and permanent-income models).

The literature has considered three approaches to estimating the effect of income shocks on consumption. One identifies episodes in which income changes unexpectedly and seeks to evaluate, in a quasi-experimental setting, how consumption reacts. A second estimates the marginal propensity to consume with respect to income shocks using the covariance restrictions imposed by theory on the joint behavior of consumption and income growth. The third estimates the impact of shocks by combining realizations and expectations of income or consumption in surveys where data on subjective expectations are available. Each of these approaches has pros and cons, as we discuss in this chapter. Selected studies using them are summarized in Table 9.1.

Table 9.1. SUMMARY OF LITERATURE FINDINGS ON THE EFFECT OF UNANTICIPATED INCOME CHANGES

Authors	Data	Empirical Strategy	Main findings
Bodkin (1959)	1950 CEX	Used dividend payments for WWII veterans as an unanticipated income shock	Marginal propensity to consume non-durables out of the shock was as high as 0.72, a sharp contradiction of the permanent-income model.
Wolpin (1982)	1968–71 panel of rural Indian farm households	Used weather shocks as a case of unanticipated income shocks	Permanent-income elasticity estimates ranged from 0.91 to 1.02, supporting the permanent-income model.
Hall and Mishkin (1982)	1969–75 PSID	Specified income process, and used covariance restrictions to identify the parameters of the response of consumption to shocks	The response of consumption to innovations in transitory income was 29% (too high to be consistent with the theory).
Hayashi (1985)	1981–82 panel of Japanese households	Exploited subjective expectations about consumption and income	Permanent income applied to about 85% of the population and income changes explained only a small fraction of the movements in expenditure.

Table 9.1. CONTINUED

Authors	Data	Empirical Strategy	Main findings
Paxson (1993)	1975–76, 1981, and 1986 Thai Socioeconomic Surveys (SES)	Used weather shocks as a case of unanticipated income shocks	High propensity to save out of transitory weather shocks, but also a propensity to save out of permanent shocks above zero.
Gruber (1997)	1968–87 PSID	Impact of unemployment as unanticipated and anticipated income shock on consumption	For anticipated layoffs unemployment insurance did not have a smoothing effect. For unanticipated layoffs UI had a large smoothing effect. A 10% rise in the replacement rate reduced the fall in consumption upon unemployment by about 3%.
Browning and Crossley (2001b)	1993 Canadian Out of Employment Panel (COEP)	Impact of unemployment as income shock on consumption exploiting legislative changes to Canadian UI system	Elasticity of expenditures with respect to UI benefit was 5%. Elasticities were as high as 20% for low-asset individuals (consistent with the presence of liquidity constraints).
Stephens (2001)	1968–92 PSID	Impact of job displacement and disability as permanent income shocks on consumption	The percentage change in consumption was less than that in income, especially at the time of the shock. Displaced households responded to an increase in the probability of job losses by reducing consumption prior to a job loss.
Pistaferri (2001)	1989–91 panel of the Italian Survey of Household Income and Wealth (SHIW)	Combined income realizations and subjective expectations to identify transitory and permanent income shocks separately	Consumers saved most of the transitory shocks and very little of the permanent shocks.
Gertler and Gruber (2002)	1991, 1993 panel data collected as part of Indonesian Resource Mobilization Study (IRMS)	Impact of illness as income shocks on consumption in developing countries	People smoothed the effect of minor illnesses well (could be interpreted as transitory shocks, or anticipated events), but the effect of major illnesses less well (which could be interpreted as permanent shocks).

(continued)

Table 9.1. CONTINUED

Authors	Data	Empirical Strategy	Main findings
Jappelli and Pistaferri (2006)	1987–95 panel of the Italian Survey of Household Income and Wealth (SHIW)	Exploited the implications of the theory on the transition matrix of consumption	Rejected simple representations of the consumption decision rule, and revealed that households smooth income shocks to a lesser extent than implied by the PIH.
Blundell, Pistaferri, and Preston (2008)	1978–92 PSID and 1980–92 CEX (using imputation)	Specified income process, and used covariance restrictions to identify the parameters of the response of consumption to shocks	Consumption was nearly insensitive to transitory shocks (somewhat more sensitive among poor households), and response to permanent shocks was significantly lower than 1, suggesting that households are able to partially insure permanent shocks.
Guvenen and Smith (2014)	1978–92 PSID and 1972–73, 1980–92 CEX (using imputation)	Specified income process with heterogeneity and advanced information which is resolved in a Bayesian manner	Consumers know a good deal about the evolution of their income process (about 80% of the uncertainty about the random trend component was resolved in the first period).
Kaufman and Pistaferri (2009)	1995–2001 panel of the Italian Survey of Household Income and Wealth (SHIW)	Used subjective income expectations to distinguish superior information from partial insurance	A large part of the transitory variation in income was either anticipated or the result of measurement error, while about two-third of the permanent variation in income could be labeled as a true innovation.
Primiceri and Van Rens (2009)	1980–2000 CEX	Specified income process with heterogeneity and advance information and used covariance restrictions to identify sources of consumption and income inequality	All of the increase in income inequality over the 1980–2000 period was attributed to an increase in the variance of permanent shocks, and most permanent income shocks were anticipated by individuals, hence consumption inequality remained flat.

Table 9.1. CONTINUED

Authors	Data	Empirical Strategy	Main findings
Agarwal and Qian (2014)	Proprietary data from leading Singapore bank, 2010–12	Exploited announcement and implementation of Singapore's Growth Dividend Program, consisting of a one-time cash payout between $80 to $700 per resident (foreigners excluded)	The MPC is 0.8 in the ten months following the announcement; 0.15 in the 2-month period between announcement and actual cash payout. Credit card financed spending during the announcement period, and debit card after the actual cash payout.
Di Maggio, Kermani, and Ramcharan (2015)	Administrative data on mortgage loans originated 2005–13	Focus on borrowers with ARMs originated in the 2005–07 period featuring automatic interest rate resets after 5 years	Monthly household car purchases increased 40% after mortgage rate reset. MPC is higher for low-income and underwater borrowers.
Gelman et al. (2015)	Administrative data on financial transactions from online financial manager platform	Focus on behavior of US Federal employees (treatment group) vs. non-government employees (control group) around the 2013 US Federal government shutdown	Little effect on consumption, due to ability to postpone recurrent payments (such as mortgage and credit card bills).
Baker and Yannelis (2015)	Administrative data on financial transactions from online financial manager platform	Focus on behavior of US Federal employees (treatment group) vs. non-government employees (control group) around the 2013 US Federal government shutdown	Consumption is excessively sensitive to the income drop associated with the shutdown. Households use home production to adjust the composition of their spending during the shutdown.

9.1. THE QUASI-EXPERIMENTAL APPROACH

The approach we discuss in this section does not require estimating an income process, or even observing the individual shocks. Rather, it compares households that are exposed to shocks with households that are not (or the same households before and after the shock), positing that the difference in consumption arises from the realization of the shock.

The first such effort dates to a study by Bodkin (1959), who set out all the ingredients of the quasi-experimental approach more than fifty years ago. This pioneering study examined the consumption behavior of war veterans after the receipt of unexpected dividend payments from the National Service Life Insurance. Bodkin assumes that the dividend payments are an unanticipated windfall, finding a point estimate of the marginal propensity to consume non-durables out of this windfall income as high as 0.72, which represents a sharp contradiction of the permanent-income model.

More recently, and in rather different contexts, Argarwal and Qian (2014) and Di Maggio et al. (2016) have assessed the effect of unanticipated positive income changes on consumption. Agarwal and Qian exploit the announcement of the Singapore government's Growth Dividend Program in 2011. The program included a one-time cash payout ranging from $80 to $700 per resident. Foreigners were excluded and thus serve as the control group. The authors use a panel data set of consumers' financial transactions to study their response. They find a marginal propensity to consume (MPC) of 0.8 during the ten months after the announcement. They also find a strong announcement effect, as consumers increased spending during the two months between the announcement and the payout (an MPC of about 0.15). Di Maggio et al. focus on US households who purchased homes with adjustable rate mortgages (ARMs) between 2005 and 2007 with an automatic reset of interest rates after five years. The loose monetary policy of the post-recession period and the consequent fall in mortgage rates resulted in an average monthly drop in mortgage interest payments of $900, a substantial income inflow for most households. The authors show that following the reset the probability of car purchase increased by 45 percent. On average, 40 percent of the income increase was used to purchase durables or non-durable goods.

Two other papers use administrative spending and balance-sheet data from online financial managers (such as Mint.com or Check.com in the United States) to test whether government employees smoothed their spending during the US federal government shutdown in 2013, when they were left without their regular paycheck for about two weeks (with no change in permanent income). Gelman et al. (2016), using non-government employees as control group, find that the shutdown did not cause a drop in consumption because many individuals rescheduled recurrent expenditures (such as mortgage or credit card payments) to overcome the temporary reduction in liquidity and attenuate the impact on total consumption. However, Baker and Yannelis (2015), using data from a different online financial manager, report that consumption does appear to have responded to the shutdown, violating the permanent-income hypothesis (PIH). They show that increased home production and changes in time allocation are important household responses.

Other studies have looked at the economic consequences of illness, disability, unemployment, and, in the context of developing countries, weather shocks and crop losses. Some of these shocks are transitory (i.e., temporary job loss), and others are permanent (i.e., disability); some are positive (i.e., dividend payouts), others negative (i.e., illness). The framework in Section 9.2 suggests that it is important to distinguish between these various types of shock because in theory consumption should change almost one-to-one in response to permanent income shocks (positive or negative) but may react asymmetrically to transitory ones. Indeed, if households are credit-constrained (can save but not borrow), they will cut consumption sharply in the face of a negative transitory shock, but will not react much to a positive one.

Other works that take this quasi-experimental approach have looked at how unemployment shocks alter consumption and considered the smoothing effect of unemployment insurance (UI). As is pointed out by Browning and Crossley (2001b), unemployment insurance provides two benefits to consumers. First, it offers "consumption smoothing benefits" by transferring resources from low- to high-marginal-utility states. If individuals are unable to borrow, in case of job loss they would need to adjust their consumption sharply downward, so UI benefits are even more significant in the presence of credit constraints. Second, it reduces the conditional variance of consumption growth and hence the need to accumulate precautionary savings.

One early effort to estimate the welfare effect of unemployment insurance is Gruber (1997). Using the PSID, he constructs a sample of workers who lose their job between period $t-1$ and period t, and regresses the change in food spending over the same time span against the UI income replacement rate an individual would be eligible for (i.e., potential benefits).[1] Gruber finds a large smoothing effect of UI; specifically, a 10-percentage-point rise in the income replacement rate reduces the fall in food consumption upon unemployment by about 3 percent.[2] He also finds that the fall in consumption at zero income replacement is about 20 percent, suggesting that consumers face liquidity constraints.[3]

---

1. Potential instead of actual benefits are used for three reasons: (a) the endogeneity of UI receipts, (b) the large errors in reported UI benefits, and (c) the greater policy interest in the effect of potential UI benefits (which can be determined by the government) than received benefits (which cannot).

2. If the gauge used were total consumption rather than just food, the estimated effect would presumably be larger, given that food is only one item in total consumption, and perhaps one of the least easy to compress.

3. Gruber also tests whether layoffs that are anticipated (measured using "seasonal" and "serial" layoffs) have an impact on consumption, and finds no rejection of the hypothesis that they do not. Given that he is considering anticipated income declines, this result is not inconsistent with the finding of the large impact of an unemployment

Browning and Crossley (2001b) extend Gruber's idea to a different country (Canada instead of the United States), using a more comprehensive measure of consumption (not just food) and legislative changes to unemployment insurance instead of state-time variation. Moreover, their data are rich enough to identify households that are presumably liquidity-constrained (in particular, they have data on assets at the time of job loss). Browning and Crossley estimate a low elasticity of expenditure with respect to UI benefits (5 percent). But this small effect masks substantial heterogeneity, with low-asset households exhibiting elasticities as high as 20 percent. This is consistent with the presence of liquidity constraints.

A critique of the approach is that the response of consumption to unemployment shocks is confounded by three sets of issues (similar arguments apply to papers that look at unpredictable income changes due to illness or disability, such as Stephens, 2001). First, some of these shocks may not actually come as a surprise, and individuals may have saved in anticipation of them. For example, being laid off by Chrysler in 2009 can hardly be called an unexpected event. Second, the theory says that consumers should smooth the marginal utility of consumption, not consumption per se. If an unemployment shock brings more leisure and if consumption is a substitute for leisure, then an excess response of consumption to the transitory shock of job loss does not necessarily violate the theory. Third, even if unemployment shocks are truly unanticipated, they may be partially insured against through government programs such as unemployment benefits (or disability benefits). An attenuated consumption response to a permanent income shock due to disability, rather than representing a failure of the theory, may be explained by the availability of government-provided insurance. Therefore, a complete analysis of the impact of unemployment or disability shocks requires explicit modeling of the type of insurance available and of the possible interactions between public and private insurance.[4]

The foregoing suggests that it might be easier to test the theory in contexts in which no insurance except self-insurance is available, as in developing countries.[5] Gertler and Gruber (2002) study the consumption impact of income shocks due to serious illness in Indonesia. They find that while people smooth the effect of minor illnesses well (these could be interpreted as transitory shocks or as anticipated events), they experience considerably greater

shock. Moreover, for some individuals—those close to retirement age, say—an unemployment shock could be persistent.

4. Some of these interactions reflect the fact that most welfare programs are means-tested. For example, in the US individuals with more than $2,000 in liquid assets are not eligible for food stamps, Medicaid and other popular welfare programs even if they have no income. The disincentives to saving (self-insurance) induced by public insurance (generally not subject to time limits) have been studied by Hubbard, Skinner and Zeldes (1995).

5. On the other hand, in these countries there may be stronger family networks.

difficulty in smoothing the impact of severe illnesses (which could be interpreted as permanent shocks).

Wolpin (1982) and Paxson (1993) study the effect of weather shocks in India and Thailand, respectively. In agricultural economies, weather shocks affect income directly through the production function, and deviations from normal weather conditions are truly unanticipated events. Wolpin (1982) uses Indian regional time series data on rainfall to construct long-run moments (average yearly rainfall) as instruments for current income (which is assumed to measure permanent income with error). The estimated permanent-income elasticity ranges from 0.91 to 1.02 depending on the measure of consumption—strong support for the permanent-income model. Paxson (1993) uses Thai regional weather data to measure transitory shocks and finds that Thai consumers have a high propensity to save out of transitory weather shocks, again supporting the theory. However, she also finds that they have a positive propensity to save out of permanent shocks, which rejects the certainty equivalence version of the permanent-income hypothesis.

Quasi-experimental studies using measurable variations to define shocks to household income have the obvious advantage of being clear and easy to explain and understand. The countervailing limitation is that they can capture only one type of shock at a time, for instance illness, job loss, drought, extreme temperatures, or crop loss. One may wonder, for example, whether the estimates obtained by Gruber (1997) and Browning and Crossley (2001b) in a sample of job losers have external validity for examining the effect of other kinds of shock (especially those that are harder to insure against, such as shocks to one's productivity).

A second limitation of the approach is that some of the income shocks (in particular, unemployment and disability), cannot be defined as truly exogenous. For instance, for some people unemployment is a voluntary choice; for others disability could be reported (or claimed) just in order to obtain benefits (a moral hazard issue). For this reason, not all income variability is necessarily unanticipated or independent of the agent's own action (Low, Meghir, and Pistaferri, 2010). The lesson of the literature is that it is very hard to identify episodes of genuinely exogenous and unanticipated income changes. One such case is weather conditions, at least insofar as people do not move to different regions to offset bad weather.

9.2. COVARIANCE RESTRICTIONS

A different approach to identifying the consumption response to unanticipated income shocks makes specific statistical assumptions about the income process and uses covariance restrictions to identify the parameters that characterize the joint behavior of consumption and income.

But how to identify income shocks? Two methods have emerged in the literature. One, discussed in this section, relies on panel data (or pseudo-panel data) and measures shocks as deviations from observable income determinants (MaCurdy, 1982). To be valid, this method requires several assumptions: that in forming expectations all individuals condition on the same set of variables; that the people studied and the econometrician have the same information set; and that the econometrician knows the stochastic process that generates individual income expectations. A second strategy, which we discuss in Section 9.3, relies on quantitative subjective expectations.

There are several advantages to the statistical decomposition of income shocks. First of all, it allows the simultaneous estimation of the marginal propensity to consume with respect to shocks of various kinds and persistence. The main variable of interest in the statistical decomposition is income, so one can estimate the response of consumption to all types of income shock, not only to specific events (such as bad weather or job loss). Finally, there is a sharper (if econometrically derived) distinction between transitory and permanent shocks. The method also has some shortcomings, however. Since it assumes that income and consumption follow a particular process, it is structural in nature and may suffer from specification bias for the consumption rule. It is more demanding in terms of data, because it requires repeated observations on income and consumption, although not necessarily in the same dataset or for the same households. Finally, it makes it harder to distinguish between the effects of positive and negative income shocks.

To explain how the method works, consider again a slightly modified version of the consumption rule (9.1), to which we append an equation for income growth:

$$
\begin{aligned}
\Delta \ln c_{it} &= z'_{it} \lambda^c + \phi_1 \zeta_{it} + \phi_2 u_{it} + \phi_3 v_{it} + \Delta \xi_{it} \\
\Delta \ln y_{it} &= z'_{it} \lambda^y + \zeta_{it} + \Delta u_{it} + \Delta v_{it}.
\end{aligned}
\tag{9.2}
$$

This expanded consumption rule (9.2) states that consumption growth depends on preference shifts z (such as age and family size), as well as income shocks, and nests many of the models that we have discussed. In this specification ζ represents a permanent shock (the innovation of a martingale process), and u and v are i.i.d. components, measuring transitory shocks and income measurement error, respectively. The parameters ϕ_1 and ϕ_2 measure the marginal propensities to consume with respect to permanent and transitory income shocks, respectively, and can be interpreted as the degree to which households insure income shocks, and therefore capture the degree of market completeness. The literature typically imposes $\phi_3 = 0$

because consumption does not respond to income noise. But note that this assumption has behavioral content if v captures anticipated transitory changes in income that the econometrician does not observe. In the rest of this section we follow the literature and impose $\phi_3 = 0$. Lastly, ξ is measurement error in consumption.

According to the permanent-income model, consumption responds fully to permanent income shocks ($\phi_1 = 1$) and negligibly to transitory shocks ($\phi_2 \approx 0$), because consumers use accumulated assets to smooth temporary income fluctuations. The buffer stock model has similar implications, possibly allowing for slightly lower values of ϕ_1. In the complete-market benchmark model, consumption is completely insulated from transitory as well as permanent shocks ($\phi_1 = \phi_2 = 0$). Finally, models with precautionary saving or partial insurance hypothesize that consumers can insure permanent shocks to a larger extent than in the PIH ($0 < \phi_1 < 1$).

Identification of the model with panel data on income and consumption growth can be approached by considering a set of covariance restrictions. Defining the residual term $\Delta \ln \tilde{x}_{it} = \Delta \ln x_{it} - z_{it}' \lambda^x$, they are:

$$\text{var}\left(\Delta \ln \tilde{c}_{it}\right) = \phi_1^2 \sigma_\zeta^2 + \phi_2^2 \sigma_u^2 + 2\sigma_\xi^2$$
$$\text{cov}\left(\Delta \ln \tilde{c}_{it}, \Delta \ln \tilde{c}_{it-1}\right) = -\sigma_\xi^2$$
$$\text{var}\left(\Delta \ln \tilde{y}_{it}\right) = \sigma_\zeta^2 + 2\left(\sigma_u^2 + \sigma_v^2\right)$$
$$\text{cov}\left(\Delta \ln \tilde{y}_{it}, \Delta \ln \tilde{y}_{it-1}\right) = -\left(\sigma_u^2 + \sigma_v^2\right)$$
$$\text{cov}\left(\Delta \ln \tilde{c}_{it}, \Delta \ln \tilde{y}_{it}\right) = \phi_1 \sigma_\zeta^2 + \phi^2 \sigma_u^2$$
$$\text{cov}\left(\Delta \ln \tilde{c}_{it-1}, \Delta \ln \tilde{y}_{it}\right) = -\phi_2 \sigma_u^2.$$

Note that the model is underidentified, because unless ϕ_2 is known, the variance of the transitory shock σ_u^2 and the variance of the measurement error in income σ_v^2 cannot be identified separately. One solution is to identify σ_v^2 by means of outside information, such as the results from income validation studies, as suggested by Meghir and Pistaferri (2004).

The first paper to decompose income shocks in order to estimate the marginal propensity to consume is that of Hall and Mishkin (1982), who work with PSID data on income and food consumption. Their setup assumes quadratic preferences (and hence examines consumption and income changes), imposes $\phi_1 = 1$, and leaves only ϕ_2 free for estimation. They find that the response of consumption to innovations in transitory income is 29 percent, which is too high to be consistent with the theory.

Blundell, Pistaferri, and Preston (2008) show that equation (9.2) can be obtained as an approximation of the lifetime budget constraint in conjunction with a log-linearized Euler equation under isoelastic utility. They use panel data with a comprehensive consumption measure for the PSID, obtained through an imputation procedure based on food demand estimates from the

CEX. They find that consumption is practically insensitive to transitory shocks (the estimated ϕ_2 parameter is around 5 percent, but higher among poor households), while their estimate of ϕ_1 is significantly lower than 1 (around 0.65 overall, but lower for the college-educated and those near retirement and higher for poorer or less educated households), suggesting that households are able to insure at least part of the permanent shocks. Kaplan and Violante (2010) report that these estimates conform to theoretical values of the marginal propensities to consume calculated by calibrating a theoretical model with income risk and a natural borrowing constraint (discussed in Chapter 6).

The results of Blundell, Pistaferri, and Preston (2008) help to show why consumption inequality in the United States has grown less than income inequality over the past two decades. Their findings suggest that the increasing divergence between consumption inequality and income inequality is due to the change in the durability of income shocks. In particular, the increasing variance of permanent shocks in the early 1980s gave way toward the end of the decade to steady growth in the variance of transitory income shocks. Since they find little evidence that the degree of insurance with respect to shocks of different durability changed over this period, it is the relative increase in the variability of more insurable shocks rather than greater insurance opportunities that explains the disjuncture between income and consumption inequality.[6]

A small response of consumption to permanent shocks may reflect not only the possibility of insurance but also advance information. To exemplify, suppose we find that consumption responds little to what the econometrician labels a permanent shock. Does this happen because the income change is not really a surprise from the point of view of the consumer (i.e., it was anticipated) or because it is mostly insured? The variation that is measured in the data may reflect both information known to the econometrician and superior information held by the individual. Two recent papers inquire seriously into this information issue. Primiceri and van Rens (2009) assume that consumers are unable to smooth permanent shocks and that any attenuation of the response measures the amount of advance information that they have about developments in their permanent income. Using CEX data, they find that the entire increase in income inequality between 1980 and 2000 can be attributed to an increase in the variance of permanent shocks but that individuals anticipate most permanent income shocks; hence consumption inequality remains flat even though income inequality increases.

---

6. Hryshko (2014) allows the transitory and permanent shocks to be correlated with each other and shows, using simulations, that such a correlation can be very important in interpreting life-cycle consumption. This additional feature cannot be identified with income data alone and thus provides an example of the importance of considering the income and consumption processes jointly for identification purposes. Following the method of Blundell, Pistaferri and Preston (2008), he finds that the MPC with respect to permanent shocks is about 0.63.

While their results challenge the consensus that permanent shocks were important only in the early 1980s (Card and DiNardo, 2002), they might actually reflect the poor quality of income data in the CEX.

In related research, Guvenen and Smith (2014) assume that the income process is the sum of a random trend that consumers must learn about in Bayesian fashion, an AR(1) process with AR coefficient below 1, and a serially uncorrelated component. They extend Blundell, Pistaferri, and Preston's consumption imputation procedure to create panel data from the PSID data on income and consumption and find that consumers know a good deal about the evolution of their income process (about 80 percent of the uncertainty concerning the random trend component is resolved in the first period).

This discussion suggests that although the method of setting restrictions on the covariance between the income and the consumption processes allows estimation of the sensitivity of consumption to permanent income shocks, it still does not isolate the reasons these shocks appear to be smoothed. In particular, the approach cannot distinguish between insurance, on the one hand, and differential information between consumer and econometrician, on the other.

Kaplan and Violante (2014) introduce a distinction between liquid and illiquid assets. The standard model assumes that consumers can run down their assets in response to transitory shocks at no cost. Kaplan and Violante consider instead a model in which the use of high-return illiquid assets is subject to a transaction cost. This allows them to identify "wealthy hand-to-mouth" consumers who hold sizable amounts of wealth in assets that can be liquidated only at a cost, such as housing, big-ticket durables, and retirement accounts, but little or no liquid wealth, such as checking and saving accounts. The presence of such households can explain the puzzling finding of excess sensitivity of consumption to transitory shocks among the rich. Kaplan, Violante, and Weidner (2014) find that a third of all US households live hand-to-mouth, that over two-thirds of these are "wealthy-hand-to-mouth" households, and that the latter behave similarly in terms of consumption to the poor-hand-to-mouth, both with high marginal propensity to consume out of small income changes.

9.3. CONSUMPTION MOBILITY

A different way to estimate the impact of income shocks on consumption is to consider the implications that the model has for consumption mobility. Mobility is defined as the change in a household's position in the distribution of consumption between two successive time periods, while inequality measures the dispersion of the distribution of household consumption at a given point in time. Panel data are thus necessary to study mobility, while repeated cross-sectional data are sufficient to study the dynamics of inequality (as we shall see in Section 9.4).

To see how consumption mobility can be used to estimate the impact of income shocks, assume that the income process is the sum of a permanent component and a transitory component:

$$\Delta \ln y_{it} = \zeta_{it} + \Delta u_{it}.$$

Consider first the extreme case of complete markets. On this hypothesis, the cross-sectional distribution of the marginal utility of consumption of any group of households is constant over time. Of course aggregate consumption can increase or decrease, so that for any single household the marginal utility can increase or decrease, but the relative position of each household in the cross-sectional distribution of marginal utilities does not change. The complete-market hypothesis thus embodies strong predictions about the entire distribution of marginal utilities, not just its mean or variance. In particular, consumption insurance implies that there is no mobility of the marginal utility of consumption between any two time periods, regardless of the nature of the individual income shocks or the time frame. If one observes people moving up and down in the distribution of marginal utilities, therefore, one must conclude that some people are not insulated from idiosyncratic shocks, which contradicts the consumption insurance hypothesis.

The opposite extreme case is one in which households simply set consumption equal to income in each period, or "rule-of-thumb" consumers. Given that any change in current income translates into an equivalent change in consumption, one should expect a relatively high degree of consumption mobility if the shocks are not correlated with the rank in the initial distribution of consumption.

In a simplified version of equation (9.1), consumption reacts to permanent unanticipated income shocks but is almost insensitive to transitory ones. Households will therefore move up and down in the consumption distribution only in response to permanent shocks. Thus, in the absence of measurement error one should expect a degree of mobility that is intermediate between the level predicted by the complete-market model and the prediction of the rule-of-thumb model.

The following equation nests the complete-market, rule-of-thumb, and permanent-income models:

$$\ln c_{it} = \ln c_{it-1} + \varphi \left(\zeta_{it} + \frac{\lambda + r}{1 + r} u_{it} - \lambda u_{it-1} \right). \tag{9.3}$$

The two parameters λ and φ allow one to distinguish various forms of departure from the stylized models of intertemporal choice. Consider first the case in which $\varphi = 1$. The parameter λ represents the extent to which consumption responds to income over and above the amount warranted by the PIH, that is, the excess sensitivity of consumption to current and past income shocks. One way to interpret this parameter is to imagine that each household sets consumption equal to income with probability λ and follows the PIH with probability $(1-\lambda)$. Note that with $\lambda = 0$ the expression (9.3) reduces to the PIH, while with $\lambda = 1$ one obtains the rule-of-thumb model.

Consider now the situation in which $\varphi = 0$. Income shocks play no role in the complete-market model. But intermediate cases in which $0 < \varphi < 1$ are interesting and potentially informative, providing presumptive evidence for the precautionary saving or partial-insurance hypothesis.

To gauge the impact of income shocks, the study of consumption mobility may be more suitable than that of consumption inequality. In fact, the distribution of consumption at time t might have the same variance as at time $t-1$ (suggesting no changes in consumption inequality) even if there is mobility in the underlying distributions, which signals that income shocks have an effect on consumption. For instance, suppose that a poor household and a rich one switch ranks in the consumption distribution. This will not change the cross-sectional variance of consumption, but examination of this mobility will reveal that it is income shocks that are behind the rank switches.

Jappelli and Pistaferri (2006) estimate the parameters of the consumption function (9.3), λ and φ, by minimizing the distance between the empirical and the simulated transition matrix of the consumption distribution.

Table 9.2 reports the simulated transition probabilities and (in parentheses) the empirical transition probabilities for the 1993–95 SHIW panel. The closeness of the comparison between the two sets of numbers is striking: regardless of cell, the difference between the empirical and the simulated

Table 9.2. THE TRANSITION MATRIX OF CONSUMPTION, DATA AND MODEL

1993 Quartile	1995 Quartile			
	1st	2nd	3rd	4th
1st	0.6748	0.2515	0.0677	0.0061
	(0.6700)	(0.2528)	(0.0660)	(0.0112)
2nd	0.2513	0.4111	0.2748	0.0628
	(0.2416)	(0.4259)	(0.2665)	(0.0660)
3rd	0.0675	0.2764	0.4175	0.2386
	(0.0660)	(0.2653)	(0.4346)	(0.2341)
4th	0.0061	0.0613	0.2401	0.6926
	(0.0237)	(0.0549)	(0.2332)	(0.6883)

Note: The table is reproduced with permission from Jappelli and Pistaferri (2006).

values is at most 2 percentage points. In formal estimation, the hypothesis that $\varphi = 1$, consistent with the permanent-income model, cannot be rejected. The authors also find some excess sensitivity with respect to transitory shocks $(\lambda = 0.16)$ and asymmetric responses to transitory income shocks according to educational attainment. In particular, the better-educated group has a lower MPC with respect to transitory income shocks than the less-educated group. To the extent that the low-education households are less likely to have access to credit and insurance markets than those with more education, these findings support the hypothesis that excess sensitivity stems from borrowing constraints rather than other factors.

9.4. CONSUMPTION INEQUALITY

In Section 9.2 we derived covariance restrictions that can be used to estimate parameters when panel data of individuals are available. Sometimes such data are not available but useful covariance restrictions can still be derived using repeated cross sections, as shown by Blundell and Preston (1998). As we shall see, the main difference is that while genuine panel data use moments of income and consumption growth, in repeated cross section the only restrictions available are those involving the growth of income and consumption moments (since individual growth rates are not available).

Blundell and Preston (1998) use the link between the income process and consumption inequality to investigate how income shocks affect the evolution of inequality in income and consumption, as measured by their variances. They work with repeated cross-sectional data from the UK Family and Expenditure Survey, define cohorts based on the year of birth of the household head, and decompose the cohort-specific variance of log income into a transitory component, an initial component, and the cumulation of past permanent shocks:

$$\operatorname{var}\left(\ln y_{it}\right) = \operatorname{var}\left(u_{it}\right) + \operatorname{var}\left(p_{i0}\right) + \sum_{j=1}^{t}\operatorname{var}\left(\zeta_{ij}\right),$$

where period 0 corresponds to the age of entry of this cohort into the labor market. With repeated cross sections one can write the change in the variance of log income for a given cohort as:

$$\Delta\operatorname{var}\left(\ln y_{it}\right) = \operatorname{var}\left(\zeta_{it}\right) + \Delta\operatorname{var}\left(u_{it}\right).$$

Hence, a rise in inequality (the left-hand side of this equation) may be due to a rise in the "volatility" $\Delta\operatorname{var}(u_{it}) > 0$ or to the presence of a persistent income shock, $\operatorname{var}(\zeta_{it})$. In repeated cross sections the problem of distinguishing between the two sources is insoluble if one focuses just on income data. Suppose instead that we have access to repeated cross-sectional data on consumption (which, conveniently, may or may not come from the same dataset—the use of multiple datasets is possible as long as samples are drawn randomly from the same underlying population). Then we have that the change in consumption inequality for a given cohort is:

$$\Delta \operatorname{var}\left(\ln c_{it}\right) = \varphi_1^2 \operatorname{var}\left(\zeta_{it}\right) + \varphi_2^2 \Delta \operatorname{var}\left(u_{it}\right),$$

assuming one can approximate the variance of the change with the change in the variances (see Deaton and Paxson 1994 for a discussion of the conditions under which this approximation is acceptable). In the case of certainty equivalence, we have $\varphi_1 = 1, \varphi_2 = \left(\dfrac{r}{1+r}\right)$. Here one can see that the growth in consumption inequality is dominated by the permanent component. Indeed, assuming $r \approx 0$, we have:

$$\Delta \operatorname{var}\left(\ln c_{it}\right) \cong \varphi_1^2 \operatorname{var}\left(\zeta_{it}\right)$$

and

$$\Delta \operatorname{cov}\left(\ln c_{it}, \ln y_{it}\right) = \varphi_1 \operatorname{var}\left(\zeta_{it}\right).$$

It follows that the marginal propensity to consume with respect to permanent shocks can be identified using:

$$\varphi_1 = \frac{\Delta \operatorname{var}\left(\ln c_{it}\right)}{\Delta \operatorname{cov}\left(\ln c_{it}, \ln y_{it}\right)}.$$

Note that, unlike the identification strategy of Section 9.2, which requires genuine panel data, this strategy can make do with repeated cross-sectional data. However, it may break down in the presence of serially correlated shocks, measurement error, or lack of cross-sectional orthogonality.

9.5. SUBJECTIVE EXPECTATIONS

Identifying income shocks is difficult because people may have information that is not observed by the econometrician. For instance, they may know in advance that they will face a temporary change in their income (a seasonal layoff, say). When the event occurs, the econometrician will count as a shock what was in fact expected. The literature based on subjective expectations attempts to circumvent the problem by asking people to report quantitative information on their expectations, an approach forcefully endorsed by Manski (2004). This literature accordingly relies on survey questions and not on retrospective data, to elicit information on the conditional distribution of future income, and it measures shocks as deviations of actual realizations from the elicited expectations.

Hayashi (1985) was the first to adopt this approach. His study uses a four-quarter panel of Japanese households containing respondents' expectations about expenditure and income in the following quarter. Hayashi works with disaggregated consumer expenditures, allowing each component to have a different degree of durability. He specifies a consumption rule and, allowing for measurement error in expenditures, estimates the covariances between expected and unexpected changes in consumption and expected and unexpected changes in income. His results are in line with Hall and Mishkin (1982), suggesting a relatively high sensitivity of consumption to income shocks.

Pistaferri (2001) combines income realizations and the quantitative subjective income expectations contained in the Italian Survey of Household Income and Wealth (SHIW) to identify transitory and permanent income shocks separately. To see how subjective income expectations allow us to estimate transitory and permanent income shocks for each household, consider the income process (in levels):

$$y_t = p_t + u_{it}$$
$$p_t = p_{t-1} + \zeta_{it}. \tag{9.4}$$

The assumption of rational expectations implies that the transitory shock at time t can be identified by:

$$u_{it} = -E\left(\Delta y_{it+1} \middle| \Omega_{it}\right), \tag{9.5}$$

where Ω_{it} is the individual's information set at time t. Using equations (9.4) and (9.5), the permanent shock at time t is identified by the expression:

$$\zeta_{it} = \Delta y_{it} - E\left(\Delta y_{it} \middle| \Omega_{it-1}\right) + E\left(\Delta y_{it+1} \middle| \Omega_{it}\right),$$

that is, the income innovation at time t adjusted by a factor that takes into account the arrival of new information concerning the change in income between t and $t+1$. Thus, the transitory and permanent shocks can be identified if one observes, for at least two consecutive periods, the conditional expectation and the realization of income, a requirement satisfied by the 1989–93 SHIW. Pistaferri estimates the saving-for-a-rainy-day equation as

$$s_{it} = \left(1 - \phi_1\right)\zeta_{it} + \left(1 - \phi_2\right)u_{it},$$

where ϕ_1 and ϕ_2 are the MPC with respect to permanent and transitory shocks, respectively. He finds that consumers save most of the transitory shocks ($\phi_2 \cong 0$) and very little of the permanent shocks ($\phi_1 \cong 1$), supporting the rainy-day model described in Chapter 4.

Kaufmann and Pistaferri (2009) use the same Italian survey to distinguish between superior information and insurance, an issue mentioned in Section 9.2. Considering the covariance restrictions implied by the theory on the joint behavior of consumption, income realizations, and subjective quantitative income expectations, they show that the degree of insurance of income shocks is upward-biased when only income and consumption data are considered. They also find that a large part of the transitory variation in income is either anticipated or due to measurement error, while about two-thirds of the permanent variation can be labeled as a true innovation.

A different source of subjective information is survey questions containing responses to hypothetical income changes. Jappelli and Pistaferri (2014), for instance, rely on a useful question contained in the 2010 Italian SHIW. The survey is designed to elicit information on how much people would consume or save if they unexpectedly received a reimbursement (or transfer) equal to their average monthly income. The responses to this question provide the sample distribution of the MPC in Figure 9.1.

In their sample, the average MPC is 48 percent, at the high end of current estimates based on survey data on observed consumption and income changes. Most important, they find substantial heterogeneity of responses. Households with low cash on hand exhibit a much higher MPC than affluent

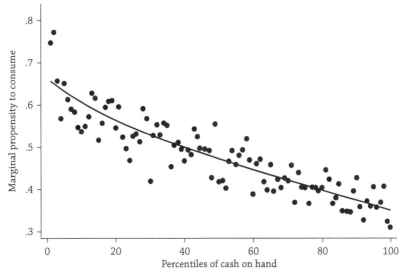

Figure 9.1: The sample distribution of the MPC by percentiles of cash on hand
Note: The figure is reproduced with permission from Jappelli and Pistaferri (2014).

households, which is in agreement with models that assign a major role to income risk or liquidity constraints.

Christelis et al. (2017) use the responses from a survey of Dutch households that asks how much of an unexpected, transitory and positive income change they would consume, and by how much an unexpected, transitory and negative income change would reduce their consumption. Their results are broadly in line with models with precautionary saving and borrowing constraints.

Studies that use subjective expectations are subject to the usual doubts concerning the reliability and information content of subjective data, and in practice subjective expectations are still rarely available alongside consumption and income data, or else are confined to special survey modules. However, there is considerable promise in the use of subjective expectations to evaluate the validity of various consumption models.

9.6. SHOCKS TO LIFETIME RESOURCES

An important source of permanent income shocks is events that affect the amount of future pension benefits. In calculating their lifetime resources, in fact, consumers should count not only their future earnings but also their pension benefits after retirement. Furthermore, in the case of public retirement systems, shocks to future income may derive from legislation (on the payroll tax, the award formula, or pension indexation rules). Several papers in the last two decades have sought to measure the effect of shocks to pension wealth on current consumption or saving. One of the most difficult problems is how to measure pension wealth itself, as it depends on many unobservable variables and on the long-run value of several variables (inflation, income growth, and rates of return many years ahead).

This is exemplified by the following expression for the present discounted value of future benefits from pension and social security wealth, PW:

$$PW_t = \sum_{\tau=N}^{T_{max}} b_\tau p(\tau|N) \left(\frac{1+g}{1+r} \right)^{\tau-t}.$$

This indicates that any estimate of PW involves knowledge of survival probabilities, $p(\tau|N)$, the stream of future benefits b, the expected retirement age N, and the expected growth rate of national income. For this reason, any estimate of pension wealth is necessarily approximate if not arbitrary.

A first generation of studies sought to estimate the *wealth replacement effect* associated with social security by simply regressing private wealth on pension wealth (Feldstein, 1974). The coefficient of PW in this regression should equal −1 if pension wealth totally crowds out private wealth: individuals should treat the two forms of wealth identically, so they should offset an increase in pension wealth by reducing private wealth one-for-one. Most empirical studies find some offset of pension wealth on private wealth or saving, but less than full: that is, values that are negative but higher than −1, suggesting a degree of substitution between the two sources of wealth that is substantially lower than predicted by the theory. There are many possible explanations for this finding. Since there is no space to discuss all of them in detail, here we limit ourselves to a broad summary.

Starting with Feldstein (1974), a growing literature has used individual data on the degree of substitution between private wealth and pension wealth in the United States and other countries, imputing pension wealth on the basis of legislation (Gale, 1998 and Bernheim, 2002). The microeconometric evidence suggests that pension wealth does crowd out discretionary wealth, but considerably less than one-for-one. Influential related research has looked at how pension entitlements affect the retirement and labor market participation decisions of the elderly and simulated the effects of policy reforms (Gruber and Wise, 1999, 2004).

There are several factors potentially countering complete crowding out. Bequest motives, myopia, liquidity constraints, and non-marketable future benefits are among the most commonly cited reasons why the offset might well be less than one-for-one. Precautionary saving can have similar effects. An increase in private wealth offset by a decline in pension wealth may reduce uncertainty and thus increase current consumption. In this case too the offset is less than complete. Moreover, consumers may respond to changes in pension wealth by adjusting the time of retirement, an effect that will tend to attenuate the offset between private and pension wealth. A related issue, lastly, is consumers' uncertainty about the long-run solvency of the social security system and the prospect of future pension reforms. This could lead them to revise their social security wealth expectations downward and save more in the current period.

The main limitation of this first generation of studies is that in a cross section the correlation between private wealth and pension wealth could be due to a number of unobservable variables that are omitted from the regression; for instance, people with a strong propensity to save might also work harder and longer, and so receive larger pensions. A second generation of studies exploits pension reforms in the United Kingdom and Italy that have affected the resources of some cohorts of future retirees but not others. Using SHIW data for the years 1989–95, Attanasio and Brugiavini (2003) exploit the changes in pension wealth across cohorts and employment groups induced by Italy's 1992 pension reform. They model the response of the change in private wealth relative to income (the saving rate) to the level of social security wealth relative to income. Attanasio and Rohwedder (2003) exploit three major UK pension reforms as natural experiments to investigate the relationship between pension wealth and savings. Using time-series and cross-sectional variation from the Family Expenditure Survey, they find that the earnings-related tier of the pension scheme has a negative impact on household saving, with relatively high substitution elasticities.

Bottazzi, Jappelli, and Padula (2006), also using the SHIW, study the impact of the sequence of Italian pension reforms of the 1990s. These reforms lowered income replacement rates and raised retirement ages, with different effects on different cohorts and occupational groups. This exogenous variation in replacement rates allows inquiry into the effect of pension reforms on expectations of social security benefits and estimation of the extent to which changes in expected social security wealth were reflected in private wealth accumulation decisions. They find that the pension reforms did indeed affect expectations of retirement benefits, but that the revision of expectations was far from complete even years after the reform. Moreover, the offset between pension wealth and expected private wealth is only partial, considerably less than one-for-one.

In a related study, Jappelli and Padula (2016) consider the effect of a reform of the traditional system of Italian severance pay for public employees. Until 2000, severance pay was proportional to the final salary before retirement; under the new regime, it is proportional to lifetime earnings. This reform entailed substantial losses for future generations of public employees, in the range of €20,000–€30,000, depending on seniority. Using a difference-in-difference framework, the authors estimate that a €1.00 reduction in severance pay reduced the average propensity to consume by €0.03 and increased the wealth-income ratio by 0.3. The response is stronger for younger workers and for households in which both spouses are public sector employees.

9.7. THE WEALTH EFFECT

While this chapter, as its title indicates, has investigated changes in income, traditionally considered the model's only source of uncertainty, equation (9.1) (which we reproduce for convenience below) is agnostic regarding the type of shock π_{it} that could induce revision of the optimal consumption path:

$$\Delta \ln c_{it} = z'_{it}\lambda + \alpha E_{t-1}\Delta \ln y_{it} + \sum_{k=1}^{K} \phi^k \pi_{it}^k + \xi_{it}.$$

We now allow that π_{it} may also reflect the separate impact on consumption of unanticipated changes in house prices and stock market prices (in accordance with the "wealth effect" literature).

Standard models of intertemporal choice suggest that unexpected, permanent drops in wealth reduce consumption, and that the reduction should be equal to the annuity value of the wealth decline—in the case of an infinite horizon, $r/(1+r)$. However, there is considerable disagreement over the magnitude of the impact. Most of the literature is based on two implicit assumptions: (a) wealth shocks (whether due to house price changes or movements in stock prices) are not predictable, and therefore not anticipated by consumers; and (b) current asset prices are the best predictors of future prices, so changes in asset prices constitute a permanent wealth shock. According to the permanent-income hypothesis, from (a) and (b) it follows that wealth shocks should have a relatively large impact on consumption, equivalent to the annuity value of the shock (from 2 to 5 percentage points, depending on the real interest rate assumed).

The "pure" wealth effect that is studied by most of this literature is the response of consumption to unanticipated changes in wealth (capital gains and losses). Paiella and Pistaferri (2017) use subjective interest rate expectations to isolate exogenous changes in wealth (due only to asset price shocks) from anticipated changes (due to, for example, planned portfolio rebalancing). They also consider the impact of positive and negative wealth changes (expected and unexpected) and find evidence of asymmetric responses consistent with binding liquidity constraints.

Several studies, relying on macroeconomic or regional data, regress the logarithm of consumption, consumption growth, or saving on shocks to housing or financial wealth, but no consensus has yet emerged on the link between house prices and consumption.[7] Studies using microeconomic data allow researchers to inquire more thoroughly into this link. While changes in stock prices imply unambiguous wealth effects on consumption, as observed by Sinai and Souleles (2005), Campbell and Cocco (2007), and Attanasio et al. (2009), the consumption response to a fall in house prices is quite heterogeneous across the population. Most empirical analyses using micro data refer to the United States and the United Kingdom. Engelhardt (1996) estimated an MPC of 0.03 or higher for the United States in the 1980s, and Juster et al. (2006) found an even higher MPC for stock price changes. On the other hand, Hoynes and McFadden (1997) found that households who had experienced housing capital gains increased their saving rather than their spending, and Hryshko, Luengo-Prado, and Sørensen (2010) find that after a job loss homeowners smooth consumption more easily than tenants in times of higher house prices. For the United Kingdom, Disney, Gathergood, and Henley (2010) find a relatively low

7. Davis and Palumbo (2001) estimate that the MPC out of total wealth is in the range of 0.04–0.06. Case, Quigley, and Shiller (2005) provide estimates from a panel of developed countries and a panel of US states. In both they find an MPC for housing wealth of around 0.03–0.04 and a small and insignificant MPC for stock market wealth. Carroll, Otsuka, and Slacalek (2011) estimate the longer-run effects of housing wealth changes on consumption (beyond the next quarter) to be larger than the effects of financial wealth shocks.

MPC out of housing wealth (of the order of 0.01), whereas Campbell and Cocco (2007) show a relatively strong response for older households that own their homes. Attanasio et al. (2009) conclude that the co-movements in consumption and house prices reflect not a causal link but the action of common factors, contradicting the findings of Campbell and Cocco (2007).

The recent financial crisis has spurred a large amount of research on the relation between housing booms and busts, their effect on consumption, and how households with different balance sheets respond to house price shocks. Mian and Sufi (2016) have contributed to this literature by exploiting exogenous variation in house prices across US cities. They interpret this variation as due to differences in housing supply elasticities that arise from different geographical and institutional constraints (such as terrain elevation, presence of water bodies, and building regulations). Before the Great Recession, cities with the strongest house price boom experienced also a debt expansion and strong consumption growth. After the house price collapse, the same cities saw a stronger decline in consumption, particularly where debt had risen most.

Christelis, Georgarakos, and Jappelli (2015) examine the effects of the recent crises in the US housing market and stock market on household spending, using micro data from the 2009 Internet survey of the Health and Retirement Study. They find that real estate and financial losses have a substantial negative effect on household consumption, and the same is true in the case of job loss by a household member. In particular, they estimate that the marginal propensities to consume with respect to housing wealth and financial wealth are 1 percent and 3.3 percent, respectively. They also distinguish the effect of perceived transitory and permanent wealth shocks. In line with the standard models of intertemporal choice, they find that consumption responds more strongly to permanent wealth shocks than to shocks perceived as transitory.

On balance, the results based on micro data too are mixed. Some papers find large responses of expenditure to housing and securities price shocks, others find smaller effects. This literature suffers from a series of limitations, however. First, movements in house and stock prices are likely to be correlated with other economic events that may well have an impact on income expectations. Second, most of these studies rely on aggregate measures of house price changes (at national, regional, or county level), while house price risk also has an idiosyncratic component specific to each dwelling. Third, the current studies do not usually distinguish between transitory and permanent wealth shocks, which should affect consumption differently. Finally, consumers may tend to smooth consumption when income or wealth changes are large but may be less likely to do so when the changes are small and the cost of adjusting consumption is not trivial (Browning and Collado, 2001). Indeed, it is quite possible that the literature has been unable to get more precise estimates of the MPC with respect to wealth shocks because some of the shocks are small, while consumers may react mostly to large shocks.

CHAPTER 10

The Response of Consumption to Income Risk

In several parts of this book we have made the point that empirically, the actual growth rate of consumption is higher than would be implied by the certainty equivalence model. What is more, many studies have found, again counter to the theory, that consumption is sensitive to expected changes in income. Both of these facts can be explained by the precautionary motive for saving, which the certainty equivalence model does not contemplate. To understand this, consider the Euler equation derived in Chapter 6:

$$E_t \Delta \ln c_{t+1} = \gamma^{-1} \left(E_t r_{t+1} - \delta \right) + \frac{\gamma}{2} \mathrm{var}_t \left(\Delta \ln c_{t+1} - \gamma^{-1} r_{t+1} \right). \qquad (10.1)$$

This equation is derived assuming that the utility function is isoelastic and that consumption growth and the interest rate are jointly normally distributed. Increases in the expected real interest rate and in the anticipated variability of consumption growth are associated with a higher rate of growth in consumption. The second term of the equation is the precautionary saving component of consumption growth, because uncertainty about future consumption induces prudent consumers to defer consumption and increase savings. In equilibrium, the growth rate of consumption is higher than in the certainty equivalence model, where consumers do not respond to uncertainty.

Suppose now that we want to test for the excess sensitivity of consumption with respect to expected income growth, as described in Chapter 8. We can write the ex-post Euler equation (after the realizations of the random variables of the model, income and the interest rate), and augment the equation with the expected income growth rate:

$$\Delta \ln c_{t+1} = \gamma^{-1}\left(E_t r_{t+1} - \delta\right) + \frac{\gamma}{2}\text{var}_t\left(\Delta \ln c_{t+1} - \gamma^{-1} r_{t+1}\right) + \alpha E_t \Delta \ln y_{t+1} + \varepsilon_{t+1}. \quad (10.2)$$

There is evidence for excess sensitivity if the coefficient α is statistically different from zero—that is, if expected income growth affects the growth of consumption. However, if the variance term is not included in the regression, there is a standard problem of omitted variable bias. The coefficient of expected income growth could be statistically different from zero simply because it is correlated with the error, which now also includes the conditional variance term.

Precautionary saving therefore offers a possible explanation for the excess sensitivity of consumption when the estimated Euler equation omits the conditional variance term. As is observed by Carroll (1997), an increase in expected future income is associated with greater variability of future consumption and more precautionary saving. In turn, this raises the expected growth rate of consumption (and therefore $\alpha > 0$).

Other versions of the excess sensitivity test use current income in lieu of expected income, but they face a similar problem. An increase in current income, given expected future resources, reduces the variability of future income and thus that of future consumption. Since the precautionary saving term declines, so does the expected growth rate of consumption.

Tests of the importance of precautionary saving follow several research strategies. One aims to find a variable (or set of variables) that can approximate the variance of the growth rate of consumption in equation (10.1). A second strategy seeks to estimate a reduced form for the level of consumption and wealth with proxies for income risk. A third approach simulates the path of consumption and wealth in models with precautionary saving, matching simulations with the observed distribution of wealth and consumption. Other studies provide indirect evidence for or against the precautionary saving hypothesis. Finally, some papers test the null hypothesis of the precautionary saving model (or more generally, self-insurance), in which risks can only be insured via private savings, against specific alternatives in which researchers make the source of market incompleteness explicit (positing, for instance, that it is due to private information). Before presenting these empirical strategies, we discuss the question of how to measure income risk.

10.1. MEASURING INCOME RISK

Three approaches have emerged in the literature to extract moments of the distribution of future income from observable variables and to relate it to decisions on consumption and asset accumulation. The first approach relies on panel data and infers expectations and possibly higher moments of the individual distribution from past income realizations. The method typically proceeds in two steps. In the first step, researchers estimate a univariate ARMA process for earnings, taking the variance of the residuals as a reasonable measure of risk. Some variants of this procedure allow for different income shocks (transitory and permanent), but the basic idea is broadly the same: the history of earnings provides information about earnings volatility. In the second step the relevant variable chosen (assets, saving or consumption) is regressed on the risk measure obtained in the first step. In the simulation studies discussed in Section 10.4, the income variance is instead used as an important analytical input.

Using earnings history to measure income risk requires us to assume that in forming their expectations all individuals condition on the same set of variables (past income, say), that individuals and the econometrician have the same information set, and that the econometrician knows the stochastic process that generates individual expectations.

To avoid the need for such strong assumptions, some research relies on survey questions, not retrospective data, to elicit information on the conditional distribution of future income. The main advantage of surveys over realization-based inferences is that they do not require the econometrician to know which variables individuals consider in forming their expectations. Of course, to derive empirical measures of subjective income expectations and income risk, one must design appropriate questions to characterize either the density or the cumulative distribution function of future income. The literature includes both approaches.[1]

The simplest way to elicit income risk is to ask respondents for the minimum and maximum amounts they expect they could earn in the year following the survey. Assuming that the income distribution is uniform, one can then readily compute the moments of the distribution. More sophisticated techniques ask the consumer to report the probabilities with which future income will exceed a series of thresholds, or else extend the time horizon of the income forecasts (for instance, to five years or the entire lifetime). Of course, estimation of the distribution of future income is more reliable when the interviewees provide more information, but this comes at a cost: a lengthy survey is more likely to result in non-responses. One of the main advantages of the subjective expectations approach is that researchers can estimate a different income distribution (and therefore a different measure of income risk) for each consumer.

1. Guiso, Jappelli, and Terlizzese (1992) is based on survey questions from the 1989 Italian Survey of Household Income and Wealth (SHIW). Dominitz and Manski (1997), Das and Donkers (1999), and Guiso, Jappelli, and Pistaferri (2002) follow the alternative approach using, respectively, US, Dutch, and Italian data.

A third approach to measuring income risk uses natural experiments to identify exogenous changes in institutions and relates them to saving behavior. For instance, Kantor and Fishback (1996) take as an exogenous change the introduction of workers' insurance (mandatory insurance covering accidents on the job) in the United States, which reduced the degree of labor income risk among the workers covered.

In the rest of this chapter we will see how the different approaches have been implemented in tests of the precautionary saving model. However, it is important to stress that each has limitations. One problem is that it is not clear where risks come from. Earnings may vary from year to year for many reasons, such as movements in and out of work, variations in hours worked, or changes in productivity (as reflected in wages). Distinguishing among them is important because different risks entail different opportunities for insurance. For instance, it is relatively easy for a government to provide insurance against job loss due to a firm's closure (an event that is observable and hard for an individual worker to manipulate), but much harder to insure against low wages (owing to problems of private information or limited commitment).

The second problem is that researchers commonly interpret income variability as risk, while in some cases it may reflect choice. For instance, low income variability may reflect a worker's choice to be employed in a sector with low employment risk (such as the public sector). Similarly, unemployment may reflect a firm's decision to lay the worker off (job destruction) or a worker's decision to quit (voluntary unemployment), a distinction ordinarily drawn by unemployment insurance programs, which are generally targeted to involuntary job loss rather than voluntary resignation. As for productivity, health shocks such as work-related accidents represent true risk, while job mobility, with the associated productivity changes due to match-specific effects, is often a choice, not a random event. We will come back to these issues at the end of the chapter.

10.2. EULER EQUATION ESTIMATES

The main problem in estimating the Euler equation with precautionary saving is that the conditional variance of consumption growth in equation (10.1) is not observable. And the variance itself is an endogenous variable. Researchers have proxied this unobserved term with some measure of income risk (such as the conditional variance of income). But apart from the case of exponential utility and specific assumptions about the income process (in which the conditional variance of consumption growth coincides with that of income growth), the relationship between the variances of income and consumption is not straightforward. For example, consumers with more volatile income processes tend to procure more self-insurance by accumulating larger buffer stocks of wealth, and they may also alter their behavior in other ways to off-set the impact of this labor income uncertainty on consumption.

The first to seek to identify the precautionary saving term in the Euler equation was Dynan (1993), who used the approximation of the Euler equation derived by Blanchard and Mankiw (1988):

$$\frac{c_{it+1} - c_{it}}{c_{it}} = \alpha + \sigma r_{t+1} + \varphi E_t \left(\frac{c_{it+1} - c_{it}}{c_{it}} \right)^2 + \varepsilon_{it+1}, \qquad (10.3)$$

in which the term ε_{it+1} reflects innovations to consumption growth and approximation errors. If one could measure the expectation on the right-hand side of equation (10.3), then one could estimate the equation by ordinary least squares (OLS) and identify the coefficient φ, which is proportional to relative prudence. However, the expectation is not observed, and Dynan replaces it with the realization $\left(\frac{c_{it+1} - c_{it}}{c_{it}} \right)^2$, which is clearly correlated with the Euler equation error term.

To address this endogeneity problem, Dynan uses an instrumental variables approach applied to panel data drawn from the US Consumer Expenditure Survey. Her instrument set includes, among others, education and occupation, assuming that these characteristics are correlated with the expected variance. Overall, however, Dynan's results are disappointing. The instruments have little power, so the estimate of the coefficient of relative prudence is impre-cisely estimated. Furthermore, the data are quarterly, meaning that the vari-ability of consumption may capture seasonal phenomena rather than genuine uncertainty.

Dynan's approach has been refined by Bertola, Guiso, and Pistaferri (2005), who use the subjective variance of income as an instrument for $\left(\frac{c_{it+1} - c_{it}}{c_{it}} \right)^2$. They find that this more appropriate, more powerful instrument delivers cred-ible results. In particular, the coefficient of prudence is around 2 and is pre-cisely estimated, providing support for the precautionary saving model.

Christelis, Georgarakos, Jappelli and van Rooij (2015) use subjective expec-tations on future consumption drawn from the Dutch Center Internet Panel to construct measures of expected consumption growth and expected con-sumption risk that can be used to estimate the degree of prudence in equation (10.3), avoiding the use of realized consumption values in the Euler equation and the need for an instrument. They too estimate a statistically significant coefficient of relative prudence of around 2.

10.3. EVIDENCE FROM WEALTH REGRESSIONS

Workers in different occupations or industries face different degrees of income risk. For example, the self-employed have more volatile income prospects than public sector employees. In keeping with this idea, Skinner (1988) runs a reduced-form regression of wealth on occupational dummies. However, such risk proxies are almost invariably correlated with other attributes, and it is hard to tell whether they are truly measuring risk or instead capturing preferences for risk or other effects. More fundamentally, any risk indicator is subject to the problem of self-selection. Individuals in risky categories may have chosen to belong to that category simply because they are less risk-averse, in which case their wealth accumulation behavior might be no different from the average even if they have a precautionary saving motive.

A different approach is to use subjective measures of income risk obtained from survey data. As observed above, the Italian Survey of Household Income and Wealth elicits the respondents' income expectations. These data have been used by Guiso, Jappelli, and Terlizzese (1992) to test whether changes in the subjective variance of future income changes consumption and wealth in the directions suggested by the precautionary saving model. They find that in both regressions the results are consistent with precautionary saving, but the effects are quantitatively modest. For example, the assets accumulated in response to income uncertainty form only about 2 percent of total wealth.

Rather than relying on subjective expectations, one can estimate a proxy for income risk from the estimation of a process for earnings using panel data. Carroll (1997) and Carroll and Samwick (1997) assume that log earnings can be decomposed into a transitory component and a permanent component. They estimate the variance of transitory and permanent income shocks for each individual in the Panel Study of Income Dynamics. In the second step they regress wealth on their measure of income risk, finding that wealth increases with the variance of both permanent and transitory shocks, but that its sensitivity to risk is much smaller than is implied by the standard precautionary saving model. They argue that this agrees, especially for the younger age groups, with the buffer stock model of saving, which posits a precautionary saving motive but also impatient consumers.

As we know from Chapter 7, in the buffer stock model consumers have a unique and stable ratio between cash on hand (wealth plus disposable income) and the permanent component of income, which is termed the target ratio of wealth to permanent income. The model postulates that consumers save only if wealth is below target. Jappelli, Padula, and Pistaferri (2008) use a survey question on precautionary wealth available in the 2002 and 2004 Survey of Household Income and Wealth to devise a direct test of this implication of the model. People are asked how much savings they think they need for emergencies, similar to a question in the 1995 and 1998 waves of the Survey of Consumer Finances (Kennickell and Lusardi, 2004). Taking the answers as information on target wealth in a buffer stock model, they test the proposition that people with a below-target ratio of actual wealth to permanent income expect to save, while those with a ratio above target expect to dissave. Their results reject this basic implication of the buffer stock model and instead are more consistent with standard life-cycle models of wealth accumulation.

Hurst et al. (2010), with data from the Panel Study of Income Dynamics from the 1980s and 1990s, find that in samples of both business owners and other respondents precautionary savings against labor income risk are modest, amounting to less than 10 percent of total household wealth. They point out that higher estimates of precautionary balances emerge only if the two groups are pooled. However, such pooling is inappropriate given that business owners face higher income risk and accumulate more wealth for reasons unrelated to precautionary motives.

10.4. ESTIMATION BY SIMULATION METHODS

An analytical solution for the consumption function under uncertainty exists only with quadratic utility (Chapter 4) or with exponential utility (Chapter 6). In both cases, consumption is a linear function of wealth, but both also imply rather implausible assumptions about preferences for risk.

In more realistic cases, there is no analytical solution. In particular, when the utility function is of the constant relative risk aversion type, the properties of the consumption function can be characterized only by approximations or numerical simulations. The simulation studies require parameters of the utility function and of the income process. In the first generation of such studies, these parameters were either taken directly from outside sources or calibrated to fit the distribution of consumption and wealth.

One of the earliest and most influential studies to take this approach is by Hubbard, Skinner, and Zeldes (1994). They assume that consumers face not only labor income risk but also uncertainty about the length of life and medical expenses. To simulate their model, they estimate the income and health spending process, using realistic baseline values for the preference parameters (a coefficient of relative risk aversion of 3 and a discount rate of 3 percent) and imposing a non-negative constraint on wealth.

Figure 10.1 shows the asset accumulation profile over the life cycle for high school graduates in four different scenarios. The "all certain" profile arises from the case where people die with certainty at age eighty and have no income or health spending risk. In the first ten years, the borrowing constraint binds, households set consumption equal to income, and wealth is zero. Afterward, one observes the familiar life-cycle profile of wealth in which the only reason for saving is to smooth consumption during retirement. In the scenario

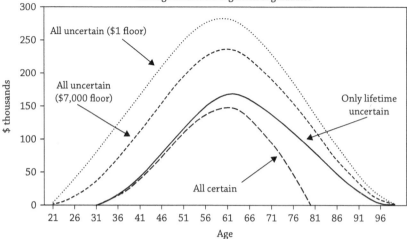

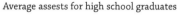 Average assests for high school graduates

Figure 10.1: Wealth accumulation under four scenarios
Note: The figure is reproduced with permission from Hubbard, Skinner, and Zeldes (1994).

labeled "only lifetime uncertain," they introduce uncertainty about the length of life, as we will do in Chapter 11. In this case, people have a life expectancy of eighty years but may live up to one hundred. The primary consequence of introducing lifetime uncertainty is to moderate the decumulation of wealth during retirement. In the remaining two scenarios, households face income, health spending, and longevity risk. In the scenario labeled "all uncertain ($1 floor)," consumers can only self-insure against these risks and the wealth profile shifts upward and at its peak (around age sixty-two) is twice as high. The last scenario, "all uncertain ($7,000 floor)," shows the role of social insurance in the form of a $7,000 consumption floor (provided, say, by food stamps) to those who qualify on the basis of income and asset tests. The pattern of wealth accumulation is intermediate between "all uncertain" and "all certain". This comparison highlights the importance of precautionary saving as an explanatory factor in the pattern of wealth accumulation over the life cycle and its interaction with government programs.[2] In fact, in their model social insurance crowds out private asset accumulation.

In a companion paper, Hubbard, Skinner, and Zeldes (1994) show that asset testing for eligibility for social insurance is equivalent to an implicit tax on savings. They show that the combination of social insurance programs and income risk can explain both the extent of heterogeneity in wealth accumulation and the minimal accumulation of wealth by individuals at the bottom of

---

2. The results of these simulations depend on the degree of persistence of income shocks. The more persistent the shocks, the higher the share of wealth accounted for by the precautionary motive.

the income distribution (for which high school educational attainment serves as a proxy).

A second generation of studies uses estimation-by-simulation methods to match empirical and theoretical moments of the income, consumption, and wealth distributions under precautionary saving. The basic idea behind estimation-by-simulation is described in the appendix to Chapter 7. Following this line of research, Gourinchas and Parker (2002) assume isoelastic preferences and labor income uncertainty. They first construct consumption and income profiles of men for five education groups and four occupations using the Consumer Expenditure Survey. Labor income uncertainty is measured using data from the Panel Study of Income Dynamics. Given the estimates of the income process, they estimate the relevant parameters (time preference and risk aversion) by minimizing the distance between the actual and theoretically predicted life-cycle profiles of consumption. Setting the real interest rate to 3 percent, they estimate a rate of time preference of about 4 percent and an elasticity of intertemporal substitution of 0.51, corresponding to a coefficient of relative risk aversion of around 2. Since the model is overidentified, a way to test precautionary saving is to compare the theoretical life-cycle consumption profiles generated by these estimates with the actual profiles. The match is quite good, supporting the precautionary saving model. In addition, they find that young consumers (under forty) accumulate little wealth, behaving like buffer stock agents. It is only in middle age that people start accumulating assets for retirement.

Cagetti (2003) estimates the same preference parameters as Gourinchas and Parker (2002) (the rate of time preference and the coefficient of risk aversion) by matching simulated and actual median wealth profiles over the life cycle, using data from the PSID and the Survey of Consumer Finances. He finds higher estimates of time preference and of risk aversion (around 4 for the high school sample). He then uses his estimates to assess the importance of the precautionary motive in determining the pattern of wealth accumulation. Cagetti confirms the main finding of Gourinchas and Parker: that people accumulate wealth in response to income risk early on in the life cycle and start saving for retirement as they begin to approach retirement age.

The interplay between precautionary saving and demographic variables is the subject of Attanasio, Banks, Meghir, and Weber (1999). They assume that preferences are affected by demographic and labor supply variables, such as family size and the spouse's leisure, and estimate the preference parameters by the Euler equation rather than matching simulated and actual consumption or wealth profiles. They then use their estimates to simulate consumption profiles in alternative scenarios, and show that they are best explained by a model with precautionary saving and preferences that depend on demographic variables.

10.5. GROUP COMPARISONS

A fruitful strategy is to compare the saving behavior of different groups of individuals (or the same individuals over time) who face different levels of risk. For instance, one can compare the behavior of the self-employed (who have highly variable earnings) with that of public employees (who face quite limited income and employment risk). Other things equal, the difference in saving rates between the two groups can be read as an indirect estimate of the importance of precautionary saving.

An early example of this approach is Friedman (1957), who compares the saving rates of the self-employed and employees. His puzzling finding, later confirmed by Skinner (1988), was that employees have higher saving rates. Two explanations for this puzzle have been proposed. One is simply that precautionary saving is not important, because individuals behave as in the certainty equivalence model. A second is that people self-select into more or less risky jobs according to their risk preferences: those who choose jobs with greater income uncertainty will be less risk-averse (and hence will save less) than those who choose more stable jobs.

Fuchs-Schündeln and Schündeln (2005) tackle the self-selection problem by using the German unification shock as a quasi-experiment. Their main assumption is that the self-selection problem is present in West Germany, whereas in East Germany labor income risk was practically non-existent regardless of occupation, and occupational choice was often restricted by political considerations. At unification, East Germans employed in risky occupations faced an exogenous increase in income risk if they decided to remain in their previous occupation.

Figure 10.2 summarizes the importance of self-selection using a standard precautionary saving model in which people differ in risk aversion and type of job selected. The left panel plots the life-cycle wealth profile without selection,

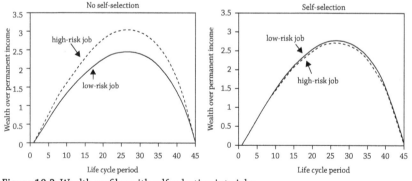

Figure 10.2: Wealth profiles with self-selection into jobs
Note: The figure is reproduced with permission from Fuchs-Schündeln and Schündeln (2005).

where people with different degrees of risk aversion are allocated randomly to high- or low-risk jobs. In this case differences in wealth accumulation are driven exclusively by precautionary motives. The right panel illustrates the case of selection, in which highly risk-averse consumers are sorted into low-risk jobs. In this case, there would be no differences in wealth accumulation between individuals in high- and low-risk jobs, leading to the false conclusion that precautionary saving is not important.

Fuchs-Schündeln and Schündeln (2005) regress wealth on permanent income and a proxy for low income risk (i.e., civil servant status) separately for East and West Germany. Neglecting the selection bias, one would conclude that the precautionary motive for saving explains only about 10 percent of total wealth accumulation, while adjusting for the bias raises the proportion to about 22 percent. Their results support the precautionary model and also demonstrate the importance of the selection bias induced by the correlation between risk preference and income risk.[3]

Another study taking the group comparison approach was done by Kantor and Fishback (1996), who test whether the introduction of compulsory workers' insurance in different US states reduced the propensity to save, the demand for health insurance, and the demand for life insurance. In 1915 the federal law on workers' compensation required employers to offer compulsory insurance against accidents on the job to all employees. The law was implemented gradually, state by state, between 1916 and 1930. Before the law workers bore the burden of insuring against workplace accidents. The reform was thus an exogenous change in the amount of risk workers faced and provides a quasi-experiment to test the main tenet of the precautionary saving model. Kantor and Fishback conclude that the reform actually reduced saving by about 25 percent.

10.6. BEYOND INCOME RISK

Some of the works discussed in the previous section suggest that fluctuations in income often reflect choices. To give a few examples, risk-averse individuals choose safer occupations; some workers can choose their labor supply, at least partially; others change firms in response to better matches; productivity shocks may reflect events that are partly under the worker's control, such as education and health. Looking inside the black box of earnings fluctuations and disentangling genuine risk from choice is an ongoing task for research. The distinction is also important from the policy standpoint, in that different

3. Guiso, Jappelli, and Pistaferri (2002), measuring individual risk aversion by lottery questions and income risk by subjective expectations, find a strong correlation between the two variables.

types of shock may be differentially insurable, and policy makers can better characterize behavior or improve welfare policy design.

In a key contribution, Abowd and Card (1989) consider joint movements of hours and wages. Their starting point is that fluctuations in earnings, which would normally be the preferred measure of risk, can be decomposed into exogenous fluctuations in wages and endogenous choices on hours. It is only the first type of fluctuation that represents genuine risk, although variation in hours has welfare costs, insofar as people value leisure.[4] Their conclusion is that the common components in the variation of earnings and hours cannot be explained by productivity shocks alone.

Low, Meghir, and Pistaferri (2010) model labor supply and job mobility in a search and matching framework. This approach distinguishes between shocks and responses to shocks and between employment risk (e.g., exogenous job destruction and lack of job offers when unemployed) and productivity shocks (e.g., health shocks or poor matches). Their welfare experiments show that in the United States people are much more willing to pay to eliminate productivity risk than unemployment risk, because the relatively short duration of unemployment means unemployment shocks are essentially temporary, while productivity shocks are more persistent. In contrast, people are willing to pay for endogenous job mobility, as they can always accept better job opportunities and turn down the bad ones.

Low and Pistaferri (2015) model productivity risk by distinguishing between health shocks (disability risk) and shocks to the price and quantity of skills (perhaps related to skill-biased technological changes). Their welfare analysis highlights the importance of a social insurance program such as public disability insurance, because disability triggers dramatic wage and job losses but has a relatively low probability of occurring, so precautionary saving against it represents a very costly insurance mechanism.

In addition to earnings risk, people face a number of other uninsurable or only partly insurable risks that can affect saving behavior. Among these, we have already discussed the risk of future liquidity constraints (Chapter 7) and shocks to asset prices, including house prices (Chapter 9). Here we will briefly touch on health expenditure and the risk of family breakup.

Individuals face substantial uncertainty over future health spending. In countries without universal health care, people are only partially insured against the risk of major medical expenditure shocks. For instance, in the United States some medical expenses are covered only partially or not at all and can constitute large out-of-pocket shocks to consumption. Indeed, 10 percent of the elderly spend more than 20 percent of their income on health

---

4. Of course, changes in hours worked are also driven by shocks to labor demand, not only by voluntary adjustments, and hence represent genuine risk. Disentangling demand and supply shocks is difficult in the extreme.

(not including nursing homes). The probability that a sixty-five-year-old will enter a nursing home at some point is about 50 percent. The average stay is longer than a year. About 5 percent of the elderly have nursing home expenses that exceed 40 percent of their income. Faced with these large potential costs, it comes as no surprise to find that uncertainty over medical costs leads the elderly to decumulate wealth more slowly than if they were fully insured.

The first work to inquire seriously into this issue was Palumbo (1999). This paper assumes that health status h evolves exogenously as a Markov process. Health costs m depend on h and a random term. That is, health expenditure is not a normal, freely chosen consumption good but can be interpreted as the "maintenance" costs of keeping a machine (one's body) running. In most of his specifications Palumbo assumes that utility is not state-dependent, that is, $\partial^2 u / \partial c \partial h = 0$, and that the preferences between consumption and health are separable.

Relaxing state dependence could imply that health problems may reduce the enjoyment of certain goods. For example, food consumption may go down during an illness as the patient loses appetite. In this case, good health and consumption are Frisch complements, or $\partial^2 u / \partial c \partial h > 0$. Bad health may also increase the consumption of certain goods. For example, individuals with a broken leg may need to take a taxi to go out, or will rent more DVDs if they stay at home. In this case good health and consumption are Frisch substitutes, or $\partial^2 u / \partial c \partial h < 0$. Scholars who have used data on consumption and health (Lillard and Weiss, 1997; Low and Pistaferri, 2015) have found evidence that consumption and good health are Frisch substitutes, whereas those who have used proxies for utility such as happiness (Finkelstein, Luttmer, and Notowidigdo 2013) have found evidence of Frisch complementarity.

Palumbo (1999) finds that individuals who face considerable medical expenditure risk do decumulate their wealth more slowly, but even so, the puzzle of slow decumulation remains: "elderly families typically dissave their financial assets more slowly than even the baseline health uncertainty model predicts is optimal" (395).[5]

Another important study is De Nardi, French, and Jones (2010). Estimating a rich structural model of behavior in old age using Asset and Health Dynamics Among the Oldest Old (AHEAD) data, they show that for many elderly people the risk of major health care expenses in very old age is an important explanation for the slow decumulation of wealth after retirement. They also emphasize the role of social insurance programs. On the one hand, a program like Medicaid

5. Another observation may also be consistent with this conclusion. In most European countries almost all health shocks are insured, yet there too, the decumulation of wealth is slow. Of course, in some countries public health care may be perceived to be of poor quality, which would help to resolve the puzzle of slow decumulation even in the presence of full insurance of health shocks.

discourages asset accumulation by the very poor, who incur ineligibility if they save up more than the asset test threshold. On the other hand, Medicaid is the health insurance program of last resort even for wealthier families, who may access it in the worst case, when they are unable to afford the medical care they need or have exhausted all their wealth due to large medical bills.

Another major risk is marital breakup. Divorce and separation entail substantial costs: legal and relocation expenses and the loss of the economies of scale and risk-sharing opportunities of marriage. Hence, the risk of divorce may lead some individuals to increase their precautionary saving. Marital status shocks appear to influence saving to about the same extent as earnings shocks (Cubeddu and Rios-Rull 2003). The costs of divorce are aggravated in many countries by the imposition of equal division of the couple's assets between the spouses, which may not reflect the actual allocation of resources within the marriage. Compared to a situation in which spouses have separate assets, equal division may lead risk-averse couples to increase their savings in order to allow both spouses to smooth consumption in the case of divorce (Voena, 2015).

10.7. ENDOGENOUS INCOMPLETE MARKETS

The model of precautionary saving developed in Chapter 6 posits that markets are incomplete and that the only way the individual can buffer income risk is by self-insurance. Many economists are dissatisfied with the assumption that market incompleteness is exogenous and the failure to specify the source of the incompleteness. They have developed models that treat incomplete markets endogenously, assuming that the incompleteness stems from problems of private information or limited commitment. The goal is then to test self-insurance (or full insurance) against specified alternatives, such as endogenous incomplete markets resulting from one or the other of the problems just mentioned.

An example of this approach is Ligon (1998), who in studying risk sharing in Indian villages notices that the intertemporal allocation of consumption depends on one's assumption concerning the source of market incompleteness. When incompleteness is exogenous and self-insurance is the only way to protect against risk, a standard Euler equation applies:

$$u'(c_t) = \frac{(1+r_{t+1})}{(1+\delta)} E_t u'(c_{t+1}). \qquad (10.4)$$

Next, Ligon considers the possibility that consumers may conclude risk-sharing agreements through a social planner. As is explained in Chapter 3, the planner equalizes consumption over time and across states; that is, equation (10.4) will hold state by state, rather than just in expectation. Finally, Ligon considers the case in which consumers have private information about their income. Again as in Chapter 3, this prevents the emergence of full insurance as a Pareto-optimal solution. However, we can consider a Pareto-optimal solution in which the planner chooses consumption *conditional on private information*. Mathematically, in addition to the usual resources constraint, one needs an incentive compatibility constraint, that is, a restriction that makes truth-telling optimal for the household. As Rogerson (1985) demonstrates, when markets are endogenously incomplete due to private information, the intertemporal allocation of consumption chosen by the planner is characterized by an inverse Euler equation:

$$\frac{1}{u'(c_t)} = \frac{(1+r_{t+1})}{(1+\delta)} E_t \frac{1}{u'(c_{t+1})}. \tag{10.5}$$

This equation characterizes the behavior of households who agree to share risks *conditional on private information*. Hence, while there is no full risk sharing, there is more insurance than in a simple model in which households only self-insure. To interpret this equation, assume for simplicity $r_{t+1} = \delta$. Jensen's inequality implies that $E_t \frac{1}{u'(c_{t+1})} > \frac{1}{E_t u'(c_{t+1})}$. Hence the inverse Euler equation implies that $u'(c_t) < E_t u'(c_{t+1})$, or that (if preferences are concave) consumers save (privately) less than in the pure self-insurance model (equation (10.4)). This is simply because when bad events occur the planner transfers some resources to them (although less than in a complete market setting, owing to the private information). We refer readers to Ljungqvist and Sargent (2004) for an excellent introduction to these models.

To see with a simple example how one can use this framework for empirical testing, assume that the preferences are isoelastic, $u(c) = \dfrac{c^{1-\gamma}}{1-\gamma}$, so that (10.4) and (10.5) can be rewritten, respectively, as:

$$E_t\left[\frac{(1+r_{t+1})}{(1+\delta)}\left(\frac{c_{t+1}}{c_t}\right)^{-\gamma} - 1\right] = 0$$

$$E_t\left[\frac{(1+r_{t+1})}{(1+\delta)}\left(\frac{c_{t+1}}{c_t}\right)^{\gamma} - 1\right] = 0.$$

It follows that one can nest the two cases of exogenous and endogenous incomplete markets (due to private information problems) by estimating the parameter θ in the moment condition:

$$E_t\left[\frac{(1+r_{t+1})}{(1+\delta)}\left(\frac{c_{t+1}}{c_t}\right)^{\theta} - 1\right] = 0.$$

If the estimated $\theta > 0$, there is evidence for private information, while if $\theta < 0$ the evidence tells more in favor of simpler self-insurance.

Ligon (1998) finds strong evidence in some of the Indian villages he studies that markets are incomplete because of private information, and hence that the data on intertemporal consumption allocation are characterized better by the presence of some risk sharing, not only simple self-insurance mechanisms such as saving and borrowing. In other villages, the self-insurance model provides a better characterization.[6] A explanation of this result is that in some village economies close ties of kinship or community participation allow members to share and diversify risks more efficiently than in other, more complex settings. In principle, the larger a community, the easier it should be to insure individual risks, but at the same time, the weaker the bonds of solidarity, hence the lower willingness to help the less fortunate. For this reason, many scholars believe that a model with complete markets (or endogenous incomplete markets) is more appropriate for small communities in developing countries or underdeveloped economies than to entire industrialized countries.

To summarize the evidence discussed in this chapter, the primary risk that people face—income risk—is hard to measure and may mix together choice with genuine risk. Nor is income risk the only source of uncertainty; indeed, for many people and some stages in the life cycle, it is not even the most important (health risk is a prime alternative). Simulations suggest that income risk could have a powerful impact on asset accumulation and that its effect is tempered by social insurance programs, which in many developed countries keep consumption from falling below a certain (poverty) threshold.

The evidence from empirical analysis of the relationship of consumption growth or wealth to income risk is mixed. Most studies have found a positive correlation consistent with the precautionary saving model, but the magnitude of the effect, while varying considerably from one study to another, tends on net to be on the small side. This does not warrant the conclusion that precautionary behavior is marginal, however, because accumulated wealth can be put to use in multiple ways, so that people who have saved assets for retirement may also use them as a buffer against emergencies. This makes it difficult for formal empirical tests to account for the different motives for saving. Finally, we have discussed tests of the precautionary saving model (or, more generally, of the self-insurance hypothesis), in which risks can only be insured by private savings, against specific alternatives in which the incompleteness of markets is explicitly modeled (as the product, for instance, of private information issues).

6. Nested tests to distinguish among market completeness scenarios have also been conducted in other settings. For example, Kocherlakota and Pistaferri (2009) consider the implications for asset pricing of the models of complete markets, self-insurance, and endogenous incomplete markets due to private information.

CHAPTER 11

Lifetime Uncertainty

U p to this point we have worked on the assumption that consumers face no uncertainty about the length of their planning horizon. In reality, however, one's life span is not certain, and this uncertainty affects consumers' choices, especially in old age. Lifetime uncertainty represents an additional risk that affects intertemporal choice, because consumers may live longer than expected and run the risk of exhausting the resources accumulated for retirement. In principle, this longevity risk can be insured by a policy that pays out an annuity (a certain stream of income until death) in exchange for the payment of a premium. In practice, as we will discuss, these contracts are not very common, owing to problems of moral hazard and adverse selection.

Factoring lifetime uncertainty into models of intertemporal choice has a number of significant effects. First, it introduces an incentive to consume earlier in life because consumers discount future utility at a higher rate, so their rate of time preference must take survival probability into account. Second, since in each period there is some positive probability that the consumer will not survive to the next period, the terminal condition on wealth corresponds effectively to a liquidity constraint similar to that examined in Chapter 5. Third, with lifetime uncertainty, the decumulation of wealth by the elderly is slower than predicted by the life-cycle model, because people choose to maintain a certain level of resources even at very old ages in order to insure against the danger of living longer than they had expected and running out of resources. Finally, the model with lifetime uncertainty generates transfers of wealth across generations even without an express bequest motive, through what we can term involuntary or accidental bequests.

Many of the ideas presented in this chapter come from the seminal study by Yaari (1965). Yaari was the first to consider the intertemporal choice problem with lifetime uncertainty and compare optimal consumption profiles with and without annuity contracts. His model has been applied by Davies (1981), who uses simulations to calculate the effect of lifetime uncertainty on the propensity to consume, and Hurd (1987), who studies the profile of consumption and wealth of the elderly with lifetime uncertainty and with a bequest motive. As in previous chapters, we first illustrate the key elements in a simple two-period model and then generalize to the multi-period context. The chapter concludes by highlighting the necessity of accounting for lifetime uncertainty when interpreting empirical age-wealth profiles estimated from microeconomic data.

11.1. A TWO-PERIOD MODEL

The two-period model is particularly useful to isolate the effect of lifetime uncertainty from other risks. Suppose that the consumer is alive in period 1 and with probability p survives to period 2 and with probability $(1-p)$ does not. In this model, the duration of life is the sole source of uncertainty. Denoting the discount factor by $\beta = 1/(1+\delta)$, we assume that the consumer maximizes expected utility:

$$\max u(c_t) + \beta E_t u(c_{t+1}) = \max u(c_t) + \beta p u(c_{t+1}) \qquad (11.1)$$

$$\text{s.t.} \quad a_{t+1} = (1+r)(a_t + y_t - c_t) \geq 0 \qquad (11.2)$$

$$a_{t+2} = (1+r)(a_{t+1} + y_{t+1} - c_{t+1}) = 0, \qquad (11.3)$$

and a_t is given. In previous chapters the terminal condition on wealth was simply expressed as $a_{t+2} = 0$. With perfect capital markets and a perfectly known planning horizon, the consumer can borrow as long as the intertemporal budget constraint is satisfied. If life duration is certain, this is sufficient to ensure that wealth is non-negative at the end of period 2. With lifetime uncertainty, wealth cannot be negative even at the end of the first period, for otherwise there is the risk that the consumer will die in debt (with negative net assets). The dynamic budget constraint (11.2) is then formally identical to a liquidity constraint that prevents the consumer from carrying debt from the first period to the second.

The consumer's intertemporal budget constraint is consequently kinked and has slope $-(1+r)$ in the region above the kink. Consumption in the first period is constrained by the resources available in that period:

$$c_t \leq a_t + y_t.$$

This constraint may or may not bind. If desired first-period consumption does not exceed $a_t + y_t$, the intertemporal budget constraint is:

$$c_t + \frac{c_{t+1}}{1+r} \leq a_t + y_t + \frac{y_{t+1}}{1+r}. \tag{11.4}$$

Figure 11.1 plots the optimal (c_t, c_{t+1}) allocation assuming that the optimal amount of wealth a_{t+1} to be carried to the next period is positive. The optimal consumption profile is at the point of tangency A between the indifference curve and the intertemporal budget constraint. Note that the constraint is kinked due to the liquidity constraint on wealth implied by lifetime uncertainty. If the constraint does not bind, the first-order condition for utility maximization is:

$$u'(c_t) = p\beta(1+r)u'(c_{t+1}). \tag{11.5}$$

The Euler equation (11.5) shows that in equilibrium the marginal utility of consumption in the first period equals its discounted marginal utility in the second period multiplied by the survival probability. To see how this differs from the case of certainty, set $\delta = r$, thus $\beta(1+r) = 1$. With $p = 1$ (no lifetime uncertainty) the consumption profile would be constant. If $p < 1$ and the utility function is concave, the marginal utility of consumption in the first period is less than in the second period, $u'(c_t) < u'(c_{t+1})$. It follows that first-period consumption exceeds second-period consumption, $c_t > c_{t+1}$. That is,

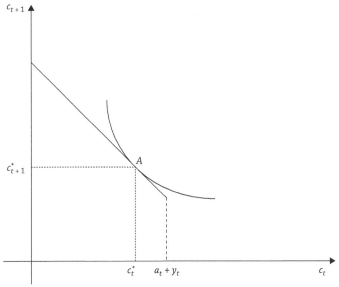

Figure 11.1: Interior solution

uncertainty over life span makes consumers more impatient, less willing to defer consumption.

Note that lifetime uncertainty and income uncertainty have different effects on the allocation of consumption. As we know from Chapter 6, the effect of income uncertainty depends on the convexity of marginal utility (measured by the coefficient of prudence). The effect of lifetime uncertainty depends instead on the concavity of the utility function (measured by the degree of risk aversion). While income uncertainty tends to reduce current consumption and increase saving, lifetime uncertainty has the opposite effect.

Let us now focus on the case in which the first-period consumption that would be chosen in the absence of lifetime uncertainty exceeds available resources, $c_t^* > (a_t + y_t)$, and hence the constraint on wealth is binding. Consumption allocations will now be given by a corner solution, just as in the model with liquidity constraint (see Figure 11.2), and consumption is equal to available resources in each period:

$$c_t = a_t + y_t$$
$$c_{t+1} = y_{t+1}.$$

Although formally identical to the case of liquidity constraints, the situation depicted in Figure 11.2 is unlikely to be relevant for young people, who have high survival probabilities. It is hard to maintain that the young are unable to borrow because banks fear that they will die before repaying the

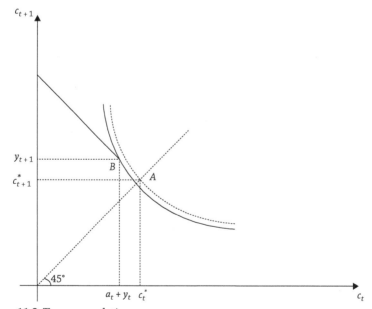

Figure 11.2: The corner solution

debt. It is much more likely that credit rationing for young consumers stems from credit market imperfections than from lifetime uncertainty (the relationship between age and survival probability is analyzed in Section 11.3).

11.2. ANNUITY CONTRACTS

In this section we consider how the solution changes if consumers can purchase annuities, contracts whose payoff is conditional on surviving to future periods. Annuity contracts differ from term life insurance, which pays a lump sum to the surviving beneficiary upon the death of the insured. Absent a bequest motive, in the two-period model set out above there is no demand for term insurance. Consumers may instead be willing to purchase an annuity, insuring against longevity risk, that is, the danger of surviving into the second period with insufficient resources.

With annuity contracts, the consumer transfers a portion of first-period savings to an insurance company in exchange for the latter's undertaking to refund the same amount (plus interest) if the consumer survives to the second period. In case of death, the insurance company keeps the premium. While saving can only transfer resources over time, annuities transfer them between states of nature and accordingly address longevity risk more efficiently than self-insurance.

While longevity is a risk for the single individual, insurance companies can diversify it by pooling individual life histories. By the law of large numbers, an insurance company that stipulates a sufficiently large number of such contracts knows the fraction of the insured population that will survive to the second period. Thus, from the point of view of the insurance company p is not a random variable. Let us further assume that insurance is actuarially fair and hence the insurance company makes zero profit. This implies that the expected value of discounted future payouts is equal to current revenues (premiums received). Under these conditions, the return on a dollar invested in a safe asset is equal to the expected return on the annuity,

$$(1+r) = p(1+\omega), \tag{11.6}$$

where ω indicates the return on the annuity. Since $p < 1$, $(1+\omega) > (1+r)$ and the return on the annuity is higher than the market return if the consumer survives. Under actuarial fairness, insurance companies are able to commit to a higher return than the market interest rate because they can redistribute to those alive in the second period the resources of those who have predeceased them. Since annuity contracts dominate other forms of saving, consumers will always choose to annuitize all of their wealth.

With annuities, the dynamic budget constraint depends on the state that is realized in the second period. At the beginning of the period, wealth (now held entirely in the form of annuity entitlements) takes two possible values, depending on whether the consumer survives or not:

$$a_{t+1} = \begin{cases} (1+\omega)(a_t + y_t - c_t) & \text{with prob. } p \\ 0 & \text{with prob. } (1-p) \end{cases}$$

The expected intertemporal budget constraint is:

$$c_t + \frac{pc_{t+1}}{1+r} = a_t + y_t + \frac{py_{t+1}}{1+r} = a_t + E(h_t), \tag{11.7}$$

where $E(h_t)$ denotes the expected discounted value of future income. The expected intertemporal budget constraint has slope $-(1+r)/p$ and has no kink. The first-order condition for utility maximization is the same as in a model with no lifetime uncertainty:

$$u'(c_t) = \beta(1+r)u'(c_{t+1}). \tag{11.8}$$

Without annuities, lifetime uncertainty makes the consumer more impatient and less willing to defer consumption to future periods. Annuities instead encourage saving and offset this effect. However, the intertemporal budget constraint in the case of lifetime uncertainty is different from that of certainty, so the consumption function is not the same. Here we cannot compare the consumption functions in the two cases, because the planning horizon is different (two periods given certainty, $1+p$ periods given lifetime uncertainty). In the remainder of this chapter, we develop a multi-period model that allows comparison of the two solutions, holding the expected planning horizon constant.

11.3. THE MULTI-PERIOD MODEL

Our multi-period analysis is cast in continuous time. The length of life T is a random variable with support $[0, T_{max}]$, where T_{max} is the oldest possible age that a consumer can reach.[1] Assume that T has a probability distribution function $\varphi(T)$ such that:

$$\Phi(s) = \Pr(T \leq s) = \int_0^s \varphi(T)dT \tag{11.9}$$

1. There are two interpretations of T_{max}. One is that it is fixed and determined by biological constraints, implying that in the long run improving health will increase the mass of the distribution located near T_{max}. A second interpretation is that T_{max} is time-varying and is itself affected by improvements in medical technology.

is the cumulative distribution function, or the probability of dying before a given age s. Hence, $\Phi(0) = 0$ (all individuals survive past the initial age) and $\Phi(T_{max}) = 1$ (no individual will survive past age T_{max}). Since T is a random variable, the consumer maximizes expected utility:

$$\max_{\{c_t\}_0^T} E(V(T)) = \int_0^{T_{max}} \varphi(T) \left[\int_0^T u(c_t) e^{-\delta t} dt \right] dT$$

$$= \int_0^{T_{max}} \left[\int_t^{T_{max}} \varphi(T) dT \right] u(c_t) e^{-\delta t} dt$$

$$= \int_0^{T_{max}} \left[1 - \Phi(t) \right] u(c_t) e^{-\delta t} dt.$$

To see where the second equality comes from, denote as p_j the probability of surviving to period j and as u_j the utility derived from consumption in period j. The discrete-time equivalent of the first integral is then $p_1 u_1 + p_2 (u_1 + u_2) + \dots + p_{T_{max}} (u_1 + u_2 + \dots + u_{T_{max}})$, which can be rewritten as $(p_1 + \dots + p_{T_{max}}) u_1 + (p_2 + \dots + p_{T_{max}}) u_2 + \dots + p_{T_{max}} u_{T_{max}}$. The third equality comes from the fact that $\int_t^{T_{max}} \varphi(T) dT = \Phi(T_{max}) - \Phi(t) = 1 - \Phi(t)$, where $1 - \Phi(t)$ is the probability of surviving after age t. The consumer's problem can therefore be written as:

$$\max_{\{c_t\}_0^{T_{max}}} \int_0^{T_{max}} \left[1 - \Phi(t) \right] u(c_t) e^{-\delta t} dt \qquad (11.10)$$

$$\text{s.t. } \dot{a}_t = r a_t + y_t - c_t$$

$$a_t \geq 0 \qquad \forall t \in (0, \dots, T_{max}).$$
$$a_{T_{max}} = 0$$

In the absence of insurance markets the sequence of constraints $a_t \geq 0$ obliges the consumer to choose a consumption path in which wealth is never negative, since no one would be willing to grant a loan to a consumer who can die before repaying the debt. Below we assume that the non-negative wealth constraint never affects the consumer's problem in the sense that optimal consumption never exceeds the resources available in any period.[2]

The Hamiltonian function of the problem is:

$$H_t = \left[1 - \Phi(t) \right] u(c_t) e^{-\delta t} + \mu_t (r a_t + y_t - c_t).$$

2. Yaari (1965) shows that when the constraint is binding, consumption follows a "constrained" phase when it is equal to income and an "unconstrained" phase in which it follows the Euler equation. The problem is formally identical to that with liquidity constraints considered in Chapter 5.

The first-order conditions are:[3]

$$[1-\Phi(t)]u'(c_t)e^{-\delta t} = \mu_t \qquad (11.11)$$

$$\mu_t r = -\dot{\mu}_t. \qquad (11.12)$$

Taking the log of (11.11), deriving with respect to time, and substituting the result into (11.12) gives the growth rate of consumption:

$$\frac{\dot{c}_t}{c_t} = EIS[r - \delta - m(t)], \qquad (11.13)$$

where $EIS = -\dfrac{u'(c_t)}{c_t u''(c_t)}$ is the elasticity of intertemporal substitution and $m(t) = \dfrac{\varphi(t)}{1-\Phi(t)}$ is the instantaneous mortality rate at age t given survival up to that age (the hazard function). Compared with the case of certainty, the novel aspect of the Euler equation (11.13) is the term $m(t)$. In each period the consumer must take the change in survival probability into account. Since $m(t) > 0$, lifetime uncertainty increases the rate at which future marginal utility is discounted and reduces the rate of growth in consumption, just as in the two-period model. The intuition is that the fear of dying before exhausting their wealth induces people to anticipate consumption.

Quite clearly, longevity risk is the risk of living too long—or, from the insurance company's standpoint, of policyholders living too long. Lifetime uncertainty has the opposite effect on consumption from income risk. We know from Chapter 6 that when marginal utility is convex the consumer is prudent and responds to increased income risk by reducing current consumption. The precautionary saving motive therefore results in greater consumption growth. Lifetime uncertainty works in the opposing direction, insofar as it leads consumers to transfer consumption from the future to the present, reducing the growth rate of consumption. This result requires only that the consumer be risk-averse.

To see the implications of longevity risk for the age-consumption profile, consider that mortality rates are not constant but vary with age. Figure 11.3 plots the survival function and the mortality function for American men and women. Note in particular that mortality increases with age at an increasing rate.

---

3. Note that the transversality condition is $a_{T_{max}} \mu_{T_{max}} = 0$.

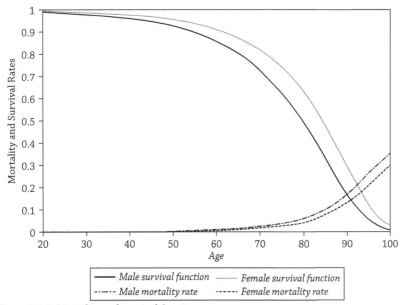

Figure 11.3: Mortality and survival functions

Note: Data are drawn from US mortality tables. *Source:* US actuarial life tables (www.ssa.gov).

For consumers with a certain planning horizon, the sign of the difference $(r - \delta)$ is all that is needed to establish whether consumption is increasing $r > \delta$ or decreasing $(r < \delta)$ over the life cycle. With lifetime uncertainty, the growth rate of consumption is no longer constant, because $m(t)$ varies with age. Equation (11.13) implies that consumption is increasing or decreasing depending on whether the interest rate r is less or greater than the rate of time preference adjusted for mortality, $\delta + m(t)$.

When $r < \delta$, so the consumer would want a decreasing consumption profile in the case of certainty, mortality reinforces the effect of δ and consumption falls at an even faster rate. The case $r > \delta$ is more interesting, because it generates a concave consumption profile. Figure 11.4 plots an example of such a profile (solid line) obtained assuming $\delta = 0$, $r = 0.02$, $EIS = 1$, and the mortality function plotted in Figure 11.3 and normalizing consumption at age twenty-five to be 1. For comparison, we also plot the consumption profile under certainty (dashed line). For young people, the mortality rate is low and consumption growth is positive, as the effect of the interest rate dominates the mortality-adjusted effect of the rate of time preference. According to the actuarial tables for men, the mortality rate equals 0.02 at age sixty-eight, implying that at that age $r = \delta + m(t)$ and consumption peaks. At later ages, mortality is higher and consumption declines.[4] This is a further reason the

---

4. In Chapter 1 we saw that another reason the consumption profile may be concave over the life cycle is changing family size.

empirical consumption profile discussed in Chapter 2 may be concave over the life cycle. Notice, however, that in this case consumption peaks about twenty years later than family size.

While mortality/longevity risk makes the consumer more impatient and unambiguously reduces the growth rate of consumption, there are no clear-cut implications regarding the relation between mortality and the *level* of consumption. Whether or not consumption under uncertainty is greater than under certainty depends on the degree of risk aversion (Davies, 1981).

To compare the two consumption solutions, under certainty and uncertainty respectively, Davies considers a consumer who has a given, certain lifetime and one who has the same life expectancy but with longevity risk. To obtain a closed-form solution for consumption, he assumes that the utility function is isoelastic and that wealth in the initial period is zero. Using realistic preference parameters and US data on income and actuarial tables, he finds that at age forty the marginal propensity to consume lifetime resources in the case of lifetime uncertainty is 8 percent lower than under certainty, implying that lifetime uncertainty reduces not just the growth of consumption but also the level of consumption, as depicted in Figure 11.4, adapted from Davies (1981).

Because consumers never reach T_{max} but plan as if they had a positive probability of doing so, the model with lifetime uncertainty implies that all consumers die with some unspent wealth, thus leaving accidental or involuntary bequests.

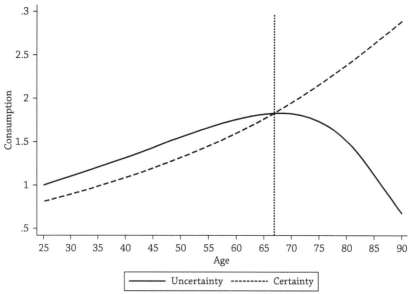

Figure 11.4: The profile of consumption with and without lifetime uncertainty
Note: Consumption is normalized to one in the uncertainty case.

11.4. COMPLETE MARKETS

Let us now examine how the consumer's problem changes when annuity insurance is available. The demand stems from the consumer's desire to avoid dying with unspent resources. We discussed this possibility in the two-period model of Section 11.2, and as we know, if annuity contracts are available, the consumer transfers wealth to an insurance company in exchange for a perpetual annuity. If the contracts are actuarially fair, insurance companies pay out $[r+m(t)]$ for every dollar paid in.[5] Hence, in this model there is individual uncertainty but not aggregate uncertainty. Note that from the insurer's point of view $m(t)$ is not a random variable. Thus this is a complete-market model. The return on annuities $[r+m(t)]$ exceeds the market return because the number of policyholders exceeds the number of beneficiaries (survivors), and annuities accordingly dominate self-insurance.

If annuities are available, the objective function of the consumer is:

$$\max_{c(t)} \int_0^{T_{max}} \left[1-\Phi(t)\right] u\!\left(c_t\right) e^{-\delta t}\, dt$$

$$\text{s.t. } \dot{a}_t = \left[r+m(t)\right]a_t + y_t - c_t.$$

The Hamiltonian function of the problem is:

$$H_t = \left[1-\Phi(t)\right]u\!\left(c_t\right)e^{-\delta t} + \mu_t\left\{[r+m(t)]a_t + y_t - c_t\right\}.$$

The first-order conditions are:

$$[1-\Phi(t)]u'\!\left(c_t\right)e^{-\delta t} = \mu_t \tag{11.14}$$

$$\mu_t\left[r+m(t)\right] = -\dot{\mu}_t. \tag{11.15}$$

Deriving with respect to time the logarithm of (11.14) and using (11.15), we get:

$$\frac{\dot{c}_t}{c_t} = EIS(r-\delta). \tag{11.16}$$

Given complete markets, $m(t)$ does not appear in the Euler equation, which is therefore identical to the case of certainty. The reason is that annuities

---

5. The term $[r+m(t)]$ is the equivalent, in continuous time, of the term $(1+r)/p$ in discrete time.

encourage the accumulation of wealth by raising the return to saving and eliminating accidental bequests. All wealth is therefore invested in annuities. As noted above, this does not imply that the level of consumption is the same as under certainty, since intertemporal budget constraints still differ.

11.5. THE ANNUITY PUZZLE

There are several types of annuity contracts to protect against longevity risk. A common one is a life insurance policy that guarantees a fixed stream of payment in exchange for a lump sum policy premium. A second instrument is the reverse annuity mortgage, which allows individuals to run their housing equity down through a series of payments from a financial institution, which takes ownership upon the insuree's death. The most important forms of annuity, however, are social security and defined-benefit pension plans, which guarantee a stream of payments until the death of the insured or a surviving partner.

While uncertainty about the date of death offers a plausible explanation for the slowness with which retirees decumulate wealth, at the same time it poses a different puzzle. If uncertainty about the date of death is really the motive, why don't people buy annuities? Purchasers of life annuities give a fixed sum of money for a continuous stream of benefits as long as they live. If people have no bequest motive, they should actually have an incentive to annuitize *all* of their wealth. But this is rarely observed in reality. For example, according to Johnson, Burman, and Kobes (2004), only 4 percent of workers with defined-contribution pension plans who left work after age fifty-five converted their retirement plan assets into annuities; for workers leaving after age sixty-five, the figure rises to 10 percent, still almost negligible by comparison with the 100 percent implied by the model described in this chapter.[6]

There are many reasons the annuity market is so underdeveloped. First, people may have a bequest motive, hence no incentive to annuitize their wealth. If insurance contracts provide a higher return than the market, then individuals without a bequest motive should always choose to convert their assets into annuities, even when the return is less than fair. Those who do have a bequest motive must weigh the advantage of higher returns against the disadvantage of having a smaller estate to bequeath. Bernheim (1991) shows that in this case the share of capital converted into an annuity is less

---

6. The puzzle refers to "private" wealth, as social security wealth and defined-benefit pensions are in fact annuitized. However, these annuities cannot be used as a test of rationality because no individual choice is involved.

than 100 percent, even when the return is actuarially fair. We discuss bequest motives further in Chapter 12.

A second reason is that a large fraction of wealth is already annuitized in the form of social security benefits, which stop with the consumer's or surviving spouse's death. Moreover, total annuitization leaves households with no resources to deal with unexpected contingencies such as health shocks. Asymmetric information between the insurer and the insured may induce market failure because of adverse selection: the demand for annuities may be concentrated among individuals who are in good health and expect to live longer. To the extent that the availability of annuities itself creates incentives to live longer (possibly by investing more in one's health), moral hazard too may be an issue. In this case, a rational insurance company will not offer annuity policies.

Another possibility is emphasized by Brown and Poterba (2000), who also develop a method to evaluate the consumer's incentive to purchase annuities grounded in the intertemporal consumption model with lifetime uncertainty. The simplest measure of the value of an annuity is the "money's worth ratio" (MWR) between the expected present value of the payments promised by the annuity and the cost of the premium. If the ratio is greater than 1, consumers expect to receive more than they pay in. This measure, however, assumes that consumers are risk-neutral and are not capable of comparing the annuity with other financial options.

Brown and Poterba (2000) develop a more sophisticated measure, defining as annuity equivalent wealth (AEW) the amount of additional wealth that an individual who purchases an annuity would need in order to maintain the same utility as if there were no annuity market. The AEW can be computed in three steps, solving first a life-cycle model with annuities and then the same model without annuities before comparing the utility in the two models. This more sophisticated measure therefore depends on the entire set of parameters of the intertemporal model, including preference, the structure of the household, demographic parameters, and the tax treatment of annuities and other income. The authors note that the utility gain from annuitization is smaller for couples than for singles because there is risk sharing within the couple, in that if one member of the couple lives a long life, he or she may inherit the spouse's remaining resources. Since most potential buyers of annuities are married, this factor may explain the smallness of the annuity market.

In a study that adopts the same theoretical framework, Butler and Teppa (2007) use data from Swiss employer-based pension plans to study the annuitization decision at retirement. They find that the AEW measure explains a good deal of the option to annuitize wealth at retirement. However, they also find that the decision to annuitize is heavily influenced by the default option of the plans' sponsors, which in most cases is the annuity. According to Benartzi, Previtero, and Thaler (2011), failure of self-control, inertia, and lack of financial sophistication inhibit some households from providing adequately for retirement, and these behavioral factors are also important in understanding the demand for annuities. We return to the issue of default options in Chapter 14.

Another factor that might discourage people from annuitizing their wealth is inflation risk, if (as often happens in practice) annuities are not indexed to inflation. Yet while inflation risk was important in the 1970s and 1980s, it is unlikely to be a good explanation for the smallness of the annuity markets in the 1990s and 2000s. Finally, the low take-up rate could be due to the actuarial unfairness and high cost of annuity contracts. However, the loads on annuity insurance are typically no greater than on casualty or property insurance, at least in the United States.

11.6. THE AGE-WEALTH PROFILE WITH LIFETIME UNCERTAINTY

We now turn to the implications that the model with life uncertainty carries for the age-wealth profile when markets are incomplete. Since mortality among young people is low, lifetime uncertainty mainly affects the behavior of the elderly. We know from Section 11.3 that with lifetime uncertainty the consumption of the elderly decreases faster than with a certain planning horizon. This result is quite general, because it depends only on mortality rates, not on risk aversion or other preference parameters. However, if the coefficient of risk aversion is high, the propensity to consume is lower under uncertainty than under certainty.

In the baseline life-cycle model of Chapter 1, the wealth profile is hump-shaped and wealth is completely exhausted at the time of death. This general feature holds even when income risk, credit market imperfections, and the role of demographic variables such as family size are factored in. Although each of these factors changes the shape of the age-wealth profile, the central tenet of the life-cycle model, that wealth is exhausted by the time of death, remains. This no longer applies, however, when the date of death is uncertain and markets are incomplete. In particular, in these circumstances the rate at which wealth is depleted is lower than under certainty and consumers leave unintended bequests.

Figure 11.5 compares the wealth profile by age of a consumer having a known, certain horizon (the dashed line), living with certainty V years, with that of an uncertain one (the solid line), who may live to T_{max} but on average only lives to V, and both retiring at age N. In our example, the peak of wealth comes later and is higher with lifetime uncertainty than with certainty (although this is not necessarily the case for different parameter values). Moreover, the elderly decumulate at a lower rate, and wealth is not exhausted even at very old ages.

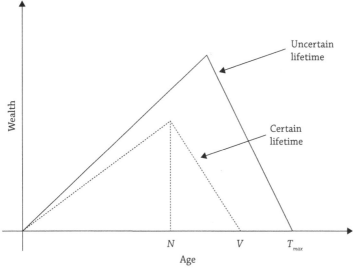

Figure 11.5: Wealth by age with certain horizon and uncertainty about the duration of life

The low rate of decumulation by the elderly has been found by a good number of empirical studies, some of which are reviewed in Section 2.6 in Chapter 2. While this is often interpreted as evidence against the life-cycle model and in favor of models in which bequests are important, this is not necessarily so. The figure shows that a very slow decumulation or even an increase in wealth (as happens, in our example, between age N and the age of the wealth peak under uncertainty) does not automatically imply rejection of the life-cycle model. Indeed, the figure suggests that the age profile of wealth alone is not an adequate test of the model's validity. This issue is discussed further in Chapter 12, on bequest motives.[7]

Comparing age-wealth profiles in the empirical data with theoretical benchmarks may be complicated by significant measurement problems. In repeated cross sections, there may be systematic bias, induced by differential mortality. If wealth and mortality are correlated (i.e., poorer consumers die younger), then the average wealth profile estimated from repeated cross sections may be biased upward—that is, it might show lack of decumulation even though all consumers run their wealth down. This point was first made by Attanasio and Hoynes (2000).

Figure 11.6 provides a simple example with three individuals who differ in initial wealth. They follow the life-cycle hypothesis with no lifetime uncertainty and have identical decumulation rates, but they die at different ages

7. The mortality rate differs considerably between men and women. This poses a difficult problem in interpreting the age profile of household wealth and the very definition of the age of the household (which is usually, but somewhat arbitrarily, taken as that of the head).

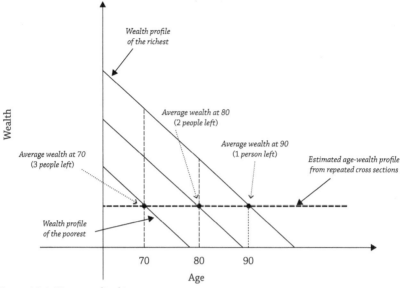

Figure 11.6: The mortality bias

(the poor die earlier). The average wealth profile estimated from the data at each age, starting at seventy, is given by the corresponding dot. At age eighty the poorest consumer has died, and average wealth appears not to have changed simply because of a compositional effect. At age ninety only the wealthiest consumer is left, and again the composition of the sample has changed, producing misleading evidence of a constant wealth profile even though all three consumers decumulate wealth precisely in keeping with the life-cycle hypothesis. Once recognized, the problem can be solved by constructing mortality-adjusted age profiles of wealth, obtained by multiplying the observed wealth averages by survival probability according to wealth at any age.

Figure 11.7, adapted from Attanasio and Hoynes (2000), is based on data from the Survey of Income and Program Participation and shows that taking mortality bias into account significantly affects both the mean and the median wealth accumulation profiles. Up to age sixty, the mortality bias is negligible, but by age eighty-four, both mean and median wealth are about 25 percent less when adjusted for the longer life expectancy of wealthier individuals compared to poorer individuals.

This chapter has shown that uncertainty over the length of life can have profound implications for consumption behavior. A first important consequence is that lifetime uncertainty makes consumers more impatient. Second, it reduces the growth rate of consumption and under plausible assumptions may turn the consumption profile hump-shaped. Third, the elderly decumulate wealth at a lower rate than that implied by the certainty

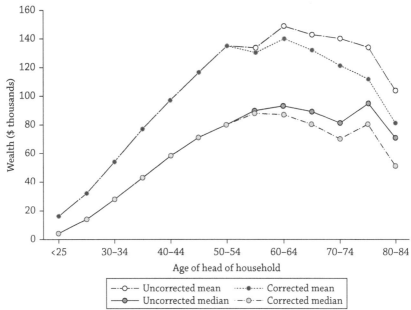

Figure 11.7: The effect of mortality bias on the age-wealth profile
Note: Figure reproduced with permission from Attanasio and Hoynes (2000).

model. Finally, wealth is not entirely depleted by the time of death, and this gives rise to involuntary or accidental bequests even in the absence of any bequest motive.

The type of lifetime uncertainty analyzed in this chapter is idiosyncratic, since some people die before their life expectancy and some after. However, it should be noted that lifetime uncertainty also has an aggregate component, which, for instance, may stem from unforeseen medical advances that increase longevity. Since insurance companies cannot diversify aggregate risks, market failure may arise from the inability to cope with such developments (i.e., committing to overgenerous annuities and then finding that the average duration of life is greater than had been factored in when pricing the annuities). Given medical progress and the uncertainties surrounding the estimation of mortality tables, this issue is likely to be of growing importance in the future.

CHAPTER 12
Bequest Motives

We have repeatedly highlighted the difference between models with finite and infinite time horizons. Bequest motives play a crucial role in this distinction. For instance, the life-cycle hypothesis with finite planning horizon posits that the elderly decumulate all their wealth to finance consumption during retirement. As we saw in Chapter 11, with lifetime uncertainty wealth decumulation is slower, and wealth is not run down to zero at the time of death.[1] Although individuals thus leave bequests, these are involuntary and unplanned. The use of a model with infinite horizon is usually justified by assuming that consumers are characterized by feelings of altruism, providing a strong link between generations in the form of intergenerational transfers. The study of bequests is therefore crucial to distinguishing between these different models of intertemporal choice.

Various explanations of individual attitudes toward bequests have been proposed. In addition to altruism, the literature has considered strategic bequests, in which intergenerational transfers are a reward for services provided by the heir, and models in which bequests, like any other good, directly influence utility. The literature on bequest motives is vast, and here we limit ourselves to a summary of the main approaches. We first clarify the distinction between altruistic and strategic bequest motives. Next we consider the choice between bequests and gifts. Then we derive the Euler equation when bequests are an argument of the utility function (a model with "joy of giving"). In the

---

1. Lifetime uncertainty alone does not justify the presence of involuntary bequests in life-cycle models. With efficient insurance markets, consumers could choose to hold all their wealth in the form of annuities, which cannot be passed on to heirs. As we saw in Chapter 11, however, annuities are not common because of informational asymmetries and transaction costs.

second part of the chapter we address the difficult issues of how to measure bequests and how to tell the different bequest motives apart empirically, and discuss the link between transfer taxes and the accumulation of wealth.

12.1. ALTRUISM

Those who believe that bequests are mostly voluntary must explain why individuals should deliberately deprive themselves of some of their resources in order to transfer them to their heirs. Intertemporal models with altruism assume that consumers draw utility not only from their own consumption but also from the utility of their offspring. A formal definition of altruism in a static context is given by Becker (1981), who defines person h as altruistic toward person w if h's utility function is:

$$u_h = u(c_h, u_w);$$ (12.1)

that is, the welfare of person h depends not only on his own consumption, c_h, but also on the utility of person w (think of h and w as husband and wife). Note that altruism implies not only that u_w is an argument of u_h but also that $\dfrac{\partial u_h}{\partial u_w} > 0$. The husband's budget constraint is:

$$c_h + d = y_h,$$

where d is the amount transferred from husband to wife and y_h is husband's income. Since the model is static, there are no savings and income coincides with total expenditure. The consumption of the wife is:

$$c_w = d + y_w,$$

where y_w is wife's income. Substituting d into the budget constraint of the husband gives the budget constraint of the household:

$$c_h + c_w = y_h + y_w = y.$$

The allocation of resources within the family is obtained by maximizing the utility of h subject to the household budget constraint. Maximization leads immediately to an equilibrium condition between the marginal utility of consumption of husband and wife:

$$\frac{\partial u_h / \partial c_h}{\partial u_w / \partial c_w} = 1.$$

The most important implication of altruism is that a redistribution of resources within the family does not change the distribution of consumption between husband and wife. In other words, individual consumption depends on total household income, not on individual income (note the similarity to the model with complete markets). Moreover, if w's income is reduced, w's consumption drops by less than her income because h will increase the amount he transfers to w. Altruism thus implies that the family shares individual risks and provides partial insurance against uncertainty. Becker further shows that this result is true regardless of the attitude of w toward h: even if w is not altruistic, and thus her goals are different from h's, it is in h's best interest to behave as if w were altruistic.

Barro (1974) proposed a multi-period model in which the welfare of parents depends on the utility of children. Like that of the husband in the example above, the objective function of the parent can be written as:

$$u_b = u(c_b, u_{b+1}),$$

(12.2)

where c_b indicates a sequence of consumption of cohort b (for example, from year zero to year T). Since $u_{b+1} = u(c_{b+1}, u_{b+2})$, the utility of the parent also depends upon the utility of the grand-child, with a recursion that extends to all future generations. For this reason, models with intergenerational altruism necessarily consider the welfare of a "dynasty" rather than that of an individual consumer. As the planning horizon becomes effectively infinite, the relevant budget constraint no longer refers to the individual but to the entire dynasty, as in Becker's static model in which the relevant budget constraint is no longer on the individual but on the household. The main difference between the static problem and the intertemporal problem is that husband and wife consume in the same period (and therefore transfers are contemporaneous, or *inter vivos*), while parent and child consume in periods that do not completely overlap (so the transfers can take the form of inheritances).

Barro (1974) shows that, in the absence of growth, the problem of cohort b can be written as:

$$\max u_b = \int_0^T u(c_t) e^{-\delta t} dt + \int_T^{2T} u(c_t) e^{-\delta t} dt + \ldots = \int_0^\infty u(c_t) e^{-\delta t} dt,$$

subject to the intertemporal budget constraint:

$$\int_0^\infty e^{-rt} c_t \, dt = a_0 + h_0,$$

where h_0 is the discounted value of the earnings of all the dynasty's members.

Since the horizon is infinite, the dynasty behaves exactly as predicted by the permanent-income model. In particular, the redistribution of resources within the dynasty does not change the distribution of consumption between the different members. That is, each member's consumption depends on the resources of the dynasty, not on individual income. A redistribution of resources between generations does not affect the allocation of consumption and is offset by transfers between generations. For example, if a parent believes that the resources of future generations will diminish, he or she will choose to increase transfers.

In an economy with growth, children might be richer than parents, so the optimal solution requires that young people make transfers to the elderly, and not vice versa. Bequests and intergenerational transfers (in both directions) are the means by which the dynasty smooths consumption between generations. It is therefore quite natural to interpret the model with altruism as one way to justify the assumption of an infinite horizon and to take the evidence for or against altruism as evidence for or against infinite horizon models.

The implications of altruism are discussed in various passages in the previous chapters. At the microeconomic level, the main implication is that if the consumer is part of a dynasty, we should not find wealth decumulation after retirement. Macroeconomically, we have stressed that positing an infinite horizon greatly simplifies the problem of aggregation. Furthermore, this assumption may imply equivalence between debt and taxes as a means of financing a given public expenditure and also between pay-as-you-go and funded pension systems.[2] These equivalence propositions follow directly from the fact that policies that redistribute resources between generations do not alter a dynasty's intertemporal budget constraint.

12.2. STRATEGIC BEQUESTS

Another strand of research considers bequests as the result of services provided by children to their parents, not just altruism. These theories are known in the literature as models with a *strategic bequest motive*. To understand the basic issues, let us assume that parents and children are selfish and that the parents' utility function depends only on their own consumption and services s received by an only child, that is, $u_b = u(c_b; s_{b+1})$, and similarly for the child: $u_{b+1} = u(c_{b+1}; -s_{b+1})$. The variable s_{b+1} appears with a negative sign in the child's utility function because it has a utility cost, while it appears with a positive sign in the parent's utility function because parents like to be cared for by their children.

---

2. The result holds when there is no uncertainty, there are no credit market constraints, and taxes are lump sum.

Table 12.1 THE GAME BETWEEN PARENT
AND CHILD

Child	Parent	
	Leave a bequest	Do not leave a bequest
Care for the parent	5; 5	0; 8
Not care for the parent	8; 0	1; 1

Consider first the case in which the parent can credibly threaten to totally disinherit the child. The main insight of this simple model is easily grasped with an example adapted from the prisoner's dilemma game, as shown in Table 12.1.

The parent can leave a bequest or not. The child can choose to provide care for the parent or not. Table 12.1 assigns ordinal utility values to the possible strategies of child and parent. The first number in each cell represents the child's utility, the second the parent's. As in the prisoner's dilemma, the Nash equilibrium of the game is not Pareto efficient: the dominating strategy for the parent is not to leave a bequest, and the child's best strategy is not to assist the parent, even though the alternative (assist the parent; leave a bequest) could provide a higher payoff to both. Under limited commitment, no other equilibrium is sustainable and no bequest will occur.

In reality, parents cannot always credibly commit to disinherit; for instance, there may be restrictions on the share of the estate that the testator can freely dispose of. Moreover, as noted by Bernheim, Schleifer, and Summers (1985), parents may be altruistic even when children are purely selfish. The utility functions are therefore modified as $u_b = u\left[c_b; s_{b+1}; u\left(c_{b+1}; -s_{b+1}\right)\right]$, while for the child, as before, $u_{b+1} = u\left(c_{b+1}; -s_{b+1}\right)$.[3] Furthermore, the presence of more than one child makes the threat of disinheriting one child more credible because of competition among the children. In this situation there will be a greater incentive for children to provide care and for parents to leave bequests. Bernheim, Schleifer, and Summers (1985) show that in such cases, strategic bequests can arise in equilibrium and that children's provision of services is directly related to the parents' estate. To test this prediction empirically, they compare the supply of services to parents by only children with the supply by two or more children. If the strategic motive is important, one should observe more competition for bequests among the offspring of parents with two or more children. Looking at visitation rates, they find that they increase with potential

3. This is a variant of the so-called rotten-kid theorem.

bequests in families with two or more children, while they decline with potential bequests in families with an only child. Both findings are consistent with the strategic bequest model.

12.3. *INTER VIVOS* TRANSFERS

The timing of bequests is, by nature, unpredictable, and only by chance will a child receive a bequest when it is most needed. A parent who is truly interested in the utility of the child should prefer to transfer wealth *inter vivos*, with gifts, rather than with a bequest at the time of death.[4] *Inter vivos* transfers are obviously voluntary and are particularly important when the child is subject to credit constraints. In the absence of credit constraints, the allocation of consumption across periods is independent of the distribution of resources during the life cycle. With credit constraints, however, children are not indifferent about the timing of bequests, precisely because they cannot borrow against future income, much less against bequests.

To illustrate the relationship between credit market constraints and intergenerational transfers, we present a model similar to that elucidated by Cox (1987). It extends Becker's model (described in Section 12.1) to a dynamic context. Consider a family consisting of a parent and a child. Since we are only interested in *inter vivos* transfers, we take a two-period model (t and $t+1$), when both parent and child are alive. For example, in period t the parent is forty years old and the child is twenty; in period $t+1$ the parent is sixty and the child forty. In period t the child (k) cannot borrow against future income, so his consumption, c_{kt}, equals income in that period, y_{kt}, plus any transfer received from the parent, d_t. We assume that the parent is not credit-constrained and is altruistic, in the sense that his or her utility depends on the utility of the child. Thus the parent's objective function is:

$$u\left[c_{pt}, v(y_{kt} + d_t)\right] + \frac{u\left[c_{pt+1}, v(y_{kt+1} + d_{t+1})\right]}{1+\delta},$$

where u and v indicate, respectively, the utility of parent and child, c_{pt} the consumption of the parent, and δ the rate of time preference (which is assumed to be identical for parent and child). The functions $u(.)$ and $v(.)$ are increasing and concave in each of their arguments and satisfy the Inada conditions $\lim_{c\to 0} u'(c) = \infty$, $\lim_{c\to\infty} u'(c) = 0$, $\lim_{c\to 0} v'(c) = \infty$, $\lim_{c\to\infty} v'(c) = 0$. The parent maximizes the

---

4. Another reason why parents transfer resources *inter vivos* is for intertemporal exchanges; for instance, parents may support children's education in exchange for being cared when old.

objective function subject to his or her own intertemporal budget constraint and the two dynamic budget constraints faced by the child:

$$c_{pt} + \frac{c_{pt+1}}{1+r} + d_t + \frac{d_{t+1}}{1+r} = y_{pt} + \frac{y_{pt+1}}{1+r}$$

$$c_{kt} = y_{kt} + d_t$$
$$c_{kt+1} = y_{kt+1} + d_{t+1},$$

where y_{pt} denotes the parent's income in period t and r is the real interest rate. The model also allows for the possibility that transfers in the first period are actually loans rather than gifts. If the interest rate on these loans does not exceed the market interest rate, the discounted flow of transfers cannot be negative:

$$d_t + \frac{d_{t+1}}{1+r} \geq 0. \tag{12.3}$$

If the constraint on transfers is binding, then intergenerational transfers are, de facto, loans at market rates (as long as $d_t > 0$; in fact, loans from child to parent would require $d_t < 0$). Alternatively, if the constraint is not binding, then they represent a subsidy by the parent to the child's consumption.

Since parents have access to the credit market, their Euler equation is satisfied:

$$\frac{\partial u(.)}{\partial c_{pt}} = \frac{1+r}{1+\delta} \frac{\partial u(.)}{\partial c_{pt+1}}.$$

Furthermore, the first-order conditions with respect to the transfers are:

$$\frac{\partial u(.)}{\partial v(.)} \frac{\partial v(.)}{\partial c_{kt}} - \lambda - \mu = 0$$

$$\frac{1}{1+\delta} \frac{\partial u(.)}{\partial v(.)} \frac{\partial v(.)}{\partial c_{kt+1}} - \frac{\lambda}{1+r} - \frac{\mu}{1+r} = 0,$$

where μ is the multiplier on the constraint (12.3). Assuming that the constraint on transfers is not binding, these first-order conditions imply that the Euler equation holds for the child as well:

$$\frac{\partial v(.)}{\partial c_{kt}} = \frac{1+r}{1+\delta} \frac{\partial v(.)}{\partial c_{kt+1}}.$$

Note that the Euler condition holds also in the case in which intergenerational transfers are actually loans at market rates. In this case the child uses the parent as a financial intermediary, which shows that an informal loan market (between parents and children) may overcome the constraints in formal credit markets. As in Becker's model, the result holds regardless of the attitude of the child to the parent (altruistic or not).

Since intergenerational transfers help children to smooth consumption, a change in the timing of income will change the timing of transfers. For example, a child with a steep income profile receives (other things being equal) proportionally more in the first period than a child with a flat earnings profile.[5] If the child were not credit-constrained, transfers would not affect the profile of consumption but would reduce the difference between the parent's total resources and those of the child. When the child is subject to credit market constraints, however, the timing of gifts plays a crucial role in stabilizing consumption.

To summarize, the model shows that if the child is credit-constrained, the amount of *inter vivos* transfers should be correlated negatively with the child's current income and positively with future income. Put another way, the idea is that *inter vivos* transfers should be directed to those who have low current income and high lifetime resources.

The model also suggests that if parents were truly motivated by altruism, they should transfer their assets to heirs *inter vivos* (i.e., in the first period) and not at death (the end of the second period). There are at least two other reasons altruistic parents should prefer *inter vivos* transfers to inheritances. First, many transfers are intended to subsidize the purchase of goods to which parents allocate a special value (in particular, education, weddings, and homes) and which generally are relevant only for the young. The second consideration relates to the tax system: in some countries the treatment of *inter vivos* transfers is more favorable than that of bequests, not to mention the relative ease of evading taxes and concealing assets in life than after a will.

Altruism implies that we should observe very few bequests and many *inter vivos* transfers. In reality, however, we find the opposite: most intergenerational transfers are in the form of bequests. This empirical fact suggests that a large proportion of bequests are not motivated by altruism but are accidental or strategic.[6]

---

5. Altonji, Hayashi, and Kotlikoff (1996) show that in this model with altruism the condition $\dfrac{\partial d_t}{\partial y_{pt}} - \dfrac{\partial d_t}{\partial y_{kt}} = 1$ holds. The condition states that if the parent's income is reduced by a dollar and the child's increases by a dollar, the amount transferred is reduced by a dollar. Thus there is full crowding-out of transfers when the distribution of resources between generations changes. The authors test the hypothesis of full crowding-out and find that the offset is only 10 percent, thus rejecting the altruistic model.

6. Models with strategic motives in fact reach the opposite conclusions from altruistic models: the parent chooses to defer the transfer as long as possible so as not to lose the ability to influence the children and receive their assistance.

Empirical research on *inter vivos* transfers is vast and we cannot do full justice to it. Overall, the evidence suggests that in some cases families offset some of the constraints that young people face in official credit markets, but research has also shown that the family is a very imperfect substitute. For instance, first-home buyers who do not have access to mortgage markets receive gifts or loans from their parents to help them with the down payment. But the proportion is low and the majority of young people denied credit do not get subsidies from their parents. Engelhardt (1996) finds that the vast majority of first-time US home buyers accumulate their down payments from their own savings, while no more than 20 percent receive some kind of help from relatives. Guiso and Jappelli (2002), using Italian data, find that *inter vivos* transfers increase the hazard rate of purchasing the first home by about 20 percent. These findings imply that while many households do have access to gifts or loans to overcome down-payment constraints, the vast majority may be truly constrained by down payments even considering access to family networks.

12.4. JOY OF GIVING AND THE AGE-WEALTH PROFILE

Some authors have proposed to study the role of intergenerational transfers with the assumption that donors derive direct utility from giving, and not from the well-being of their heirs or from the assistance services they receive. These "joy of giving" or "warm glow" models treat bequests essentially like any other commodity. They are not entirely satisfactory because they simply assume the bequest motive and fail to specify why donors should be willing to transfer assets to their heirs, but they do simplify the analysis in multi-period models drastically and allow researchers to obtain analytical implications for the consumption and wealth profiles in the presence of bequests.

To show the main differences between the models with and without joy of giving, Figure 12.1 plots the age-wealth profiles in two scenarios. Both assume that there is no lifetime uncertainty. The lower line is the same age-wealth profile given in Chapter 1, obtained assuming a constant consumption profile throughout life and a constant income profile up to retirement. The upper line maintains these assumptions but in addition posits the presence of consumers who experience the joy of giving. In the absence of productivity growth across generations, individuals receive a bequest in the initial period and leave the same amount (labeled "target bequest") when they die.[7] The

7. If there is no growth, the bequests received are equal to those passed on to the next generation. Aggregate net saving is zero, and the aggregate wealth-income ratio is constant. In a growing economy, bequests increase from one generation to the next because the number of people leaving bequests and their lifetime resources are growing. It is easy to show that in this case aggregate net saving is positive even if the individual profiles of income, consumption, and wealth are all constant throughout life.

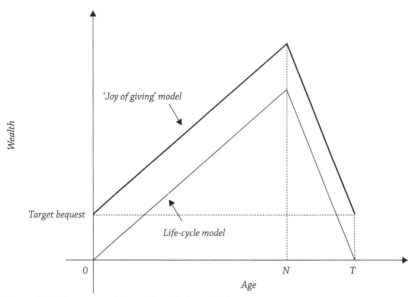

Figure 12.1: The age-wealth profile with joy of giving

age-wealth profile with joy of giving is simply a scaled-up version of that without bequests. The figure explains why people do not run their assets down to zero at the time of death, but not why the elderly decumulate wealth at a slower rate than in the standard life-cycle model.

The joy-of-giving model is more interesting when combined with lifetime uncertainty (Chapter 11). We follow Hurd (1992) and, in keeping with the notation in Chapter 11, posit continuous time. The consumer's objective function now includes a term that depends directly on terminal wealth (or bequest):

$$\max_{c(t),a(t)} \int_0^{T_{\max}} [1-\Phi(t)]u(c_t)e^{-\delta t}dt + \int_0^{T_{\max}} m(t)v(a_t)e^{-\delta t}dt. \qquad (12.4)$$

The first term represents the expected utility of consumption between 0 and T discounted at the rate of time preference δ. As in Chapter 11, $T_{\max}$ indicates the highest possible age to which people can live, and $[1-\Phi(t)]$ is the probability of surviving up to time t. The second term is the expected utility of leaving a bequest (again discounted at rate δ), and $m(t)$ is the probability of death at time t. The second term indicates that the consumer derives utility from the bequest made, which occurs when he or she dies, so that the timing (as well as the size) of transfers is uncertain. The parent thus needs to discount all potential utility streams coming from the bequest and weight them by the probability of death at each age.

As in Section 11.3 of Chapter 11, we assume that the consumer cannot purchase annuities and maximizes function (12.4) subject to the following constraints:[8]

$$a_0 \text{ given}$$

$$\dot{a}_t = ra_t + y_t - c_t$$

$$a_t = a_0 e^{rt} + \int_0^t (y_t - c_t) e^{r(s-t)} ds \geq 0 \quad \text{for every } t.$$

The first two constraints are the same as in the problem without bequests: an exogenous value for initial wealth and a dynamic budget constraint. The third constraint states that bequests can never be negative and thus that it is impossible to pass debt on to one's heirs. Since the probability of death is positive at every point in time, the constraint on wealth must hold in every period; therefore wealth can never be negative.

Note that the model is best suited to describing the wealth and consumption trajectories of an individual who is already retired. If the constraint on terminal wealth does not bind, the Hamiltonian function of the problem is:

$$H_t = \left[1 - \Phi(t)\right] u(c_t) e^{-\delta t} + m(t) v(a_t) e^{-\delta t} + \mu_t \left(ra_t + y_t - c_t\right),$$

and the first-order conditions for a maximum are:

$$[1 - \Phi(t)] u'(c_t) e^{-\delta t} = \mu_t \tag{12.5}$$

$$m(t) v'(a_t) e^{-\delta t} + \mu_t r = -\dot{\mu}_t, \tag{12.6}$$

and the transversality condition $\mu_T a_T = 0$. Multiplying both terms of (12.6) by the integration factor e^{rt} and integrating it between any two points in time t and τ, $\tau > t$, we have:

$$\int_t^\tau m(s) e^{(r-\delta)s} v'(a_s) ds = -\int_t^\tau (\dot{\mu}_s + r\mu_s) e^{rs} ds.$$

Using the fact that $(\dot{\mu}_t + r\mu_t) e^{rt}$ is the primitive function of $\mu_t e^{rt}$, we get:

$$\int_t^\tau m(s) e^{(r-\delta)s} v'(a_s) ds = -(\mu_\tau e^{r\tau} - \mu_t e^{rt}). \tag{12.7}$$

8. Initial wealth (a_0) should in principle include pension wealth, which, however, cannot be freely bequeathed. For simplicity, we assume that there are neither pensions nor a market for life insurance (Hurd considers this case as well).

Multiplying (12.5) by the same factor of integration e^{rt}, we get

$$[1-\Phi(t)]e^{(r-\delta)t}u'(c_t) = \mu_t e^{rt}. \qquad (12.8)$$

Considering (12.8) at time t and τ, subtracting one from the other, and using (12.7), we finally obtain the Euler equation:

$$u'(c_t)[1-\Phi(t)] = u'(c_\tau)[1-\Phi(\tau)]e^{(r-\delta)(\tau-t)} + \int_t^\tau m(s)v'(a_s)e^{(r-\delta)(s-t)}ds. \qquad (12.9)$$

The integral on the right-hand side of (12.9) is the marginal benefit of leaving a bequest between time t and time τ. The equation indicates that postponing consumption from t to τ increases the expected value of discounted future consumption (just as when there are no bequests) but also the probability of leaving a bequest between the two points in time. Note that given the non-negativity constraint on wealth, the last term of the integral is always positive.

Equation (12.9) thus establishes the first important result of the model with bequests as consumption goods. Given $u'(c_\tau)$, the bequest motive (the last term of equation (12.9), absent in the no-bequest model) increases $u'(c_t)$. Current consumption falls relative to future consumption, so the growth rate of consumption is higher.

If consumers obtain no utility from bequests, equation (12.9) collapses to the following, which is equation (11.13) in Chapter 11:

$$\frac{\dot{c}_t}{c_t} = EIS[r-\delta-m(t)].$$

Since the focus here is the consumption profile of the elderly, the mortality rate is sufficiently high, $(m(t)>r-\delta)$, as to predict a declining consumption profile. And for an analogous reason, with a bequest motive the wealth profile is flatter. To see why, take the budget constraint for an old person (with $y_t = 0$):

$$\frac{da}{dt} = ra - c.$$

Take the derivative with respect to time, giving:

$$\frac{d^2a}{dt^2} = r\frac{da}{dt} - \frac{dc}{dt}.$$

Since after retirement $\frac{dc}{dt} < 0$, it must be that wealth too declines $\left(\frac{da}{dt} < 0\right)$. Suppose by contradiction that it does not $\left(\frac{da}{dt} > 0\right)$. Then $\frac{d^2a}{dt^2} > 0$ and wealth

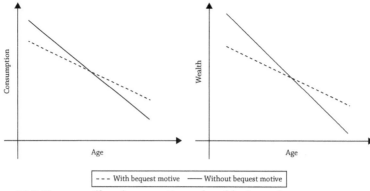

Figure 12.2: The age profiles of consumption and wealth after retirement

will increase at an increasing rate, which violates the terminal condition $a_{T_{max}} = 0$. It follows that wealth must decline with age.

When the individual draws utility from terminal wealth, $v'(a) > 0$, and hence from (12.9) the decline in consumption will be more moderate, insofar as the bequest motive leads people to postpone consumption. The decline in wealth according to age is also attenuated in the joy-of-giving model by the fact that people get utility from having some positive assets at the time of death. In short, with a bequest motive the consumption and wealth profiles of the elderly are both flatter, as is shown qualitatively in Figure 12.2. A bequest motive therefore implies not only that the elderly do not exhaust their wealth before they die, but also that wealth decumulation is slower than predicted by the pure life-cycle model.

It should be clear by now that the age profile of wealth per se does not provide much information about the bequest motive. In fact, altruistic parents should transfer assets to their children when they are most in need, in the form of *inter vivos* transfers rather than bequests. More important, predicting whether a large portion of wealth is passed from one generation to the next—rather than built up during the course of a lifetime—requires knowledge of the motives for bequests. In fact, even very substantial bequests do not necessarily imply a powerful bequest motive: in the absence of well-functioning annuity markets, people save against longevity risk, and most bequests are involuntary.

Hurd (1987) overcomes some of these identification problems by supposing that only families with children should have an incentive to leave bequests. Even if the wealth profile provides no information on the bequest motive, a divergence between the wealth profiles of families with and without children can be interpreted as evidence for the bequest motive. Using longitudinal data from the Retirement History Survey, Hurd shows that wealth falls rapidly after age sixty-five, but that couples with children actually decumulate faster than couples without (–17% versus –2% over a ten-year horizon).

Hurd's finding can be explained in many ways. First, it is not self-evident that only couples with children should have a bequest motive. Indeed, childless people may care for some other relatives (nephews, nieces, etc.). Kopczuk and Lupton (2007) note that Hurd's test requires a known sample separation rule (couples with children versus childless couples). They estimate a switching regression model with unknown sample separation and find that 75 percent of the elderly have a bequest motive. Bequeathed wealth accounts for 78 percent of all wealth at death, and half of it is for an explicit bequest motive. Second, parents may feel that children themselves represent insurance against health or other shocks, while childless couples need to keep a higher level of assets to self-insure against such contingencies. Indeed, there are significant differences in wealth and mortality rates between people with and without children. Third, altruism could take the form of *inter vivos* transfers rather than bequests. However, Hurd (1987) shows that eliminating the households that make these transfers does not change the basic result, and couples with children still decumulate wealth faster. Finally, remember the importance of social security wealth. Hence, to assess the validity of the life-cycle model, one must consider that a sizable share of the elderly's wealth consists of pension annuities that cannot be passed on to future generations.

12.5. THE SIZE OF INTERGENERATIONAL TRANSFERS

In the life-cycle model wealth is accumulated during the working years in order to provide for retirement. In models with an infinite time horizon, wealth is accumulated for transfer to heirs. Accordingly, in the former model most wealth is accumulated during one's own lifetime, whereas in the latter it is mostly inherited from previous generations. Hence the estimated share of inherited wealth and the extent of decumulation of wealth by the elderly can be seen as crucial in distinguishing between the two models. This explains why the measurement of bequests has received so much attention from applied research.[9]

Calculating the share of bequests in aggregate wealth is not easy, as is shown by the well-known dispute between Kotlikoff and Summers (1981) and Modigliani (1988). Starting with different assumptions and calculation methods, they reach significantly different conclusions about the proportion of inheritances in total wealth. According to Kotlikoff and Summers, inherited wealth accounts for about 80 percent of US national wealth; according to

9. Not all bequest motives clash with the life-cycle model. For example, the strategic motive is quite easily reconciled with it. The utility of bequests is reflected directly in the donor's utility function through the care and attention of potential heirs.

Modigliani, just 20 percent. Most of the difference depends on the treatment of the interest earned on transfers. Kotlikoff and Summers consider the interest earned on transfers as part of the inheritance, whereas Modigliani counts it as part of life-cycle accumulation. Therefore, according to Modigliani wealth comes largely from savings accumulated during life by the different generations, while Kotlikoff and Summers see it as mostly transferred from previous generations.

In addition to this methodological problem, measuring the share of inherited wealth poses a good many practical difficulties. One is defining the economic unit that receives and makes transfers. If this unit is the individual, then we should count transfers between spouses (inherited after the death of one of the two) as "intergenerational" transfers. If instead, perhaps more appropriately, we take the family as the decision unit, then transfers between spouses do not constitute inheritance. Unfortunately, surveys often do not distinguish between bequests or gifts from the spouse and from other donors.

The second problem is transfers to children. Whereas in principle one could consider children's consumption as a form of intergenerational transfer, it is more reasonable to consider it as parental consumption, as long as the children still live in the parental home. But in practice drawing a line is difficult. Kotlikoff and Summers treat expenditures on education for children over eighteen as an intergenerational transfer, not parental consumption, whereas Modigliani counts spending on the education of children who are not yet independent as parental consumption. The difference is not trivial: Kotlikoff and Summers calculate that expenditures on education account for about 10 percent of inherited wealth.

One way to distinguish altruism from other bequest motives is to analyze the composition of transfers. Gifts are only a fraction of total transfers, but they are unquestionably voluntary and so shed some light on transfer motives. Gale and Scholz (1994) use the US Survey of Consumer Finances to provide direct estimates of transfer wealth, distinguishing between gifts to other household members and bequests. They estimate that gifts account for at least 20 percent of net worth, so a significant portion of US wealth accumulation cannot be explained by the life-cycle model of wealth accumulation and consumption during the individual's lifetime.

A second research strategy is to analyze the distribution of inheritances among heirs. Models positing altruism suggest that transfers should be directed to the less fortunate children: these children have a higher marginal utility of consumption and thus benefit more from transfers (Tomes, 1981). But this hypothesis is contradicted by a series of empirical findings to the effect that the correlation between the income of the heirs and the share of assets inherited is essentially zero since the main tendency is to divide assets equally among children, in clear violation of any principle of altruism. However, McGarry and Schoeni (1995), using data from the Health and

Retirement Survey (HRS), show that equal transfers to all children are the exception rather than the rule, and that in most cases parents transfer less to wealthier children, and thus less to those with than without housing wealth.

Further, analysis of the distribution of inheritances among children poses difficult measurement problems. The data requirements are severe, because one needs data on testators (for instance, wills), not just the resources of the heirs. Furthermore, whereas most common-law countries place no restrictions on the share of the estate that a testator may bequeath to a single child, in civil law countries there may well be binding limits (Ellul, Pagano, and Panunzi 2010). In addition, the division of wealth itself may not be indicative of transfer motives, because altruistic parents may transfer resources to their less fortunate children in the form of gifts rather than bequests. Light and McGarry (2004) use direct HRS questions to mothers on expectations of *inter vivos* transfers. Only 8 percent of these mothers fall into the "unequal bequests" category. Those who say they intend to divide their estates unequally are asked to explain why, but only 25 percent provide an explanation that is consistent with altruism (e.g., "the oldest son has more assets than the youngest son").

The bottom line is that examination of the amount of bequests or of expectations of leaving bequests has very little to tell us about the validity of the life-cycle model or the validity of the various theories intended to explain bequests.

12.6. TRANSFER TAXES

Intergenerational transfers are taxed in most developed countries, including the United States and practically all of Europe. Two main taxes are levied on bequests: the estate tax on the total estate of the donor, regardless of the characteristics and number of recipients, and the inheritance tax, which is levied on the transfers the heirs receive. In most countries there is also a gift tax levied on inter vivos transfers.

Figure 12.3 shows that in OECD countries the proceeds of transfer taxes have fallen from 1 percent of total tax revenue in 1965 to 0.4 percent in recent years. Despite this low share, transfer taxes are the subject of intense controversy both in the United States and in Europe. Partly in response, some countries have eliminated transfer taxes entirely (e.g., Sweden), others have raised exemption levels (Italy), and still others have reduced tax rates on intergenerational transfers.

Economists disagree on the appropriateness and efficiency of transfer taxes, and have set forth arguments both for and against such taxation. It is claimed that transfer taxes inhibit capital accumulation and economic growth, threaten the survival of family businesses, depress entrepreneurial activity, and disproportionally penalize thrifty individuals who work and save. Opponents of

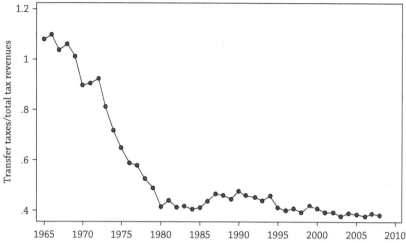

Figure 12.3: Total proceeds of transfer taxes (percentage of total tax revenues in OECD countries)

Note: Data are drawn from OECD, *Revenue Statistics 1965–2009* (Paris: OECD, 2011).

transfer taxes also claim that they are easy to avoid, produce little revenue, and are therefore not very effective in reducing inequality. Advocates of transfer taxes emphasize the positive redistributive effect and the negative externalities of the concentration of wealth, arguing that estate taxes are not distortionary because they are levied at death and are fair because they bear on unearned resources and are paid by only a few, very wealthy people.[10]

These academic and policy debates lack the support of reliable estimates of the effect of transfer taxes on the propensity to bequeath, and hence on fiscal revenues, wealth transmission and intergenerational mobility. As we know, bequests may be accidental, altruistic, strategic, or ascribable to a utility that consumers may derive from terminal wealth. The simplest case is one in which bequests are accidental. Since the length of life is uncertain, people may die with positive assets even in the absence of an explicit bequest motive. In this case transfer taxes mechanically reduce the inheritance left to future generations but have no effect on parents' wealth accumulation or the amount transferred. When bequests are accidental, their elasticity with respect to transfer taxes is equal to zero.

A second possibility is that potential donors derive utility from their own consumption and from terminal wealth, a situation that is termed "joy of

10. The fact that different institutional arrangements generate similar (and low) tax revenues could be seen as evidence that intergenerational transfer taxes produce little redistribution, but data limitations and other concurrent economic trends have prevented researchers from establishing with much confidence whether or not the reduction in transfer taxes is responsible for the increase in the inequality of wealth and income in many OECD countries in the last two decades.

giving". To illustrate this case, we assume, as in Blinder (1975), that consumers solve the following problem:

$$\max \int_0^T \frac{c_t^{1-\gamma}-1}{1-\gamma}e^{-\delta t}dt + \rho\frac{b_T^{1-\eta}-1}{1-\eta}e^{-\delta T}, \tag{12.10}$$

where δ is the discount rate, γ the elasticity of intertemporal substitution, η the elasticity of the marginal utility of bequests, ρ the intensity of the bequest motive, T the length of life, and b_T bequests net of estate taxes; we further assume $\gamma > 0$, $\delta > 0$, $\eta > 0$, and $\rho \geq 0$. The intertemporal budget constraint can be written as:

$$\int_0^T c_t e^{-rt}dt + \frac{b_T}{1-\tau}e^{-rT} = a_0 + h_0, \tag{12.11}$$

where r is the interest rate, τ is the tax rate on bequests, and the right-hand side of (12.11) is the sum of initial wealth and the present discounted value of lifetime income.

Maximization of (12.10) subject to the intertemporal budget constraint (12.11) delivers the following first-order conditions:

$$c_t^{-\gamma}e^{-\delta t} - \mu e^{-rt} = 0 \quad \text{for all } t$$

$$\rho b_T^{-\eta}e^{-\delta T} - \frac{\mu}{1-\tau}e^{-rT} = 0,$$

where μ is the multiplier associated with the intertemporal budget constraint. If $\eta = \gamma$, we obtain the following expressions for c_t and b_T:

$$c_t = c_0 e^{\frac{(r-\delta)t}{\gamma}} \tag{12.12}$$

$$b_T = c_0\left[\rho(1-\tau)e^{(r-\delta)T}\right]^{\gamma^{-1}}. \tag{12.13}$$

Combining (12.12), (12.13), and the intertemporal budget constraint, it is immediately clear that an increase in the transfer tax rate τ reduces net bequests, that is, $\partial b_T / \partial \tau < 0$.[11]

---

11. The negative effect of taxes on net bequests applies also if $\eta \neq \gamma$. Furthermore, Gale and Perozek (2001) show that the effect carries over to the case of altruistic donors who care about their own consumption and the utility of their children, transferring wealth to their heirs until the marginal utility of their own consumption is equal to that of increasing the children's consumption. The negative effect also arises when bequests are compensation for the services that donors receive from recipients, as in Bernheim, Shleifer, and Summers (1985), because estate taxes raise the pre-tax cost of the services and lower the demand for them.

The relation between transfer taxes and bequests has been the subject of a number of empirical analyses. Holtz-Eakin and Marples (2001) use HRS data and construct a measure of individual projected estate taxes using federal and state-specific transfer tax rates. Net worth is then regressed on this measure of taxes, controlling for other determinants of wealth accumulation. The parameter estimates are sensitive to model specification, but in any event the authors find a negative relationship between wealth accumulation and the estate tax. Kopczuk and Slemrod (2001) use estate tax returns from 1916 to 1996 and find that an aggregate measure of reported estates is negatively correlated with summary measures of the level of estate taxation, holding other influences constant. From a quantitative point of view, these papers conclude that the elasticity of estates with respect to transfer taxes is negative but small, between –0.1 and –0.2. Using Italian survey data and exploiting a sequence of reforms that culminated with the outright abrogation of the transfer tax in 2001, Jappelli, Padula, and Pica (2014) reach qualitatively similar conclusions. They estimate that the abolition of the tax increased the probability of making a real estate transfer by 2 percentage points. None of these studies, however, can distinguish the effect of the taxes on wealth accumulation from the effect on tax avoidance.

This chapter emphasizes two important points. First, the theories on the nature of bequests are numerous. Bequests may be involuntary (arising from lifetime uncertainty even in the absence of a specific bequest motive) or voluntary (induced by pure altruism, strategic considerations, or joy of giving). Second, distinguishing between these motives empirically is difficult, because they often lead to observationally equivalent empirical implications. In particular, a declining age-wealth profile later in life may arise either because people have no bequest motive whatsoever or because they are so altruistic as to transfer resources to their children at the time they need them most. For these reasons, empirical analysts have marshaled additional information, such as data on parental care, demographics (couples with and without children), direct information on wills, and the demand for annuities. The distinction between bequests and *inter vivos* transfers has proved more fruitful for empirical analysis, generally providing strong evidence against the pure altruistic model and also showing that, at least in part, intergenerational transfers compensate for credit market imperfections.

The study of bequests, their origin, and their size is of primary importance to understand the source of wealth inequality (De Nardi, 2015). A first source of inequality is found in any model of intertemporal choice, even in the absence of bequest motives. People have equal initial endowments, but they receive different income shocks during their working life, invest in different financial assets, and die unexpectedly, producing different wealth trajectories. Another factor in wealth inequality, of course, is that some people choose to become entrepreneurs, with access to high-return technologies. However, bequest motives add a further important source of heterogeneity, and like entrepreneurship they are particularly important in explaining the concentration at the top of the wealth distribution, hence the increase in the inequality of wealth.

CHAPTER 13

Time, Habits, and Consumer Durables

Up to this point we have assumed that the utility function for each period depends only on consumption in that period and not on other variables (such as demographics, leisure, or health), nor on consumption from other periods. This hypothesis is known as *preference separability*. We have also assumed that the household, while composed of many members, behaves as a single decision-making unit. In many cases, however, these assumptions are inappropriate.

We will now distinguish between intratemporal and intertemporal non-separability. Intertemporal (or time) non-separability is a dynamic concept that takes account of such factors as consumption habits and durability (i.e., the fact that consumers derive utility from some goods over many periods). Intratemporal non-separability is more of a static concept, a way of explaining the potential dependence of consumption on individuals' occupational status or health.

This chapter reviews the most important sources of non-separability. In models with *habit formation* the marginal utility provided by today's consumption depends on past consumption (internal habits) or on the level of aggregate consumption (external habits). Habits have been used to study the demand for addictive goods (such as cigarettes, drugs, and alcohol), and their importance depends on the intensity of their consumption.

The analysis of *durable goods* is similar in most respects to models with habits. Durable goods put a wedge between expenditure (which takes places in one period) and consumption (over multiple subsequent periods). For example, cars provide services for a number of years, not just the year in which they are bought. The current marginal utility of these services may depend on the timing of the expenditure: it will be greater if the car has been purchased recently and is thus in better condition than an older car.

Another type of non-separability is that between *consumption and leisure*. For example, the utility from reading a book depends on the amount of leisure time one has available, so presumably those who do not work and thus have more time on their hands get different utility from reading than those who work.

Another important deviation from the model with separable preferences is *home production*. Models incorporating home production assume that consumers allocate their time among three activities: work, leisure, and home production. Home production may include cooking, cleaning, gardening, child care, and so forth—that is, producing goods that could otherwise be purchased on the market at a cost. This is a further reason consumption and spending may differ. While durability introduces an intertemporal wedge between consumption and spending, home production inserts the wedge within a single period: some of the goods that the household consumes are self-produced and not bought in the market.

Finally, *collective models* of behavior assume that household members have different preferences with regard to individual consumption, individual leisure time, and public (shared) goods. Here non-separability may arise as a result of one household member's caring about another's consumption.

13.1. NON-SEPARABLE UTILITY FUNCTIONS

Before considering specific cases, it is useful to start with a formal definition of separability. Suppose that a consumer draws utility from three goods x, w, and z. We can classify various forms of non-separability with the following examples of utility functions defined over the three goods:

$$U = \begin{cases} V_1(x) + V_2(w) + V_3(z) & (13.1) \\ V_1\left(V_2(x,w), z\right) & (13.2) \\ V_1(x,w,z). & (13.3) \end{cases}$$

Case (1) is the additive separable case, in which the marginal utility of any good is independent of the amount of the other goods. Formally,

$$\frac{\partial^2 U}{\partial x \partial z} = \frac{\partial^2 U}{\partial x \partial w} = \frac{\partial^2 U}{\partial z \partial w} = 0.$$

Note that this restriction implies that the marginal rate of substitution between any two goods is independent of all other goods. Case (2) assumes that there is only weak separability between x and w, on the one hand, and z, on the other. In this case the marginal utility of x and w depends on z, but the marginal rate of substitution between x and w is independent of z. More formally:

$$\frac{\partial \left(\dfrac{\partial U / \partial x}{\partial U / \partial w} \right)}{\partial z} = 0.$$

Case (3) is the most general, because the marginal utility of any good and the marginal rate of substitution between any two goods depend on all the other goods.

Hypothesizing case (2) serves to reduce the dimensionality of the problem so that one can model only the goods one is really interested in. For instance, suppose that x and w represent expenditure on two goods (determining total consumption today, c_t), and z is total future consumption, c_{t+1}. The key aspect of weak separability above is that the choice of consumption in period $t+1$ is independent of the allocation of consumption between x and w in period t. This property is known as "two-stage budgeting". First consumers decide the intertertemporal allocation between consumption today and consumption tomorrow; then they decide the intratemporal allocation of first-stage consumption among the various goods. We refer the reader to Deaton and Muellbauer (1980) for further analysis of the issue of separability.

In previous chapters we used utility functions that depend only on consumption and assume additive (time) separability. For instance, in Chapter 1 we assume that in the life-cycle model consumers maximize the following objective function:

$$U = \sum_{t=0}^{T-1} \frac{u(c_t)}{(1+\delta)^t}.$$

Moreover, throughout the book we discuss intertemporal consumption choices without reference to leisure. This can be justified either by assuming that people do not care about leisure (i.e., they get no utility from it) or by making an explicit assumption that preferences for consumption and leisure are additively separable. For example, if:

$$U = \sum_{t=0}^{T-1} \frac{u(c_t)}{(1+\delta)^t} + \sum_{t=0}^{T-1} \frac{v(l_t)}{(1+\delta)^t},$$

preferences are separable both between periods and within each period. It is easy to see that maximizing U breaks down into separate maximization of the functions $\sum_{t=0}^{T-1} \frac{u(c_t)}{(1+\delta)^t}$ and $\sum_{t=0}^{T-1} \frac{v(l_t)}{(1+\delta)^t}$.[1]

---

1. We do not consider the problem of choosing leisure over the life cycle. See Blundell and MaCurdy (2000) for a survey of life cycle labor supply choices.

In this chapter we consider cases in which the marginal utility of current consumption is potentially affected by leisure and consumption from other periods. There are several cases of interest. First, if $U = \sum_{t=0}^{T-1} u_t \left(c_t, c_s \right) + v_t \left(l_t, l_s \right)$ with $s \neq t$, preferences are separable between consumption and leisure intra-temporally but not between periods (that is, consumers are characterized by habits, or goods by durability). We develop this case in Sections 13.2 and 13.3. Second, if $U = \sum_{t=0}^{T-1} \dfrac{u \left(c_t, l_t \right)}{\left(1 + \delta \right)^t}$, preferences are separable intertemporally but not intratemporally (work status affects the marginal utility of current consumption). Finally, the more general case (which we do not discuss) is $U = \sum_{t=0}^{T-1} u_t \left(c_t, c_s, l_t, l_s \right)$ with $s \neq t$, in which preferences are non-separable both between and within periods.

13.2. HABITS

Assume that utility in period t depends not only on consumption in that period but also on consumption in period $t - 1$, a case of time non-separability known as *internal habits*: $u \left(c_t, c_{t-1} \right)$.[2] The sign of the cross-derivative $\dfrac{\partial^2 u \left(c_t, c_{t-1} \right)}{\partial c_t \partial c_{t-1}}$ determines whether current and past consumption are complements or sub-stitutes in utility. If $\dfrac{\partial^2 u \left(c_t, c_{t-1} \right)}{\partial c_t \partial c_{t-1}} > 0$, current and past consumption are substitutes and the marginal utility of current consumption falls with c_{t-1}, whereas if $\dfrac{\partial^2 u \left(c_t, c_{t-1} \right)}{\partial c_t \partial c_{t-1}} < 0$, they are complements. In general, consumption in periods s and t are complements if an increase in consumption in period s increases the marginal utility of consumption in period t. They are substitutes if the sign of the derivative is negative.

Consider the problem of a consumer with infinite horizon under uncertainty and a generic utility function $u \left(c_t, c_{t-1} \right)$. The objective is to maximize:

$$\max E_t \sum_{\tau=0}^{\infty} \left(1 + \delta \right)^{-\tau} u \left(c_{t+\tau}, c_{t+\tau-1} \right),$$

subject to the dynamic budget constraint:

$$a_{t+1} = \left(1 + r \right) \left(a_t + y_t - c_t \right).$$

2. More general functional forms allow dependence on all past consumption levels, the entire "stock of habits".

As in previous chapters, one can use the Euler equation to describe intertemporal consumption behavior. Note that in this case there are two state variables: wealth, as in the standard problem, and the level of past consumption (which determines the consumer's habits). The value function can therefore be written as:

$$V_t\left(a_t, c_{t-1}\right) = \max_{a_{t+1}, c_t} u\left(c_t, c_{t-1}\right) + \frac{1}{1+\delta} E_t V_{t+1}\left(a_{t+1}, c_t\right),$$

subject to the constraint $a_{t+1} = (1+r)(a_t + y_t - c_t)$.

The first-order conditions of the problem are:

$$\frac{\partial u_t}{\partial c_t} - \frac{1}{1+\delta}(1+r)E_t \frac{\partial V_{t+1}}{\partial a_{t+1}} + \frac{1}{1+\delta}E_t \frac{\partial V_{t+1}}{\partial c_t} = 0 \qquad (13.4)$$

$$\frac{\partial V_t}{\partial a_t} = \frac{1+r}{1+\delta} E_t \frac{\partial V_{t+1}}{\partial a_{t+1}}, \qquad (13.5)$$

where we use the notation $u_{t+\tau} = u(c_{t+\tau}, c_{t+\tau-1})$ for every $\tau = 0,1,...$ As in the standard problem without habits, equation (13.5) implies that (when $r = \delta$) the marginal utility of wealth follows a martingale process even with habits.

Taking the derivative of the objective function with respect to the second argument of the utility function, one obtains:

$$\frac{\partial V_t}{\partial c_{t-1}} = \frac{\partial u_t}{\partial c_{t-1}}. \qquad (13.6)$$

Using (13.6) and (13.5), the first-order condition for consumption can be rewritten as:

$$\frac{\partial u_t}{\partial c_t} + \frac{1}{1+\delta} E_t \frac{\partial u_{t+1}}{\partial c_t} = \frac{\partial V_t}{\partial a_t}. \qquad (13.7)$$

Considering the value of (13.7) in period $t+1$ and taking expectation as of period t yields:

$$E_t \frac{\partial u_{t+1}}{\partial c_{t+1}} + \frac{1}{1+\delta} E_t \frac{\partial u_{t+2}}{\partial c_{t+1}} = E_t \frac{\partial V_{t+1}}{\partial a_{t+1}}. \qquad (13.8)$$

And finally, multiplying both sides by $(1+r)(1+\delta)^{-1}$:

$$\frac{1+r}{1+\delta}\left[E_t \frac{\partial u_{t+1}}{\partial c_{t+1}} + \frac{1}{1+\delta} E_t \frac{\partial u_{t+2}}{\partial c_{t+1}} \right] = \frac{1+r}{1+\delta} E_t \frac{\partial V_{t+1}}{\partial a_{t+1}}. \qquad (13.9)$$

Since the right-hand sides of (13.8) and (13.9) coincide (from equation (13.5)), one can equate the left-hand sides and obtain the following Euler equation:

$$\frac{\partial u_t}{\partial c_t} + \frac{1}{1+\delta} E_t \frac{\partial u_{t+1}}{\partial c_t} = \frac{1+r}{1+\delta} \left[E_t \left(\frac{\partial u_{t+1}}{\partial c_{t+1}} + \frac{1}{1+\delta} \frac{\partial u_{t+2}}{\partial c_{t+1}} \right) \right]. \qquad (13.10)$$

If preferences are intertemporally separable, $\dfrac{\partial u_{t+1}}{\partial c_t} = \dfrac{\partial u_{t+2}}{\partial c_{t+1}} = 0$, and equation (13.10) collapses to the standard Euler equation without habits.

To interpret the Euler equation (13.10), suppose that $\dfrac{\partial u_{t+1}}{\partial c_t} < 0$, that is, current utility decreases with past consumption so that levels of consumption in the two periods are substitutes in utility. In other words, having consumed a lot in period t reduces the utility of additional consumption in period $t+1$, so that when the consumer considers consuming more in period $t+1$, the total utility obtained is reduced by the high consumption of the previous period. Therefore, habits reduce the variability of consumption across time and ensure that individuals seek to maintain the same levels of consumption as in the past. While in the standard case the marginal utility of consumption follows a martingale, with habits it does not (equation (13.10)), so in this case the optimal consumption rule is more complex than under time separability. Whenever an individual chooses consumption, intertemporal choice involves more than just a sequence of two periods: consumption today depends on consumption yesterday, and by the same token also affects tomorrow's consumption decisions.

One implication of the model with habits is that the Euler equation no longer has the property that consumption innovations are independent of lagged variables. Depending on the number of lags in habits, in the case of time non-separability one must modify the orthogonality condition to account for lags that affect current consumption. To see this, consider the case with quadratic utility,

$$u\left(c_t, c_{t-1}\right) = a\left(c_t + \alpha c_{t-1}\right) - \frac{b}{2}\left(c_t + \alpha c_{t-1}\right)^2,$$

and assume $r = \delta = 0$. In this case, equation (13.10) reduces to:

$$\alpha E_t \Delta c_{t+2} + \left(1 + \alpha^2\right) E_t \Delta c_{t+1} + \alpha \Delta c_t = 0.$$

If $\alpha = 0$, we obtain the standard random walk equation $E_t \Delta c_{t+1} = 0$. However, if $\alpha \neq 0$, changes in consumption are autocorrelated and are affected not only by past changes in consumption but also by the expectations of future changes. This example may be used to explain both a failure of the orthogonality test (because expected changes in consumption depend on past changes) and excess sensitivity of consumption changes to expected income changes (because the latter determine future consumption changes). Failure of the orthogonality test and excess sensitivity may therefore be signs that preferences are misspecified.

Among the many empirical studies that support the habit hypothesis, one of the most original and complete is offered by Meghir and Weber (1996). These authors propose a model with consumption habits and borrowing constraints and report no evidence of excess sensitivity of consumption to expected income changes when they take consumption habits into account. The study concludes that excess sensitivity results exclusively from the misspecification of the utility function.

13.3. DURABLE GOODS

Unlike non-durables, which are consumed practically when purchased, durable goods are consumed over more than one period, for as long as their services last. A general formulation of the utility function assumes that utility depends on consumption of non-durable goods c as well as the stock of durable goods k. Assuming for simplicity that the horizon is infinite, the consumer's problem is:

$$\max E_t \sum_{\tau=0}^{\infty} (1+\delta)^{-\tau} u(\phi c_{t+\tau} + \eta k_{t+\tau}). \tag{13.11}$$

This utility function considers not expenditure on durable goods but the stock of durables k available to the consumer. However, the stock k is linked to the flow of spending on durable goods, c^d, through the following law of motion:

$$k_{t+1} = (1-\lambda)k_t + c_{t+1}^d, \tag{13.12}$$

where λ is the rate of depreciation of the stock of durables. For example, in each period the market value of a car k_t is reduced by an amount equal to λk_t. At the same time, in every period the owner might face a cost c_{t+1}^d that increases the value of the car in the next period (for example, repairs, accessories, etc.). If $\lambda = 1$, the good is non-durable and the model reduces to that considered in the previous chapters.[3]

---

3. In this model the depreciation rate is a technological parameter. Browning and Crossley (2009) show that an important source of consumption smoothing is slowing down the replacement of certain small durable goods (such as socks, pillows, and plates).

Note that the objective function (13.11) exhibits both intertemporal non-separability—because stocks of durables are intertemporally linked through the law of motion (13.12)—and intratemporal non-separability between non-durable consumption and the stock of durables (if $\eta \neq 0$). For example, the marginal utility of taking an old car to the car wash is less than that of taking a brand-new one.

For simplicity, however, in this section we follow Mankiw (1982) and consider a case in which the utility function depends only on the stock of durable goods (i.e., we assume that $\phi = 0$ and $\eta = 1$):

$$\max E_t \sum_{\tau=0}^{\infty} (1+\delta)^{-\tau} u(k_{t+\tau}).$$

Using identity (13.12) we can write the dynamic budget constraint as:

$$a_{t+1} = (1+r)\left[a_t + y_t - k_t + (1-\lambda)k_{t-1}\right].$$

The problem can be solved by writing the value function:

$$V_t(a_t) = \max_{a_{t+1}, k_t} u(k_t) + \frac{1}{1+\delta} E_t V_{t+1}(a_{t+1}),$$

subject to the constraint $a_{t+1} = (1+r)[a_t + y_t - k_t + (1-\lambda)k_{t-1}]$. The Euler equation is identical to that of the model with non-durable goods:

$$V_t'(a_t) = \frac{1+r}{1+\delta} E_t V_{t+1}'(a_{t+1}).$$

The envelope condition can be written as:

$$u'(k_t) = \frac{r+\lambda}{1+r} V_t'(a_t),$$

where $\dfrac{r+\lambda}{1+r}$ is called the user cost of a durable good. As for any investment good, the cost of holding one unit of a durable good is equal to the opportunity cost (the interest rate r) plus the depreciation rate (λ). Substituting the envelope condition into the Euler equation, we can express the marginal utility of the stock of durable goods as:

$$u'(k_t) = \frac{1+r}{1+\delta} E_t u'(k_{t+1}), \tag{13.13}$$

which is the same Euler equation that one obtains for non-durable goods.

If the utility function is quadratic, $u(k_t) = ak_t - (b/2)k_t^2$ and $r = \delta$, the Euler equation can also be written as:

$$k_{t+1} = k_t + \varepsilon_{t+1},$$

where ε_{t+1} is the innovation in the stock of durable goods, namely: $\varepsilon_{t+1} = k_{t+1} - E_t(k_{t+1})$. The stock of durables follows a martingale process, just like non-durables consumption. Using the accounting identity (13.12), it is straightforward to derive an expression for the expenditure on durable consumption goods:

$$c_{t+1}^d = c_t^d + \varepsilon_{t+1} - (1 - \lambda)\varepsilon_t.$$

Since the change in the stock of durables follows a random walk, the change in their consumption (Δc_{t+1}^d) does not follow a random walk (as in the permanent-income model of Chapter 4), but rather is an MA(1) process. From an econometric point of view it is no longer true that the change in consumption is orthogonal to past information, because $E_t(\Delta c_{t+1}^d) = -(1 - \lambda)\varepsilon_t \neq 0$. A consumer who has bought a new car in period t ($\varepsilon_t = \Delta k_t > 0$) is less likely to buy one in period $t+1$ than a consumer who has not just renewed his stock of cars. This dampening or mean reversion effect is greatest with goods with long durability (or low λ) and vanishes as $\lambda \to 0$. Therefore, the durability of some consumption components might induce a correlation between past income changes and durable purchases, so as to induce excess sensitivity of consumption to past income changes.

The lesson from this example is that the standard Euler equation relies on the assumption of separability between consumption of durables and non-durables. This poses a challenge for empirical research that relies on measures of consumption that do not distinguish goods according to durability. Even expenditures on goods that are classified as non-durable (clothing and books, to cite two) may have a significant component of durability, as they often provide services well beyond the year of purchase.

The MA(1) implication is rejected by the data (both in Mankiw's study and in subsequent research). Possible reasons for the empirical failure are that the model considers the demand for durable goods in isolation, ignoring the interaction between durable and non-durable goods and relative price dynamics. Moreover, the model assumes that the stock of durables can be changed instantly and at no cost.

An extension of the foregoing frictionless model considers that durables purchasers may face adjustment costs (search costs or imperfections in the resale market), as well as the importance of indivisibility (which typically characterizes durable goods). Two approaches have been taken to address this issue. One (Bernanke, 1984) assumes that the cost of adjusting durables is quadratic, the second (Grossman and Laroque, 1990), that it is fixed.

Bernanke shows that if the stock of "desired" durables that would be chosen in the absence of adjustment costs, k^*, is proportional to permanent income, and if the latter follows a martingale, then the actual stock of durables adjusts according to the equation: $k_{t+1} = k_t + \psi\left(k_{t+1}^* - k_t \right)$, where ψ is the speed of convergence on the optimal level. Note that when $\psi = 1$ consumers adjust immediately to the desired stock of durables and the model collapses to that of Mankiw. Bernanke cannot reject the permanent-income model with quadratic utility using PSID micro data on automobile purchases.

The main empirical problem with the quadratic adjustment costs model is that it still assumes that individuals make frequent purchases of durable goods, although not as frequent as in the frictionless model. In the real world, however, durable purchases are lumpy and infrequent. People buy a new car only every five or six years, rather than continuously renewing their stock, so that in a given cross section only a small fraction of respondents report expenditure on cars. Furthermore, people may defer adjustment toward the optimal stock according to market conditions (i.e., the price of the relevant durable goods) as well as income uncertainty, credit availability, and so forth. These considerations have led researchers to adapt a model known as (S,s), originally developed in operation research, to the context of durable goods.

Figure 13.1 exemplifies the (S,s) rule followed by consumers in this model. The optimal stock of durables is k^*, and its evolution is known as the internal return point. The actual stock of durables evolves over time because of appreciation/depreciation or changes in economic conditions. The stock is not adjusted to the optimal level (i.e., adjustment is infrequent) as long as it fluctuates between the upper S and lower s bands (called triggers). If, however, the stock hits one of the two bands (implying that the consumer has too much or too little of the good), then there is a "return" to the optimal level,

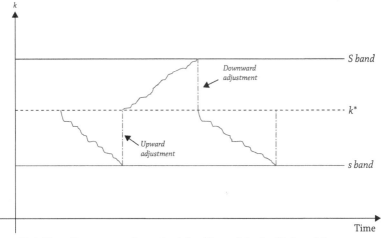

Figure 13.1: The adjustment to the optimal durable stock in the (S,s) model

implying a lumpy, large adjustment. The process starts over with another cycle of appreciation (movement toward the upper band S) or depreciation (movement toward the lower band s) until another adjustment is triggered.

In the last two decades various papers have used this framework to characterize the determinants of the optimal stock and of the (S,s) bands, expanding the basic setup to allow for credit market imperfections and income uncertainty. These models are analytically complex and hard to estimate with microeconomic data. Lam (1991) uses PSID data to estimate the parameters of a threshold adjustment model under an extended permanent-income hypothesis, finding evidence for liquidity constraints and resale market imperfections. Eberly (1994) studies car purchases using data from the SCF and finds that greater uncertainty increases the width of the inaction bands; however, she does not characterize the effects of uncertainty on the probability of adjustment. Foote, Hurst, and Leahy (2000) study not the size but the frequency of durable stock adjustment. They find that in the CEX this frequency is negatively related to the imputed variance of household income obtained from regressions estimated with PSID data (although this proxy may be contaminated by income measurement error and prediction errors due to the small dataset). Attanasio (2000) estimates a model of car purchases on a sample of US households drawn from the CEX. He characterizes trigger and return points in reduced form rather than attempting to estimate the structural parameters of the model (such as the extent of adjustment costs).

Bertola, Guiso, and Pistaferri (2005) use rich data from the Italian SHIW, with subjective measures of income uncertainty and information on stocks and purchases of three categories of durable goods (vehicles, furniture, and jewelry), to assess the effects of uncertainty (as well as of observed and unobserved heterogeneity of tastes and other factors) on the frequency and size of adjustment. In the frictionless model, consumers would attempt to keep the ratio between the stock of durables and non-durable consumption constant. The authors find that the probability of adjusting the stock of vehicles is lower when the initial ratio is higher and there is less uncertainty facing the consumer, but the size of adjustment is positively correlated with uncertainty. Both findings are consistent with an (S,s) rule. Results for furniture and jewelry are less supportive of the model.[4]

Purchases of durable goods respond to many factors affecting their user cost, including the functioning of secondary markets, and tax policy. For example, Mian and Sufi (2012) evaluate the impact of a 2009 tax incentive for car replacement in the United States. They exploit variation across cities in the number of potential beneficiaries of the program, and find that it

---

4. Padula (2004) derives a Euler equation for non-durable consumption where durable goods appear as a conditioning good.

induced a strong positive effect on car purchase in the short run; however, within a year, the effect reverses to the mean, offsetting most of the initial purchases.

13.4. LEISURE

In this section we maintain the assumption that preferences are intertemporally separable but relax intratemporal separability between consumption and leisure.[5] The model in this section assumes that a consumer can choose freely not only whether to work but also how many hours.[6] These assumptions are violated when there is labor market rationing (involuntary unemployment) or inflexible work schedules. In practice, contracts usually set minimum working hours and limit the ability of firms to use overtime work.

In a model in which consumption and leisure are non-separable, the consumer's objective function (assuming an infinite horizon) is:

$$\max E_t \sum_{\tau=0}^{\infty} (1+\delta)^{-\tau} u(c_{t+\tau}, l_{t+\tau}),$$

subject to the dynamic budget constraint for $\tau = 0,1,...,$

$$a_{t+\tau+1} = (1+r)\left[a_{t+\tau} + w_{t+\tau}(1-l_{t+\tau}) - c_{t+\tau}\right],$$

and the constraint on total available time,

$$0 \leq l_{t+\tau} \leq 1,$$

where l is leisure, $1-l$ labor supply (so l is expressed as a proportion of total time available), and w is the wage rate. We take the price of consumption as a numeraire and normalize it to 1. The wage rate is typically a random variable, and for simplicity we assume that it is exogenous. Finally, we also assume that the interest rate is constant.

Define the value function of the problem:

$$V_t(a_t) = \max_{a_{t+1}, c_t, l_t} u(c_t, l_t) + (1+\delta)^{-1} E_t V_{t+1}(a_{t+1}),$$

5. A further interesting case of intratemporal non-separability is between public and private consumption. For example, the utility from driving a car may depend on the condition of the roads.
6. Our focus will be on intertemporal consumption choices. The literature on life cycle labor supply choices is vast, and we do not cover it here. See MaCurdy (1981) and, for a recent survey, Blundell and MaCurdy (2000).

subject to the dynamic budget constraint and the time constraint. Unlike the case of habits, where we had two state variables (assets and lagged consumption) and one control variable (consumption), here we have one state variable (assets) and two control variables (consumption and leisure). From the dynamic budget constraint and the value function, one obtains two first-order conditions:

$$\frac{\partial u(c_t, l_t)}{\partial c_t} - \frac{(1+r)}{(1+\delta)} E_t V'_{t+1}(a_{t+1}) = 0, \tag{13.14}$$

$$\frac{\partial u(c_t, l_t)}{\partial l_t} - \frac{(1+r)}{(1+\delta)} w_t E_t V'_{t+1}(a_{t+1}) \geq 0. \tag{13.15}$$

Equation (13.15) holds with equality when consumers choose an interior solution $l_t < 1$. If instead the solution is at the corner $l_t = 1$, equation (13.15) holds as an inequality. With an interior solution, the marginal rate of substitution between consumption and leisure is:

$$\frac{\dfrac{\partial u(c_t, l_t)}{\partial l_t}}{\dfrac{\partial u(c_t, l_t)}{\partial c_t}} = w_t. \tag{13.16}$$

Equation (13.16) shows that this rate is equal to the relative price of leisure, that is, the wage rate.

Consider now the corner solution. The decision to work depends on the comparison between the wage offered, w, and the reservation wage w^*, defined as the wage at which a person is indifferent between working and not. It is defined implicitly by the marginal rate of substitution (13.16) evaluated at the corner solution $l_t = 1$:

$$\frac{\dfrac{\partial u(c_t, 1)}{\partial l_t}}{\dfrac{\partial u(c_t, 1)}{\partial c_t}} = w_t^*.$$

If $w \geq w^*$, the individual decides to work; if $w < w^*$, he decides not to.

In what follows we assume an interior solution $(w \geq w^*)$, so equation (13.15) holds with equality. The optimal solutions are the two policy functions relating consumption and leisure to the value of assets, $c_t^*(a_t)$ and $l_t^*(a_t)$. By the steps described in Chapter 4 to solve dynamic programming problems, we obtain Euler equations describing intertemporal consumption and leisure choices:

$$\frac{\partial u(c_t, l_t)}{\partial c_t} - \frac{(1+r)}{(1+\delta)} E_t \frac{\partial u(c_{t+1}, l_{t+1})}{\partial c_{t+1}} = 0 \qquad (13.17)$$

$$\frac{\partial u(c_t, l_t)}{\partial l_t} - \frac{(1+r)}{(1+\delta)} E_t \frac{w_t}{w_{t+1}} \frac{\partial u(c_{t+1}, l_{t+1})}{\partial l_{t+1}} = 0. \qquad (13.18)$$

If preferences are intratemporally separable, the marginal utility of consumption $\dfrac{\partial u(c_t, l_t)}{\partial c_t}$ is independent of leisure and the Euler equation for consumption is the same as those of the previous chapters. Hence, the intertemporal allocation of consumption is not affected by that of leisure. If instead $\dfrac{\partial u(c_t, l_t)}{\partial c_t}$ is a function of leisure, then the intertemporal allocation leisure does affect that of consumption.

The reallocation of consumption along the optimal intertemporal path under non-separability depends on the sign of the cross-derivative $\dfrac{\partial^2 u(c,l)}{\partial c \partial l}$.[7] In particular, consumption and leisure can be Frisch complements $\left(\dfrac{\partial^2 u(c,l)}{\partial c \partial l} > 0 \right)$ or substitutes $\left(\dfrac{\partial^2 u(c,l)}{\partial c \partial l} < 0 \right)$. For example, transportation costs produce substitutability between consumption and leisure because of commuting costs, while such public utilities as gas and electricity imply complementarity, because more time spent at home means more resources spent on heat or cooling.

Closed-form solutions can be obtained specifying a tractable utility function, assuming interior solutions and positing that consumption and leisure are jointly log-normal. For example, if $u(c_t, l_t) = \dfrac{\left(c_t^\alpha l_t^{1-\alpha} \right)^{1-\gamma}}{1-\gamma}$, equation (13.17) can be written as:

$$\frac{1+r}{1+\delta} E_t \left[\left(\frac{c_{t+1}}{c_t} \right)^{\alpha(1-\gamma)-1} \left(\frac{l_{t+1}}{l_t} \right)^{(1-\alpha)(1-\gamma)} \right] - 1 = 0,$$

7. Note that the elasticities that we discuss in the context of Euler equation estimates are all Frisch elasticities, since by the definition of Euler equation the marginal utility of wealth is constant along the optimal path. In contrast, Marshallian elasticities measure the total effect of changes in consumption with respect to changes in the price of leisure (the wage), allowing for both intertemporal substitution and wealth effects arising from changes in the budget constraint.

where α can be interpreted as the "budget share" allocated to the consumption of goods and $(1-\alpha)$ as that allocated to the consumption of leisure. Under these assumptions, one obtains an expression for expected consumption growth:[8]

$$E_t \Delta \ln c_{t+1} = \beta_0 (r - \delta) + \beta_1 E_t (\Delta \ln l_{t+1})$$
$$+ \beta_2 \operatorname{var}_t \left\{ \left[\alpha(1-\gamma) - 1 \right] \Delta \ln c_{t+1} + (1-\alpha)(1-\gamma) \Delta \ln l_{t+1} \right\}, \quad (13.19)$$

where

$$\beta_0 = \left[1 - \alpha(1-\gamma) \right]^{-1}, \beta_1 = \left[(1-\alpha)(1-\gamma) \right] \left[1 - \alpha(1-\gamma) \right]^{-1}, \beta_2 = \left\{ 2 \left[1 - \alpha(1-\gamma) \right] \right\}^{-1},$$

and the first and second moments of the joint distribution of consumption and leisure are conditional on the information set available to the individual in period t.

We can now note several interesting properties of the solution. First, the Euler equation (13.19) is an equilibrium relationship between expected consumption growth $E_t \Delta \ln c_{t+1}$ and the expected growth rate of leisure $E_t \Delta \ln l_{t+1}$, not a relationship between endogenous and exogenous variables.

Second, equation (13.19) shows that expected consumption grows because of the usual intertemporal substitution motive (if $r > \delta$), but also if the consumer expects leisure to grow in the future and consumption and leisure are complements (which requires $\gamma < 1$), because consumers have greater consumption needs in the state in which they work less.

Finally, consumption can be deferred for precautionary reasons. Here, however, both the conditional variance of consumption and that of leisure time induce precautionary saving. Greater consumption volatility is associated with higher consumption growth, as under separability (people compress current consumption and save in order to guard against low future consumption). Suppose now that leisure and consumption are complements: consumers desire more consumption when they have more leisure. Here, the expected volatility of leisure reinforces the precautionary saving effect. Low (2005) studies this case and observes that when wage prospects become more uncertain people may respond not only by precautionary saving but also by working longer hours.[9]

8. We use the approximation $\ln \left(\dfrac{1+r}{1+\delta} \right) \approx r - \delta$.

9. Pistaferri (2003) estimates the effect of an increase in the conditional variance of wage growth on labor supply and finds that while the estimate is statistically significant and in agreement with the theory, the effect of wage risk on labor supply appears negligible: a 10 percent increase in the conditional variance of future wages increases current labor supply by only 0.5 percent. Even doubling wage risk would hardly affect labor supply.

Non-separability between consumption and leisure provides an additional explanation for the excess sensitivity of consumption to expected income growth. This was first noticed by Heckman (1974) as an explanation for the correlation between consumption and income growth in a life-cycle framework. Equation (13.19) shows that expected consumption growth depends on the expected growth rate of leisure (and hence the expected growth rate of hours worked). But given a fixed wage rate, expected positive growth in hours predicts growth in earnings. If the Euler equation omits the growth rate of leisure, one may find evidence of excess sensitivity simply because of this omitted variable and not because the model fails.

Attanasio and Weber (1995) estimate the Euler equation for consumption using CEX data. Omitting leisure and demographic variables, they find a positive and statistically significant effect of (instrumented) income growth on consumption growth: 0.42. However, when they also include indicators of labor supply (the change in the spouse's labor market participation and in hours worked), the income coefficient is sharply reduced, to 0.11, and becomes insignificant. As in the case of consumer habits, this finding of excess sensitivity depends on misspecification of preferences.

There is extensive evidence of non-separability between consumption and leisure. Browning, Hansen, and Heckman (1999) discuss the empirical evidence on whether consumption and leisure are Frisch complements or substitutes. In the framework considered in this section, there is no distinction between the extensive margin (whether to work or not) and the intensive margin (how many hours to work). This issue is taken up by Blundell, Pistaferri, and Saporta-Eksten (2016) in a model of consumption and family labor supply. They find that consumption and hours are Frisch substitutes at the intensive but not at the extensive margin. One likely explanation is that certain goods are complements, with work at the extensive margin (transportation costs), while the consumption of other goods increases when people are at home, making them substitutes for work at the intensive margin (gas, heating, electricity).

13.5. HOME PRODUCTION

In home production models, the total time available is allocated not only to work and leisure but also to a third activity, home production. Hence, individuals may choose to produce certain consumption goods at home instead of purchasing them in the market. Common examples are gardening, home maintenance, and child care. One way to formalize this idea is to write a production function for home-produced goods that use as inputs home production time and goods purchased in the market.

Baxter and Jermann (1999) were among the first to introduce a formal home production model in the context of intertemporal choice. Suppose that consumers solve the problem:

$$\max E_t \sum_{\tau=0}^{\infty} (1+\delta)^{-\tau} V\left(c_{t+\tau}, x_{t+\tau}, l_{t+\tau}\right),$$

where the period utility function is $V\left(c_{t+\tau}, x_{t+\tau}, l_{t+\tau}\right) = \dfrac{\psi\left(c_{t+\tau}, x_{t+\tau}\right)^{1-\gamma}}{1-\gamma} v\left(l_{t+\tau}\right).$

Here, c stands for market goods, x refers to home-produced goods, and the function $\psi(c,x)$ is a linearly homogeneous aggregator of the two consumption goods (the simplest version of which is $\psi(c,x) = c + x$). The maximization problem is subject to three constraints for $\tau = 0, 1, \dots$. The first constraint is the dynamic budget constraint:

$$a_{t+\tau+1} = (1+r)\left[a_{t+\tau} + w_{t+\tau}\left(1 - l_{t+\tau} - n_{t+\tau}\right) - c_{t+\tau}\right].$$

The second is the time constraint,

$$l_{t+\tau} + n_{t+\tau} + h_{t+\tau} = 1,$$

where n and h are hours devoted to home production and work, respectively. Finally, home production is assumed to depend linearly only on hours devoted to home production:

$$x_{t+\tau} = A n_{t+\tau}.$$

Solving the problem delivers the modified Euler equation:

$$\frac{\partial V_t(\cdot)}{\partial c_t} = \frac{1+r}{1+\delta} E_t \frac{\partial V_{t+1}(\cdot)}{\partial c_{t+1}},$$

or

$$\psi\left(c_t, x_t\right)^{-\gamma} \frac{\partial \psi\left(c_t, x_t\right)}{\partial c_t} v\left(l_t\right) = \frac{1+r}{1+\delta} E_t \psi\left(c_{t+1}, x_{t+1}\right)^{-\gamma} \frac{\partial \psi\left(c_{t+1}, x_{t+1}\right)}{\partial c_{t+1}} v\left(l_{t+1}\right). \quad (13.20)$$

Together with the intratemporal marginal rate of substitution conditions,

$$\frac{\dfrac{\partial V_t(.)}{\partial l_t}}{\dfrac{\partial V_t(.)}{\partial c_t}} = \frac{\psi\left(c_t,x_t\right)^{1-\gamma}\dfrac{\partial v\left(l_t\right)}{\partial l_t}}{\left(1-\gamma\right)\psi\left(c_t,x_t\right)^{-\gamma}\dfrac{\partial \psi\left(c_t,x_t\right)}{\partial c_t}v\left(l_t\right)} = w_t$$

$$\frac{\dfrac{\partial V_t(.)}{\partial x_t}}{\dfrac{\partial V_t(.)}{\partial c_t}} = \frac{\dfrac{\partial \psi\left(c_t,x_t\right)}{\partial x_t}}{\dfrac{\partial \psi\left(c_t,x_t\right)}{\partial c_t}} = \frac{w_t}{A}.$$

Note that the marginal rate of substitution between leisure and market consumption equals the wage rate (exactly as in the foregoing), while the marginal rate of substitution between market and home-produced goods is equal to the price of x (w/A) relative to the numeraire (which is normalized to 1).

Baxter and Jermann consider a first-order approximation of the Euler equation (13.20), which delivers a relation between expected consumption growth and expected wage growth:

$$E_t\Delta \ln c_{t+1} = \theta_0\left(r-\delta\right) + \theta_1 E_t\left(\Delta \ln w_{t+1}\right),$$

where the parameter θ_1 is a complicated function of, among other things, the elasticity of substitution between market goods and home-produced goods. The most plausible parameter configuration is one in which $\theta_1 > 0$. The intuition here is that expected rises in the wage rate increase the cost of producing at home and hence imply that people will replace home-produced goods with goods purchased in the market, inducing positive growth in market consumption. Using macro data, Baxter and Jermann find that the permanent-income hypothesis is true but that the omission of home production generates spurious evidence of excess sensitivity insofar as market consumption responds to expected income growth due to the mechanism just described.

One of the most interesting applications of the home production model is by Aguiar and Hurst (2005). They use a version of the home production model to explain the so-called retirement consumption puzzle, which is that consumption falls after retirement even though the concurrent decline in income is very largely predictable. Aguiar and Hurst argue that while spending on market goods does indeed decline, total consumption (including home-produced goods) does not. For example, food spending falls but caloric intake does not, as pensioners either produce lettuce and tomatoes in their vegetable patch or spend some of their new leisure time shopping for better prices, as by collecting supermarket coupons. One of their findings is that about 20 percent of the fall in food spending at retirement reflects more intensive shopping (resulting in more economical purchases) and the remaining 80 percent is due to home production. In short, there is not actually any decline in food consumption.

13.6. UNITARY VERSUS COLLECTIVE MODELS

So far we have assumed that a household acts as if it were a unitary decision maker, maximizing a well-behaved utility function subject to a budget constraint that defines the possible alternatives. Consumption and labor supply are taken as the result of a process of maximization by the "household", disregarding the fact that it is composed of various members who in practice sometimes disagree on the allocation between consumption and leisure. Since this approach implicitly assumes that all households act as a single individual, it has come to be known as the unitary model of consumption.

In the past two decades the unitary model has been criticized for the empirical failure of some of its implications, chiefly the so-called income-pooling hypothesis, which holds that all resources are put in common, so their source or distribution among members does not affect the allocation of consumption and leisure. A second reason for dissatisfaction with the unitary model is its inadequacy from the policy standpoint—as when one wants to compare tax regimes allowing for couples to file joint returns with those in which each individual is taxed separately. Another interesting policy area is the effect of conditional cash transfers (payments to households who send their children to school, say), and in particular if it matters which member receives the transfer.

Taking seriously the fact that households are made up of different individuals and allowing that they may have diverging but individually rational objectives and preferences requires alternative models. We refer the reader to the excellent surveys by Vermeulen (2002) and Chiapporri and Mazzocco (2015) for an exposition of the main properties of the static unitary and collective models. In this section we first sketch the unitary model in an intertemporal context and then review some of the main results of collective intertemporal models. In both cases we use simplified versions of the models, assuming that household members draw utility only from consumption. However, most models in the literature assume non-separable utility functions defined for leisure as well as consumption and derive the demand function for them as a function of individual and household resources (avoiding our restrictive assumption).

Consider a household with two members, husband (H) and wife (W). Assume that the couple draws utility from consumption (c) and that the labor of both members is supplied inelastically (for simplicity), so they receive incomes y^H and y^W and total income is $y = y^H + y^W$. For simplicity we do not distinguish between private goods (for instance, clothing) and shared goods (such as home rental). Nor do we consider possible non-separabilities between the consumption and leisure of both household members, and we rule out home production. (Interesting extensions relaxing each of these restrictions have received attention in the literature, mostly in the static context.)

With these assumptions, in the unitary model, the problem is:

$$\max u(c_0) + \beta E_0 u(c_1)$$

s.t. a_0 *given*

$$a_{t+1} = (1+r)\left(a_t + y_t^H + y_t^W - c_t\right) \quad \text{for } t = 0, 1$$

$$a_2 = 0.$$

As we know from Chapter 4, the solution to this problem is a consumption function in which consumption depends on initial assets and the expected present discounted value of the two members' income. Consider, as a special case, quadratic preferences and $\beta = r = a_0 = 0$. Then expected consumption in both periods is:

$$c_0 = c_1 = \frac{\left(y_0^H + y_0^W\right) + E_0\left(y_1^H + y_1^W\right)}{2} = \frac{y_0 + E_0 y_1}{2}.$$

In this model, optimal household consumption in each period depends only on the sum of individual incomes $y_t = \left(y_t^H + y_t^W\right)$, but not on which member receives income or how income is distributed (i.e., distribution shares such as y_t^H / y_t).

A testable implication of the unitary model is that consumption should be independent of such distribution shares, *conditioning* on pooled income y_t. Earlier work typically rejected this implication of the model. However, since these tests amount to simply regressing consumption on pooled income and income shares, they can give spurious results if the income shares are endogenous. A number of recent papers propose testing for income pooling by considering government transfer policies that redistribute resources within households without altering the household's budget constraint. For example, Ward-Batts (2008) refutes income pooling using an exogenous change in the intrahousehold distribution of income provided by a change in the UK family allowance program. Her estimates suggest that children and mothers benefited at the expense of fathers when the new policy shifted income within households from men to women, but that there was no comparable variation among couples with no children. Attanasio and Lechene (2002), studying the Progresa program in Mexico, which transfers welfare resources exclusively to the woman within the household, also reject income pooling. In addition, they find evidence that the wife's decision-making power within the household depends on her income share.

In keeping with this empirical evidence, Chiappori (1988) introduced models in which households are treated as a collection of individual agents, each with distinct preferences and resources. To see the essential ingredients and implications of the collective models in an intertemporal context, we can modify the problem set out above to consider the case of two consumption bundles, that of the husband (c^H) and that of the wife (c^W). Assume that there is also a public good Q, shared by the two members (say, an apartment). Also, saving decisions are made jointly.

The household now has two distinct utility functions: $u_H(Q, c^H)$ and $u_W(Q, c^W)$. These preferences are said to be egotistic, because each member cares only about his or her own consumption. At the opposite extreme, one may consider altruistic preferences, in which both husband and wife are concerned directly with the other's consumption and not just with the utility that he or she derives from it, that is, $u_H(Q, c^H, c^W)$ and $u_W(Q, c^W, c^H)$. An intermediate case is Becker's "caring" preferences, in which utility functions depend on a person's own consumption as well as the spouse's utility: $v_H\left[u_H(Q, c^H), u_W(Q, c^W)\right]$ and $v_W\left[u_H(Q, c^H), u_W(Q, c^W)\right]$.

The literature adopts various assumptions concerning the way in which husband and wife make decisions and reach agreement about the distribution of resources within the household. If the spouses cooperate, decisions are Pareto efficient. If they do not, then the decision-making process ends up being a "game" between the two agents, and efficiency is not generally guaranteed. In the rest of this section we examine the cooperative case.[10]

With Pareto efficiency (and full information), the two-period collective model maximizes the weighted average of the utilities of the spouses:

$$\max \mu_H\left[u_H\left(c_0^H, Q_0\right) + \beta_H E_0 u_H\left(c_1^H, Q_1\right)\right] + \mu_W\left[u_W\left(c_0^W, Q_0\right) + \beta_W E_0 u_W\left(c_1^W, Q_1\right)\right]$$

s.t. a_0 given

$$a_{t+1} = (1+r)\left[a_t + y_t^H + y_t^W - p_t\left(c_{Ht} + c_{Wt}\right)\right] \quad \text{for } t = 0,1$$

$$a_2 = 0.$$

---

10. This case is more likely to be relevant empirically if there are mechanisms that facilitate the enforcement of Pareto-efficient equilibria, such as formal legal contracts (i.e., prenuptial agreements), love, mutual trust, or (in dynamic cases) provision for punishment when one party deviates from the equilibrium (i.e., divorce or reversion to non-cooperative decision making).

The Pareto weights μ_H and μ_W reflect the natural interpretation in terms of decision-making power: they capture the relative bargaining power of the two members and are a function of prices, income shares, and some distribution factors (for instance, divorce laws that alter the relative power of one spouse or the other). Since the solution does not change if one divides the objective function by the sum of the two weights, only the relative weights $\mu = \dfrac{\mu^H}{\mu^H + \mu^W}$ and $1 - \mu = \dfrac{\mu^W}{\mu^H + \mu^W}$ matter. In a limiting case, $\mu = 0$ or $\mu = 1$, and one of the spouses has no say in the household's decisions.

In an intertemporal framework, the solution of the problem will be given by individual rather than household Euler equations. From these, and under some assumptions regarding preferences, one can obtain individual (and public) consumption functions, which will typically depend in very complicated ways on Pareto weights (and hence the income shares of the two spouses) as well as total income and individual preferences. These collective models therefore reject income pooling, and they represent one way of rationally explaining the empirical evidence found above.

Whereas in a static context (and with no uncertainty) the Pareto weights would obviously not change over time, models of dynamic intertemporal choice posit that household members receive "news". For example, a member with a low initial income share may become the breadwinner owing to a promotion (or a negative shock to the other); or else one of the spouses may unexpectedly earn a college degree. Also, the "rules of the game" between husband and wife might be altered, as by a change in the law that reallocates assets between the two spouses and their relative bargaining power in case of divorce.[11]

How do intra-family choices change in this case? Chiappori and Mazzocco (2015) discuss two cases of interest: full commitment and limited commitment. Under full commitment, only the distribution of power at the time the household is formed matters (so that most of the conclusions of the static model extend to a dynamic context). This also implies that conditional cash transfer programs designed to empower selected household members in order to make the program itself more effective are unlikely to change intra-family consumption allocations.[12] In contrast, under limited commitment,

11. Voena (2015) examines how divorce laws affect couples' intertemporal choices and wellbeing. Exploiting panel variation in US laws, she finds that in states that imposed an equal division of property the introduction of unilateral divorce is associated with higher household savings and lower female employment.
12. One instance is Mexico's Progresa program, which offers conditional cash transfers to the rural poor in exchange for sending their children to school and regularly visiting health clinics.

household members can renegotiate the distribution of resources in the wake of shocks. We refer readers to Chiappori and Mazzocco (2015) for an excellent survey of the theoretical implications and empirical implementation of the various models.[13]

To recapitulate the main themes of this chapter, we have studied various reasons for the failure of simpler versions of the intertemporal choice model. Habits, goods durability, non-separability between consumption and leisure, home production, and collective behavior models all imply adding terms to the Euler equation for consumption that can account for a correlation between expected consumption growth and expected income growth. The second important insight is that some forms of non-separability (in particular, the durability of consumer goods and home production) drive a wedge between the concept of spending (which is what is typically observed in the data) and consumption (which is what consumers draw utility from). Incorporating the features discussed in this chapter into empirical research is a challenge that researchers are only just now coming to grips with. We know very little about the structural parameters that characterize preferences in these more realistic models. Furthermore, it is important to inquire into how the marginal propensity to consume changes with non-separability and whether this gives rise to substantial heterogeneity across consumers. Finally, while developing models that simultaneously take account of frictions in the labor market, the credit market, and the market for durables is computationally challenging, it may provide further key insights on consumption behavior.

13. Mazzocco (2008) shows that assuming a unitary framework when instead the collective model is appropriate may generate spurious evidence of excess sensitivity of (aggregate) consumption with respect to (aggregate) income. This is because the Euler equation for Δc_{it} omits the spouses' income shares (in periods t and $t-1$). This makes it possible for lagged income to enter significantly into the Euler equation simply because it serves as a proxy for the omitted variables.

CHAPTER 14
Non-Standard Preferences

Throughout what has preceded this final chapter we have assumed that consumers are rational, make dynamically consistent choices, and are fully informed about market prices, financial opportunities, and their probability distributions. We have further assumed that they invest in a single asset, not distinguishing between liquid and illiquid instruments, and that they are atomistic agents, making choices independently of other consumers.

In the real world, of course, many facts appear to conflict with these assumptions, prompting the development of alternatives to the standard life-cycle model and its main hypotheses. Some of these departures from the model are relatively minor and do not alter its basic insights and implications. Other alternatives, drawing on psychology, have integrated various psychological traits, heuristics, and social considerations into the main framework. These models have been particularly fruitful in the analysis of certain puzzles concerning saving and portfolio choice (Tversky and Kahneman, 1981). As always, our survey of these models and the evidence will be highly selective, relating only to the main applications involving intertemporal consumption decisions.

The first assumption to be rejected is that resources are fungible. Shefrin and Thaler (1988) proposed the *mental accounting model* as a way of explaining why people often treat different sources of income (current or future) and wealth in different ways. As we shall see, the main implication of the mental accounting model is that the marginal propensity to consume out of the various sources of income differs. Failure to see that the different types of income are actually fungible may be a sign of inability to solve complicated maximization problems. In these cases, people will rely on simple heuristics (rule of thumb or educated guesses) in making their decisions.

A second challenge to the life-cycle model is the substantial evidence produced by psychology, laboratory experiments, and empirical studies that people do not make time-consistent decisions. In particular, many studies have found evidence that people do not properly discount the future (they want immediate gratification, only to regret past decisions afterward). For instance, when people evaluate the utility of consumption far in the future, they are patient and plan to save for retirement, but as the future gets nearer people discount it at a higher rate and have a strong preference for current consumption. The formalization of these findings leads to the analysis of time-inconsistent preferences and *hyperbolic discounting* (Laibson, 1997), a model in which rational agents make time-inconsistent decisions.

A third critique is that people are in fact not fully informed about financial opportunities (the equity premium, say, or the virtue of diversification). In this chapter we review the literature on *financial sophistication* and present a stylized model that integrates investment in financial information into a standard model of intertemporal choice. The model emphasizes that, like other forms of human capital, financial information can be accumulated, and that the decision to invest in financial sophistication has costs as well as benefits.

A final departure from the standard approach explicitly models another important fact of life, namely, that our own choices are affected by the choices of other consumers, owing to social preferences. In some cases people emulate the choices made by a selected reference group (the "keeping up with the Joneses" model), and in others they seek to impress their peers by display of highly visible and expensive goods such as jewelry and sporty cars (the "conspicuous consumption" model).

The literature that departs from the standard life-cycle model by positing non-standard preferences, behavioral bias, imperfect information, and social preferences is vast—indeed, a full survey would require a book of its own. We refer readers to the survey in Della Vigna (2009) for many more applications.

14.1. MENTAL ACCOUNTING

According to Wikipedia, "a good is fungible if one unit of the good is substantially equivalent to another unit of the same good of the same quality at the same time and place." If we replace "good" with "money," anyone should be indifferent between spending a $10 bill and ten $1 bills. Similarly, individuals should treat an unexpected $500 tax refund in the same way as they treat $500 of their regular paycheck. According to the mental accounting model of Shefrin and Thaler (1988), however, people regularly violate this rule of fungibility. For example, some people are more reluctant to use a $10 bill to buy a $2 item because they fear that once the bill is broken they will be tempted to spend it all. Similarly, it may be more tempting to spend out of bonuses than out of regular income.

Extending this example to decisions about asset accumulation, individuals with mental accounting are more willing to spend certain sources of income or assets (for instance, a lottery prize, which can be seen as a windfall) than others (for instance, money accumulated in a college tuition plan, which requires a strong commitment over many years). In the mental accounting framework, the subjective framing of a transaction determines the utility the person expects from it. This framing effect is an example of cognitive bias, in which people react to a particular choice in different ways depending on how it is presented (Tversky and Kahneman, 1981).

One of the clearest examples of this mental accounting behavior is the observation that people appear to treat savings and debt differently, even when debt comes at a high cost. Gross and Souleles (2002) find that many individuals maintain substantial credit card debt while nevertheless holding liquid assets. Given the large difference between credit card interest rates and interest rates on saving accounts, this is extremely costly for consumers and represents a puzzle for models based on rational choice. The explanation requires factoring in psychological costs: to avoid the temptation to spend for current consumption, people use savings as a commitment device for future consumption. An alternative explanation, as we shall see, is hyperbolic discounting, a model discussed in Section 14.2.

In order to test for mental accounting, Levin (1998) compares the consumption decisions of a typical life-cycle consumer (c_L) with the decision of a behavioral consumer (c_B). For the former, consumption depends only on total wealth (the sum of human capital and other assets),

$$c_{L,0} = c_L \left(\sum_{t=0}^{T-1} \frac{y_t}{(1+r)^t} + \sum_{k=1}^{K} A_{k0} \right),$$

where y is income and the K assets $(A_1, A_2, \ldots, A_K)$ are ordered in terms of their liquidity (for instance, asset 1 is a checking account, asset 2 a savings account, etc.). According to the standard life-cycle model (Chapter 1), the consumer treats all sources of income and wealth in the same way. If income changes are transitory, the marginal propensity to consume out of each asset and initial income is the same:

$$\frac{\partial c_{L,0}}{\partial y_0} = \frac{\partial c_{L,0}}{\partial A_{1,0}} = \ldots = \frac{\partial c_{L,0}}{\partial A_{K,0}}.$$

Note that the marginal propensity to consume out of current income is higher if income shocks are persistent.

For a behavioral life-cycle individual, consumption depends not only on total resources but also on how they are divided between the various types of income and assets, or more generally,

$$c_{B,0} = c_B\left(y_0,...,y_{T-1},A_{1,0},A_{2,0},...,A_{K,0}\right).$$

For behavioral consumers, the consumption response to changes in resources is given by:

$$\frac{\partial c_{L,0}}{\partial y_0} > \frac{\partial c_{L,0}}{\partial A_{1,0}} > ... > \frac{\partial c_{L,0}}{\partial A_{K,0}}.$$

The inequalities indicate that consumers are more likely to spend from the more tempting resources, and that they will spend more from liquid than illiquid assets. Since the most tempting source of cash is regular income, the propensity to consume with respect to current income is greater than for any asset.

Levin's empirical analysis, based on the Retirement History Survey (RHS), concludes that the sensitivity of consumption to income is greater than the sensitivity to individual assets, and that the propensity to consume out of liquid assets is greater than that for relatively illiquid real estate wealth. He interprets the evidence as supporting the mental accounting model.

The mental accounting model implies that if resources can be converted into less tempting forms of wealth, they are more likely to be saved. This carries important policy implications if, say, the government wants to stimulate household saving. For instance, the mental accounting model implies that if one could shift resources from high-temptation accounts (such as checking accounts) toward low-temptation accounts (such as IRAs or 401(k)s, which are earmarked for retirement saving), total savings will increase. That is, there exists a major justification for preferential tax treatment of these assets.

For these reasons, the default options of retirement accounts are highly significant. According to this literature, people's decisions are characterized by inertia, so if they are enrolled in a pension plan automatically (by default), they will tend to stick with it. If instead they are not enrolled, they are less likely to become plan participants. As an example of this literature, Madrian and Shea (2001) examine the changes in the default clauses for 401(k) accounts at a large US company. Initially, the default option was non-participation (employees had to opt in). Later, the default option was changed to participation (employees had to opt out, although at the negligible cost of a phone call). The authors find that the default rule change increased the participation rate substantially. Accordingly, automatic enrollment in 401(k)s or other defined contribution retirement plans is a frequently advocated policy option for increasing retirement savings.

The switch to default rules that induce people to save more for retirement is what Camerer et al. (2003) call "cautious paternalism". According to this view, a default rule mandating participation in retirement saving plans helps individuals with self-control problems substantially and inflicts little or no harm on those without such problems (they would save anyhow or can opt out at a minor cost). A much stronger form of paternalism is compulsory social security. Mandatory contributions are obviously an extreme form of saving commitment, with no provision for opting out, which means they could reduce the welfare of consumers with no self-control problems (e.g., those who would like to borrow against future income).

A related issue is people's choice between an annuity and a lump sum payment at retirement. Chapter 11 shows that in the presence of lifetime uncertainty, annuities are valuable, in the sense that they allow consumers to follow an optimal consumption plan, raising the return to saving and eliminating accidental bequests. As we point out, bequest motives, the high cost of annuities, adverse selection, and moral hazard in the annuity market are the most commonly cited explanations for the low demand for annuities found in practice. Brown, Kling, Mullainathan, and Wrobel (2008) explore, as additional factors, behavioral biases and framing. They observe that the purchase of an annuity has an investment component (how much to invest) and a consumption component (how to spend the return on the investment). Rational consumers should care only about the level of consumption that they will be able to enjoy in retirement, but other consumers might adopt an investment framework and consider the return on the annuity, not the impact on retirement consumption.

We take the same two-period model as in Chapter 11, where consumers survive to the second period with probability p. In the first period they can purchase a bond with return $(1 + r)$ and no risk, or an annuity with return $(1 + r) / p$ if they survive to the second period and 0 if not. If the annuity is actuarially fair, the expected return is equal to $(1 + r)$. Brown, Kling, Mullainathan, and Wrobel (2008) argue that although it has the same expected return (and a higher return if the consumer survives), the annuity *appears* to be riskier than the bond because its return depends on a random variable (the probability of surviving). To test for this framing hypothesis, the authors present descriptions of annuities in either an investment framework or a consumption framework in an Internet survey. In practice, they use words such as "invest" and "earnings" in the investment framework, "spend" and "payment" in the consumption framework. They find that "the vast majority of individuals prefer an annuity over alternative products when presented in a consumption frame, whereas the majority of individuals prefer non-annuitized financial products when presented in an investment frame" (308). This line of research therefore suggests that many retirees do not make rational and well-informed financial decisions. As we shall see in Section 14.3, lack of sophistication is a complementary explanation for non-optimal financial decisions.

14.2. TIME INCONSISTENCY

A series of laboratory experiments and real-life situations indicates that in practice people have problems of self-control and time-inconsistent preferences. One way to formalize these notions is to rely on models of intertemporal choice with *hyperbolic discounting*.

When evaluating outcomes in the distant future, individuals with hyperbolic discounting are patient, but as the future gets nearer, their discounting gets steep, and they become impatient. For example, an individual with hyperbolic discounting prefers $x(1+\alpha)$ in period 5 to x in period 4 (with $\alpha > 0$). Nevertheless, the same individual would then prefer x in period 0 (now) to $x(1+\alpha)$ in period 1 (Angeletos et al., 2001). In this sense, the hyperbolic discounting model identifies an intrapersonal conflict between "early selves" (patient and eager to commit) and "later selves" (preferring instant gratification). With exponential discounting, this conflict does not exist and preferences exhibit time consistency (i.e., individuals who prefer $x(1+\alpha)$ in period 5 to x in period 4 also prefer $x(1+\alpha)$ in period 1 to x in period 0).

Insofar as they are rational agents, hyperbolic discounters are perfectly aware of their lack of self-control and so adopt strategies to limit the temptation for instant gratification. Like Odysseus tying himself to the mast, they try to attenuate their problem with self-control by purchasing illiquid assets that are hard to monetize, owing to penalties and other transaction costs. On the other hand, the desire for instant gratification may induce people who cannot tap this illiquid wealth to borrow excessively from expensive sources such as credit cards.[1] This may explain the credit card puzzle posed by Gross and Souleles (2002). The breakdown among liquid assets, illiquid assets, and debt therefore plays an important role in the hyperbolic discounting models. As we shall see, it is precisely the composition of wealth that distinguishes the hyperbolic model from the life-cycle model with exponential discounting.

For a formal exposition of the implications of hyperbolic discounting, we write the lifetime utility function as:

$$U_0 = u(c_0) + D_1 u(c_1) + \ldots + D_{T-1} u(c_{T-1}), \tag{14.1}$$

1. What lies behind the instant gratification effect? Psychological research shows that different parts of the brain are activated when confronted with the choice between something available in the immediate present and the same thing available, with a reward, in the future. The area of the brain that eventually dominates determines the type of decision that the individual will make. The study of how brain activity affects economic decisions (neuroeconomics), still in its infancy, holds considerable promise for understanding various behavioral anomalies in saving and financial decision-making. However, it is probably too early to say whether its findings will ever become universally accepted.

where D_{t+s} is a discount function, and we assume $D_0 = 1$. The discount function measures how much future utility is discounted to the present. In the model we have used in this book, the discount function is exponential, $D_{t+s} = \beta^{t+s}$, so the discount rate (the ratio between the function's values at two points in time) is constant:

$$\frac{D_1}{D_0} = \frac{D_2}{D_1} = \ldots = \frac{D_{t+s}}{D_{t+s-1}} = \beta.$$

The strongest theoretical argument for exponential discounting is that it is the only discount function that implies time-consistent preferences—that is, if a certain decision is considered optimal today, the same decision will be considered optimal also in the future when the time comes to make that decision. Gollier (2001) suggests two other arguments in favor of exponential discounting. With lifetime uncertainty, δ can be interpreted as the survival probability from one period to the next, so equation (14.1) can be interpreted as a function giving "the expected utility of the consumption flow at date t seen from period zero" (219). Furthermore, exponential discounting guarantees that the objective function is well defined even when the horizon is infinite.

To allow for time inconsistency, assume that the discount function is quasi-hyperbolic: $D_{t+s} = \theta\beta$, with $\theta > 1$. As before, $D_0 = 1$.[2] The discount rate is then:

$$\frac{D_1}{D_0} = \theta\beta, \quad \frac{D_2}{D_1} = \ldots = \frac{D_{t+s}}{D_{t+s-1}} = \beta.$$

In this model discount rates decline faster in the short run than in the long run. In general, the objective function of the consumer is:

$$\max u(c_0) + \theta \sum_{t=1}^{T-1} \beta^t u(c_t).$$

Note that when we set $\theta = 1$, we obtain the traditional exponential discounting model. Figure 14.1 (taken from Angeletos et al., 2001) plots two discount functions against time: exponential and quasi-hyperbolic. The main difference is that in the exponential function the decline is smooth, whereas hyperbolic discounting produces a decline that is steep initially before flattening out in the long run.

Laibson, Repetto, and Tobacman (1988) calibrate a numerical simulation model with hyperbolic discounting, with many of the traditional features of the buffer stock model, including constant relative risk aversion, a realistic

2. The more general form of hyperbolic discounting assumes that events t periods away are discounted with factor $(1 + \alpha\tau)^{-\left(\frac{\gamma}{\alpha}\right)}$, with $\alpha > 0, \gamma > 0$.

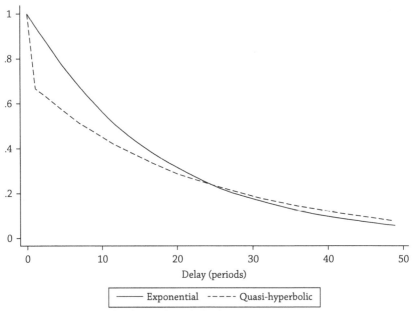

Figure 14.1: Exponential and quasi-hyperbolic discount functions

Note: The figure plots an exponential discount function, defined as $D_t = \delta^t$ (with $\delta = 0.944$), and a quasi-hyperbolic discount function, defined as $D_0 = 1$ and $D_t = b\delta^t$ for $t > 0$ (with $b = 0.7$ and $\delta = 0.957$).

income profile with uncertainty, and borrowing constraints. In the baseline model with only one liquid asset, their simulations of the hyperbolic and exponential discounting cases produce life-cycle profiles of consumption and asset accumulation that appear highly similar, although hyperbolic consumers hold less wealth early in life than exponential discounters and hyperbolic discounters are more likely to be near or under binding liquidity constraints. The explanation for both these differences is the effect of "later selves" on decision-making.

The hyperbolic discounting model implies that individuals will benefit from a default rule that penalizes early withdrawals from retirement accounts, since this meets their need for commitment devices. In fact, when consumers are allowed to invest their savings in an additional asset (defined-contribution pension plans), significant differences between simulated consumption and asset profiles under the two discounting functions emerge. With exponential discounting and a coefficient of relative risk aversion of 1, a defined-contribution plan with early withdrawal penalties of 10 to 15 percent increases the steady-state national saving rate by between 60 and 100 percent, whereas with hyperbolic discounting the increase is between 81 and 134 percent. The difference depends on the hyperbolic discounters' demand for commitment devices.

The literature on hyperbolic discounting deals with consumers who would like to consume less if they could procure a good commitment mechanism.

In discussing this work, Hall (1998) notes that some individuals may have the opposite problem—that is, they plan to consume in the future, but when the future eventually comes around, they defer consumption again and end up dying with substantial unspent wealth. These people, then, would benefit from a different commitment device, one by which they commit in one period to consume in later periods.

14.3. FINANCIAL SOPHISTICATION

The standard model of intertemporal choice posits that people maximize expected utility and choose consumption and saving at each point in time on the basis of expected lifetime resources and preference parameters.[3] Individuals are assumed to be rational and fully informed, able to project future income and interest rates and discount them appropriately. In reality, a good many studies have produced evidence that a large number of adults know little about finance and are unfamiliar even with basic economic concepts such as risk diversification, inflation, and compound interest.

Financial sophistication is relevant to assets and liabilities alike. On the asset side, sophistication is important because some financial assets have become extremely complex and opaque (such as derivatives). And even simple assets such as savings accounts or government bonds offer a variety of contracts to choose from, which makes choice difficult. Furthermore, since the end of the 1980s financial market innovation and deregulation have considerably increased the number of types of financial assets, with many new ways to invest in equities and bonds.

There is considerable evidence that financial sophistication affects saving and portfolio choices. Van Rooij, Lusardi, and Alessie (2011) find that financial sophistication is associated with greater wealth, a higher probability of investing in equities, and a greater propensity to plan for retirement. Christelis, Jappelli and Padula (2010) study the relation between cognitive abilities and stockholding based on the Survey of Health, Assets, Retirement, and Expectations (SHARE), and find that the propensity to invest in stocks directly and indirectly (through mutual funds and retirement accounts) is strongly associated with mathematical ability, verbal fluency, and recall skills. In a related paper, McArdle, Smith, and Willis (2009) find that numeracy, measured by answers to three simple mathematical questions, is a strong predictor of total wealth, financial wealth, and the fraction of wealth held in equities. Lusardi and Mitchell (2014) provide a useful survey of this emerging field of study.

3. This section is based on Jappelli and Padula (2013).

The debt-related aspects of financial sophistication have also received attention. Lusardi and Tufano (2009) analyze a sample of Americans with respect to debt literacy, financial experience, and judgment about their level of indebtedness. Measuring literacy through a set of questions about fundamental concepts involving debt, they find illiteracy in all segments of the population, and especially among women and the elderly.

One of the limitations of these studies is that the incentive to become financially literate itself depends on level of wealth and on portfolio allocation, which creates endogeneity bias in any regression of financial sophistication on wealth or portfolio choices. Jappelli and Padula (2013) and Lusardi, Michaud, and Mitchell (2015) emphasize that, like other forms of human capital, financial information can be accumulated, and that investing in financial sophistication has costs as well as benefits. To see the implications of the model, we posit that people are endowed with an initial stock of financial sophistication, which they acquire before entering the labor market, and that investing in financial sophistication gives access to better investment opportunities, increasing the returns to saving. But acquiring information also entails costs in time, effort, and resources. So the model features rational agents who choose how much to invest in financial information and how much to save.

A simple two-period model illustrates this trade-off. In period 0 consumers earn income y, and in period 1 they retire. At the beginning of period 0 they have no assets but are endowed with a stock of financial literacy, Φ_0, which depreciates at a rate λ. The initial stock is what people know about finance before entering the labor market; it is related, therefore, to schooling and parental background. The return to saving is the interest rate r, which is paid at the beginning of the second period on the wealth transferred from the first.

The key assumption is that a greater stock of financial literacy enables consumers to access better investment opportunities and to save on transaction costs and fees. Therefore, the rate of return on assets is a function of the stock of financial literacy at the beginning of period 1,

$$1+r\left(\Phi_1\right)=\Phi_1^\alpha,$$

where Φ_1 is the stock of financial literacy at the beginning of period 1 and α is the return on financial literacy. In line with the literature on human capital, investment in literacy raises asset returns, though at a decreasing rate. There is empirical evidence to corroborate the assumption that the return on wealth is correlated with financial sophistication. For example, Calvet, Campbell, and Sodini (2007), using Swedish data, find that part of the variability of returns across investors is explained by financial sophistication. In particular, they show that predictors of financial sophistication (such as wealth, income, occupation, and education) are associated with higher Sharpe ratios, and that richer and more sophisticated households invest more profitably.

Consumers can increase their stock of financial literacy by acquiring it during period 0. The relative cost of financial information in terms of the consumption good is p, which includes both monetary and time costs. The stock of literacy therefore evolves according to:

$$\Phi_1 = (1 + \lambda)\Phi_0 = \phi,$$

where ϕ denotes investment in financial information. In the first period people choose saving and investment in financial information to maximize:

$$u(c_0, c_1) = \ln c_0 + \beta \ln c_1,$$

subject to the dynamic budget constraints:

$$c_0 + s + p\phi = y \quad \text{and} \quad c_1 = \Phi_1^\alpha s,$$

where β is the discount factor and s is first-period saving. The first-order conditions with respect to s and ϕ are:

$$\beta^{-1}\frac{c_1}{c_0} = \Phi_1^\alpha \tag{14.2}$$

$$p = \frac{\alpha \beta c_0 s \Phi_1^{\alpha-1}}{c_1}. \tag{14.3}$$

The first equation is the standard Euler equation for consumption, stating that the marginal rate of substitution is equal to the interest rate, which in turn depends on investment in financial information. The second equation states that in equilibrium the marginal cost of literacy (p) equals the marginal return.

Equations (14.2) and (14.3) implicitly define optimal investment in financial information. To show this, Figure 14.2 plots the marginal cost of investing in financial information (p) and the marginal benefit as a function of the investment. While the marginal cost is the constant p, the marginal return decreases as the investment rises.[4]

The model implies that optimal saving is a function of the initial stock of information and that the incentive to invest in financial literacy depends on the return to literacy as well as the amount saved in the first period. The implication is that financial sophistication and saving are positively

4. Using the Euler equation and the budget constraint, one can rewrite condition (14.3) as $p = \dfrac{\alpha\beta(y - p\phi)}{[(1-\delta)\Phi_0 + \phi](1+\beta)}$.

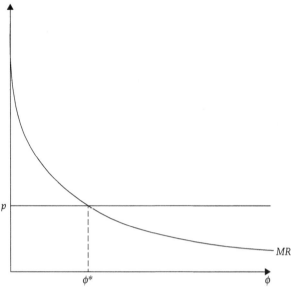

Figure 14.2: The optimal decision to invest in financial information
Note: Figure reproduced with permission from Jappelli and Padula (2013).

correlated. However, one cannot conclude from this that a larger stock of current financial sophistication "causes" higher saving, because both variables are endogenous.

To study the dynamics of wealth and financial sophistication over the life cycle, one can generalize this model to a multi-period context with isoelastic utility, income uncertainty, and a more generic return function, $1+r(\Phi_t)=f(\Phi_t)$. Under these assumptions, the Euler equation for consumption is:

$$\Delta \ln c_{t+1} = \gamma^{-1}\ln \beta + \gamma^{-1}\ln f\left(\Phi_{t+1}\right) + \varepsilon_{t+1}.$$

The growth rate of consumption is higher for those who have a greater incentive to save in the current period, whom we may call "high-information, high-returns" individuals. This equation is not a reduced form but an equilibrium condition between consumption growth and financial information.

Baseline simulations of the age profiles of wealth and financial sophistication are plotted in Figure 14.3, under two scenarios: with and without a public pension system.

The upper panel shows that wealth has the hump-shaped profile typical of life-cycle models. The stock of literacy (lower panel) is similarly shaped, increasing in the first portion of the life cycle and decreasing after retirement, when net investment in financial information becomes negative, owing to depreciation of the stock and the reduced incentive to acquire information.

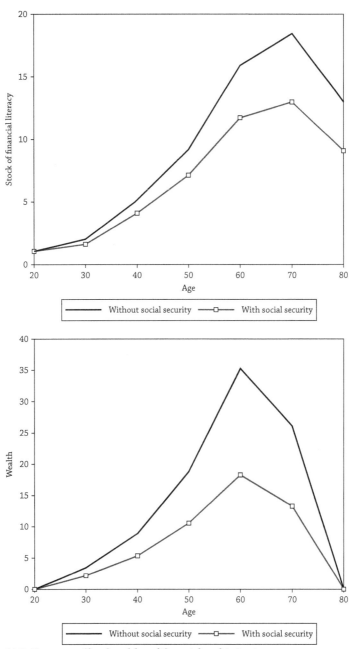

Figure 14.3: The age profile of wealth and financial sophistication

Note: Figure reproduced with permission from Jappelli and Padula (2013). The simulation assumes that the utility function is isoelastic with an elasticity of intertemporal substitution equal to 0.5, the rate of time preference is 0.03, the return to financial literacy (α) is 0.03, the price of literacy (ρ) is 0.1, the initial levels of income and of financial sophistication are both equal to 1, that consumers retire after 40 periods, and that income is constant throughout life. In the scenario with social security, the system is assumed to be actuarially fair and the social security contribution rate equals 20%.

A social security system attenuates not only the incentive to accumulate assets but also the incentive to invest in financial literacy. The reduction in wealth accumulation is the familiar displacement effect induced by social security: given the presence of mandatory saving and pension benefits, people need to accumulate a smaller amount of private wealth during their working life to finance retirement consumption. Since the incentive to invest in financial information depends on the amount saved, with social security consumers also accumulate less information. This might explain why in countries with more generous public retirement systems households participate less in financial markets and have relatively simpler portfolios. Indeed, cross-country microeconomic data from the Survey of Health, Ageing and Retirement in Europe suggest a strong correlation between initial financial sophistication and level of wealth and degree of financial sophistication later in life (Jappelli and Padula 2013).

14.4. SOCIAL PREFERENCES

The standard model of intertemporal choice assumes that consumers do not interact with one another and that their actions do not affect others' choices. However, there is a respected school of economics that studies how social factors influence consumption behavior. Veblen (1899) wrote that "in any community where goods are held in severalty it is necessary, in order to ensure his own peace of mind, that an individual should possess as large a portion of goods as others with whom he is accustomed to class himself; and it is extremely gratifying to possess something more than others" (38). Veblen also stressed that this social effect would be stronger in the case of what he called "conspicuous consumption": "The competitor with whom [an individual] wishes to institute a comparison is ... made to serve as a means to the end. He consumes vicariously for his host at the same time that he is a witness of that excess of good things which his host is unable to dispose of singlehanded" (65). The relative income hypothesis of Duesenberry (1948) also emphasized social influences on consumption: "The strength of any individual's desire to increase his consumption expenditure is a function of the ratio of his expenditure to some weighted average of the expenditures of others with whom he comes into contact."

The study of social influences on consumption behavior has developed in two different directions. First, there is the problem of network formation, with the related problem of defining the relevant reference group that generates peer effects on consumption. Second, there is the problem of measuring and understanding the sources of these peer effects. Three models have been proposed. The first is "keeping up with the Joneses", in which individual utility depends on the current average consumption of one's peers.[5] The second group of studies revisits Veblen's idea of conspicuous consumption and suggests that the allocation of consumption may be tilted toward goods that are more "conspicuous", such as jewelry, luxury cars, restaurant meals, and so forth. A final reason an individual's consumption may be correlated with that of a reference group is unrelated to social preferences but arises from the insurance opportunities offered by friends, co-workers, or neighbors.

To see how peer consumption effects may influence intertemporal choice, we consider a two-period model where consumers' utility is isoelastic,

$$U_t = \frac{(c_t^{1-\gamma} - 1)}{1-\gamma} \bar{c}_t^{-\theta} + (1+\delta)^{-1} \frac{(c_{t+1}^{1-\gamma} - 1)}{1-\gamma} \bar{c}_{t+1}^{-\theta},$$

and $\bar{c}$ is the average consumption of peers. Under the usual budget constraint, one obtains a modified Euler equation,

$$\Delta \ln c_{t+1} = \gamma^{-1}(r - \delta) + \gamma^{-1}\theta \Delta \ln \bar{c}_{t+1} + \epsilon_{t+1},$$

where $\theta \neq 0$; the additional term with average peers' consumption changes the intertemporal allocation of consumption. In particular, when $\theta > 0$, people try to imitate the consumption of their peers. By contrast, if consumers derive utility from deviating from their peers' behavior, then $\theta < 0$.

Using Danish administrative data, De Giorgi, Frederiksen, and Pistaferri (2015) find that peer effects are positive and quantitatively important. Moreover, in their test to distinguish between the "keeping up with the Joneses" model and the "conspicuous consumption" model, they find evidence in favor of the former.

There are at least two reasons social influences on consumption are interesting. First, one would like to understand the welfare implications of peer effects. Since conspicuous goods are typically luxuries (most notably cars and jewelry), peer consumption effects could well have appreciable consequences for welfare (in the form of "wasteful" excess consumption).[6] In the "keeping up with the Joneses" model, the saving profile would diverge from the optimal profile that we observe when agents act atomistically. This will lead to undersaving (or overborrowing) if peers' consumption is on a growing trend, or possibly to underconsumption in the opposite case.

Evaluating the peer effect on consumption empirically is also important for policy reasons, because peer effects in consumption are related to social

5. When utility depends on lagged average peer consumption, as in Ljungqvist and Uhlig (2000), this model becomes "catching up with the Joneses".

6. This is not the case if peers provide "information" about, say, better prices, and so forth. If this information factor is important, we should see it emerging mostly among goods with more pronounced informational asymmetries (as reflected in pricing).

multiplier for the evaluation of economic policy measures. For instance, a tax change affecting the wealthiest might have consequences not only for the specific target group but also for those who interact socially with them, thus expanding the effect of the policy. At the aggregate level, the total effect of the measure depends on the initial shock, the response of the target group, the magnitude of the social multiplier, and the degree of connectedness between the social groups that are affected and unaffected.

This chapter has reviewed models in which people's behavior deviates from some of the main assumptions of the life-cycle model. In many circumstances, modifying the standard model provides insights that are invaluable in reconciling theory and evidence. The hyperbolic discounting model has implications for the age-wealth profile that are practically identical to those of exponential discounting, but it can explain why people engage in costly borrowing while at the same time holding substantial assets in liquid form. The model that factors in financial sophistication, where people incur costs of collecting and processing financial information, also delivers a hump-shaped age-wealth profile. This model adds an important source of heterogeneity in wealth trajectories: initial differences in the endowment of financial sophistication. This may be an explanation for inequality of wealth. Sophisticated consumers have access to high-return assets and end up with greater wealth than the less sophisticated, who end up with less wealth. Models with social preferences, like many of the models presented in this book, lead to a modified Euler equation in which the slope of consumption depends not only on the incentive for intertemporal substitution but also on the growth of peers' consumption.

In sum, many of the models discussed in this concluding chapter modify the standard life-cycle model in important ways while preserving some (but not all) of the basic assumptions and implications, most important among them the hump-shaped age-wealth profile.

There is of course an alternative interpretation that views the evidence against the life-cycle model as so damning as to require different modeling frameworks, ones in which individuals' decisions are influenced by inertia, heuristics, myopia, status quo bias, and so on. However, even those who depart more radically from the model still recognize its usefulness as a normative paradigm. Very few would disagree that people would be better off following the life-cycle model rather than making heuristic decisions based on some rule of thumb. For instance, in considering how common compulsory public pension systems are, one might well note that this represents broad social approval for plans to guarantee that people have adequate reserves to be spent during retirement. In essence, forcing or inducing people to behave as in the life-cycle model, accumulating resources during one's working life and drawing assets down after retirement, seems to be viewed as an optimal policy.

Conclusions

This book examines the way in which consumers respond to changes in their economic environment and circumstances and how they react to the risks faced during the life cycle. In addressing these issues we have augmented the basic life-cycle permanent-income model (in which the key factors determining the dynamics of consumption are retirement saving and income shocks) with other significant features of consumers' preferences and environment: precautionary motives for saving, borrowing constraints, life span uncertainty, intergenerational transfers, non-separability between consumption and leisure, habits, and degree of financial sophistication.

These matters are highly important for assessing the effectiveness of macroeconomic stabilization policies, both fiscal and monetary. Their relevance became manifest during the global financial crises of the first decade of the twenty-first century. On many of the themes analyzed here, a consensus among economists has emerged. A first element of agreement, at least since the early 1990s, is that if we intend to analyze models of intertemporal choice with individual heterogeneity, we need genuine microeconomic panel data. For different reasons, both aggregate data and pure cross-sectional data may produce erroneous conclusions if they are applied to predict the consumption behavior of individuals. As we illustrate in this volume with a series of examples, except in certain special—and unrealistic—cases, the aggregate consumption function is not a good approximation of the individual consumption function, and may even diverge radically from it. With cross-sectional data, cohort effects cannot be distinguished from age effects; furthermore, these data seldom contain the information required to identify income shocks and their impact on consumers' behavior. Evidence based on cross-sectional data is therefore often misleading, producing incorrect inferences, as when one attempts to estimate consumption and life-cycle profiles of wealth or to measure the impact of shocks on consumption and saving decisions. The increased availability of high-quality panel data with relatively long time horizons has improved applied research considerably.

By the mid-1990s, a very prominent role in our field had been taken by estimation of the Euler equation for consumption. At first the possibility of estimating preference parameters using only the first-order conditions for intertemporal maximization had sparked great interest among applied economists. But the initial enthusiasm for this approach has given way to a realization that it has not come up to scholars' high expectations for it. The principal legacy of the work based on this approach has been to highlight the complex econometric problems that plague the estimation of risk aversion, prudence, intertemporal substitution, and discount rates using only the first-order conditions. For instance, there is still a great deal of uncertainty over the magnitude of the coefficient of relative prudence, hence the importance of precautionary saving.

The problems associated with the estimation of the Euler equation, which we have pointed out repeatedly, prompted a subsequent generation of studies that followed a different route, using simulation and estimation methods that fully specify the intertemporal consumption model, the budget constraint, the environment in which the consumer operates (the severity of borrowing constraints and the extent of insurance opportunities, the role of welfare programs, etc.), and the income process. Unlike the Euler equation studies, this type of analysis fully incorporates the consumer's budget set and not only the first-order conditions. In some special cases, the stochastic dynamic programming problem for consumption delivers a closed-form solution between consumption and cash on hand, but in many more cases no such solution is available, so researchers turn to numerical solutions. Simulation methods are also widely used to estimate the parameters of the utility function and the income process. Of course, such estimates require a much larger set of assumptions than the Euler equation approach, but they enable researchers to conduct policy analyses and to trace the consumption impact of fiscal reforms, social security arrangements, and permanent and transitory income shocks.

A second method that has proven useful in consumption analysis relies on quasi-experimental evidence, an approach that has been shown to be most fruitful in labor economics and many other fields of applied economics. In the context of consumption analysis, this approach can do without estimating an income process and even without observing individual resources and shocks. Instead, it compares the households that are exposed to shocks with those that are not (or the same households before and after the shock) and assumes that the difference in consumption is due to the shocks.

Since mid-2000 simulations and quasi-experimental studies have provided fresh evidence relevant to the central question that we have addressed: how household consumption responds to changes in income or to tax and welfare reforms, knowledge of which is crucial to the design of effective stabilization policies. In this volume, in the course of reviewing the literature, we have addressed two distinct questions. First, does household consumption respond to changes in income that were anticipated? And second, does it respond to unexpected income changes?

The body of work on this subject is vast and accordingly hard to summarize. Nevertheless, some consensus has emerged in the literature, both on method and on substance. On method, it is clear that distinguishing between negative and positive income changes and between transitory and permanent shocks can shed light not only on the response of consumption to income but also on the validity of the various theories of intertemporal choice. A series of approaches can be fruitfully explored in analyzing these issues: the identification of specific episodes of anticipated income declines or increases, the estimation of sophisticated income processes to distinguish between transitory and permanent shocks, and the use of data that include subjective consumption or income expectations.

On substance, by now there is quite strong evidence that consumption responds to anticipated income increases more than would be implied by the standard model of consumption smoothing. Although the reasons for this failure of theory are not yet well understood, there is evidence from diverse sources, studies, and countries that, at least locally, one of the chief causes is liquidity constraints. Indeed, in cases where liquidity constraints have no bearing, consumption appears to be less responsive to anticipated income declines (such as those that come with retirement).

A second finding that this volume brings out is that consumption tends to respond much more sharply to permanent income shocks than to transitory ones. There is also evidence, at least in the United States, that consumers do not fully adjust their spending to permanent shocks. Taken together, these findings are consistent with the hypothesis that a significant role in determining consumption is played by precautionary saving and perhaps even by insurance over and above self-insurance (such as government welfare programs, family labor supply, or family networks). In each of these dimensions, the heterogeneity of households is important, because liquidity constraints apparently account for the higher estimated marginal propensity to consume that is found especially in the population subgroups (above all low-income and low-education households) that are less likely to be able to access credit markets.

One challenge for future empirical work is distinguishing between the information set available to consumers (which might possibly be determined by better data, by the specification of an income process that acknowledges the possibility of advance information, or by observing subjective expectations) and insurance (the gauging of which may require better modeling of the sources of consumption smoothing that consumers can tap over and above their own savings). The fiscal stimulus packages implemented in virtually all countries in response to the Great Recession will certainly enable researchers to probe more deeply and gain further insights into the response of consumption to income changes. It is also likely that future research will increasingly exploit large-scale administrative data with detailed information on households' consumption and financial portfolios. Given the extremely large number of households covered, these datasets will enable economists to answer questions that cannot be addressed using traditional surveys, in particular those regarding heterogeneity of responses within specific population groups.

Readers who have had the patience to follow us to this point will certainly have realized that in our view the life-cycle hypothesis is still the most appropriate theoretical framework for thinking about intertemporal consumption decisions, especially when the baseline framework is extended to include precautionary saving, liquidity constraints, and lifetime uncertainty. Of course, the life-cycle hypothesis does not explain all the behavioral facts that are observed (for instance, that people borrow at outrageously high interest rates on credit cards when they have funds available in savings accounts). Equally clearly, in the real world many people do not have the financial sophistication that the theory necessarily postulates.

In this book we have discussed and summarized the evidence on a series of tests of the life-cycle hypothesis. By and large, one can reconcile some puzzling facts present in the empirical data with the hypothesis by means of relatively modest modifications of the basic version, such as provision for home production and non-separable preferences between consumption and leisure. However, in order to explain other "anomalies" and "puzzles" observed in the actual saving and financial behavior of individuals, more important modifications to the standard framework (such as the introduction of hyperbolic discounting or mental accounting) are required. Some recent developments in behavioral economics may be interpreted as a further contradiction of the life-cycle theory. Even in the models proposed by some behavioral economists, however, consumers are assumed to understand that it would be in their best interest to conform diligently to the life-cycle consumption hypothesis, but they end up succumbing to the temptation of instant gratification. In other words, even in behavioral models the life cycle is the right frame of reference. Yet brain and other mental frictions keep behavior from being fully consistent with the theory. Furthermore, the common presence of compulsory retirement plans in numerous developed and developing countries can be interpreted as indicating fundamental social approval for programs to ensure that people have adequate reserves to finance consumption during retirement. In essence, such programs force people to behave according to the dictates of the life-cycle hypothesis, accumulating resources during their working lives and drawing these assets down after retirement. For these reasons, we believe that the life-cycle hypothesis remains the benchmark model for thinking about individual consumption decisions and consequently also for policy analysis.

REFERENCES

Aaronson, Daniel, Sumit Agarwal, and Eric French. 2012. "The Spending and Debt Response to Minimum Wage Hikes." *American Economic Review* 102, 3111–39.

Abowd, John M., and David Card. 1989. "On the Covariance Structure of Earnings and Hours Changes." *Econometrica* 57, 411–45.

Adams, William, Liran Einav, and Jonathan Levin. 2009. "Liquidity Constraints and Imperfect Information in Subprime Lending." *American Economic Review* 99, 49–84.

Agarwal, Sumit, Chunlin Liu, and Nicholas S. Souleles. 2007. "The Reaction of Consumer Spending and Debt to Tax Rebates—Evidence from Consumer Credit Data." *Journal of Political Economy* 115, 986–1019.

Agarwal, Sumit, and Wenlan Qian. 2014. "Consumption and Debt Response to Unanticipated Income Shocks: Evidence from a Natural Experiment in Singapore." *American Economic Review* 104, 4205–30.

Aguiar, Mark, and Erik Hurst. 2005. "Consumption vs. Expenditure." *Journal of Political Economy* 113, 919–48.

Aguiar, Mark, and Erik Hurst. 2007. "Measuring Trends in Leisure: The Allocation of Time over Five Decades." *Quarterly Journal of Economics* 122, 969–1006.

Aguila, Emma, Orazio P. Attanasio, and Costas Meghir. 2008. "Changes in Consumption at Retirement." Working Paper 621, RAND Corporation.

Aiyagari, S. Rao. 1994. "Uninsured Idiosyncratic Risk and Aggregate Saving." *Quarterly Journal of Economics* 109, 659–84.

Alessie, Rob, and Annamaria Lusardi. 1997. "Consumption, Saving and Habit Formation." *Economics Letters* 55, 103–8.

Altonji, Joseph G., and Aloysious Siow. 1987. "Testing the Response of Consumption to Income with (Noisy) Panel Data." *Quarterly Journal of Economics* 102, 293–328.

Altug, Somru, and Robert A. Miller. 1990. "Household Choices in Equilibrium." *Econometrica* 58, 543–70.

Alvarez, Fernando, and Urban J. Jermann. 2000. "Efficiency, Equilibrium, and Asset Pricing with Risk of Default." *Econometrica* 68, 775–97.

Angeletos, George-Marios, David Laibson, Andrea Repetto, Jeremy Tobacman, and Stephen Weinberg. 2001. "The Hyperbolic Consumption Model: Calibration, Simulation, and Empirical Evaluation." *Journal of Economic Perspectives* 15, 47–68.

Attanasio, Orazio P. 2000. "Consumer Durables and Inertial Behaviour: Estimation and Aggregation of (S,s) Rules for Automobile Purchases." *Review of Economic Studies* 67, 667–96.

Attanasio, Orazio P., James Banks, Costas Meghir, and Guglielmo Weber. 1999. "Humps and Bumps in Lifetime Consumption." *Journal of Business Economics and Statistics* 17, 22–35.

Attanasio, Orazio P., Laura Blow, Robert Hamilton, and Andrew Leicester. 2009. "Booms and Busts: Consumption, House Prices and Expectations." *Economica* 76, 20–50.

Attanasio, Orazio P., and Agar Brugiavini. 2003. "Social Security and Households' Saving." *Quarterly Journal of Economics* 118, 1075–119.

Attanasio, Orazio P., and Steven J. Davis. 1996. "Relative Wage Movements and the Distribution of Consumption." *Journal of Political Economy* 104, 1227–62.

Attanasio, Orazio P., Pinelopi Koujianou Goldberg, and Ekaterini Kyriazidou. 2008. "Credit Constraints in the Market for Consumer Durables: Evidence from Micro Data on Car Loans." *International Economic Review* 49, 401–36.

Attanasio, Orazio P., and Hilary Williamson Hoynes. 2000. "Differential Mortality and Wealth Accumulation." *Journal of Human Resources* 35, 1–29.

Attanasio, Orazio P., and Tullio Jappelli. 2001. "Intertemporal Choice and the Cross-Sectional Variance of Marginal Utility." *Review of Economics and Statistics* 83, 13–27.

Attanasio, Orazio, and Valérie Lechene. 2002. "Tests of Income Pooling in Household Decisions." *Review of Economic Dynamics* 5, 720–48.

Attanasio, Orazio P., and Hamish Low. 2004. "Estimating Euler Equations." *Review of Economic Dynamics* 7, 405–35.

Attanasio, Orazio P., and Susann Rohwedder. 2003. "Pension Wealth and Household Saving: Evidence from Pension Reforms in the United Kingdom." *American Economic Review* 93, 1499–521.

Attanasio, Orazio P., and Guglielmo Weber. 1993. "Consumption Growth, the Interest Rate, and Aggregation." *Review of Economic Studies* 60, 631–49.

Attanasio, Orazio P., and Guglielmo Weber. 1995. "Is Consumption Growth Consistent with Intertemporal Optimization? Evidence from the Consumer Expenditure Survey." *Journal of Political Economy* 103, 1121–57.

Attanasio, Orazio P., and Guglielmo Weber. 2010. "Consumption and Saving: Models of Intertemporal Allocation and Their Implications for Public Policy." *Journal of Economic Literature* 48, 693–751.

Azariadis, Costas. 1975. "Implicit Contracts and Underemployment Equilibria." *Journal of Political Economy* 83, 1183–202.

Baker, Scott, and Constantine Yannelis. 2015. "Income Changes and Consumption: Evidence from the 2013 Federal Government Shutdown." Unpublished manuscript.

Banks, James, Richard Blundell, and Sarah Tanner. 1998. "Is There a Retirement-Savings Puzzle?" *American Economic Review* 88, 769–88.

Barro, Robert J. 1974. "Are Government Bonds Net Wealth?" *Journal of Political Economy* 81, 1095–117.

Battistin, Erich, Richard Blundell, and Arthur Lewbel. 2009. "Why Is Consumption More Log Normal than Income? Gibrat's Law Revisited." *Journal of Political Economy* 117, 1140–54.

Baxter, Marianne, and Urban J. Jermann. 1999. "Household Production and the Excess Sensitivity of Consumption to Current Income." *American Economic Review* 89, 902–20.

Becker, Gary S. 1981. *A Treatise on the Family*. Cambridge, MA: Harvard University Press.

Benartzi, Shlomo, Alessandro Previtero, and Richard H. Thaler. 2011. "Annuitization Puzzles." *Journal of Economic Perspectives* 25, 143–64.

Bernanke, Ben S. 1984. "Permanent Income, Liquidity, and Expenditure on Automobiles: Evidence from Panel Data." *Quarterly Journal of Economics* 99, 587–614.

Bernheim, B. Douglas. 1991. "How Strong Are Bequest Motives? Evidence Based on Estimates of the Demand for Annuities." *Journal of Political Economy* 99, 899–927.

Bernheim, B. Douglas. 2002. "Taxation and Saving." In *Handbook of Public Economics*, vol. 3, edited by A. J. Auerbach and M. Feldstein, 1173–249. Amsterdam: Elsevier Science.

Bernheim, B. Douglas, Andrei Schleifer, and Lawrence H. Summers. 1985. "The Strategic Bequest Motive." *Journal of Political Economy* 93, 1045–76.

Bernheim, B. Douglas, Jonathan Skinner, and Steven Weinberg. 2001. "What Accounts for the Variation in Retirement Wealth Among U.S. Households?" *American Economic Review* 91, 832–57.

Bertola, Giuseppe, Luigi Guiso, and Luigi Pistaferri. 2005. "Uncertainty and Consumer Durables Adjustment." *Review of Economic Studies* 72, 973–1007.

Besley, Timothy. 1995. "Savings, Credit and Insurance." In *Handbook of Development Economics*, vol. 3, edited by J. Behrman and T. N. Srinivasan, 2123–207. Amsterdam: Elsevier Science.

Besley, Timothy, and Costas Meghir. 1998. "Tax Based Saving Incentives." Institute for Fiscal Studies, mimeo, September.

Blanchard, Olivier J., and Gregory N. Mankiw. 1988. "Consumption: Beyond Certainty Equivalence." *American Economic Review Papers and Proceedings* 78, 173–77.

Blinder, Alan S. 1975. "Distribution Effects and the Aggregate Consumption Function." *Journal of Political Economy* 83, 447–75.

Blundell, Richard, and Thomas E. MaCurdy. 2000. "Labor Supply: A Review of Alternative Approaches." In *Handbook of Labor Economics*, vol. 3, edited by Orley Ashenfelter and David Card, 1559–695. Amsterdam: North Holland.

Blundell, Richard, Luigi Pistaferri, and Ian Preston. 2008. "Consumption Inequality and Partial Insurance." *American Economic Review* 98, 1887–921.

Blundell, Richard, Luigi Pistaferri, and Itay Saporta-Eksten. 2016. "Consumption Smoothing and Family Labor-Supply." *American Economic Review* 106, 387–435.

Blundell, Richard, and Ian Preston. 1998. "Consumption Inequality and Income Uncertainty." *Quarterly Journal of Economics* 113, 603–40.

Bodkin, Ronald G. 1959. "Windfall Income and Consumption." *American Economic Review* 49, 602–14.

Borsch-Supan, Axel. 2003. *Life-Cycle Savings and Public Policy*. New York: Academic Press.

Bottazzi, Renata, Tullio Jappelli, and Mario Padula. 2006. "Retirement Expectations, Pension Reforms, and Their Impact on Private Wealth Accumulation." *Journal of Public Economics* 90, 2187–212.

Brown, Jeffrey R., Jeffrey R. Kling, Sendhil Mullainathan, and Marian V. Wrobel. 2008. "Why Don't People Insure Late-Life Consumption? A Framing Explanation of the Under-Annuitization Puzzle." *American Economic Review* 98, 304–9.

Brown, Jeffrey R., and James M. Poterba. 2000. "Joint Life Annuities and Annuity Demand by Married Couples." *Journal of Risk and Insurance* 67, 527–53.

Browning, Martin, and M. Dolores Collado. 2001. "The Response of Expenditures to Anticipated Income Changes: Panel Data Estimates." *American Economic Review* 91, 681–92.

Browning, Martin J., and Thomas F. Crossley. 2001a. "The Life-Cycle Model of Consumption and Saving." *Journal of Economic Perspectives* 15, no. 3, 3–22.

Browning, Martin J., and Thomas F. Crossley. 2001b. "Unemployment Insurance Benefit Levels and Consumption Changes." *Journal of Public Economics* 80, 1–23.

Browning, Martin J., and Thomas F. Crossley. 2009. "Shocks, Stocks and Socks: Smoothing Consumption over a Temporary Income Loss." *Journal of the European Economic Association* 7, 1169–92.

Browning, Martin J., Lars Peter Hansen, and James J. Heckman. 1999. "Micro Data and General Equilibrium Models." In *Handbook of Macroeconomics*, vol. 1, Part A, edited by John B. Taylor and Michael Woodford, 543–633. Amsterdam: Elsevier Science.

Browning, Martin J., and Annamaria Lusardi. 1996. "Household Saving: Micro Theories and Micro Facts." *Journal of Economic Literature* 34, 1797–855.

Bütler, Monika, and Federica Teppa. 2007. "The Choice Between an Annuity and a Lump Sum: Results from Swiss Pension Funds." *Journal of Public Economics* 91, 1944–66.

Caballero, Ricardo J. 1991. "Earnings Uncertainty and Aggregate Wealth Accumulation." *American Economic Review* 81, 859–71.

Cagetti, Marco. 2003. "Wealth accumulation over the life cycle and precautionary savings." *Journal of Business and Economic Statistics* 21, 339–53.

Calvet, Laurent, John Campbell, and Paolo Sodini. 2007. "Down or Out: Assessing the Welfare Costs of Household Investment Mistakes." *Journal of Political Economy* 115, 707–47.

Camerer, Colin, Samuel Issacharoff, George Loewenstein, Ted O'Donoghue, and Matthew Rabin. 2003. "Regulation for Conservatives: Behavioral Economics and the Case for 'Asymmetric Paternalism.'" *University of Pennsylvania Law Review* 151, 1211–54.

Campbell, John Y. 1987. "Does Saving Anticipate Declining Labour Income? An Alternative Test of the Permanent Income Hypothesis." *Econometrica* 55, 1249–73.

Campbell, John Y., and Joao Cocco. 2007. "How Do House Prices Affect Consumption? Evidence from Micro Data." *Journal of Monetary Economics* 54, 591–621.

Campbell, John Y., and Angus S. Deaton. 1989. "Why Is Consumption So Smooth?" *Review of Economic Studies* 56, 357–74.

Campbell, John Y., and Gregory N. Mankiw. 1989. "Consumption, Income, and Interest Rates: Reinterpreting the Time Series Evidence." In *NBER Macroeconomics Annual 1989*, edited by Olivier J. Blanchard and Stanley Fischer, 185–246. Cambridge, MA: MIT Press.

Card, David, and John E. DiNardo. 2002. "Skill-Biased Technological Change and Rising Wage Inequality: Some Problems and Puzzles." *Journal of Labor Economics* 20, 733–83.

Carroll, Christopher D. 1997. "Buffer-Stock Saving and the Life Cycle/Permanent Income Hypothesis." *Quarterly Journal of Economics* 112, 1–55.

Carroll, Christopher D. 2009. "Precautionary Saving and the Marginal Propensity to Consume out of Permanent Income." *Journal of Monetary Economics* 56, 780–90.

Carroll, Christopher D. 2012. "Solving Microeconomic Dynamic Stochastic Optimization Problems. Lecture Notes." Unpublished manuscript.

Carroll, Christopher D., and Miles S. Kimball. 1996. "On the Concavity of the Consumption Function." *Econometrica* 64, 981–92.

Carroll, Christopher D., Misuzu Otsuka, and Jiri Slacalek. 2011. "How Large Are Housing and Financial Wealth Effects? A New Approach." *Journal of Money, Credit and Banking* 43, 55–79.

Carroll, Christopher D., and Andrew Samwick. 1997. "The Nature of Precautionary Saving." *Journal of Monetary Economics* 40, 41–71.

Case, Karl E., John M. Quigley, and Robert J. Shiller. 2005. "Comparing Wealth Effects: The Stock Market Versus the Housing Market." *B.E. Journal of Macroeconomics* 5, 1–34.

Chamberlain, Gary. 1984. "Panel Data." In *Handbook of Econometrics*, vol. 2, edited by Zvi Griliches and Michael D. Intriligator, 775–1461. Amsterdam: Elsevier Science.

Chetty, Raj, John Friedman, Soren Leth-Petersen, Torben Nielsen, and Tore Olsen. 2014. "Active vs. Passive Decisions and Crowd-Out in Retirement Savings Accounts: Evidence from Denmark." *Quarterly Journal of Economics* 129, 1141–219.

Chiappori, Pierre-André. 1988. "Rational Household Labor Supply." *Econometrica* 56, 63–90.

Chiappori, Pierre André, and Maurizio Mazzocco. 2015a. "Static and Intertemporal Household Decisions." Unpublished manuscript, UCLA.

Chiuri, Maria Concetta, and Tullio Jappelli. 2003. "Financial Market Imperfections and Home Ownership: A Comparative Study." *European Economic Review*, Elsevier, 47(5), 857–75.

Christelis, Dimitris, Dimitris Georgarakos, and Tullio Jappelli. 2015. "Wealth Shocks, Unemployment Shocks and Consumption in the Wake of the Great Recession." *Journal of Monetary Economics* 72, 21–41.

Christelis, Dimitris, Dimitris Georgarakos, Tullio Jappelli, Luigi Pistaferri, Maarten van Rooij. 2017. "Asymmetric Consumption Effects of Transitory Income Shocks." CSEF Working Paper N. 467.

Christelis, Dimitris, Tullio Jappelli, and Mario Padula, 2010. "Cognitive Abilities and Portfolio Choice." *European Economic Review* 54, 18–38.

Cochrane, John. 1991. "A Simple Test of Consumption Insurance." *Journal of Political Economy* 99, 957–76.

Contreras, Juan, and Joseph Nichols. 2010. "Consumption Responses to Permanent and Transitory Shocks to House Appreciation." Finance and Economics Discussion Series, 2010-32, Board of Governors of the Federal Reserve System (U.S.).

Cox, Donald. 1987. "Motives for Private Income Transfers." *Journal of Political Economy* 95, 508–46.

Cubeddu, Luis and José-Víctor Ríos-Rull. 2003. "Families as Shocks." *Journal of the European Economic Association* 1, 671–82.

Das, Marcel, and Bas Donkers. 1999. "How Certain Are Dutch Households About Future Income? An Empirical Analysis." *Review of Income and Wealth* 45, 325–38.

Davies, James D. 1981. "Uncertain Life Time, Consumption and Dissaving in Retirement." *Journal of Political Economy* 89, 561–77.

Davis, Morris A., and Michael G. Palumbo. 2001. "A Primer on the Economics and Time Series Econometrics of Wealth Effects." Finance and Economics Discussion Series, 2001-9. Board of Governors of the Federal Reserve System (U.S.).

De Giorgi, Giacomo, Anders Frederiksen, and Luigi Pistaferri. 2015. "Consumption Network Effects." Unpublished manuscript, Stanford University.

De Nardi, Mariachristina. 2015. "Quantitative Models of Wealth Inequality: A Survey." NBER Working Paper No. 21106.

De Nardi, Mariacristina, Eric French, and John B. Jones. 2010. "Why Do the Elderly Save? The Role of Medical Expenses." *Journal of Political Economy* 118, 39–75.

Deaton, Angus S. 1985. "Panel Data from Time Series of Cross-Sections." *Journal of Econometrics* 30, 109–26.

Deaton, Angus S. 1991. "Saving and Liquidity Constraints." *Econometrica* 59, 1221–48.

Deaton, Angus S. 1992. *Understanding Consumption.* Oxford: Oxford University Press.

Deaton, Angus S. 1997. *The Analysis of Household Surveys.* Baltimore: Johns Hopkins University Press.

Deaton, Angus S., and John Muellbauer. 1980. *Economics and Consumer Behaviour.* New York: Cambridge University Press.

Deaton, Angus, and Christina H. Paxson. 1994. "Intertemporal Choice and Inequality." *Journal of Political Economy* 102, 384–94.

Deaton, Angus, and Christina H. Paxson. 1997. "The Effects of Economic and Population Growth on National Saving and Inequality." *Demography* 34, 97–114.

Deaton, Angus, and Christina H. Paxson. 2000. "Growth and Saving Among Individuals and Households." *The Review of Economics and Statistics,* 82, 212–25.

DellaVigna, Stefano. 2009. "Psychology and Economics: Evidence from the Field." *Journal of Economic Literature* 47, 315–72.

Diamond, Peter A., and Jerry A. Hausman. 1984. "Individual Retirement and Saving Behaviour." *Journal of Public Economics* 23, 81–114.

Di Maggio, Marco, Amir Kermani, Benjamin Keys, Tomasz Piskorski, Rodney Ramcharan, Amit Seru, and Vincent Yao. 2016. "Monetary Policy Pass-Through: Mortgage Rates, Household Consumption and Voluntary Deleveraging." *The American Economic Review* (forthcoming).

Dimitris Christelis, Dimitris Georgarakos, Tullio Jappelli, and Maarten van Rooij. 2015. "Consumption Uncertainty and Precautionary Saving". CSEF Working Papers No. 421.

Disney, Richard, John Gathergood, and Andrew Henley. 2010. "House Price Shocks, Negative Equity and Household Consumption in the United Kingdom." *Journal of the European Economic Association* 8, 1179–207.

Dominitz, Jeff, and Charles Manski. 1997. "Using Expectations Data to Study Subjective Income Expectations." *Journal of the American Statistical Association* 92, 855–67.

Duesenberry, James S. 1948. "Income-Consumption Relations and Their Implications." In *Income, Employment and Public Policy: Essays in Honor of Alvin H. Hansen,* edited by Lloyd A. Metzler, 54–81. New York: W. W. Norton.

Dynan, Karen E. 1993. "How Prudent Are Consumers?" *Journal of Political Economy* 101, 1104–13.

Dynarski, Susan, and Jonathan Gruber. 1997. "Can Families Smooth Variable Earnings?" *Brooking Papers on Economic Activity* 1, 229–84.

Eberly, Janice C. 1994. "Adjustment of Consumers' Durables Stocks: Evidence from Automobile Purchases." *Journal of Political Economy* 102, 403–36.

Ellul, Andrew, Marco Pagano, and Fausto Panunzi. 2010. "Inheritance Law and Investment in Family Firms." *American Economic Review* 100, 2414–50.

Engelhardt, Gary V. 1996. "House Prices and Home Owner Saving Behavior." *Regional Science and Urban Economics* 26, 313–36.

Engen, Eric M., William G. Gale, and John Karl Scholz. 1996. "The Illusory Effect of Saving Incentives on Saving." *Journal of Economic Perspectives* 10, 113–38.

Feldstein, Martin S. 1974. "Social Security, Induced Retirement, and Aggregate Capital Accumulation." *Journal of Political Economy* 82, 905–26.

Finkelstein, Amy, Erzo F. P. Luttmer, and Matthew J. Notowidigdo. 2013. "What Good Is Wealth Without Health? The Effect of Health on the Marginal Utility of Consumption." *Journal of the European Economic Association* 11, 221–58.

Flavin, Marjorie. 1981. "The Adjustment of Consumption to Changing Expectations About Future Income." *Journal of Political Economy* 89, 974–1009.

Foote, Christopher, Erik Hurst, and John Leahy. 2000. "Testing the (S,s) Model." *American Economic Review* 90, 116–19.

Friedman, Milton. 1957. *A Theory of the Consumption Function*. Princeton: Princeton University Press.

Fuchs-Schündeln, Nicola, and Matthias Schündeln. 2005. "Precautionary Savings and Self-Selection: Evidence from the German Reunification Experiment." *Quarterly Journal of Economics* 120, 1085–120.

Gale, William G. 1998. "The Effects of Pension Wealth on Household Wealth: A Reevaluation of Theory and Evidence." *Journal of Political Economy* 106, 706–23.

Gale, William G., Maria G. Perozek. 2001. "Do Estate Taxes Reduce Saving?" In *Rethinking Estate and Gift Taxation*, vol. 2001, edited by William G. Gale, James R. Hines, and Joel Slemrod, 216–47. Washington: Brookings Institution.

Gale, William G., and J. Karl Scholz. 1994. "IRAs and Household Saving." *American Economic Review* 84, 1233–60.

Garcia, Rene, Annamaria Lusardi, and Serena Ng. 1997. "Excess Sensitivity and Asymmetries in Consumption: An Empirical Investigation." *Journal of Money, Credit and Banking* 29, 154–76.

Gelman, Michael, Shachar Kariv, Matthew D. Shapiro, Dan Silverman, and Steven Tadelis. 2016. "How Individuals Smooth Spending: Evidence from the 2013 Government Shutdown Using Account Data." Unpublished manuscript.

Gerardi, Kristopher S., Harvey S. Rosen, and Paul S. Willen. 2010. "The Impact of Deregulation and Financial Innovation on Consumers: The Case of the Mortgage Market." *Journal of Finance* 65, 333–60.

Gertler, Paul, and Jonathan Gruber. 2002. "Insuring Consumption Against Illness." *American Economic Review* 92, 51–70.

Gokhale, Jagadeesh, Laurence J. Kotlikoff, and John Sabelhaus. 1996. "Understanding the Postwar Decline in US Saving: A Cohort Analysis." *Brookings Papers on Economic Activity* 1, 315–90.

Gollier, Christian. 2001. *The Economics of Risk and Time*. Cambridge, MA: MIT Press.

Gourieroux, Christian, Alain Monfort, and Eric Renault. 1993. "Indirect Inference." *Journal of Applied Econometrics*, Supplement: Special Issue on Econometric Inference Using Simulation Techniques, S85–S118.

Gourinchas, Pierre-Olivier, and Jonathan A. Parker. 2002. "Consumption over the Life Cycle." *Econometrica* 70, 47–89.

Gross, David B., and Nicholas S. Souleles. 2002. "Do Liquidity Constraints and Interest Rates Matter for Consumer Behavior? Evidence from Credit Card Data." *Quarterly Journal of Economics* 107, 149–85.

Grossman, Sanford J., and Guy Laroque. 1990. "Asset Pricing and Optimal Portfolio Choice in the Presence of Illiquid Durable Consumption Goods." *Econometrica* 58, 25–51.

Gruber, Jonathan. 1997. "The Consumption Smoothing Benefits of Unemployment Insurance." *American Economic Review* 87, 192–205.

Gruber, Jonathan, and David A. Wise. 1999. *Social Security and Retirement Around the World*. NBER Books. Chicago: University of Chicago Press.

Gruber, Jonathan, and David A. Wise. 2004. *Social Security Programs and Retirement Around the World: Micro-Estimation*. NBER Books. Chicago: University of Chicago Press.

Guiso, Luigi, and Tullio Jappelli. 2002. "Private Transfers, Borrowing Constraints and the Timing of Homeownership." *Journal of Money, Credit and Banking*, 34(2), 315–339.

Guiso, Luigi, Tullio Jappelli, and Luigi Pistaferri. 2002. "An Empirical Analysis of Earnings and Employment Risk." *Journal of Business and Economic Statistics* 20, 241–53.

Guiso, Luigi, Tullio Jappelli, and Daniele Terlizzese. 1992. "Earnings Uncertainty and Precautionary Saving." *Journal of Monetary Economics* 30, 307–37.

Guvenen, Fatih, and Anthony A. Smith. 2014. "Inferring Labor Income Risk and Partial Insurance from Economic Choices." *Econometrica* 82, 2085–129.

Haider, Steven J., and Melvin Stephens. 2007. "Is There a Retirement-Consumption Puzzle? Evidence Using Subjective Retirement Expectations." *Review of Economics and Statistics* 89, 247–64.

Hall, Robert E. 1978. "Stochastic Implications of the Life-Cycle Permanent Income Hypothesis: Theory and Evidence." *Journal of Political Economy* 86, 971–87.

Hall, Robert E. 1988. "Intertemporal Substitution in Consumption." *Journal of Political Economy* 86, 971–87.

Hall, Robert E. 1998. "Discussion of Laibson, Repetto, and Tobacman." *Brookings Papers on Economic Activity* 29, 174–77.

Hall, Robert E., and Frederic S. Mishkin. 1982. "The Sensitivity of Consumption to Transitory Income: Estimates from Panel Data on Households." *Econometrica* 50, 461–81.

Hamilton, James D. 1994. *Time Series Analysis*. Princeton: Princeton University Press.

Hansen, Lars P., and Kenneth J. Singleton. 1983. "Consumption, Risk Aversion and the Temporal Behavior of Stock Market Returns." *Journal of Political Economy* 91, 249–65.

Hayashi, Fumio. 1985. "The Permanent Income Hypothesis and Consumption Durability: Analysis Based on Japanese Panel Data." *Quarterly Journal of Economics* 100, 1083–113.

Hayashi, Fumio, Joseph Altonji, and Laurence J. Kotlikoff. 1996. "Risk Sharing Between and Within Families." *Econometrica* 64, 261–94.

Heckman, James J. 1974. "Life Cycle Consumption and Labor Supply: An Explanation of the Relationship Between Income and Consumption over the Life Cycle." *American Economic Review* 64, 188–94.

Holtz-Eakin, Douglas, and Donald Marples. 2001. "Distortion Costs of Taxing Wealth Accumulation: Income Versus Estate Taxes." NBER Working Paper No. 8261.

Honohan, Patrick. 2000. "Financial Policies and Saving." In *The Economics of Saving and Growth: Theory, Evidence, and Implications for Policy*, edited by Klaus Schmidt-Hebbel and Luis Serven, 71–106. Cambridge: Cambridge University Press.

Hoynes, Hilary W., and Daniel McFadden. 1997. "The Impact of Demographics on Housing and Nonhousing Wealth in the United States." In *The Economic Effects of Aging in the United States and Japan*, edited by Michael D. Hurd and Yashiro Naohiro, 153–94. NBER Books. Chicago: University of Chicago Press.

Hryshko, Dmytro. 2014. "Correlated Income Shocks and Excess Smoothness of Consumption." *Journal of Economic Dynamics and Control* 48, 41–62.

Hryshko, Dmytro, María José Luengo-Prado, and Bent E. Sørensen. 2010. "House Prices and Risk Sharing." *Journal of Monetary Economics* 57, 975–87.

Hsieh, Chang-Tai. 2003. "Do Consumers React to Anticipated Income Changes? Evidence from the Alaska Permanent Fund." *American Economic Review* 93, 397–405.

Hubbard, Glenn R., Jonathan Skinner, and Stephen P. Zeldes. 1994. "The Importance of Precautionary Motives in Explaining Individual and Aggregate Saving." *Carnegie Rochester Series on Public Policy* 40, 59–125.

Hubbard, Glenn R., Jonathan Skinner, and Stephen P. Zeldes. 1995. "Precautionary Savings and Social Insurance." *Journal of Political Economy* 103, 360–99.

Hurd, Michael D. 1987. "Savings of the Elderly and Desired Bequests." *American Economic Review* 77, 298–312.

Hurd, Michael D. 1989. "Mortality Risk and Bequests." *Econometrica* 57, 779–813.

Hurd, Michael D. 1992. "Wealth Depletion and Life-Cycle Consumption by the Elderly." In *Topics in the Economics of Aging*, edited by David A. Wise, 135–62. NBER Books. Chicago: University of Chicago Press.

Hurd, Michael D., and Susann Rohwedder. 2006. "Some Answers to the Retirement-Consumption Puzzle." NBER Working Paper 12057.

Hurd, Michael D., and Susann Rohwedder. 2010. "Wealth Dynamics and Active Saving at Older Ages: Do They Add Up?" RAND Corporation.

Hurst, Erik, Annamaria Lusardi, Arthur Kennickell, and Francisco Torralba. 2010. "The Importance of Business Owners in Assessing the Size of Precautionary Savings." *Review of Economics and Statistics* 92, 61–69.

Jappelli, Tullio. 1990. "Who Is Credit Constrained in the U.S. Economy?" *Quarterly Journal of Economics* 105, 219–34.

Jappelli, Tullio, and Franco Modigliani. 2006. "The Age-Saving Profile and the Life-Cycle Hypothesis." In *Long-Run Growth and Short-Run Stabilization: Essays in Honor of Albert Ando*, edited by Lawrence Klein, 12–45. London: Edward Elgar.

Jappelli, Tullio, and Mario Padula. 2013. "Investment in Financial Literacy and Saving Decisions." *Journal of Banking and Finance* 37, 2779–92.

Jappelli, Tullio, and Mario Padula. 2016. "The Consumption and Wealth Effects of an Unanticipated Change in Lifetime Resources." *Management Science* 62, 1458–71.

Jappelli, Tullio, Mario Padula, and Giovanni Pica. 2014. "Do Transfer Taxes Reduce Intergenerational Transfers?" *Journal of the European Economic Association* 12, 248–75.

Jappelli, Tullio, Mario Padula, and Luigi Pistaferri. 2008. "A Direct Test of the Buffer-Stock Model of Saving." *Journal of the European Economic Association* 6, 1186–210.

Jappelli, Tullio, and Marco Pagano. 1989. "Consumption and Capital Market Imperfections." *American Economic Review* 79, 1088–105.

Jappelli, Tullio, and Marco Pagano. 1994. "Saving, Growth and Liquidity Constraints." *Quarterly Journal of Economics* 106, 83–109.

Jappelli, Tullio, Jorn-Steffen Pischke, and Nicholas S. Souleles. 1998. "Testing for Liquidity Constraints in Euler Equations with Complementary Data Sources." *Review of Economics and Statistics* 80, 251–62.

Jappelli, Tullio, and Luigi Pistaferri. 2000a. *Risparmio e scelte intertemporal*. Bologna: Il Mulino.

Jappelli, Tullio, and Luigi Pistaferri. 2000b. "Using Subjective Income Expectations to Test the Excess Sensitivity of Consumption to Predicted Income Changes." *European Economic Review* 44, 337–58.

Jappelli, Tullio and Luigi Pistaferri. 2003. "Tax Incentives for Household Saving and Borrowing." In *Taxation of Financial Intermediation*, edited by P. Honohan, 127–169. Oxford: Oxford University Press.

Jappelli, Tullio, and Luigi Pistaferri. 2006. "Intertemporal Choice and Consumption Mobility." *Journal of the European Economic Association* 4, 75–115.

Jappelli, Tullio, and Luigi Pistaferri. 2010. The Consumption Response to Income Changes. *Annual Review of Economics*, 479–506.

Jappelli, Tullio, and Luigi Pistaferri. 2014. "Fiscal Policy and MPC Heterogeneity." *American Economic Journal: Macroeconomics* 6, 107–36.

Johnson, David S., Jonathan A. Parker, and Nicholas S. Souleles. 2006. "Household Expenditure and the Income Tax Rebates of 2001." *American Economic Review* 96, 1589–610.

Johnson, Richard W., Leonard E. Burman, and Deborah I. Kobes. 2004. "Annuitized Wealth at Older Ages: Evidence from the Health and Retirement Study." Washington, DC: Urban Institute.

Juster, F. Thomas, Joseph P. Lupton, James P. Smith, and Frank Stafford, 2006. "The Decline in Household Saving and the Wealth Effect." *The Review of Economics and Statistics* 88, 20–27.

Kamien, Morton I., and Nancy L. Schwartz. 1981. *Dynamic Optimization*. Amsterdam: Elsevier Science.

Kantor, Shawn E., and Price V. Fishback. 1996. "Precautionary Saving, Insurance, and the Origin of Workers' Compensation." *Journal of Political Economy* 104, 419–42.

Kaplan, Greg, and Giovanni L. Violante. 2010. "How Much Consumption Insurance Beyond Self-Insurance?" *American Economic Journal: Macroeconomics* 2, 53–87.

Kaplan, Greg, and Giovanni L. Violante. 2014. "A Model of the Consumption Response to Fiscal Stimulus Payments." *Econometrica* 82, 1199–239.

Kaplan, Greg, Giovanni L. Violante, and Justin Weidner. 2014. "The Wealthy Hand-to-Mouth." *Brookings Papers on Economic Activity*.

Kaufmann, Katja, and Luigi Pistaferri. 2009. "Disentangling Insurance and Information in Intertemporal Consumption Choices." *American Economic Review* 99, 387–92.

Kennickell, Arthur, and Annamaria Lusardi. 2004. "Disentangling the Importance of the Precautionary Saving Model," NBER Working Papers 10888. National Bureau of Economic Research, Inc.

Kimball, Miles S. 1990. "Precautionary Saving in the Small and in the Large." *Econometrica* 58, 53–73.

King, Mervyn A., and Louis Dicks-Mireaux. 1982. "Asset Holdings and the Life-Cycle." *Economic Journal* 92, 247–67.

Klibanoff, Peter, Massimo Marinacci, and Sujoy Mukerji. 2005. "A Smooth Model of Decision Making Under Ambiguity." *Econometrica* 73, 1849–92.

Knight, Frank. 1921. *Risk, Uncertainty, and Profit*. Boston: Houghton Mifflin.

Kocherlakota, Narayana, and Luigi Pistaferri. 2009. "Asset Pricing Implications of Pareto Optimality with Private Information." *Journal of Political Economy* 117, no. 3, 555–90.

Kopczuk, Wojciech, and Joseph Lupton. 2007. "To Leave or Not to Leave: The Distribution of Bequest Motives." *Review of Economic Studies* 74, 207–35.

Kotlikoff, Laurence J., and Lawrence Summers. 1981. "The Role of Intergenerational Transfers in Aggregate Capital Accumulation." *Journal of Political Economy* 89, 706–32.

Laibson, David. 1997. "Golden Eggs and Hyperbolic Discounting." *Quarterly Journal of Economics* 112, 443–78.

Laibson, David, Andrea Repetto, and Jeremy Tobacman. 1998. "Self-Control and Saving for Retirement". *Brookings Papers on Economic Activity*, 29, 91–196.

Lam, Pok-Sang. 1991. "Permanent Income, Liquidity, and Adjustments of Automobile Stocks: Evidence from Panel Data." *Quarterly Journal of Economics* 106, 203–30.

Levin, Laurence. 1998. "Are Assets Fungible? Testing the Behavioral Theory of Life-Cycle Savings." *Journal of Economic Behavior and Organization* 36, 59–83.

Light, Audrey, and Kathleen McGarry. 2004. "Why Parents Play Favorites: Explanations for Unequal Bequests." *American Economic Review* 94, 1669–81.

Ligon, Ethan. 1998. "Risk Sharing and Information in Village Economies." *Review of Economic Studies* 65, no. 4, 847–64.

Lillard, Lee, and Yoram Weiss. 1997. "Uncertain Health and Survival: Effects on End-of-Life Consumption." *Journal of Business and Economic Statistics* 15, 2, 254–68.

Ljungqvist, Lars, and Thomas J. Sargent. 2004. *Recursive Macroeconomic Theory.* Cambridge, MA: MIT Press.

Ljungqvist, Lars, and Harald Uhlig. 2000. "Tax Policy and Aggregate Demand Management Under Catching Up with the Joneses." *American Economic Review* 90, 356–66.

Loayza, Norman, Klaus Schmidt-Hebbel, and Luis Servén. 2000. "What Drives Private Saving Across the World?" *Review of Economics and Statistics* 82, 165–81.

Low, Hamish. 2005. "Self-Insurance in a Life-Cycle Model of Labor Supply and Savings." *Review of Economic Dynamics* 8, 945–75.

Low, Hamish, Costas Meghir, and Luigi Pistaferri. 2010. "Wage Risk and Employment Risk over the Life Cycle." *American Economic Review* 100, 1432–67.

Low, Hamish, and Luigi Pistaferri. 2015. "Disability Insurance and the Dynamics of the Incentive-Insurance Tradeoff." *American Economic Review* 105, 2986–3029.

Lucas, Robert E. 1976. "Econometric Policy Evaluation: A Critique." *Carnegie Rochester Series on Public Policy* 1, 19–46.

Lusardi, Annamaria, Pierre-Carl Michaud, and Olivia S. Mitchell. 2015. "Optimal Financial Knowledge and Wealth Inequality." *Journal of Political Economy* (forthcoming).

Lusardi, Annamaria, and Olivia S. Mitchell. 2014. "The Economic Importance of Financial Literacy: Theory and Evidence." *Journal of Economic Literature* 52, 5–44.

Lusardi, Annamaria, and Peter Tufano. 2009. "Debt Literacy, Financial Experiences, and Overindebtedness." NBER Working Paper No. 14808.

Mace, Barbara J. 1991. "Full Insurance in the Presence of Aggregate Uncertainty." *Journal of Political Economy* 99, 928–56.

MaCurdy, Thomas E. 1981. "An Empirical Model of Labor Supply in a Life-Cycle Setting." *Journal of Political Economy* 89, 1059–85.

MaCurdy, Thomas E. 1982. "The Use of Time Series Processes to Model the Error Structure of Earnings in a Longitudinal Data Analysis." *Journal of Econometrics* 18, 82–114.

Madrian, Brigitte C., and Dennis F. Shea. 2001. "The Power of Suggestion: Inertia in 401(k) Participation and Savings Behavior." *Quarterly Journal of Economics* 116, 1149–87.

Malmendier, Ulrike, and Stefan Nagel. 2011. "Depression Babies: Do Macroeconomic Experiences Affect Risk Taking?" *Quarterly Journal of Economics* 126, 373–416.

Mankiw, Gregory N. 1982. "Hall's Consumption Hypothesis and Durable Goods." *Journal of Monetary Economics* 10, 417–25.

Manski, Charles F. 2004. "Measuring Expectations." *Econometrica* 72, 1329–76.

Mazzocco, Maurizio. 2007. "Household Intertemporal Behaviour: A Collective Characterization and a Test of Commitment." *Review of Economic Studies* 74, 857–95.

Mazzocco, Maurizio. 2008. "Intertemporal Behavior and Household Structure." Unpublished manuscript, UCLA.

Mazzocco, Maurizio, and Shiv Saini. 2012. "Testing Efficient Risk Sharing with Heterogeneous Risk Preferences." *American Economic Review* 102, 428–68.

McArdle, John J., James P. Smith, and Robert Willis. 2009. "Cognition and Economic Outcomes in the Health and Retirement Survey." NBER Working Paper 15266.

McFadden, Daniel. 1989. "Models without Numerical Integration." *Econometrica* 57, 995–1026.

McGarry, Kathleen, and Robert F. Schoeni. 1995. "Transfer Behavior in the Health and Retirement Study: Measurement and the Redistribution of Resources Within Family." *Journal of Human Resources* 30, S184–S226.

Meghir, Costas. 2004. "A Retrospective on Friedman's Theory of Permanent Income." *Economic Journal* 114, 293–306.

Meghir, Costas, and Luigi Pistaferri. 2004. "Income Variance Dynamics and Heterogeneity." *Econometrica* 72, 1–32.

Meghir, Costas, and Guglielmo Weber. 1996. "Intertemporal Non-separability or Borrowing Restrictions? A Disaggregate Analysis Using a US Consumption Panel." *Econometrica* 64, 1151–82.

Mian, Atif, and Amir Sufi. 2012. "The Effects of Fiscal Stimulus: Evidence from the 2009 Cash for Clunkers Program." *Quarterly Journal of Economics* 127, 1107–42.

Mian, Atif, and Amir Sufi. 2016. "Who Bears the Cost of Recessions? The Role of House Prices and Household Debt." NBER Working Paper No. 22256.

Modigliani, Franco. 1986. "Life Cycle, Individual Thrift, and the Wealth of Nations." *American Economic Review* 76, 297–312.

Modigliani, Franco. 1988. "The Role of Intergenerational Transfers and Life Cycle Saving in the Accumulation of Wealth." *Journal of Economic Perspectives* 2, 15–40.

Modigliani, Franco, and Richard Brumberg. 1954. "Utility Analysis and the Consumption Function: An Intepretation of Cross-Section Data." In *Post-Keynesians Economics*, edited by K. Kurihara, 388–436. New Brunswick, NJ: Rutgers University Press.

Nelson, Julie A. 1994. "On Testing for Full Insurance Using Consumer Expenditure Survey Data." *Journal of Political Economy* 102, no. 2, 384–94.

Padula, Mario. 2004. "Consumer Durables and the Marginal Propensity to Consume out of Permanent Income Shocks." *Research in Economics* 58, 310–41.

Paiella, Monica, and Luigi Pistaferri. 2017. "Decomposing the Wealth Effect on Consumption," *Review of Economics and Statistics* (forthcoming).

Palumbo, Michael G. 1999. "Uncertain Medical Expenses and Precautionary Saving Near the End of the Life Cycle." *Review of Economic Studies* 66, 395–421.

Parker, Jonathan A. 1999. "The Reaction of Household Consumption to Predictable Changes in Social Security Taxes." *American Economic Review* 89, 959–73.

Paxson, Christina H. 1993. "Consumption and Income Seasonality in Thailand." *Journal of Political Economy* 101, 39–72.

Pistaferri, Luigi. 2001. "Superior Information, Income Shocks and the Permanent Income Hypothesis." *Review of Economics and Statistics* 83, 465–76.

Pistaferri, Luigi. 2003. "Anticipated and Unanticipated Wage Changes, Wage Risk, and Intertemporal Labor Supply." *Journal of Labor Economics* 21, 729–54.

Poterba, James M. 1994. *International Comparisons of Household Saving.* Chicago: University of Chicago Press.

Poterba, James M., Steven F. Venti, and David A. Wise. 1996. "How Retirement Saving Programs Increase Saving." *Journal of Economic Perspectives* 10, 91–112.

Primiceri, Giorgio E., and Thijs van Rens. 2009. "Heterogeneous Life-Cycle Profiles, Income Risk and Consumption Inequality." *Journal of Monetary Economics* 56, 20–39.

Rogerson, William P. 1985. "Repeated Moral Hazard," *Econometrica* 53, 69–76.

Scholnick, Barry. 2010. "Credit Card Use After the Final Mortgage Payment: Does the Magnitude of Income Shocks Matter?" Working Paper, University of Alberta.

Schulhofer-Wohl, Sam. 2011. "Heterogeneity and Tests of Risk Sharing." *Journal of Political Economy* 119, 925–58.

Shapiro, Matthew D., and Joel Slemrod. 1995. "Consumer Response to the Timing of Income: Evidence from a Change in Tax Withholding." *American Economic Review* 85, 274–83.

Shapiro, Matthew D., and Joel Slemrod. 2003. "Consumer Response to Tax Rebates." *American Economic Review* 93, 381–96.

Shapiro, Matthew D., and Joel Slemrod. 2009. "Did the 2008 Tax Rebates Stimulate Spending?" *American Economic Review* 99, 374–79.

Shea, John. 1995. "Union Contracts and the Life-Cycle Permanent Income Hypothesis." *American Economic Review* 85, 186–200.

Shefrin, Hersh M., and Richard H. Thaler. 1988. "The Behavioral Life-Cycle Hypothesis." *Economic Inquiry* 26, 609–43.

Sinai, Todd, and Nicholas Souleles. 2005. "Owner-Occupied Housing as a Hedge Against Rent Risk." *Quarterly Journal of Economics*, 120, 763–89.

Skinner, Jonathan. 1988. "Risky Income, Life-Cycle Consumption and Precautionary Saving." *Journal of Monetary Economics* 22, 237–55.

Slemrod, Joel, and Wojciech Kopczuk. 2001. "The Impact of the Estate Tax on the Wealth Accumulation and Avoidance Behavior of Donors." In *Rethinking Estate and Gift Taxation*, edited by William G. Gale, James R. Hines, and Joel Slemrod, 299–343. Washington, DC: Brookings Institution Press.

Souleles, Nicholas S. 1999. "The Response of Household Consumption to Income Tax Refunds." *American Economic Review* 89, 947–58.

Souleles, Nicholas S. 2000. "College Tuition and Household Savings and Consumption." *Journal of Public Economics* 77, 185–207.

Souleles, Nicholas S. 2002. "Consumer Response to the Reagan Tax Cuts." *Journal of Public Economics* 85, 99–120.

Stephens, Melvin. 2001. "The Long-Run Consumption Effects of Earnings Shocks." *Review of Economics and Statistics* 83, 28–36.

Stephens, Melvin. 2008. "The Consumption Response to Predictable Changes in Discretionary Income: Evidence from the Repayment of Vehicle Loans." *Review of Economics and Statistics* 90, 241–52.

Stokey, Nancy L., Robert E. Lucas Jr. 1989. *Recursive Methods in Macroeconomics.* Cambridge: Harvard University Press.

Tomes, Nigel. 1981. "The Family, Inheritance, and the Intergenerational Transmission of Inequality." *Journal of Political Economy* 89, 928–58.

Townsend, Robert M. 1989. "Consumption Insurance: An Evaluation of Risk-Bearing Systems in Low-Income Economies." *Journal of Economic Perspectives* 3, 83–102.

Tversky, Amos, and Daniel Kahneman. 1981. "The Framing of Decisions and the Psychology of Choice." *Science* 211, 453–58.

Van Rooij, Maarten, Annamaria Lusardi, and Rob Alessie. 2011. "Financial Literacy and Stock Market Participation." *Journal of Financial Economics* 101, 449–72.

Veblen, Thorstein. 1899. *The Theory of the Leisure Class.* New York: Macmillan.

Vermeulen, Frederic. 2002. "Collective Household Models: Principles and Main Results." *Journal of Economic Surveys* 16, 533–64.

Voena, Alessandra. 2015. "Yours, Mine and Ours: Do Divorce Laws Affect the Intertemporal Behavior of Married Couples?" *American Economic Review* 105, 2295–332.

Ward-Batts, Jennifer. 2008. "Out of the Wallet and into the Purse: Using Micro Data to Test Income Pooling." *Journal of Human Resources* 43, no. 2, 325–51.

Wilcox, David W. 1989. "Social Security Benefits, Consumption Expenditure, and the Life Cycle Hypothesis." *Journal of Political Economy* 97, 288–304.

Wolpin, Kenneth. 1982. "A New Test of the Permanent Income Hypothesis: The Impact of Weather on the Income and Consumption of Farm Households in India." *International Economic Review* 23, 583–94.

Yaari, Menachim E. 1965. "Uncertain Lifetime, Life Insurance, and the Theory of Consumer." *Review of Economic Studies* 32, 137–50.

Zeldes, Stephen P. 1989. "Consumption and Liquidity Constraints: An Empirical Investigation." *Journal of Political Economy* 97, 305–46.

INDEX